Imitations of Infinity

DIVINATIONS: REREADING LATE
ANCIENT RELIGION

Series Editors:
Daniel Boyarin
Virginia Burrus
Derek Krueger

A complete list of books in the series is
available from the publisher.

IMITATIONS OF INFINITY

Gregory of Nyssa and the Transformation of Mimesis

Michael Motia

PENN

UNIVERSITY OF PENNSSYLVANIA PRESS

PHILADELPHIA

Published by
University of Pennsylvania Press
Philadelphia, Pennsylvania 19104-4112
www.upenn.edu/pennpress

Printed in the United States of America on acid-free paper
10 9 8 7 6 5 4 3 2 1

Library of Congress Cataloging-in-Publication Data

Names: Motia, Michael, author.
Title: Imitations of infinity : Gregory of Nyssa and the
transformation of mimesis / Michael Motia.
Other titles: Divinations.
Description: 1st edition. | Philadelphia : University of
Pennsylvania Press, [2022] | Series: Divinations : rereading
late ancient religion | Includes bibliographical references
and index.
Identifiers: LCCN 2021014012 | ISBN 9780812253139
(hardcover)
Subjects: LCSH: Gregory, of Nyssa, Saint, approximately
335-approximately 394. | Imitation—Religious aspects—
Christianity.
Classification: LCC BR65.G76 M625 2022 | DDC 248.4—dc23
LC record available at https://lccn.loc.gov/2021014012

For Morgan

CONTENTS

The Mimetic Life

"Christianity is mimesis of the divine nature."[1] That was how, in the 390s, a graying Gregory of Nyssa (c. 335–395) defined Christianity for his young friend Harmonius. Modern scholars do not have many definitions of Christianity from late antiquity, so the sentence itself presents something of a historical gem. But these words are also theologically puzzling in the context of Gregory's larger thought—thought that often theorized forms of asceticism that his brother and sister founded when Gregory was still a young man, and thought that was all the more influential after 381, when Emperor Theodosius, as part of a larger project of making Christianity the religion of the Roman Empire, named him a "standard bearer" of orthodoxy. One puzzle is semantic: the Greek word mimesis carries a wide and often unstable set of meanings: imitation, representation, even an aptness with models.[2] Another is that Gregory was the first Christian to make the infinity, and therefore unknowability, of God central to his theological program. The two pieces raise even more questions: How does one imitate the infinite? Or, perhaps more importantly: If Gregory described the aim or perfection of the Christian life as "never to stop growing toward what is better and never placing any limit on perfection,"[3] how did mimesis function within that endless pursuit? And given that mimesis assumes a mode of desire—for love leads to likeness, and imitation incites, intensifies, reorients, and reinforces desire—how did a Christian love what she did not know? What was the presumed relationship between representation and the divine reality? What did Christians imitate when they imitated an inimitable God? What kinds of guidelines or practices governed this life? These questions lie at the heart of *Imitations of Infinity*.[4]

Imitation is so basic a part of human life that it can be difficult to see its meaning or purpose debated. Not only do all people imitate others, but part of becoming a self, or even a society, involves both what and how we imitate. Today, imitation's opposite is often something like "true," "authentic," or "real." An imitation is a "knockoff." Even in antiquity authors worried about the "cheapness" or "easiness" of imitation and how it could lead people away from the hard work of pursuing what is most real or true. But imitation is not always the opposite of reality; it is also a mode of relationship, a way to engage with and participate in reality. In learning to imitate, we learn not just models but what Plato called an *ēthos*,[5] a word that can mean a theatrical character, but also a characteristic or a disposition that is more the sum of any examples; we acquire skills, habits, and instinctual modes of desire that push us to unexpected places. Mimesis, that is, creates what Pierre Hadot called "a way of life." In Gregory of Nyssa, especially, we see this other view of imitation take hold.[6]

Mimetic relationships structured much of the classical Greek and Roman worlds. Archetypes and imitations frame discussions of how a teacher molds a student, how art shapes a soul, and how the creator creates creation—questions most intimate or most cosmic, questions of identity, cultivation of the self, power and persuasion, and more. The ubiquity of mimesis in the classical world and in the early Church, however, can blind readers to the different ways its conceptualization formed individuals and communities. Nearly everyone wrote about imitating, but they did not mean the same thing or imagine the same results. The ubiquity, therefore, makes the analysis of the relations of power and ontology implicit in these mimetic relationships even more important. Because mimesis could do so much work, it should not surprise modern readers that it was constantly challenged.

Gregory's most famous contributions to Christian thought—divine infinitude and the human mimicking of that infinitude in our endlessly expanding desire for God—participate in a larger late antique concern with imitating the divine. That is, Gregory carves out a new theorization of mimesis as he insists that humans imitate an infinite God not by becoming like a fixed object but by infinitely expanding their souls' love for God, endlessly growing toward an endless God. *Imitations of Infinity* shows how, for Gregory, mimesis structures a set of exercises, a way of life, aimed at Christian perfection.[7] His theological and ascetic program involves both *what* to imitate and *how* to imitate.[8] My reading of Gregory is structured, therefore, around three of his most common targets of desire: names, spaces, and characters. Each of these governs and propels Christians toward a more virtuous life and an ever-expanding desire; they are images of God that transform Christians into the image of God. It is not enough, however, simply to look at these images and assume we know what we mean by mimesis. Gregory's names, spaces, and characters carry with them modes of mimesis: the structures of desire, theorizations of participation, and practices of representation required for a virtuous life, defined as imitation of God.

Gregory's definition responds to Harmonius's question, a question that is difficult to capture in English:[9] Τί τοῦ Χριστιανοῦ τὸ ἐπάγγελμα; The difficult word here is ἐπάγγελμα. It can mean a promise, a profession, an art, or a subject (as in the subject of a treatise). What is the promise of a Christian? What is the profession of a Christian? What is the art of a Christian? What is the subject of a Christian? What is promised to a Christian? We get some sense of the question from the analogy he draws immediately after posing it:

> Just as someone who desires to be called a doctor or an orator or a geometrician is not worthy of a title until he has some education as to what it means, that is, until he discovers from experience [ἐπὶ τῆς πείρας] what he is being called, and just as the person wishing to be thus addressed in accordance with truth, so that the calling will not be proved to be a misnomer, will show himself faithful [πιστώσεται] to the title by the practice itself [αὐτῷ τῷ ἐπιτηδεύματι]; so, in the same way, if we, seeking the true aim of the profession [ἐπαγγέλματος] of a Christian, should find it, then we would not choose not to be it when the title is professed [ἐπαγγέλλεται] about us.[10]

Like doctors, Christians should, over time, grow into and then stretch out their titles. From their practice, they learn the truth of their profession.[11] Experience, education, and habits accumulate in Christians and transform them into what their name implies. Put differently, Harmonius is to become a Christian by practicing Christianity. Daily exercise of virtue informs the promise of Christianity.

Mimesis offers a promise, but also carries a threat. Mimesis constellates bodily habits that allow Christians to become what they profess, but what happens when someone is called a Christian without being one?[12] Because means and ends are so tightly intertwined, Gregory fears that some might mimic what they know of the title Christian without their soul's transformation as well. Gregory retells Lucian's story *The Fisherman* to illustrate this threat.[13] In Lucian's narrative, a man trains a monkey to dance, gives it a mask, and puts it, costumed and accompanied by musicians, on stage. Audiences generally marvel at the masked monkey. But one day, a maleficent audience member tosses some almonds in front of the dancing animal. Seeing the drupes, the monkey forgets his act, tears off his mask, and eats his fill. Gregory worries less about monkeys, of course, than about those "apelike souls [πιθηκώδεις ψυχάς]." The devil places temptations before those who "through mimesis, play the role of the Christian," causing the actors to "remove the mask of moderation or humility or some other virtue in a moment of passion."[14] Gregory's definition, which is meant to guide a life of virtue, looks surprisingly similar to the dangers of Christian acting.[15] Masks and mimesis here are not the problem. The problem is how easily Christians remove their masks and, so to speak, break character.

If, then, doctors gain experience by watching other doctors, seeing patients themselves, and blending theoretical knowledge with improvised practices of healing, and if orators enter teachers' homes and schools to learn to imitate rhetorical masters, then what is the analogue for Christians? What roles should Christians learn to play? What theoretical knowledge should be in place for successful, often ritualized, improvised encounters with the divine? What names, spaces, and characters can facilitate a mimetic relationship with an infinite God? The easy response is to say, "Christians imitate Christ." But that does not answer the question of how to imitate a Christ whose nature is unknown. Imitation requires imagining an "image of the invisible God" (Col 1:15) and fashioning a relationship with what always exceeds one's grasp.

For Gregory, mystery and mimesis together constitute the Christian life. Disciplining practices and striving toward the infinite are parts of the same profession. Harmonius surely knew that God's essential unknowability is no small thing for Gregory. It was central to the biggest theological battle of Gregory's life, that against Eunomius. For Eunomius, Gregory reported, "the title 'Christian' does not properly apply to those who claim that the divine nature is unknowable."[16] Eunomius argued that Christians had to know who God is in order to worship God. Gregory spent years arguing just the opposite: Christians must profess the infinitude and therefore unknowability of God's nature. But this unknowability does not leave Christians aimlessly peering into the void. Their "total ignorance"[17] must be conducted—both in the sense of a channel moving water and in the sense of a conductor leading an orchestra—and this happens also through mimesis. To be a "Christian," he insists, is to imitate that which one cannot know.

Mimesis, Ontological and Aesthetic

Imitations of Infinity argues that Gregory's definition of Christianity brought together two conceptual discussions of mimesis: one ontological and one aesthetic. That is, mimesis entails both ontological participation in God and aesthetic representation of God. Ontological participation is about who one is. While it is common today to think of oneself as a stand-alone unit, ancient theorists understood themselves to be "participating" in God. Who they "were" was a question of what they were an imitation of, and how they stood in relationship to their archetype. Aesthetic representation is about the kinds of practices, often literary or analogous to an artistic practice, that it takes to represent an archetype.[18]

The connection between ontological participation and representation is, in fact, the central concern that leads up to Gregory's definition: "Christianity is mimesis of the divine nature."[19] Participation "unites" Christians to Christ, making them "synonymous with [Christ] whose incorruptible nature is beyond names. . . . For just as by participating [τῇ μετοχῇ] in Christ we are given the title Christian, so it follows that we are also drawn into a share in the sublime names which belong to it."[20] A series of names gathers around Christ, and, in becoming synonymous with him, the Christian "exhibits in his life" what the title "Christian" indicates. Christ is "ineffable, incomprehensible, and exceeding all thought,"[21] and, at the same time, "it is not possible to be a Christian (that is, truly a Christian) without displaying in oneself a participation in these names [justice and purity and truth and separation from all evil]."[22] Only by connecting these two sides of mimesis, therefore, can one be a true imitator of God.

If, then, these two conceptions work together in Gregory's fashioning of mimesis, this book also highlights how God's transcendence troubles mimesis. As soon as he gives his definition of the Christian life, Gregory stages his reader's reaction: How do you imitate the infinite? "Let no one object to this saying [λόγον] as being immoderate and overstepping the lowliness of our nature; it does not go beyond our nature."[23] Instead, Gregory writes,

"The promise of Christianity [ἡ τοῦ χριστιανισμοῦ ἐπαγγελία] is to bring humanity back to its original inheritance."[24] For "If humanity was originally a likeness of God [τὸ ἀρχαῖον θεοῦ ὁμοίωμα], perhaps our definition [ὁρισμὸν] is not outside the bounds when we declare that Christianity is mimesis of the divine nature."[25] Humans were made "in the image of God," and while they can turn away from God, they nevertheless live and move and have their being in God; their existence marks them as images and draws them back to their origin.

Humanity's mimetic relationship with the divine, then, is grounded in an original, ontological givenness, but Gregory follows this with an account of the aesthetic aspect. Gregory's tethering of ontological participation and aesthetic representation in his understanding of Christian mimesis appears striking in the following long quote.

Assume that a professional [ἐπαγγελλόμενος] painter is commissioned by a superior to draw the form of the king [χαράξαι τὴν τῆς βασιλείας μορφήν] for those living far away. If he depicts a ridiculous and ugly shape [εἶδος] on the wood and calls this ungracious figure an image of the king [εἰκόνα βασιλέως], would it not be likely that the powers that be would be irritated, because the beautiful archetype [ἀρχετύπου κάλλους] has been insulted through this bad painting among the ignorant [i.e., those who had never seen the king]? For they will necessarily think that the original is what the form on the image shows him to be. If, then, the definition says that Christianity is mimesis of God [θεοῦ μίμησιν τὸν χριστιανισμὸν], the one who has never been given an account of this mystery [τοῦ μυστηρίου τὸν λόγον], believing that the life he sees among us is a correct mimesis of God [μίμησιν θεοῦ κατορθοῦσθαι], will also suppose the divine to be what he sees among us. Therefore, if someone should see among us models of complete goodness, he will believe that the divine revered by us is good; but, if someone is emotional [ἐμπαθὴς] and brutal, changing from one passion to another, and puts on [ὑποδυόμενος] many forms of animals in his character [ἤθει] (for it is easy to see how, in the deviations of our nature, we are changed into beasts), then, should such a one call himself a Christian, when it is clear to all that the promise [ὑπόσχεσις] of the name professes [ἐπαγγέλλεται] an imitation of God, that person in his own life makes what we believe to be divine an object of blame among unbelievers.[26]

Those who participate in God are to make their life an artistic image of that which is unknown and unseen. No one has seen God, but through art, subjects do have a sense of the king, and those images can govern a life faithful to the king. Images, in turn, allow Christians to participate in God. Rather than see the artistic work as only a process of "expression," Gregory insists that because representation and participation function together, Christians are constituted by mimesis; their mimetic relationship forms their "character" (ἦθος). To live the promise and profession of their name, Christians participate in that which they represent and represent that in which they participate. Representation and participation ground each other and together "run out to infinity."[27]

Again Gregory, having brought together the two aspects of mimesis, anticipates his skeptical reader's question about the inimitability of God: "How could it be possible for the earthly to be like the One in heaven, the very difference in nature proving the unattainableness of the imitation?"[28] He responds again, "Human and divine natures need not be combined [συγκρίνεσθαι], but we do need to imitate in life the good actions, as much as possible."[29] The all-important distinction between creator and creation— one infinite, the other finite—does not lead Gregory away from emphasizing a mimetic relationship; it makes it imperative. He repeats the earlier discussion of humans being made in the image of God, and then, quoting the Psalms, argues that God's presence already saturates human nature. "If I ascend to heaven, you are there. If I descend into hades, you are present. If I take up my wings at dawn or dwell at the bottom of the sea, indeed, there, your hand will guide me. Indeed, your right hand will hold me fast."[30] Unless humans "by choice" separate themselves from God, they already "live in heaven."[31] Christians are called to "be perfect as your Father is perfect," but to be "perfect," for Gregory, is not to dwell in "the firmament of heaven as some remote habitation [κεχωρισμένον ἐνδιαίτημα] of God."[32] It is to represent the ineffable who is always already near. Self-sabotage and external tragedy threaten to "corrode" the soul, and the devil constantly removes the masks of virtue.[33] Yet Christian perfection is available not by "overstepping our nature" or by escaping to "some remote habitation." It is forged through the daily practices that over time accumulate into a homed desire that can respond to a God it never fully knows.

Harmonius, therefore, did not receive a specific prescription from Gregory.[34] The letter assumes familiarity with scripture, shared rituals, a disciplined regimen, an orientation toward a promise always yet to come, and faith that participation in and representation of an unknown God center that promise. But there was no to-do list. Mimesis of the divine nature could not work that directly when human transformation was as endless as the God it worships. Endless transformation could not happen according to preexisting patterns; practice must generate the patterns that, in turn, shape a soul.

Gregory framed this endless growth with a metaphor of debt and interest.[35] He hoped his definition would be seed money that compounded over time. It was meant to accrue and expand as Harmonius gained experience in his calling. Putting his treasure in heaven by conducting his love of God should continue to grow Harmonius's sense of what it means to call himself a Christian. "Because of the nature of the One receiving the deposit," Gregory writes, "it is altogether necessary that the return be enlarged [μεγαλύνεσθαι]."[36] And with that dilation of desire should come new images and new understandings of what is ultimately beyond all comprehension.

If the letter's goal is to elicit more questions, it surely succeeds. Gregory's definition exhorts Harmonius to a life that he assumes Harmonius is already living, but modern readers (and likely ancient ones as well) are left wondering: What kinds of guidelines or practices help govern this life? What disciplines must Christians assume if they want to choose this life of Christian perfection? What do Christians imitate when they imitate the divine? Gregory does not quite answer any of these in this letter. Looking to other texts, especially texts from around this time late in his career, reveals how mimesis, for Gregory, became both the way and the goal of Christian perfection. To put it differently, Gregory's definition offers a lens for reading Gregory.

Mimesis and the Study of Religion

In addition to providing a more nuanced understanding of mimesis in Gregory, *Imitations of Infinity* has three broader implications: for the study of late antiquity, for the genealogies of mimesis, and for the discipline of religious studies. First, late antiquity is often defined as a time when Christian leaders applied classical practices of representation to new subject matter.[37] Reading practices once applied to Homer now work on the Bible.[38] I argue that these new subjects emerged among shifting understandings of mimesis. While Gregory is the main character of my story, his life displays many of the qualities that have made late antiquity a distinctive time period: hybridity and competitions for order, asceticism and classical education, assemblages of a new set of imagined and institutionalized authorities within an empire with a long memory, and glacial changes from civic *euergetism* to ecclesial power emphasizing "the poor."[39]

His own family lived in the intricate world of late Roman landed aristocracy, although his grandparents suffered as confessors under the persecution of Maximin Daia. Gregory of Nazianzus described them as "trainers of virtue for others—living martyrs, breathing monuments, silent proclamations."[40] His grandmother and mother instilled the family's religious roots that went back to Origen of Alexandria's student Gregory Thaumaturgus, while his father, a rhetorician, rebuilt the family's fortunes during a time when large portions of Pontus converted to Christianity. His oldest sister, Macrina, and his brothers experimented with forms of asceticism and institutionalized poverty relief. And his brother Basil, who studied in Athens at the same time as Julian (later known as "the Apostate"), knew well both the power politics and pastoral care involved in theological debates.[41]

Gregory's life and thought were constituted by all these issues—legacies of martyrdoms, Origen's contemplative practices, rhetoric, asceticism, Christianization of knowledge, imperial-level politics, pastoral care, care of the poor, and theological debate. His life was filled with questions about both *what* and *how* to imitate. Both the objects of mimetic desire and the practices of mimesis were up for debate in his life, and, because mimesis governed questions of cosmology, education, aesthetics, and much more, how it was theorized and deployed was hotly contested. With Gregory, moreover, we see imitation move from a temporary tool to the very aim of the Christian life. While many earlier writers saw imitation as a way to achieve a kind of self-sufficiency, Gregory understood mimesis to lock Christians into a life always governed by an archetype.[42]

This shift in the function of mimesis leads to the book's second goal: in addition to providing a thicker description of Gregory's account of mimesis, this book plants seeds for a new history of mimesis. Many of the best studies on the concept skate easily from Plato, to Aristotle, to Neoplatonists, to . . . Michelangelo, and then march toward Derrida and the present. No one study can do it all—and this one certainly does not try—but the persistent break in the story is worthy of note. That these studies plot a similar arc with a similar cast of characters does not make them invalid or even repetitive. Many, however, assume a stability in the contours of conceptualizations of mimesis that can survive the "jump" from ancient philosophical schools to arguments about imitation of nature in the Renaissance. In an attempt to lay the groundwork for reading a particular theorist, these narratives often highlight the texts that were key to the theorist; there are advantages to this approach, but often at the cost of reinforcing a narrow path through history.[43] *Imitations of Infinity* suggests that there is more to this story than these narratives allow. By stretching mimesis to cover this gap, I hope to add more than another plot point in this (secularization) story. Examining mimesis in late ancient Christianity shows that something is lost when modern historians, philosophers, and classicists pass over these religious reflections on mimesis. Mimesis for early Christians formed a "way of life," and erasing late antique Christianity from these narratives obscures the ways mimesis became a way to say the unsayable that involved the reshaping of an entire life.

Mimesis is both a concept and a practice; it organizes the world and gives people something to strive toward. Early Christian theoretical concerns over mimesis emerged from, responded to, and vied for the shape of the basic patterns of a Christian life. We need to see those contests to see what was at stake in conceptions of mimesis. At the same time, to examine the practice without attending to conceptual frameworks that make them meaningful is to assume a rather flat version of mimesis, which makes it difficult to see why mimesis incited so much controversy. It is commonplace to say that Christians imitated Christ. What we need to know is how and why that could be problematic. In focusing on mimesis in late antiquity, and especially in Gregory, we can see how conceptual frameworks and ascetic practices work together to stylize religious subjects as well as their sacred objects. We can only see the stakes of theories of mimesis by looking at the practices just as we can only understand the practices by seeing the theories underpinning them. By showing how debates around mimesis that began with Plato became in late antiquity an especially dense intersection of concepts and practices, I hope readers can begin to see the outlines of a different story of mimesis.

More specifically, including late ancient Christianity helps us see tension between imitation and inimitability. While earlier thinkers of mimesis (e.g., Plato or Origen) emphasized that no representation could adequately capture its archetype, Gregory's stress on the infinitude of God put a different kind of pressure on mimesis. The problem for Gregory is not that representations are not good enough (with the underlying assumption being that with more able intellects they could be); it is that the reality they represent cannot be bounded and therefore is unrepresentable.[44] How does mimesis happen when there is a necessary and unbridgeable gap between representation and reality?[45]

The third goal of *Imitations of Infinity* is to take up questions that are central to religious studies about how subjectivity is constantly constituted through mimetic relations. Gregory's names, spaces, and characters form both religious beliefs and what Talal Asad calls the "sensibilities and attitudes that are distinct from beliefs."[46] While few might have been able to follow Gregory's argument with the "Eunomians" or "Macedonians," forming relationships with the names, spaces, and characters that Gregory asked his audiences to imitate formed a kind of common sense—shared, structured dispositions and desires.[47] His writings provided patterns of identification and attachment that included and exceeded any specific claim about *epinoia* or the Trinity. They constructed models of selfhood as they taught people both how and what to desire. Theorizing mimetic relationships was key to this subjectivation. Questions of what to imitate, that is, intertwined with questions of how to imitate.

Like religion, mimesis is a mix of practices and organizing frameworks. And like religion, mimesis is a way to make sense of our lives and a way to feel out the edges of our existence. While questions about mimesis often begin from an account of how art both reflects and creates worlds, the line between art and life is often quite thin. We create the images that create us. Turning back to late antiquity allows us to see how traditional categories of literary analysis became central to contests over how to fashion a way of life that could represent another world, a heavenly sphere, or even the divine.

Critical theorists such as Michel Foucault have observed how literature, institutions, and bodily practices both limit and model possibilities of selfhood.[48] They become archetypes to imitate and worlds to participate in. Foucault, in his rethinking of the modern subject, compares modern notions of the self with ancient ones and notes how the modern self as an autonomous source of meaning is related to a cauterizing of art from life. "What strikes me is the fact that in our society, art has become something which is related only to objects and not to individuals, or to life. That art is something which is specialized or which is done by experts who are artists. But couldn't everyone's life become a work of art? Why should the lamp or the house be an art object, but not our life?"[49] Bodies in space, Foucault argues, can both show the "signs of the time" and kindle other possibilities, can make other forms of life recognizable.

Foucault and his best readers often emphasize how the mimetic relations that create us as subjects carry with them a kind of excess that cannot be captured in their archetype.[50] Robert Orsi includes Foucault's work in what he calls "the tradition of the more," a strand of scholarship that emphasizes (even praises) the "excess" as what escapes representation, positivism, and control, and what holds open the possibility of another way of being.[51] Theorists in this strain often turn to mystical theology to demonstrate how something escapes or exceeds dominant forms of representation and control, and that excess keeps alive possibilities of being otherwise.[52] But what that alternative might be can be quite vague. What might it look like to practice this alternative? Turning to Gregory allows for a more detailed, nuanced analysis of "the more." Transcending oneself, for Gregory, is not an escape from discipline; discipline attempts to shape experiences of transcendence. That God, and therefore all faithful "images" of God, cannot be captured in imitations is his starting point of reflection on Christian perfection.[53] Mystery and mimesis worked together, as new names, spaces, and characters populated the early Christian imagination and shaped practices of Christian perfection.

Outline

The first half of this study situates Gregory's writings within Greco-Roman and early Christian discourses around mimesis. I begin with Plato, who establishes what I call the "two tracks of mimesis," aesthetic representation and ontological participation. On the one hand, Plato theorizes the relationship between representation and reality. He asks how the stories and images that mirror the world affect humans in their pursuit of the Good. On the other hand, within the dialogue named after him, Timaeus theorizes mimesis as primarily a matter of ontology. His universe is created as a series of imitations or microcosms held together by participatory relationships in which creatures are held in existence by their cause. A creature imitates its makers not as a separate, contained existing entity attempting to capture the likeness of another separate, contained existing entity, but as something completely dependent on that which it imitates.

These two aspects of mimesis, moreover, correlate with two erotics or modes of desire. Representational mimesis excites readers to ascend a ladder of desire, which leads from individual images (or bodies) to more abstract loves. Once ascended, philosophers can also differently perceive those bodies: they become flashes of beauty or points of intensity. In ontological mimesis, by contrast, Timaeus does not climb a ladder. He gazes directly at the "first principles" and longs for the perfect circle of the universe in his mind. Transcendence here is that of an uninterrupted contemplation without growth or movement. After laying these two tracks, the chapter concludes with a discussion of Greco-Roman rhetorical training, which happens largely through concentrated practices of imitation. Gregory himself taught rhetoric before his ordination and so would have been familiar with how these teachers emphasized a complex mix of mimetic theory and practice by which students acquired the habits needed to imitate often "inimitable" qualities of the best speakers.

Chapter 2 examines what happens when these two tracks cross, as readers attempt to synthesize Plato's writings into one philosophical system. In late antiquity, readers of Plato—Christian and non-Christian—become particularly concerned with the role of mimesis in the philosophical life. I examine how mimesis forms "a conceptual vein that leads to the heart" of Plotinus's and Iamblichus's philosophical programs, and also how their different conceptions of mimesis lead to quite different organizing concepts and practices.[54] For Plotinus, mimesis is a stepping stone toward a non-mimetic goal in which human souls are united to the One, which is beyond all representation. Iamblichus, however, convinced that souls are too damaged to contemplate the divine without help, weds his philosophy to more specific theurgic rituals that require mimesis. In ritual, theurgists encounter "symbols," which are not representations of another reality, but an activating force for something otherwise inaccessible in humans. Only in performing these rituals and engaging the symbols do theurgists imitate and unite with the gods. The chapter finally turns to the emperor Julian, whose devotion to Iamblichean philosophy spread its popularity across the empire, especially in Cappadocia. Susanna Elm argues that what Julian saw in Iamblichus was "a consistent system that merged everything."[55] His theory of everything challenged Christian theologians to come up with their own in response.

Before turning to Gregory, however, we need to set his work in another, competing discourse. Philosophers, after all, were not the only ones concerned with mimesis. Chapter 3 examines a wide range of early Christian debates around mimesis. Paul's request that the Corinthians "imitate me as I imitate Christ"[56] binds Christian formation to practices of imitating those who show what Christ looks like. Martyrs and saints, too, are cast as imitators of Christ, or even "other Christs."[57] But with the multiplication of "other Christs," questions emerge around proper relationships with these holy women and men: Should they be imitated (and if so, by whom?), or are there other modes of participation (e.g., awe, reverence, wonder) that can quicken early Christians? By situating Gregory within these larger debates, I hope it is clear that his writings operate within lively and contested discourses concerning mimesis. Late antiquity transformed much of classical culture (e.g., religion, politics, gender norms, ascetic ideals), and with these transformations came a shift in understandings of mimetic relationships.[58]

Having presented these two tracks and shown how their crossing became a problem in late antiquity, in the second half of this study, I show how these two aspects of mimesis played out with respect to three kinds of images that Gregory insisted are not divine: names, spaces, and characters.[59] These names, spaces, and characters are finite and therefore, Gregory argued, cannot be God. And yet, what Gregory takes away ontologically he gives back mimetically. This triptych, I argue, forms not only Gregory's most common targets of mimetic desire, but also form Gregory's own "theory of everything," his way to connect heaven and earth. Throughout the first part of this study we will have seen how questions of mimesis are inseparable from the formation of desire. Put strongly, imitation is what desire looks like. When we turn to Gregory's names, spaces, and characters, we see how these three kinds of images fill souls and make participation in God possible, and how, in their combination, they govern and propel Christian desire.

Chapter 4 examines Gregory's treatise *On Perfection* and what he calls "the names we take into the soul." A seeming distinction frames the treatise: those names that "we have room for, we imitate, and those that our nature does not have room for in imitation, we revere and worship."[60] That distinction between imitation and worship was a fourth-century commonplace. For Gregory, however, it was one to overcome. When Christianity is imitation of the divine nature, he argues, Christians cannot be satisfied with worshipful participation alone. They must also push at their own edges as they imitate what always exceeds them. Said differently, inimitable things are the only things worth imitating. Gregory insists that Christians will never fully imitate the divine and that there is, indeed, a danger in "arriving too quickly" at imitation. But worship and imitation remain in a dynamic relationship for Gregory. The push and pull between them govern Christian perfection, which Gregory describes as "never to stop growing toward what is better and never placing any limit on perfection."[61] These names, like water entering a ductile container, stretch what they fill. Taking on the name of Christ requires Christians to constantly expand that name by adding more names to it.

Chapter 5 examines two literary practices Gregory often deploys involving "mimetic space." First, I look to his *Treatise on the Inscriptions of the Psalms* to show how Gregory repeatedly maps the Christian life and asks Christians to make a journey through the stations he curates. After examining this practice of mapping, I focus on the production of affective spaces or spatial images that provide particularly intense sites of the divine. These spaces not only stylize the infinite, they also teach Christians to feel it. Gregory conjures and invites his audience into a space that, in his words, "contains the Uncontained," and there invites them to become an infinite space as well.[62] Drawing on Henri Lefebvre's threefold understanding of space—perceived spaces of practice, conceived spaces such as maps, and spaces of representation or the spaces by which we understand ourselves—the chapter argues that Gregory maps spaces and creates scenes or places that link heaven and earth.

Finally, Chapter 6 turns to what might be the most obvious mimetic relationships Gregory hopes to inculcate, those with characters. These characters are not only moral examples, but also images of God. In Gregory's writings on Moses, Paul, and Macrina, each character's holiness contains a mystery that encourages both representation and participation. Watching a saint's infinite growth, for Gregory, is as close as readers can get to a representation of an infinite God, and their endless expansion invites others to join in their expansive love. These characters both exhort and reveal, spurring imitation by becoming containers of the uncontainable. Through these characters, we will also see Gregory's insistence that, in imitating an unknowable God, Christians become unknowable.

The book concludes by asking questions about the ethical and theological implications of imitating what one does not know. What are the demands and dilemmas of containing the uncontained? The question for Gregory arose with respect to God, humans, and all of creation. In forging those mysterious relationships, Gregory theorized Christian perfection as the endless stretching, intensification, and progression of love of God. These names, spaces, and characters governed and propelled the life of Christian perfection, guiding an ever-expanding desire toward a God who was at once infinitely beyond and acutely present to all. Through them, Christians could live the mimetic life.

CHAPTER 1

Two Tracks of Mimesis

In a speech celebrating Plato's birthday, the Athenian Neoplatonist Proclus (412–485 CE) posed a problem for himself: "How could there be any reconciliation between the man who, in the *Phaedo* [95a] is called by Plato a 'divine poet' and the one shown in the *Republic* [10.597e] to be 'third in line from the truth?' These cannot be woven together like two linen threads: the same individual could not possibly take both positions. In the first assertion, we have a Homer who has transcended all human and partial notions in his poetry and has rooted his own thought among the gods; in the second, a Homer who knows only images of truth and strays far from wisdom about the divine."[1] In an earlier essay, Proclus asks the question a little differently: "If, according to [Plato], poetry has something divine in it, how is it that it is rejected from the divine state? And if it does not, why is it given divine honors?"[2] If art produces the "timely stimulation [καιρῷ κινήσεως]"[3] necessary for divinization, how can Socrates reject it? Why does Socrates banish from the Republic those who practice the mimetic arts, when the next day, in Timaeus's discussion of the creation of the world, readers find that all of creation is held together by the thread of mimesis?[4]

For Proclus, Homer was not only "the originator of tragedy." He also fashioned Plato's "whole mimetic style [πραγματείας τῆς μιμητικῆς]" as well as the "whole of his philosophical perspective [τῆς φιλοσόφου θεωρίας ὅλης]."[5] Plato is both artist and philosopher; and, in this conceptualization, Proclus brings together two discourses that run parallel in Plato's writing: aesthetic representation and ontological participation.

The relationship between representation and participation was hotly debated in late ancient intellectual and religious circles. Human participation in the divine is described as mimetic. Humans come into being because of, and by becoming an image of, their creator. The status of both that dependency and of that image, however, was ambiguous. Proclus's *Commentary on the Republic* is itself of two minds about such questions. Mimesis, Proclus first argues in the fifth essay of the treatise, functions squarely in the realm of imitable things. All poetry is mimetic, and Proclus smooths out a wrinkle in Plato by distinguishing between accurate and inaccurate imitations:[6] Plato encourages accurate imitations, but inaccurate ones must be banished. By the sixth essay, however, poetry has a theurgic function and has the power to transcend the material realm and to deify the soul. Poetry, Proclus argues, mirrors the soul: tripartite art for tripartite souls.[7] The lowest levels are sensible and are "called nothing other than 'mimetic' [οὐδὲν ἀλλ᾽ ἢ μιμητικὴ καὶ οὖσα καὶ λεγομένη]."[8] These words are mere images of the real world; they represent reality without drawing readers into participation. And this drift from reality also makes them unethical. "They do not incline to virtue and education and they are not useful to lawmakers for the correct upbringing of the young."[9] These representations stir up "the trivial passions to enormous volume and [impress] the listener with such words and expressions and chang[e] the various dispositions of the soul."[10] This art, aimed at entertaining, encourages people to let loose their imaginations, dispositions, and base desires.[11]

To keep the passions in check requires a different kind of poetic encounter. And to that end, Proclus sees at least two more ways poetry functions. The second mode of engagement with poetry "draws together the knower and the known into the same entity, and reproduces the image of the intellective substance, drawing together into one the nature of the noetic objects."[12] This is an encounter with that which "know[s] the essence of the things that exist and love[s] the spectacle of good and beautiful deeds and discourses." This poetry "offers . . . participation [μετουσίαν] in practical wisdom [φρονήσεώς] and the other virtues."[13] Poetry here does not direct the mind to different thoughts spurred on by powerful images; it allows a contemplation in which the mind replicates the noetic world, which links participants into the virtues. The mind so perfectly mirrors the heavenly spheres, in fact, that the line between imitator and imitated fades and the mind shares in the nature of its object.

The third, and most notable, kind of poetry corresponds to the highest part of the soul. "Careful listeners" move beyond vision and imitation into inspiration. While "the mimetic poet has no natural link to the rational part of the soul," Proclus writes, "the inspired poet addresses his discourse to the divine part of the soul."[14] He later adds, "To the extent that he is possessed by the Muses, he is divine, and to the extent that he is an imitator, he is third from the truth. This is how Plato is able to call him as a witness to the greatest of doctrines and also to expel him from his state."[15] In some poetry, language does not describe but joins that in which it participates. "It creates a single divine bond and unifying mixture of that which is participated in and that which participates [τοῦ μετεχομένου καὶ μετέχοντος], rooting all that is inferior in that which is better, arranging that what is more divine, alone, is active, while the lower has contracted and hidden its own individual identity in that which is greater."[16] Participation in this language dissolves the mimetic distance through which signs and things are linked, and enters what Sara Rappe describes as "non-discursive" language, where words find meaning only in transcending meaning and activating another faculty that allows for contact with the divine.[17]

Proclus calls this third kind of language symbolic (συμβολικὴ) rather than mimetic.

> How, moreover, could the term "mimetic" be applied to that poetry which interprets the divine by means of symbols? For symbols are not imitations of those things they symbolize. Things could never be imitations of their opposites (good imitating bad, natural imitating unnatural), but the symbolic mode [ἡ . . . συμβολικὴ θεωρία] indicates the nature of things even by means of their complete opposites. Therefore, if a poet is inspired and reveals to us through symbols the truth about things that are, or if he uses systematic knowledge to reveal to us the order of things, this poet is not an imitator and cannot be found wanting by the arguments we are discussing.[18]

The contrast between mimetic and symbolic language for Proclus makes possible divinization, as the symbol opens into a ritual space in which the poet (or the one who is made a poet by experiencing poetry) is united to truth.

Proclus, we should note, refers here not to two different texts, but two ways of encountering a text.[19] Homer is both imitator and divine. The philosophical life is preparation for a symbolic encounter with poetry. This encounter "sets in motion the cycles of the divine souls."[20] The symbol is, in Rappe's words, "a divinely installed switch, so to speak, that operates within the context of ritual. Symbols function as crossroads, as junctures that allow the soul to trace its path back to its origins."[21] Language, that is, "reiterates the hierarchical nature of reality,"[22] and it creates a sacred space in which theurgists participate.

Most importantly for us, Proclus connects aesthetics and ontology. Theurgy and poetry, Peter Struck writes, "reverse the process of emanation, and open up an avenue by which we might retrace the ontological movement that produced the universe back up from material to divine."[23] Aesthetics and ontology weave together in Proclus's soteriology and cosmology, and they make the encounter with language a driving force of the philosophical life. Aesthetics are not a stepping stone toward an encounter with truth; poetry summons what is most ontologically real. Bluntly, good readers, in the right space, with the right texts, have access to the divine.

This connection between the two sides of mimesis—aesthetics and ontology—concerns much of late antique thought. Yet for this book's main character, Gregory of Nyssa, Christianity is not a symbol of the divine nature; it is an imitation of it. Where Proclus finds a path beyond mimesis, Gregory insists on a mimetic relation with a God beyond all mimesis. Paradoxically, Christians are united to Christ, while a gap between creator and creation remains and fosters desire. Understanding the significance of that gap and the ways in which participation and representation happen in it is at the heart of this study. But to discuss this, we need to ask: How did we get here? Proclus's tethering of aesthetics and ontology emerges from years of wrestling with Plato's writings, and it is to those writings that this chapter turns.

Plato: The Two Tracks

Proclus's reading helps situate this chapter on Plato in two ways. First, it shows how late antiquity inherits and develops a long, rich discourse around mimesis. The word mimesis traces back at least to the fifth century BCE, with origins in discussions of ritual action and the repetition of myths.[24] Early Christians also developed their own understandings of the term, but much of what came to organize late ancient understandings of mimesis emerged from engagement with Plato. Beginning this chapter in late antiquity also serves as a reminder that my reading of Plato is meant to help us understand Gregory of Nyssa, not to try to provide a full study of Plato's own writings on mimesis.[25]

Proclus helps us see what I hope to highlight in this chapter: two tracks that run parallel in Plato's writing on mimesis: aesthetic representation and ontological participation. In Plato's *Republic* and *Symposium*, discussions of mimeses address questions of art, of representation and reality, and of how representations shape souls.[26] Discussions of mimesis in the *Timaeus*, by contrast, address the structure of the universe (τὸ πᾶν) and humanity's participation in it. The universe is created mimetically with each level of creation made in the image of and dependent on its maker. While these two understandings of mimesis—aesthetic representation and ontological participation—each take up significant and sustained places in Plato's writings, how they relate remains an open question. They are spoken by different characters in different settings, and the form of the dialogues does not require them to merge. But how they relate will occupy much of late ancient thought. As we can see with Proclus, the relationship between these conceptions of mimesis was not obvious to late ancient readers.

The two understandings, moreover, also correlate with two conceptions of eros.[27] For both, eros allows imitators to move from representation to reality or from a lower level of being to a higher one. But these two discourses of mimesis focus not only on different intellectual questions but also on different structures of desire. For Proclus, philosophy is the "most erotic [ἐρωτικωτάτην]" life, but within Plato's writing, how desire functions in the pursuit of wisdom is far from clear.[28] In the *Symposium*, bodies and images intensify and anagogically direct desire, whereas in the *Timaeus*, desire for the intelligible spheres encourages a telescopic vision undisturbed by aims of desire.

Track 1: Aesthetic Mimesis

The "examined life" requires examples. "The higher ideals, dear friend, can only be shown by means of examples [παραδείγμασι]," Socrates says in the *Statesman*. Without them, "each of us seems to know everything in a dreamy sort of way, and then to wake up and know nothing."[29] But throughout Plato's writings, these examples are as powerful as they are dangerous. They have the capacity to distract from truth as well as to lead to it. Teachers, therefore, must be careful in choosing the examples and the artistic representations they champion, because bad art makes bad people.

In Plato's writings on the aesthetics of mimesis, we see the stakes and possibilities of engaging with representations. Engaged with properly, art offers the possibility of gaining some distance on one's life in order to find oneself in another. Through that identification, philosophers may better themselves, but the power of stories to seep into a soul means that they must come under critique.[30] Plato's writings on aesthetic mimesis show a concern about the influence that these models have over human lives and offer ways to work with and against them to model citizens.

Republic Books 2–3: Mimetic Formation, Crossing Boundaries, and Noble Lies

When Proclus sought to reconcile Plato's two tracks, he noticed, as many modern readers do not, that Plato's treatment of mimetic art begins not in Book 10 of the *Republic* but in Books 2 and 3. These books concern the formation of citizens, and this formation happens in large part through the aesthetics of mimesis.

The *Republic* introduces mimesis around a high-stakes issue: the origin of war. Imitators (μιμηταί)—those concerned with poets, actors, figures, colors, music, and "feminine adornment" (373b–c)—want more than is just, more than their place. They want not a "healthy" city but a "luxurious one," filled with all kinds of "heavy things." Socrates, that is, links mimesis to a kind of transcendence: imitation pushes women and men beyond their place and dissolves the boundaries of the well-ordered city. The results are catastrophic: greedy citizens, unsatisfied with their place in the city, agitating for war.

This bleak entrance into mimesis offers no clear exit. There is no getting rid of imitation. It must be tactically deployed, not jettisoned. Mimesis, specifically, is necessary for education and for friendship. The formation of children, like the formation of anything, Socrates argues, is "most plastic" at the beginning. "Each thing assimilates itself to the model whose stamp anyone wishes to give to it" (377b). But humans cannot stamp truth directly onto a soul. (Only gods can do that.) "Don't you understand," Socrates tells Glaucon and his brother Adeimantus, "that first we tell tales to children? And surely they are, as a whole, false, though there are true things in them too. We make use of tales with children before exercises" (377a). Formation requires starting with sensible stories and moving from there, "little by little," toward Beauty and Goodness. Friendship too, Socrates says, requires lying—lying to our friends' enemies, lying to keep our friends safe, and lying to our friends to keep them from doing foolish things. To pursue the good life, even within the best city, requires lying, and lying, too, is about mimesis: effective lies must appear true, and the most effective lies tell people what they want to hear. "The lie in speeches is a kind of imitation [μίμημά τι] of the affection [παθήματος] in the soul, a phantom [εἴδωλον] of it that comes into being after it, and not quite an unadulterated lie" (382b).

While readers are introduced to mimesis in Book 2, mimesis first becomes a serious concern in Book 3, when Socrates and Adeimantus discuss the style (λέξεως) of speech that will be efficacious for the city (392c). This discussion of mimesis and speech is a metonym for larger questions of fashioning women and men. Socrates suggests that human nature finds completion only when it properly imitates the narrow range of examples for which it is capable. The problem with imitation, that is, is not with imitation itself; rather it is with the desire to imitate more than one can. "Human nature . . . is unable to make a fine imitation [καλῶς μιμεῖσθαι] of many things," Socrates says (395b). When citizens reach beyond their capacity, they stop imitating "the things themselves" and imitate the imitation; they perform a simulacrum instead of doing the slow work of acclimating themselves to the ideal. This misdirected mimesis causes citizens to desire representations rather than reality. Socrates and Adeimantus, therefore, warn against the hubris of trying to access multiple professions, or even multiple worlds. This accusation is especially aimed at the poets, who represent many professions and entire worlds without knowing any of them well.

The first problem with mimesis, then, is simply that the citizen spreads herself out too thin. "The same person isn't able to imitate [μιμεῖσθαι] many things as well as one" (394e). Concerning the guardians, Socrates says,

> If, then, we are to preserve the first argument—that our guardians must give up all other crafts and very precisely be craftsmen of the city's freedom and practice nothing other than what tends to it— they also mustn't do or imitate anything else. And if they do imitate, they must imitate what's appropriate to them from childhood; men who are courageous, moderate, holy, free, and everything of the sort; and what is slavish, or anything else shameful, they must neither do nor be clever at imitating, so that they won't get a taste for the being from its imitation. Or haven't you observed that imitations, if they are practiced continually from youth onwards, become established as habits [ἔθη] and nature, in body and sounds and in thought [διάνοιαν]? (395b–d)

Imitation is both ubiquitous and undeniably influential. For Socrates, then, the state (or more specifically the ruling philosopher [401b]) must control the representations to which a guardian is exposed because he will imitate those imitations. This starts with "childhood" and continues into adulthood, such that the habits and styles of reasoning take root deep in human nature. If a guardian, especially if he is young, gets a "taste" of a bad representation and learns to imitate it, not only will he be corrupted, but, moreover, the very nature of what it will mean to be a guardian has the potential to change, which threatens the structure of civic life.[31] The poet receives the sharpest critique because he allows citizens to believe that his mimetic creations are real possibilities, and thus he threatens both the individual and political body. For the guardian, who spends years training to become a single-minded protector of freedom, the vice-rich characters of the epics open false, if deeply seductive, possibilities.

It is not only the content that is dangerous, according to Socrates. A "style" of imitation exceeds any particular example and destabilizes any direct line between example and imitation. Poetry is an unstable force— pushing a soul in ways that are at once indirect and yet constitutive. The potency of poetry leads to Socrates's skepticism more broadly of poetic music, especially "panharmonic instruments," such as the flute (399d). Who knows where a poem could lead a soul? Who knows how a song can refigure a sense of self? An instrument is acceptable if it can maintain a direct connection between its sound and its effect (e.g., the pipe to call sheep), but more often than not art's effects are too uncertain for responsible rearing (393d–394b). The disconnect between intention and consequence gives rise to the possibility of new natures being formed, natures that could be quite corrupt. And yet citizens need music in the same way that they need stories (377a–378e). Like the unexamined life, the artless life is not worth living.

Citizens need music because of this second aspect of aesthetic mimesis. Music and stories, when performed well, teach a "rhythm," which is also necessary to perform the proper roles. They not only provide images to which citizens should assimilate, but also shape the "disposition [ἤθει] of the soul" (400d). Those who grow accustomed to different rhythms take on different natures. Good speeches, with a "fine style," are possible only in a person who is trained in the arts, and training in the arts is meant to shape a good disposition. "Good speech, good harmony, good grace, and good rhythm accompany good disposition, not the folly that we endearingly call 'good disposition,' but that understanding truly trained to a good and fair disposition" (400d–e). Successful education for Socrates focuses on the soul and these rhythms.

The word ἦθος captures these two aspects. The word, on the one hand, carries theatrical resonances (e.g., a dramatic persona or literary character whom one can imitate). But it also suggests something closer to a trait, a characteristic, or, more broadly, a disposition or habitual character, which one imitates in a less direct way. Mimesis works at both of these levels as it habituates citizens. We see this clearly in the way music shapes a soul:

> "So Glaucon," I said, "isn't this why the rearing in music is most sov-
> ereign? Because rhythm and harmony most of all plunge themselves
> into the inmost part of the soul [καταδύεται εἰς τὸ ἐντὸς τῆς ψυχῆς]
> and most vigorously lay hold of it in bringing grace with them; and
> they make a man graceful if he is correctly reared, if not, the oppo-
> site. Furthermore, it is sovereign because the man properly reared on
> rhythm and harmony would have the sharpest sense for what's been
> left out and what isn't a fine product of craft or what isn't a fine prod-
> uct of nature. And, due to his having the right kind of dislikes, he
> would praise the fine things; and, taking pleasure in them and re-
> ceiving them into his soul, he would be reared on them and become
> a gentleman. He would blame and hate the ugly in the right way
> while he's still young, before he's able to grasp reasonable speech.
> And when reasonable speech comes, the man who's reared in this
> way would take most delight in it, recognizing it on account of its
> being akin?" (401d–402a, trans. altered)

Citizens become attuned to certain rhythms, modes, and styles, even before they can produce "reasonable speech." Music dives down into the deepest parts of the soul and creates a kind of common sense or "reasonableness," out of which speech and action will arise. Civic life depends on this common sense. The question for Socrates is not whether, but what kinds of aesthetic styles will be beneficial for it. What kinds of affective relations do they encourage? What kinds of representations—in both form and content, if that is still a meaningful distinction—will shape the people of the city? What ethos should they foster?

To be a protector of the city, Socrates argues, guardians must be so ha-bituated to the beautiful things, so attuned to the styles of the good, that they will not be carried away by flashy poems. Stories of previous guardians and musical rhythms must be so deeply engraved into their souls that their bodies and their judgments need not struggle with questions of which model to imitate, but move to the rhythm that has shaped their nature and allow it to direct their desire to do the proper thing (395b–d). Shaping politically responsible guardians is about cultivating citizens who most desire what is most beautiful (κάλλιστον ἐρασμιώτατον) (402d).

Mimesis now has a double movement. On the one hand is what I might call a literal imitation, where mimesis is a form of assimilation. Guardians look to exemplary guardians and ought "to practice nothing other than what tends to" their role in the city (395b–c). As they learn to imitate, they become habituated. If they do not, as we saw in Book 2, they will carry the city off to war. On the other hand, imitation molds a disposition toward the world that makes those models attractive in the first place.[32] It creates styles or "types" of citizens and fosters desires that allow them to know what is worth protecting and what should be left out.

Aware of its dangers, Socrates concedes that mimesis forms citizens by constellating the order, growth, and desire needed for the virtuous life. Mimesis has the power to arouse and to sustain a disciplined life, even if it can draw citizens away from the ordered world and into the land of myth and adornment. It makes growth and desire possible, even if its risks are unavoidable. Through slow, deep engagement with what is most beautiful, mimesis can encourage the guardians' desire to protect and even live in the style of what ought to continue.

Republic Book 10: An Old Quarrel

Plato returns to questions of mimesis in Book 10, where he continues to describe the double-edged nature of mimesis: necessary but dangerous. In Book 10, the focus turns to the role of myth and what Stephen Halliwell summarizes as "the powerful 'sympathy' that can draw audiences of poetry into deep emotional absorption in the experiences of the characters depicted."[33]

For as much as it is studied, the critique of poetry in Book 10 remains strange. Few readers who have made it through the previous nine books can miss the irony of Socrates accusing Homer of telling tales, of not governing a city, of not giving advice in battle, of not entering the daily grind of everyday politics, and of rousing citizens out of the common sense that allows the city to function—all charges that could easily be brought against Socrates.

So why deport the poets? Socrates, importantly, denounces not poetry, but "any part of [poetry] that is imitative [μηδαμῇ παραδέχεσθαι αὐτῆς ὅση μιμητική]." (595a).[34] (Recall Proclus's claim that there is a non-mimetic language that can provide access to truth.[35]) At first blush, at least, there are two different problems that Socrates addresses when he takes up mimetic poetry. First, he asks what imitation is in general (μίμησιν ὅλως) (595c). In the second and "greatest accusation" (605c), Socrates argues that mimetic poetry, in particular, dulls the mind, softens the soul, and threatens the city, making people unconcerned with truth and goodness.[36] These problems are related, but I take them in turn.

The general case against poetry is well known and easily summarized. Poetry and painting are three removes from reality.[37] There is one source of all reality; this source makes the *ideas* (the form of the table or the bed); the technician imitates this form when he makes a table or a bed; and the artist imitates that imitation. Rather than touching a divine form, this play of images is merely "an ordinary thing having intercourse with what is ordinary, producing ordinary offspring" (603b). These representations, severed from the forms, "look like they *are*; however, they surely *are* not in truth" (596e). Art here is cheap, easy. Mimesis degrades. "It is not hard" for an artist to create an entire world. "You could fabricate [all things that an artisan would make] quickly in many ways and most quickly, of course, if you are willing to take a mirror and carry it around everywhere; quickly you will make the sun and the things in the heaven; quickly, the earth; and quickly, yourself and the other animals and implements and plants and everything else that was just now mentioned" (596d–e). Mirrors capture appearance but flatten (and thus hide) reality. And from this general critique, we see hints of the ethical concerns in the repetition of the adverb "quickly" (ταχὺ). When the discussion shifts from poetry to the immortality of the soul, Socrates asks, "What that is great could come to pass in a short time?" (608c).[38] The ease of representing the world makes impossible the kind of slow, soul-forming learning advocated in Book 3. To put a point on it, Socrates makes the contrast like this: the poet "doesn't understand; but he imitates" (601a).[39] And settling for fast and facile imitations without true knowledge runs counter to the philosophical life.

Producing these images may be "easy," but they are not easily ignored.[40] And this is "the greatest accusation": the charge not that the art is false (which it is), but that it causes citizens to care for false things.[41] Stories open citizens to passions they would usually resist. And worse still, the representations might become models to imitate in life. These stories alter the mimetically formed common sense and attract citizens to characters that would be otherwise undesirable. In other words, mimetic poetry indulges the worst of the citizens. "It fosters and waters [the desires, pains, and pleasures in the soul] when they ought to be dried up," and it encourages similar behavior (606d). What almost no one recognizes, Socrates says, is that "the enjoyment of other people's sufferings has a necessary effect on one's own" (606b). Both levels of mimesis that Socrates mentions in Book 3 reappear in the deformation of the audiences. They lose themselves in their identification with characters. And they are attracted to the affective intensity that the characters suffer, so they imitate the causes of such stirrings. The poet "awakens [the worst] part of the soul and nourishes it, and, by making it strong, destroys the calculating part" (605b). Even those with well-formed souls submit to these passions and thus threaten both the soul and the city (605c–d). The problem is only amplified when Socrates reminds his hearers that human souls are formed by the very loves that these myths activate. The lies, needed to form children's moral dispositions, predispose citizens to want the myths to be true. Like the music that plunged into the depth of the souls, myths—which, indeed, are difficult to distinguish from mimetic poetry—are indispensable.

Representations are indispensable, but, Socrates insists, not irresistible. His philosophical program requires struggling with and against them: "Just like the men who have once fallen in love with someone, and don't believe the love is beneficial, keep away from it even if they have to do violence to themselves; so we too—due to the inborn love of such poetry we owe to our rearing in these fine regimes—we'll be glad if it turns out that it is best and truest." That fatal attraction requires strenuous, disciplined opposition, which is exactly philosophy's job: "when we listen to poetry," Socrates says, "we'll chant this argument we are making to ourselves as a countercharm, taking care against falling back again into this love, which is childish and belongs to the many." The real threat is that our lingering attraction will lead us to believe that poetry is "a serious thing, laying hold of truth" (607e–608b). Mimetic poetry might be three levels removed from the truth, but the solution to the problem of the formation of the soul through mimesis is not to contemplate the forms directly. This would, for Socrates, imply exchanging one kind of unexamined life for another. Socrates instead suggests that the philosophical life provides the chance to make what Allan Bloom translates as "countercharms [ἐπῳδήν]." Philosophers will not—and should not—rid the world of the charms of poetry, but examining their lives and the stories that make them allows for the possibilities of productive resistance. Philosophers' arguments emerge from and inspire new stories, new ways of stretching toward the virtuous life.

In short, poetry confirms our childish desires, whereas the philosophical life must work with and against stories. Stories abound; they order desire and create the possibility for "reasonable speech." But they also are full of lies—lies that sometimes make friendships possible, but that sometimes cause humans to go to war; lies that lead toward truths and lies that distract from them; lies that teach citizens how to love and lies that keep them in violent relationships, in thwarted love. Philosophers must not ignore or jettison these stories; they must examine them and their own lives to see what kinds of values and virtues they offer and what vices they instill. They must work to gain some distance from those stories that most fully shape them in order to see the best in them and avoid their harmful delights.

Across the *Republic*, mimesis is necessary, powerful, and dangerous. As individuals and as a political body, citizens are formed by imitations and by imitating them. They hear stories and assimilate to them, and their own desires move with the rhythms, images, characters, and narratives that sink into or even rip open the soul. Philosophers are to examine their role in the city, to form souls that can resist the charms of appearances, and to cultivate desires satisfied only with the truth.[42] It is to that movement from image to transcendent truth that I turn next.

Aesthetic Eros and the Ladder of Beauty

Critias skeptically says, "Everything we say must indeed be imitation and representation."[43] If seeking truth does not move philosophers away from mimesis, it does, nevertheless, require an ordered ascent that can transform the way one encounters the images.[44] If the soul is to be reformed as a lover of truth, mimesis and eros must work together. Philosophers, like the guardians, must be trained to desire most what is most beautiful (κάλλιστον ἐρασμιώτατον) (402d). This reformation is largely a matter of combining and shifting perceptions.[45] Philosophy weaves patterns that move from images to truth, and then, in turn, allows truth to shape the way one sees images. The philosopher described in the divided line moves from images and shadows, to the images on which they are based (that is, animals and artifacts), from there to mathematical hypotheses, to the forms, and finally to

the Good beyond being; and then can move back down as well. Image reading is at the heart of the examined life. And as we will see, changes in perception become changes in desire. Learning *what* to love is also about
learning *how* to perceive and how to love.

We see this change in perception and desire perhaps most clearly in
Diotima's speech and in the conclusion of Plato's *Symposium*.[46] After the
previous five speeches in praise of Eros, Socrates takes his turn. Instead of a
direct speech, however, he invokes a character, Diotima, to say what he cannot. In Diotima's speech in honor of Eros, lovers learn to love by moving
from loving one body, to two bodies, to all beautiful bodies, then from bodies to souls and laws, from souls and laws to wisdom, from wisdom to a unified knowledge, and finally to the beautiful (211b–d). Each of these loves is
like a "rising stair," as mimesis and transcendence come together to lead
lovers onward toward the beautiful (211b–d, trans. Nehamas and Woodruff). For the sake of brevity, I will quickly pull out a few key pieces of the
speech in order to show how mimesis carries with it an erotic pull toward
the beautiful as well as a need to create in the presence of the beautiful. Desire for the beautiful both attracts the lover, spurring him onward in ascent,
and compels him to make representations.

As in Socrates's critique of art in the *Republic*, the speech has two parts.[47]
First, it asks, "who and what sort of being is Love [ὁ Ἔρως]?" It then discusses Love's "works [ἔργα]" (201e). Unlike the gods, who are happy, Diotima begins, Eros occupies a space between mortal and immortal. Lack is
at the heart of Eros, that "great spirit [δαίμων μέγας]," who is the child of
resource and poverty (202e). Eros aches, needs, and strives toward what it
knows it does not have. This aching, straining spirit, moreover, mediates
between the human and divine, so that it can "bind the all together with itself [τὸ πᾶν αὐτὸ αὑτῷ συνδεδέσθαι]" (202e–203a, trans. altered). Eros
without being immortal itself has the capacity to encompass and transcend
physical relations, uniting forms and bodies, and gods and humans, in a
combination of endless need and wholeness. Anne Carson writes, "An edge
between two images cannot merge in a single focus because they do not derive from the same level of reality—one is actual, one is possible. To know
both, keeping that difference visible, is the subterfuge called eros."[48] Like the
pursuit of wisdom, Eros is the way one tracks the scent of the beautiful
things that lead to ineffable Beauty (203d–204a). Eros then is a great spirit,
motivated by lack and cunning, that links mortal, embodied creatures to
the beautiful.

What then are the works of love? Or how do lovers pursue the beautiful? The answer is deceptively simple.⁴⁹ "It is giving birth in the beautiful both in body and in soul [ἔστι γὰρ τοῦτο τόκος ἐν καλῷ καὶ κατὰ τὸ σῶμα καὶ κατὰ τὴν ψυχήν]" (206b, trans. altered). Despite our best efforts, Diotima continues, humans are transient. Humans are not immortal, but "reproduction goes on forever; it is what mortals have in place of immortality" (206e, trans. Nehamas and Woodruff). Everything moral "is preserved . . . not by keeping it exactly the same forever, like the divine, but by replacing what goes away or is antiquated with something new, something like what it was [οἷον αὐτὸ ἦν]" (208a–b, trans. altered). All humans, Diotima explains, are pregnant, and "when what is pregnant draws near the beautiful, it becomes gentle and joyfully disposed and gives birth and reproduces. . . . This is the source of the great excitement about beauty that comes to anyone who is pregnant and already teeming with life: beauty released them from their great pain. . . . What Love wants is not Beauty . . . [but] reproduction and birth in Beauty" (206d–e, trans. altered from Nehamas and Woodruff). Human "immortality"—which we all desire, according to Diotima—is achieved here in the production of new images in the presence of the Beautiful. Love's work, then, is the production of these images.

This insistence on Love desiring Beauty in order to give birth to the beautiful introduces the "love matters [τὰ ἐρωτικὰ]" into which Diotima will, perhaps, initiate (μυηθείης) Socrates. The initiation takes the form of a structured ascent. First, the lover "must be in love with one particular body" (210a). Learning to love one body and then another, "he must make himself a lover of all beautiful bodies" (210b). The lover of bodies can then love souls, which are more beautiful than bodies. Only then can he detach from the "slavery of a single image" and, having been acclimated to the love of beautiful things, turn "toward the main ocean of the beautiful" in philosophy (210d). Finally, "having been tutored in the lore of love, passing from view to view of beautiful things, in the right and regular ascent," Diotima says, in a long, influential speech,

> suddenly [ἐξαίφνης] he will have revealed to him [κατόψεταί], as he draws to the close of his dealings in love, a wondrous vision, beautiful in its nature [τὴν φύσιν καλόν]; and this, Socrates, is the final object of all those previous toils. First of all, it is ever-existent and neither comes to be nor perishes, neither waxes nor wanes; next, it is not beautiful in part and in part ugly, nor is it such at such a time and

other at another, nor in one respect beautiful and in another ugly, nor
so affected by positions as to seem beautiful to some and ugly to others.
Nor again will our initiate find the beautiful presented to him in the
guise of a face or of hands or any other portion of the body, nor as a
particular description or piece of knowledge, nor as existing somewhere in another substance, such as an animal or the earth or sky or
any other thing, but existing ever in singularity of form independent
by itself, while all the multitude of beautiful things partake of it in
such way that, though all of them are coming to be and perishing, it
grows neither greater nor less, and is affected by nothing. So when a
man by the right method of boy-loving ascends from these particulars
and begins to descry that beauty, he is almost able to lay hold of the final secret. Such is the right approach or induction to love-matters. Beginning from obvious beauties he must for the sake of that highest
Beauty be ever climbing aloft [ἐπαναβασμοῖς], as on the rungs of a ladder, from one to two, and from two to all beautiful bodies; from personal beauty he proceeds to beautiful observances, from observance to
beautiful learning, and from learning at last to that particular study
which is concerned with the Beautiful itself and that alone; so that in
the end he comes to know the very essence of Beauty. (210e–211d)

This revelation of the Beautiful not only allows one to see beauty, but seeing
beauty, unlike seeing a mimetic performance, transforms the viewer such
that "he sees by that which is visible concerning the Beautiful." In this highest stage, the lover "gives birth not to images of virtue (because he is in touch
with no images), but to true virtue (because he is in touch with true Beauty)"
(212a, trans. altered). We can see a contrast here between the poet in the
Republic and the lover. It is not quite that one works with images and the
other deals in reality; rather it has to do with the ability to imitate that in
which one participates. Humans continue to seek immortality in replicating
beauty. The lover here, however, is taken into the Beautiful, seeing it with its
sight, touching it with its touch. What the lover produces in the Beautiful is
inseparable from Beauty—images born from within the archetype.

At the opening of this section, I noted that, in the divided line, philosophers work their way up from image reading to trust and up to a kind of
unknowing of the Good beyond being, but that philosophers do not dwell in
the heavens; they also move back down. Revelation of Beauty transforms
both perception and desire. As the *Symposium* comes to a close, too, the

dialogue discloses another ladder. Just as Diotima's speech climaxes when "suddenly [ἐξαίφνης] Beauty appears," so the dialogue ends with three shocks of sudden beauty.[50] First, Alcibiades, Socrates's drunken lover, "suddenly [ἐξαίφνης]" comes crashing through the doors (212c). Readers—having been led up the ladder by Diotima's myth and then rapidly taken back down with Alcibiades's arrival—encounter the shock and intensity of a single body. The lover disrupts the ordered image-making party. Alcibiades, however, is shocked to find Socrates "suddenly [ἐξαίφνης]" appear before him (213c). This second shock leads Alcibiades to tell his own tale through images (δι'εἰκόνων), a tale full of aching, lack, and cunning, which describes how he was led to the *agalmata* in Socrates (a beauty, here, not beyond the body, but in it [222a]).[51] Alcibiades's love in the presence of his beloved, then, does not lead him away from images but to an image of love that allows readers a glimpse into the beauty within Socrates. If readers were still on the outside watching the love story unfold, the final shock comes when Alcibiades's speech concludes because the crowd "suddenly [ἐξαίφνης]" crashes the party (223b). Readers move from the shock of Alcibiades, to the shock of his relationship with Socrates, to the shock of "everyone" joining the erotic party. That is, readers move "from one to two, and from two to all beautiful bodies," and, perhaps, beyond, as Eros binds all things together and strives toward the ineffable.

*   *   *

In examining Plato's aesthetics of mimesis, then, we have seen, first, that mimesis is key to the formation of citizens. Imitation fashions subjects. It governs the most basic building blocks of political life and lays out the roles on offer for civic life and the means to fulfill those roles. It trains both inclinations and affects. But the affective power of representation cuts more than one way. It can slice off bad taste and undisciplined habits, but it also can split the seams of self-control that hold a city together. In the *Symposium*, moreover, mimesis teaches philosophers to love and also animates a mode of ascent that can lead beyond mimesis altogether, and from that transcendent point, encourages the creation of beautiful images, moving philosophers up and back down the ladder of ascent. The *Republic*'s concern that mimesis will lead to misshapen citizens is not done away with in the *Symposium*, but we see how, when properly arranged, representations can spur desire. This directed desire ascends from what is most intimately loved, and leads to higher and higher forms of love, until one finally stands in the presence of what is beyond all representation. Philosophers, then, learn both to love beautiful bodies and to love Beauty—indeed, the two loves are inseparable. For the one who has been "initiated," certain bodies or images can crack open a love both beyond and within bodies and images.

In the *Republic* and (at least until the climatic moments of) the *Symposium* there is a distance between viewer and viewed. Imitations work on philosophers, and philosophers work with and against imitations. But alongside this discourse on mimesis, Plato also offers a different kind of mimetic relation, one that does not theorize the viewer viewing a representation, or the movement from life to art. To see the other of these tracks, we need to move from aesthetic mimesis to ontological mimesis.

Track 2: Ontological Mimesis

While there is an implicit ontology underpinning the *Republic*'s critique of mimesis and the *Symposium*'s ladder of ascent, the relationship between imitation and ontology never becomes explicit in these texts.[52] That task is left for the day after the *Republic*, in the *Timaeus*. The dialogue, titled for its main character, opens with a similar cast of characters explicitly recalling their previous day's discussions. Socrates compares the city he describes in the *Republic* to a still painting of an animal and then asks Timaeus to show what that animal would look like in motion; specifically, what the city would look like at war (19c).[53]

Critias begins to tell such a story when Timaeus breaks in and creates an ordered cosmos out of words, or at least an "image" (εἰκών) of such a cosmos.[54] As Catherine Zuckert notes, it is difficult to see how this is a response to the request of Socrates. At best, the speech is a prelude to Socrates's request; more likely it is an avoidance of it altogether. (My conclusion tries to unpack some implications of Timaeus's unresponsiveness.) Timaeus's questions seem to be: How is the cosmos ordered? How did it come to be? And what is the role of the human in it? He sets out to explain: the intelligible order, the relation of the intelligible to the sensible, and the construction of humans and their role in the cosmos.[55] For our purposes, the details of the creation story are less important than the theorization of imitation and eros that the text proposes. My reading, then, moves quickly through Timaeus's speech, highlighting different functions of mimesis within it. When the *Timaeus* discusses mimesis, we will see, it is not (primarily, at least) about the power of artistic representation of reality; it is about the way creation is structured, and about the way humans participate in it. We will see, too, that Timaeus's account of eros differs from Socrates's (or Diotima's), not intensifying, expanding, and climbing through different loves, but attempting to shed the lower orders from a pure desire for what is eternal.

The "Most Important" Distinction: Being and Becoming

Timaeus begins his account with what he calls the "most important" distinction. "What is that which always is and has no becoming? And what is that which also is becoming but never is?" The former is unchanging and grasped by thought with reason. The latter is grasped by opinion with unreasoning sensation (27d–28a, trans. altered). This "most important" distinction between Being and Becoming is crucial because, as Peter Kalkavage argues, it is "precisely what must be overcome in some way so that Becoming can be what Timaeus insists it is—an image or likeness of an eternally changeless model or paradigm."[56] It is clear to Timaeus that "this Cosmos should be an image of something [εἰκόνα τινὸς]" (29b, trans. altered). Creation, that is, is mimetic, and "mimesis," Halliwell writes, becomes "a sort of key to the system of correspondences that supposedly connect and hold together different zones of reality, especially the noetic and the sensory."[57] This archetype-image structure, moreover, links Being and Becoming and provides intelligibility to the "blooming, buzzing confusion" of the sensible, which allows Timaeus to reason from the works of the demiurge back up to what is eternal.[58]

Aristotle quipped that Plato simply swaps the Pythagorean term "mimesis" for his fancy term, "participation" (μέθεξις, μετέχω).[59] For Plato, however, mimetic participation speaks both to a likeness and to the dependency of the creature on the creator, image on archetype. Imitation is not a matter of two independently existing things resembling one another; imitation is an outgrowth of providence and dependence. The creator, being good and unenvious, "desired that all should be, so far as possible, like unto himself" (29e). But without being held in Being, creatures as distinct creatures vanish. Every creature exists precariously: it "comes into being and perishes and never really exists. Everything that comes into being must by necessity come into being because of some cause. For without a cause, it is impossible for anything to come to be" (28a, trans. altered). This principle of dependency and resemblance structures Timaeus's universe and his understanding of mimesis.

Mimetic Intellect

To discuss these dependent creatures, Timaeus needs to tell a "likely story [εἰκότα μῦθον]" (29d). How exactly humans come to recognize the higher forms in which they participate is too complex to account for here. What we need to establish is that creatures can recognize that stable order of creation in which our moving bodies participate. His myth constructs a beautifully ordered world. For the cosmos to be most beautiful, which is what the demiurge desires (29e), it must be the case that creatures have intellect along with a soul so that the cosmos would be both intelligible and alive (30a–b). The demiurge makes the cosmos as an image of what is eternal, but things brought into being, by definition, cannot be eternal, so the demiurge made the cosmic soul "a moving image of eternity" (37d, trans. altered). This movement forms the cosmic intelligible soul, which moves in a circle, repeating without variation (40a–b). And because of its constant, unchanging repetition, humans can know them:

> The cause and purpose of that greatest good, we must maintain, is this: that God devised and bestowed upon us vision to the end that we might behold the revolutions of intellect [τοῦ νοῦ . . . περιόδους] in heaven and that we might use them for the revolutions [περιφορὰς] of the thinking [διανοήσεως] within us and, by learning and participating in [μετασχόντες] calculations which are correct by their nature, by imitation [μιμούμενοι] of the absolutely unvarying [ἀπλανεῖς] revolutions of the god we might stabilize [καταστησαίμεθα] the variable [πεπλανημένας] revolutions within ourselves. (47b–c, trans. altered)[60]

This desire to still the turning of the mind, making it an "unvarying" imitation of the unvarying cosmic intellect, will become relevant for us, because it describes not only Timaeus's anthropology, but also his practice of philosophy. His goal here is both to learn the proper calculations of the revolutions of the gods and to participate in them. When this happens, the philosopher is made in their image. But before unpacking Timaeus's concerns about the instability of human circuits and the need to stabilize them through contemplation, we need to examine that gap between Being and Becoming.

Where Mimesis Happens: χώρα

To explain what and why things are, Timaeus tells the story of Being and Becoming. But to explain *how* anything comes into being, Timaeus needs to introduce a third category, the "space" or "field" (χώρα) in which the sensible copies of intelligible things are made.[61] Space is the necessary "third thing" in which chaos is ordered and in which participation happens. The space itself has no form, and, having no form, the *khōra* is difficult to describe. After trying other images (mother, nurse, receptacle), Timaeus suggests: "if we describe her as an invisible and unshaped sort of thing, all-receptive, and, in a most perplexing and most baffling way, partaking of the intelligible, we will not deceive ourselves" (51a–b, trans. altered). *Khōra* is herself "barely an object of belief [μόγις πιστόν]" such that a kind of "bastard reasoning" is required in considering the relation of archetype and image (52b).[62]

For Timaeus, however, even if she cannot be described directly, *khōra's* function is clear. She is the space in which images can be made, but not a thing in and of herself. "If the stamped copy is to assume diverse appearances of all sorts, that substance wherein it is set and stamped could not possibly be suited to its purpose unless it were itself devoid of all those forms which it is about to receive from any quarter" (50d). The mimetic structure of creation, that is, requires a third thing in order to keep things distinguished in the stream of becoming (47e–53c).[63] This spacing both makes images possible (by making a space for them to exist at all) and keeps them different from their archetypes (because the space provides some indefinable but real distance from their cause). The implication of this spacing is that philosophers can deploy a "true argument [ἀληθὴς λόγος]" about what really exists (Being), but Becoming, because it is an image situated in this spaceless space, always exists "in the other so that the same thing becomes simultaneously both one and two" (52c–d). Participating creatures are at once joined to their cause and set off from it. There is no "thing" separating them and yet only in this spacing can they exist at all.

Mimetic Humans

So far we have seen that the cosmos is made mimetically—in imitation of and dependent on its archetype and cause; that the cosmos is intelligible and has a soul; and that to account for how things come into being, Timaeus posits a "space" in which Being and Becoming meet. Participating creatures are "both one and two," linked to their cause while distinct from it. When Timaeus focuses explicitly on the creation of humans, he notes that human beings occupy this space of dependent flux as imitations of the gods. The demiurge orders the cosmos into "a single living creature," but then leaves "the structure of mortal things . . . [to] his own engendered sons to execute" (69c). Humans are made by an imitation (three steps removed from reality). And like the three parts of creation (intelligible, sensible, and necessary), humans have three parts, all of which are interrelated.

> The imitators [μιμούμενοι] [i.e., the sons of the demiurge], having taken the immortal origin of the soul, they proceeded next to encase it within a round mortal body [i.e., the head], and to give it the entire body as its vehicle. And within the body they built another kind of soul as well, the mortal kind, which contains within it those dreadful but necessary disturbances: pleasure, first of all, evil's most powerful lure; then pains, that make us run away from what is good; besides these, boldness and also fear, foolish councilors both; then also the spirit of anger hard to assuage, and expectation easily led astray. These they fused with unreasoning sense perception and all-venturing lust, and so, as was necessary, they constructed the mortal type of soul. (69c–d, trans. altered from Zeyl)

Souls link the "sensible flux to intelligible order," such that well-made souls can align themselves perfectly with the intelligible order—an impossible goal because of its "necessary" disturbances, perhaps, but a goal nonetheless.[64] Sensations of pain, pleasure, anger, sadness, and lust are to be overcome in order to follow the perfect revolutions of the spheres (77b, 90e–92c). Bodies have a preparatory role in providing control over the lower part of the soul and knowledge, but ultimately both ought to give way to the intelligible part of the soul.[65]

What is important for us is the relationship between, on the one hand, the triangulation of movement (or flux), dependence, and likeness at the heart of being a creature, and, on the other hand, the project of philosophy offered in the *Timaeus*. We can now read the passage to which I promised to return. Timaeus assumes that what one participates in is intelligible, and that even if the philosopher will spend a lifetime (or more) in search of that intelligible form (or maker), what is sought is essentially knowable. The goal of philosophy is that "through learning and participating in [μετασχόντες] calculations which are correct by their nature, by imitation [μιμούμενοι] of the absolutely unvarying [ἀπλανεῖς] revolutions of the God we might stabilize [καταστησαίμεθα] the variable [πεπλανημένας] revolutions within ourselves" (47b–c, trans. altered). Humans are made as imitations, and, in their mimetic participation, they try to stabilize the flux, pulling taut the mimetic chain that holds all of creation together. They become one and two—united to what is eternal by repeating the eternal thoughts eternally, and, in so doing, making the mind an image of the eternal. While human existence within the *khōra* means that this stability will never be final, philosophy, for Timaeus, is about intellectually assimilating to the intelligible order of the cosmos. The stability of the cosmos and humanity's mimetic relation to it make it possible for humans to set their mind toward that intelligible order and to themselves become an image of it. Humanity's participation allows it to mirror its cause, becoming an image of that on which it depends. Bodily existence is useful (and perhaps necessary) in connecting the sensible to the intelligible, but it ultimately must give way to the intelligible.[66]

Ontological Eros

We can compare Timaeus's practice of philosophy to that in the *Symposium*. Socrates's ascent to the beautiful moved from one image or body to bodies to principles and laws to the beautiful.[67] Timaeus's desire for knowledge of the ordered cosmos defines the philosophical life differently. Timaeus's one account of eros that does not connect it to damaging effect describes that "lover of intellect and knowledge [νοῦ καὶ ἐπιστήμης ἐραστὴν]." This lover "must necessarily pursue the first causes, which belong to the Intelligent Nature, and put second all things which are moved by others, and themselves, in turn, move others because they cannot help it" (46d–e, trans. altered). The philosopher's desire here is to "duplicate the intelligible order of the cosmos in the mind of the philosopher who contemplates it."[68] To do so requires that philosophers "keep distinct" the first causes from other, lesser sites of desire. To pursue the former is to transcend the latter (46e). Intellectual desire, that is, does not emerge from other kinds of desire. Timaeus's other discussion of eros calls it "dreadful but necessary." It exists as a kind of flaw. The mortal part of human souls is created, in part, by lesser gods, and these gods' inability to create something as well as the demiurge leaves humans with irrational sensations and ever-veering desires (69c–d). Philosophy practices and enables an escape from this dreadful erotic pull by quelling the mortal soul and making one's mind an image of the first principles.

In this comparison, we can see two competing structures of eros operating in Plato's writings. Both Socrates and Timaeus see eros as essential to knowledge. Socrates's ventriloquism of Diotima, and especially what follows in the *Symposium*, suggests an intensified progression that expands the reach of one's desire. Socrates contemplates only what one can see (directly, as with the Beautiful or through mediation, as with all the stages leading up to Beauty). Timaeus by contrast asks philosophers to understand first the proper orderly motions of the cosmos and to duplicate it intelligently in the soul. Catherine Zuckert frames the distinction like this: "For Timaeus, human eros is merely the sign of our incompleteness; it becomes part of the human soul only after it is joined to a mortal (as opposed to a starry, cosmic) body. Eros heightens the confusion and disorder caused by the bodily desires; it does not direct human effort and striving toward the noble and good. Timaeus does not, therefore, like Socrates, urge his listeners to seek self-knowledge by examining their opinions to see what they truly desire. He urges them rather to look outside themselves to the heavens to find an order they can not only comprehend but also incorporate."[69] The Socrates of the *Symposium* as well as of the *Republic* sees friendship, erotics, and community—limiting spaces in which bodies bump into each other and share arguments and stories—as necessary for gaining any knowledge worth having. Working with and through limitations is part of the philosophical life. It fosters the love needed to ascend the ladder toward the beautiful. Timaeus's philosophical life, by contrast, "is not pleasant so much as it is painless. He selflessly forgets the limitations imposed by his own body by contemplating the eternal order of the whole."[70] His solitary project keeps active only the immortal soul, which participates in the immortal revolutions. In the *Republic* and the *Symposium*, viewers are changed by their ascent to the good or the beautiful, but their transformation keeps them in relationships. Timaeus can give an account of all of creation (he does not ignore bodies), but his paramount concern is that the creation he orders is anchored to the revolutions, that no image gets in the way of the one focal point that can put all other things in perspective.

To conclude, we can look back to the transition between the *Republic* and the *Timaeus*. When Socrates completes his review of the *Republic* with his companions, he urges Timaeus to join in the discussion, to build upon the image of the city and move toward something higher, or more refined. Socrates asks, "Are we yearning [ποθοῦμεν] for something further in what was said, my dear Timaeus, something that's being left out?" Timaeus is not interested. "Not at all," he replies (19b).[71] Timaeus does not so much build upon Socrates's work—he never answers the question of what a city at war would look like, which was Socrates's request—as transcend all direction and look directly to the "first principles." Socrates suggested countercharms to the myths, but Timaeus's "likely story" is a different myth, not a starting point for dialectic and community.

Put bluntly, Socrates's philosophical program directs desire; Timaeus's stabilizes it. For all of Socrates's warnings about the power and danger of images, Timaeus remains fixed on (fixated by?) his own, almost as if it actually reproduced the movements of the heavens in the soul. The dialogue ends not by turning back to the other characters in the dialogue, but by a solitary celebration of his consummated mimetic relation, one attracted only to what is unchanging: "Let us now declare that our account of the universe has reached its end [τέλος]. For having received the living creatures both mortal and immortal and thereby having been fulfilled, this, our cosmos, has a visible living creature embracing the visible creatures, a perceptible god made in the image of the intelligible [ζῷον ὁρατὸν τὰ ὁρατὰ περιέχον, εἰκὼν τοῦ νοητοῦ θεὸς αἰσθητός], greatest and best and beautiful and perfect [μέγιστος καὶ ἄριστος κάλλιστός τε καὶ τελεώτατος]—even this one heaven, being the only one of its kind [μονογηνὴς]" (92c, trans. altered). Timaeus's own "likely story" fulfills him and takes him out of himself as he joins in his perfect image.

*   *   *

This chapter does not present a comprehensive view of mimesis in Plato. Rather, it lays out two conceptions of mimesis in Plato's works and traces correlating erotics to these accounts, both of which will reappear in late antiquity. I hope to have shown that Plato provides two ways of discussing mimesis that are also tethered to two erotic modes. One conception organizes a discourse around representation and reality, about the images, rhythms, and stories that shape (or undo) souls. This aesthetic mimesis is tethered to a mode of desire in which lovers of beauty and truth, by loving from what is most intimate, love what is most transcendent. The other conception organizes a discourse around ontological participation, about dependency on and imitation of an archetype in which one has life and existence. Here desire does not begin with intimate desires, but longs for "first principles." All other kinds of desire are not rungs on a ladder but distractions, pulling attention away from the truth. Finally, we saw too how these different modes of desire lead to different practices of philosophy. Socrates sees the telling of stories and sharing of arguments as necessary for the examined life; Timaeus, by contrast, is less interested in dialogue, seeing the philosopher's goal, instead, as making her intellect an image of that in which she participates.

In large part these conceptual tracks of mimesis run parallel, each assumed or ignored by the other. By the time of Proclus, however, readers were intent on reconciling them. In the next chapter, we see how two of Plato's readers, Plotinus and Iamblichus, pick up and combine these two discourses. Plotinus and Iamblichus both argue that representation and participation must work together to form the ideal life, but they do not agree on how that is best done. The importance of these debates and the lack of consensus around them intensify the debates into which Gregory of Nyssa will enter.

Imitation, Education, Rhetoric

Before moving to the late ancient philosophical schools and their readings of Plato, however, I want to sketch quickly one other area in which Plato's mimetic pedagogy becomes especially important in late antiquity: education, especially rhetorical education. Most narrowly for this study, Gregory taught rhetoric before he became a bishop; more broadly, debates around mimesis in late antiquity (and beyond) largely emerged through rhetorical education.[72]

Even in his own generation, those who knew Socrates and supported him saw his pedagogy as primarily mimetic. His good, disciplined, pious life, Xenophon wrote in his *Memorabilia*, is inseparable from his teaching. "By letting his own light shine, he led his disciples to hope that they through imitation [μιμουμένους] of him would attain to such excellence."[73] This process of mimetic education was not unique to Socrates, nor did Plato's critiques of rhetoric prevent rhetoricians from drawing on his writings. Aristotle, in addition to his own understanding of how mimetic art allowed for a cathartic release, saw the capacity for imitation as what separates humans from animals, and emphasized imitation as part of a larger process of habit formation (ἕξις).[74] Education involved habituation into theories and principles and learning to imitate approved models, be they ideas, plots, models, or teachers.[75] Plato's contemporary, the rhetorician Isocrates, argued that teachers of rhetoric had two jobs: the exposition of principles and the offering of an example. Bringing clarity and precision to concepts helps to orient learners, and "for the rest," Isocrates says, the teacher "must present himself as an example [παράδειγμα], so that the students who have taken form [τοὺς ἐκτυπωθέντας] under his instruction and are able to pattern themselves [μιμήσασθαι] after him will directly show in their speaking a degree of grace and charm which is not found in others."[76]

Imperial and late Roman rhetorical education emphasized aesthetic mimesis as what Tim Whitmarsh calls a "strategy of self-making."[77] "Both literary style and life-style alike are affected by the didactic processes of *mimēsis*, which are thus focused not narrowly upon linguistic etiquette, but on the whole person. . . . Both life and literature should be conducted as a mode of eclectic *mimēsis* of the paradigms of the past."[78] For Quintilian, "imitation," in addition to the memory required to grasp and retain examples, "is the mark of a teachable nature."[79] Cicero's "first counsel [*primum in praeceptis*]" for teachers of rhetoric was to "show the student whom to copy, and to copy in such a way as to strive with all possible care to attain the most excellent qualities of his model."[80] Choosing the right model and learning how to mimic it formed the cornerstone of rhetorical training, for students would learn from and even become those they imitate. Libanius, for example, wanted to "install Demosthenes in [his students'] souls."[81]

How transformation happened drove much of rhetorical theory and practice.[82] The earliest surviving Roman rhetorical handbook, *Rhetorica Ad Herennium*, lays out three "means" to becoming an orator: "Theory, Imitation, and Practice [*arte, imitatione, exercitatione*]": "By theory is meant a set of rules that provide a definite method and system of speaking. Imitation is that by which we are impelled [*Imitatatio est qua impellimur*] to attain, in accordance with a studied method [*ratione*], the effectiveness of certain models in speaking. Practice is assiduous exercise and experience in speaking [*adsiduus usus consuetudoque dicendi*]."[83] Theory provides a set of rules or norms, and students can transform into orators only by making oration an established habit (*consuetudo*). The treatise opens noting that "theory without continuous practice in speaking is of little avail."[84] But imitation here is the key and the most difficult piece to understand. Colin Burrow argues that theory lays out a method for practice but that the handbook's anonymous author describes imitation less as a plotting through the required steps and more as "a drive, by which we are impelled (*qua impellimur*) to be like another person in speaking."[85] Imitation has a mysterious—and untheorized in the treatise—power that compels the student to both theory and practice. It *is* theory and practice, and yet how imitation happens cannot be reduced to simple hard work and rule following; the kind of imitation that makes for the best orators requires something extra, a force that drives students to imitate.

By studying the examples, a larger transformation happens in the soul. The fragments that remain of Dionysius of Halicarnassus's *On Imitation* contain an exhortation to students: "spend time with the writings of the ancients, so that we can acquire from them not merely material from our arguments but also emulation of their expressions [ὁ τῶν ἰδιομάτων ζῆλος]. For, by constant observation, the reader's soul attracts a likeness of the style [χαρακτήρ]." To make the point, Dionysius told a story of an ugly farmer who, afraid that he would have ugly children, "fashioned beautiful images [εἰκόνας] and made his wife look at them regularly; when she had looked at them he would sleep with her and was rewarded with beautiful children." For Dionysius, the point was clear: "in literature also, likeness is born through imitation whenever someone emulates what seems excellent in each of the ancients and, as it were, constructs a single stream from many rivulets and channels this into his own soul."[86] The ancient examples formed grooves in the soul and, by attending to them, by looking at their beauty, an ugly flood of words could transform into a flow of beautiful speeches.

Burrow rightly notes that this story is a subtle critique of Plato in two ways. The first questions the argument that representations degenerate. In this story, the lesson seems to be: "Make good pictures and you could have beautiful children."[87] The second critique engages the time it takes to educate. Dionysius shows aesthetic imitation to be something more akin to what we saw in the slow learning of the guards in Book 3 of the *Republic* than the sudden shock experienced in the theater in Book 10. "Imitation," Burrow writes, "is the acquisition of a *hexis* or a *habitus*, of learning how to write like someone else as the result of a long process of writing and training."[88]

Rhetorical exercises, therefore, placed students in a tightly curated hall of examples. Quintilian advised providing enough variation that students were saturated by examples, such that when they inevitably fell short of any one example, they fell into other models of excellence.[89] "Since it is scarcely given to man to produce a complete reproduction of a chosen author, let us keep the excellences of a number of authors before our eyes."[90] Ideally, students developed their own style by saturating themselves in and repeating these masters' words until they became their own.[91] Seneca suggested, "we should so blend those several flavours into one delicious compound that, even though it betrays its origin, yet it nevertheless is clearly different from that whence it came."[92]

Essential to this saturation was memorizing long swaths of texts that conditioned students for the more advanced disciplines, including the ability to inhabit those characters (ἦθος), making arguments in their voice and from their perspective. In this imitation, students became sensitized both to the nuances of speech making and to the examples and virtues valued in speeches. Well into late antiquity, for example, "the crown of the curriculum" remained, for sophist schools, "the declamation."[93] In these exercises, advanced students would present an argument by assuming the character of a famous orator and would make an argument in their style.[94] These exercises trained students in the art of suasion, and, just as important, like the music in Book 3 of the *Republic*, imprinted Roman values onto their souls. They learned the argots, anxieties, virtues, and desires of the empire and thrived off of amplifying and distorting them in their mimetic performances. In representing "the best of art and culture," students sharpened their desires and grew into citizens capable of representing the ideals of a society.[95] How exactly that happened, of course, was somewhat mysterious. The theories and techniques settle into the soul and create a kind of *charactēr*, Burrow notes, "in the sense of being an imprint of a particular type of person or a particular set of repeating characteristics of style."[96] Mimesis is both a theory and a practice, and yet, in that intertwining, a stylized subject emerges.

More than any ancient example, however, students learned from their own teachers. Teachers, as Libanius's school shows, became objects of mimetic desire. As Raffaella Cribiore writes, "Affection for his teacher (*erōs*) made a student's work a product of imitation."[97] For Quintilian, students "should love their teachers as they do their studies, and think of them as the parents not of their bodies but of their minds. The feeling of affection [*pietas*] will do much for their studies. They will be ready to listen, have confidence in what is said, and want to be like the teacher [*esse similes concupiscent*]."[98] Why must the student love the teacher? Because the kind of imitation these educators desired involved imitating far more than "the obvious" things. Cicero writes, "there is nothing easier than to imitate someone's style of dress or pose or gait."[99] The soul-forming imitation requires imitating something deeper: "the form" (*formam*), or, Cicero turns to the Greek to be more precise, the "*charactēr*," or the distinctive, often ineffable style of speaking.[100] There is some "inimitable talent, or *ingenium* of the text or the person imitated."[101] As in the *Symposium*, seeing the form of the orator requires moving through an ordered process but also renders the viewer passive, lovingly imitating something that they can only know indirectly. Desire for the teacher, then, leaves in question exactly what one imitates when they imitate their teacher.

This love of the teacher of course fostered jealousy and competition that propelled students toward even more imitations. Even imitations of the classics were ultimately extensions of their love for their teacher.[102] Libanius may have wanted Demosthenes on students' souls, but more often than not, he produced little Libani. Mimesis here, as in Plato's writings, taught students both how to love and what to love. Education filled students so completely with models that students became blended versions of their models. The model's words imprinted on the student's soul as teachers educated desire, directing and intensifying it until students became what they loved.

Rhetorical educators continued to debate how imitation should shape students, and yet their debates were, in Burrow's words, "metaphor rich and concept poor."[103] Practices normalized, desires intensified, but orators focused less on conceptual clarity around ontological questions than on the ability to speak persuasively and live ethically. Metaphors could guide those practices, but without clarifying the relationship between imitated and imitator, the work of moral formation in these mimetic relationships was something of a black box—and perhaps it was all the more powerful for remaining mysterious.[104] By the time Gregory of Nyssa was teaching, however, philosophers were debating how these mimetic relationships form and what kinds of bonds tie imitator to imitated. The two conceptions of mimesis—aesthetic representation and ontological participation—that we saw in Plato would merge, and they merged with full knowledge of the centrality of mimesis not only for literary and philosophical theories but for the formation of desiring subjects.

CHAPTER 2

Crossing Tracks: Mimesis in Neoplatonism

The previous chapter laid out two tracks that sit side by side in Plato's writings on mimesis. Aesthetically, mimesis was removed from truth and allowed humans to move toward it. Reflection spurred desire for goodness and beauty in those who knew how to relate to them. Ontologically, mimesis was the way the world is structured: lower levels of the world were microcosmic images of that which created them and that on which they depended. These two tracks of mimesis also correlated with two modes of desire or eros. Aesthetic mimesis encouraged desire that ascended from intimate love toward transcendent beauty (from loving one body, to two bodies, to laws that govern those bodies, and up to the beautiful). Ontological mimesis, by contrast, began with a desire for the whole and from there shed or shook off loves that would distract from contemplating that object of desire.

By late antiquity, those tracks crossed. Gregory of Nyssa's insistence on imitating an infinite God by infinitely desiring God, I argue, is best understood as a combining and working out of these two discourses. But it was not Gregory alone who combined these discourses; he was part of a much larger philosophical discussion. In some of Plato's keenest readers, especially Plotinus (c. 204/205–270) and Iamblichus (c. 240–325), the two conceptions of mimesis and their correlated erotics overlapped. Or, perhaps more precisely, the shift from Plato's dialogue to a more systemized reflection on those dialogues in these late ancient philosophers required a more precise accounting of the relationship between the aesthetics and the ontology of mimesis. In these theorizations, the art that formed a soul increasingly submerged into a larger system to the point that, in different ways, the aesthetic eventually gave way to the ontological. Images led past imitation. A desire for truth surpassed a desiring relationship between image and archetype, into an assimilation that stilled or cut off direction, as philosophers imitated the circularity of the timeless Forms or gods in which they participated and even became one with the One.

We pick up our story, then, around 250 CE, nearly six centuries after Plato wrote. In that gap, his works were read, taught, commented on, deified, and disagreed with. They mixed with, among others, the writings of Aristotle; Stoics such as Seneca, Epictetus, or the emperor and philosopher Marcus Aurelius; Neopythagoreans such as Apollonius of Tyana and Xenocrates; rhetoricians such as Quintilian; and Jewish philosophers such as Philo.[1] And they constituted much of the common core of Greco-Roman culture. My goal over the next two chapters is not to give a reception history of Plato on mimesis. Instead, I describe an intellectual climate in which readers can productively locate Gregory's understanding of a mimetic relationship with an infinite God.

When Gregory wrote that "Christianity is mimesis of the divine nature," he carved out a mimetic style or way of life within a world questioning what it meant to imitate the divine. He joined an intellectual scene in which the lines between Christian and non-Christian often blurred or became contested. Christians and non-Christians studied together and shared norms around social behavior, moral education, and metaphysical assumptions. They shared a *paideia*, which Peter Brown describes as a "common culture that was held to be the distinguishing mark of the diffused governing class of the empire, shared alike by the notables of each region and by the personnel of the imperial government."[2] *Paideia* "bridged the distances of a vast empire" and "provided a shared imaginative landscape for those whose careers took them, increasingly, far from their native cities."[3] Gregory's concern about imitation and incomparability, that is, cut across the Roman Empire as well as across modern distinctions between Pagan and Christian. To read him well requires broadening the scope of our question to include a wide range of intellectual circles.

Plotinus's synthesis and ordering of Plato's dialogical and occasional writings reshaped the intellectual world. Teaching in third-century Rome, he was recognized in his own time as a philosopher to reckon with, even by his critics such as Longinus.[4] As we will see, this reshaping was in large part due to his view of mimetic relations and their role in structuring metaphysics. Stephen Halliwell writes, "If, in Plotinus's scheme of things, being or reality 'flows' down the cosmos from top to bottom, mimetic affinities are one way of talking about the process by which all being endeavors to revert, upward, to its source."[5] Mimesis facilitated a return but also marked

a separation from the desired presence. The gap between image and archetype allowed for the graded ordering of the universe, while also keeping it
all tethered to the same end. A mimetic trail remained, and philosophers
followed it back to its cause. Achieving a mimetic relation, however, was
only the first step in this return. Mimesis was a step toward the larger goal of
overcoming imitation and becoming one with the One.

Around the turn of the fourth century, Iamblichus left his teacher Porphyry and set up a school in Apamea, a city near Antioch in Syria. We may
never fully know why he left, but one reason is clear: a theological disagreement over the nature of the soul and the best way to imitate the divine. Plotinus's (and Porphyry's) mimetic world made it too easy, according to
Iamblichus, to ascend through the heavens. For Iamblichus, the injunction
to imitate the gods could only be accomplished with the help of the gods.
This help came in the shape of the liturgies, which the gods provided as a
point of contact between heaven and earth. The liturgies "imitated" the gods
and invited humans to participate in that already established relationship.
Iamblichus tells us little about what these liturgies look like. They seem to
have connected to the Chaldean Oracles, involved some kind of sacrifice,
and presumed familiarity with Egyptian as well as Homeric myths. Beyond
that it is difficult to know much.[6] The text theorized these rituals in opposition to Porphyry and for those who were already practicing them. It gave an
account of how what was intimately known, in fact, works, and in so doing,
created a tradition in which others could join.[7]

The ritual spaces were filled with what Iamblichus called "symbols"
(σύμβολα)—images, statues, words, animals, plants, or even smells—which
can transport humans into the presence of God (*Myst.* 5.23).[8] The symbols
were not mimetic in the sense that they provided a descriptive image of that
which they symbolize. Nor were they convenient names arrived at in community to refer to an object. The theurgist's aim was not to assimilate to
what symbols signify. Symbols did not quite "mean" anything. Iamblichus
referred to them as "meaningless names [ἄσημα ὀνόματα]" (*Myst.* 5.4–5).
Instead, they were "suspended" from the higher orders of creation, and
lower orders could "link" into that on which they depend through this point
of contact (*Myst.* 1.3). He calls them pure "receptacles [ὑποδοχὰς]," invoking
the *Timaeus*'s discussion of *khōra*, the unformed "space" or "mother" in
which anything that comes into being emerges (*Myst.* 5.23). Humans engaging with these symbols could dip into those receptacles and experience an
"ecstatic release" (*Myst.* 3.12), a release that united humans with the gods. In

that ecstatic union, humans were not annihilated; instead, they imitated the gods by doing what the gods do, namely, create.[9]

Especially notable in Iamblichus's writing is the link between contemplation and action. Plotinus's return centered what happens in and beyond the mind. For Iamblichus, humans, imitating the gods, need not shake off the world in order to contemplate. Instead, participating in the Good meant acting as the gods did. Like the gods who reach down to the orders of being below them in order to entice philosophers to the higher way, philosophers too could create places—or even a social order—where humans could be transformed.[10] Debates about the philosophical life, then, were also debates about governing, about providing ways for fellow Romans to align themselves with the gods.

This link between contemplation and order was especially attractive to the emperor Julian. Julian's conversion spread Iamblichian thought, which, as Susanna Elm has shown, posed a challenge to Christian theologians, especially those living in Cappadocia.[11] Julian's religious and philosophical politics did more than require Christian theology to provide a response to a competing philosophical system. (Christianity had been doing that for a long time.) In adopting Iamblichus's system, which allied the material and divine worlds, Julian highlighted the confluence of theology with all of life, from governance to God. This confluence achieved what Dominic O'Meara calls "a divinization of political life."[12] This divinization was not radically new, but it nevertheless helped define the expectations around what theology needed to provide. In this light, Gregory's emphasis on mimetic names, spaces, and characters can be seen as an attempt to place the pursuit of Christian perfection within a larger frame that links doctrine and desire and contemplation to the concrete practices of daily life that legitimated social norms. Gregory too provided a mimetic life that could move from governance to God.

Plotinus

Stephen Halliwell argues, "Any investigation of the place of mimesis in the philosophy of Plotinus must start with the fundamental observation that the language of mimesis pervades his writings, forming a conceptual vein that leads to the heart of his thinking."[13] By following that vein, we can see how Plotinus combines Plato's two conceptions of mimesis and offers his own account of philosophical desire that eventually moves beyond mimetic participation and into union with the one.

From Plato to Plotinus

This is not the place to get lost in the dazzling complexity of Plotinus's metaphysics, but some broad brushstrokes provide context for his understanding of mimesis.[14] Plotinus's synthesis of Plato depicts a universe with slotted levels of reality held together by mimetic bonds. Lower orders of reality mimic higher ones, reflecting them, desiring to be united to them, and participating in them. Lower orders, we will see, both *are* and *are like* their higher counterparts. They have no existence outside their cause, and they exist as an image of their archetype. A tension between the *are* and the *are like* animates the philosophical quest for reunion or assimilation with the One.

More specifically, three graded hypostases, or principles of reality—the One (sometimes called "the Good"), the Intellect, and the Soul—structure Plotinus's universe. *Ennead* 5.1, *On the Three Primary Hypostases*, provides the most sustained discussion of these principles. The treatise raises the question: How does something other than the One come into being? If the One is simple and singular, how is there something other than the One? The simplest version of the answer is: through a series of emanations or overflows. The isolated, transcendent source of all things is the One, from which "emanates" (περίλαμψις) the Intellect, from the Intellect "emanates" the soul, as a ghost (or image, εἴδωλὸν) of the Intellect, and from the Soul, Nature, and so on, all the way down to matter, which is the final product of these causal emanations. But why emanation? For Plotinus—expanding Diotima's statement about humans producing images in the presence of the beautiful (*Symposium* 206b)—anything that is perfect, such as the One, produces images: "All beings, so long as they persist, necessarily, due to the power present in them, produce from their own substantiality a real, though dependent, existent around themselves directed to their exterior, a sort of image of the archetypes [εἰκόνα . . . ἀρχετύπων] from which it was generated. . . . Perfumes show this particularly clearly, for so long as they exist, something flows from them around them, and what is near them enjoys their existence. And all things as soon as they come to perfection produce [Καὶ πάντα δὲ ὅσα ἤδη τέλεια γεννᾷ]" (*Enn.* 5.1.6, trans. altered). Perfection, for Plotinus, requires producing a kind of excess from which something else can come into being. Creation is made from the drifting scent of existence.

It has its existence as its cause, though a lesser form or intensity of its cause, and it desires to return to its source (*Enn.* 5.1.6).

To call this entire process "emanation," however, is to move too quickly. As Charles Stang writes, emanation is "only one step in an elaborate choreography."[15] Zooming in on that first procession from the One to the Intellect, we see that the radiation of the One outward does not itself create the Intellect. That radiation is "indefinite [ἀόριστος]," a "power [δύναμις]" or vitality without boundaries. There is a step between what Plotinus describes as "an encompassing reality [ὑπόστασιν] directed to their exterior," and "a kind of image of the archetypes from which it was produced" (*Enn.* 5.1.6, trans. altered). In the first procession he describes that in-between step as an "encompassing reality," or "something like the Intellect in the One which is not Intellect; for it is one" (*Enn.* 6.8.18). The Intellect becomes something determined only as it "turns" (ἐπιστροφή) and, in that "turning," takes on form by becoming an "image" of its "archetype" (*Enn.* 5.1.7). The Intellect's perfection or "completion" results in its separation from the One (even if the One is still present to it as its cause), and its production of an image of what it sees. The Intellect, then, "is its objects" as it becomes *like* what it sees, that is, becomes an image of what it sees.[16] If we still want to call this choreography an "emanation"—as Plotinus occasionally will—then emanation is mimetic.

Before examining how images and archetypes relate, I need to pause on what is perhaps the most significant shift we will track in the move from Plato to Plotinus: Plotinus's metaphysics is also an anthropology. The human soul, for Plato, ascends to the Forms and the Good, but for Plotinus, there is no need to go somewhere else, as the soul is already divine and needs only to realize it. Philosophy is not so much a project of migration, as it seems to be in the *Phaedo*, but of a homecoming. Philosophy is ultimately a project of "self-knowledge." As Sara Rappe writes, "However elaborate their metaphysics may sometimes appear, the structures reported and discovered by Neoplatonists are part and parcel with self-discovery."[17] In Plotinus's words, "Just as in nature these . . . three [principles] are found, so it is necessary to believe as well that they are in us" (*Enn.* 5.1.10). Humans do not have representations of the principles in them, as if the One existed somewhere else and creatures were Russian dolls inside but separable from it. The principles are even more constitutive than that.[18] Humans rely on and are made up of that which transcends them. The principles that make the universe are "present in us."[19]

The phrase "in us," for Plotinus, refers to what Plato calls "the inner human being [εἴσω ἄνθρώπον]," or the soul, which "is a divine thing." In a move that will be controversial in later Platonism, our souls, for Plotinus, have not descended all the way into matter (e.g., *Enn.* 5.1.10, 5.3.49). We exist as "parts of the intelligible, neither bounded off nor cut off but by belonging to the whole. For even now we are not cut off" (*Enn.* 6.4.14). The soul does not require a full-scale ontological transformation in order to be united to the divine. "We must 'fly from here' [*Theaetetus* 176a–b] and 'separate' [*Phaedo* 67c] ourselves from our accretions, and not be the ensouled composite body. . . . For each of us is double, one is a sort of complex and one the self" (*Enn.* 2.3.9). The goal here is to shake off something that has been added. Philosophers need not know or become something else to arrive at their goal. Their souls remain tethered to the Intellect, as an image of it, and retain both the desire and power to unite with the Intellect and with the One. By contemplating and ordering desire, philosophers clear away material accretions and return the soul to what it is.

This redefined soul, then, fits somewhere between what Plotinus calls "two kinds of likenesses [ἡ ὁμοίωσις διττή]" (*Enn.* 1.2.2, trans. altered). This first kind of likeness unites things that are in the same "level" of reality around something shared. It "requires that there be something identical in things that are the same, such that their sameness derived equally from that which is identical" (*Enn.* 1.2.2). The other is a nonreciprocal likeness, which "must be taken in a different sense . . . since likeness has come about in a different way [εἴπερ κατὰ τὸν ἕτερον τρόπον ὡμοίωται]." This likeness, by contrast, results from a causal relationship; the image is like the archetype that caused it (*Enn.* 1.2.2).[20] Plotinus's distinction structures his *askesis*,[21] which attempts to reconcile these two kinds of likeness—becoming like (a perfect image of what remains an archetype) and then becoming one (uniting into the same principle).[22]

Plotinus welds together the two modes of desire we saw in Plato (on the one hand, the *Symposium*'s ladder of love in which one learns to love the Beautiful by loving what is closest to oneself and ascending through it to the Form of Beauty, and, on the other hand, the *Timaeus*'s practice of beginning with the whole and desiring to cut away the passions to contemplate existence and beyond).[23] Incorporating especially a Stoic emphasis on turning inward, Plotinus universalizes, orders, and internalizes the *Symposium*'s intimate ascent and the *Timaeus*'s contemplation of the principles. Human ascent, for Plotinus, is ultimately also an ascent to oneself.[24] In loving what is most intimate, one loves all.

What Can Representations Do?

Representations, at best, train the soul, but they fall on the wrong side of a basic distinction that runs throughout Plotinus, that between the true (ἀληθινός) and the imitation or representation (μίμημα).[25] "Because intellectual knowledge is not intentional, in the sense that it is not directed at things outside of itself," Sara Rappe writes, "the contents of intellect cannot be disclosed by means of linguistic representations. Nor can the metaphysical structures revealed by the intellect be described by means of propositions without suffering a great deal in the process of translation."[26] Truth for Plotinus is beyond representation, yet representations are part of a revelatory process.[27] So what can representations do?

For Plotinus, representations are the constitutive element in "thinking" (νοεῖν). Thinking is not simply reception.[28] Plotinus describes the establishment of the Intellect as a kind of "turning" that makes the Intellect an "image" of the One. While it is customary to see philosophical activity as primarily about abstract thinking, for Plotinus and much of the Neoplatonist tradition, thinking is a necessary training ground of desire, a transformation of the mind that makes it imitate what it desires.

> This is what thinking [νοεῖν] is: a movement towards the Good it desires [κίνησις πρὸς ἀγαθὸν ἐφιέμενον ἐκείνου]. For the desire generated thought [ἡ γὰρ ἔφεσις τὴν νόησιν ἐγέννησε] and caused it to exist with itself: for desire for seeing is sight. The Good itself, then, must think nothing, for the Good is not other than itself. And since whenever that which is other than the Good thinks it, it thinks it by being, "like the Good" [*Republic* 509a] and having a likeness in relation to the Good, and thinks it as the Good and as desirable to itself, and in a way having an image [φαντασίαν] of the Good. (*Enn.* 5.6.5, trans. altered)

Thinking here is mimetic. It requires positing an image and yearning for it. The image making that separates also binds and entices. The Good does not think or have any image of itself, but to unite with it requires images of it. Just as important for Plotinus, then, is that the aim of this thinking is to move beyond thinking. Philosophers become like what they contemplate, but uniting with the object of contemplation requires uniting with what is ultimately not an object at all. They must move past that appearance (φαντασία) of the Good to join the Good as the Good. Becoming *like* should eventually give way to *being* in such a way that there is no more yearning for something else.

But first, how do these images bind and entice? Some of Plotinus's clearest examples of how to move beyond mimesis and into union with the One appear, at least on first sight, to be references to representational art. They are nearly always analogies for (rather than the aim of) the philosophical life, but the continuity between art and ascent highlights the role of representation in this homecoming. We will see, moreover, that the mimetic activity most interesting to Plotinus is art that leads beyond itself, art that reaches beyond matter and into another sphere.

For Plotinus not just art, but all of nature exists *mimetically*. Because mimesis is a kind of metaphysical bonding agent, representations do not fall under Plato's critique of art as mere reflections of reality, set apart from more real beings. "Every original maker must be in itself superior [καθ᾽ αὑτὸ κρεῖττον] to that which it makes," Plotinus writes. "If anyone disrespects the arts because they make imitations of nature [Εἰ δέ τις τὰς τέχνας ἀτιμάζει, ὅτι μιμούμεναι τὴν φύσιν ποιοῦσι], we must tell him, first, that natural things imitate other things [καὶ τὰς φύσεις μιμεῖσθαι ἄλλα]. Next, he must know that the arts do not simply imitate what they see [τὸ ὁρώμενον μιμοῦνται], but they run back up [ἀνατρέχουσιν] to the expressed principles [λόγους], from which nature derives. Then also they do a great deal by themselves, and, since they possess beauty, they supply [προστιθέασι] whatever is missing [τι ἐλλείπει]" (*Enn.* 5.8.1, trans. altered). Not only is the gap between mimesis and *physis* (art and nature) closed, but mimesis can also play a supplemental role. Mimesis is both necessary and extra. It is a principle of nature, and it "suppl[ies] whatever is missing" by reaching beyond nature to the forms.[29]

This supplement comes precisely in the kinds of images art can produce. To make something already visible visible again is not really art. As with Cicero, who insisted that the best students imitate not the dress or the gait of their teacher but the teacher's "*ingenium*," their indefinite "form" (*formam*) or "*character*,"[30] here, for Plotinus, art can allow us to see what has no "model perceived by the senses." Pheidias, Plotinus explains, "did not produce his statue of Zeus from any sensible model." The sculptor "grasped [λαβὼν] what Zeus would look like if he wanted to appear before our eyes" (*Enn.* 5.8.1, trans. altered). The artist reaches above himself to the form of beauty, and in that reaching creates an image that contains more than meets the eye. In that statue, viewers too could focus their desire and lose themselves in what is not seen. The image then provides a way to become like the gods, but also allows viewers to move beyond the representation to see the model beyond the senses.

That double movement of focused attention and transcendence makes art a fruitful analogy for the philosophical life. Images train philosophers to see a beauty already present, but images also, like nature, can reach beyond themselves toward what is above them.[31] "The reality in the sensible world is false," Plotinus writes. It requires "an imported image of beauty [ἐπακτοῦ εἰδώλου καλοῦ] in order that it should appear beautiful" (*Enn.* 5.8.9, trans. altered). Starting from the outside, these images of beauty affect the philosophers as they move within and reshape their dispositions. "While something is outside us," Plotinus writes, "we do not yet see it; when it comes within, it influences us [διέθηκεν]" (*Enn.* 5.8.2, trans. altered). Real sight requires a "sort of intimate understanding and self-awareness [σύνεσις καὶ συναίσθησις αὐτοῦ]" (*Enn.* 5.8.11, trans. altered). This intimacy and perfection, then, evaporate the gap between representation and ontology, ushering in a union of soul with intellect. While the philosopher begins her quest for beauty in an unreal way—chasing after phantoms—this pursuit transforms her into what is truly beautiful, to the point that she becomes what is *not* here below. As Zeke Mazur writes, "The self must encounter itself in an autoscopy or 'self-seeing' and then overcome that staged duality of seer and seen so as to be elevated to the next stage."[32] External images serve only a penultimate good, but, until that point when imitation gives way to reality, the mimetic relationship is still the best, and perhaps the only, chance of ascending to the One.

Beautiful images become for Plotinus a mode of clearing. By "taking away" all the layers of deception—once credited *to* mimesis—philosophers learn to participate in what is most real. The Socratic dictum given by the Delphic oracle—"know thyself"—becomes the work of making oneself the beautiful image. "When we ourselves are beautiful, it is by belonging to ourselves, but we are ugly when we change to another nature. When we know ourselves we are beautiful, but when we are ignorant of ourselves, we are ugly" (*Enn.* 5.8.13, trans. altered). To know oneself is to become who one already is by making oneself an image of the beautiful. This is the first step in a larger process of reunion. Like the statue that makes present what is unseen, seeing here moves beyond sight. One must "be in beauty" in order to see it. "Seeing [beauty] as something different, he will no longer be in beauty, but will come to be it—'in it' in this extreme way. If, then, seeing is of that which is external, there should not be seeing, or else only the seeing in which one is identical with that which one sees" (*Enn.* 5.8.11). Observing beauty from a distance is impossible. One must participate in it in order to see it.

With this understanding of the supplemental quality of representations, we are in a better position to read Plotinus's well-known and most explicit exhortation for the soul's return.[33] In *On Beauty*, union is described as "working on your statue," chiseling away at the soul until the true self shines through. Just before the statue, he describes the "pangs of love . . . [and] longings and wanting to be united with [beauty]." A "painless shock" meets "with true love [ἀληθῆ ἔρωτα] and piercing desire [πόθους]" (*Enn.* 1.6.7, trans. altered).[34] Plotinus describes this yearning in mimetic terms: the creation of the self is a statue made in the image of that shock that has pierced its way inside the soul.

> Go back into yourself and look. If you do not yet see yourself as beautiful, then, be like a sculptor who, making a statue that is supposed to be beautiful, removes a part here and polishes there so that he makes the latter smooth and the former just right until he has given the statue a beautiful face. In the same way, you should remove superfluities and straighten things that are crooked, work on the things that are dark, making them bright, and not stop "working on your statue" [*Phaedrus* 252d] until the divine splendor of virtue shines in you, until you see "Self-Control enthroned upon its holy seat" [*Phaedrus* 254b].
>
> If you have become this, and have seen it, and find yourself in a purified state, you have no impediment to becoming one in this way nor do you have something else mixed in with yourself, but you are entirely yourself, true light alone, neither measured by magnitude nor reduced by a circumscribing shape nor expanding indefinitely in magnitude by being unmeasured everywhere, as something greater than every measure and better than every quantity. If you see that you have become this, at that moment you have become sight. You

can trust yourself then. And you have at this moment ascended here, no longer in need of someone to show you. Just open your eyes and see, for this alone is the eye that sees the great beauty. . . .

For no eye has ever seen the sun without becoming sun-like, nor could a soul ever see Beauty without becoming beautiful. You must first actually become wholly god-like and wholly beautiful if you intend to see god and Beauty. (*Enn.* 1.6.9, trans. altered)

What began as a "piercing desire" continues to cut, moving inward, scraping away all that is not beautiful, until the soul becomes what it sees. And yet this is a strange statue. Perfecting the statue means freeing the beauty from the stone. By cutting away, philosophers refine themselves and then lose shape altogether, becoming "unbounded" and "unmeasured." This unbounded statue is formed not by looking to an external model; readers instead are directed inward toward what is ultimately nothing but the self. The distortion and separation implied by mimesis, that is, is also the path beyond it. This assimilation beyond mimesis is what our final section on Plotinus aims to understand.

Beyond Mimesis

For Plotinus, mimetic art aims to overcome the gap in which representations dwell. Representations help usher in an ontological union in which representations are swallowed up. When "you are entirely yourself," Plotinus writes, you become nothing but "true light" (*Enn.* 1.6.9). The central work of philosophy for Plotinus, then, becomes contemplation of and assimilation to what cannot be said. If, as we saw, perfection naturally produces a kind of overflow that is not yet something else but not itself either, contemplation seems to reduce the flow and "deproduce." The philosopher becomes a kind of "nothingness" that can be refashioned as that which she contemplates, an imitation so perfect that it ceases to become imitation altogether. "Offering oneself to [that which he contemplates] as a kind of matter" enables this transformation because of previous reality: in becoming nothing, the self returns to that "indefinite" state, existing only as the overflow of that which sustains it, "being oneself then only potentially" (*Enn.* 4.4.2).

The self can move from one kind of nothingness to another kind, namely, the nothing of the One (*Enn.* 6.4.2).[35] The Soul, "having been fitted to [Intellect], . . . is united with it while not being dissolved, but both are one, while still being two" (*Enn.* 4.4.2). In this perfect alignment, the distance between image and reality collapses. Before that alignment it is "as if a shadow followed the other, or as if a weaker light ran under [ὑποτρέχοντος] the greater one" (*Enn.* 4.3.31, trans. altered), but in union, the soul "flies from multiplicity [πολλῶν], and gathers multiplicity into one, thus getting rid of the infinite [τὸ ἄπειρον]. In this way it is not involved with multiplicity but travels light and is focused on itself" (*Enn.* 4.3.32, trans. altered). Images, for Plotinus, are to be arranged in order to be ultimately abandoned. The shadows of distinctiveness give way to the light of truth, when two will also be one.

After an explication of Eros, where he argues that the things we love most in this world are only images, Plotinus provides a diagnosis and a prescription. The diagnosis: the material world has made "love . . . vulgar" (*Enn.* 6.9.9). Love in this world is full of deceit and violation. He analogizes that love in this world is like a woman in an abusive relationship: maybe it seemed fine at first, but the abused must leave and return to "her father again," if she will ever find "contentment" (*Enn.* 6.9.9).[36] And then he poses an alternative: rather than pursuing material images, return home; join in the "intelligible world . . . by participating in him [the Good] and relating to him truly." Plotinus knows this shift is hard to explain but says, "Anyone who has seen it, knows what I mean. Which is to say: the soul then acquires a new life, when it approaches him, indeed arrives at him and participates in him, such that it is in a position to know that the true provider of life is present, and that the soul is in need of nothing more." The prescription then is that "The soul should put away all other things and stop in this one thing alone, become this alone, and cut loose everything we wear. The result is that we hasten to exit from here, so we may, despite the vexation at being bound to the other side, enfold him with the whole of ourselves, and contain no part with which we do not touch god" (*Enn.* 6.9.9). Unlike other kinds of love, this true love allows the self to be fully joined to what it loves.

Plotinus no longer needs to choose between the mimetic desire that begins with desire for the whole, as in the *Timaeus*, and the mimetic desire that begins with one's nearest loves, as in the *Symposium*. For Plotinus, the structure of the universe is already within the self. By making oneself as like as possible to that which is unseen, a different kind of likeness breaks through, one that transcends sameness and difference.

When the soul is so fortunate as to meet with [Beauty], and it comes to the soul, or rather appears by being present, when the soul turns away from the things present, and prepares itself to be as beautiful as may be, and arrives at a likeness to [Beauty]—the mode of preparation and ordering are somehow clear to those who prepare themselves—the soul sees it appear suddenly, for there is nothing in between, nor are they two things; both are then one, for you cannot distinguish them, as long as it is present—in imitation of this, lovers and their beloved ones here want to mingle with one another—and the soul no longer perceives even that it is in the body, nor does it say that it itself is something else, not a human being, not an animal, not a being, nothing at all. For consideration of itself in these capacities would disturb the soul. Nor does the soul have the leisure for them, nor does it want to. Rather, since the soul sought [Beauty], it encounters it when it is present, and looks at it, instead of looking at itself. It has no leisure to look to see who it is that looks.

There, it would exchange nothing in place of [Beauty], not even if someone were to offer the whole universe, on the grounds that nothing is preferable or better. For it cannot ascend higher, and all other things, even those up there, are a descent for it. The result is that it can then very well judge and recognize that it was [Beauty] that it desired, and to assert that there is nothing better than it. For in the intelligible world, there is no deception. (*Enn.* 6.7.34)

All representation, even perfect vision, must finally cease as the soul joins the Intellect and the One, no longer seeing them from a distance or even working to be more like them.[37]

The soul, at this stage, has nowhere higher to go. It even "distains thinking— which at other times it welcomes—because thinking is motion and the soul does not want to move" (*Enn.* 6.7.35, trans. altered). In those moments,

the soul sees by a kind of confusing and annihilating [Ἡ δὲ ψυχὴ οἷον συγχέασα καὶ ἀφανίσασα] the intellect which abides within it— but rather its intellect sees first and the vision comes also to it and the two become one. But the Good is spread out over them and fitted in to the union of both; playing upon them and uniting the two it rests upon them and gives them a blessed perception and vision, lifting them so high that they are not in place nor anything other, among things where it is natural for one thing to be in another; for he is not anywhere either, but the intelligible place is in him, but he is not in another. Therefore, the soul does not move then either, because that does not move. Nor, then, is it soul, because that does not live, but is above life. Nor is it intellect, because that does not think either; for one must be made like. It does not even think that it does not think. (*Enn.* 6.7.35, trans. altered)[38]

The soul's defining qualities (movement and life) are swallowed up, as is the intellect's (for it does not think), as it assimilates to the one.

Some amount of movement and thinking is required to ascend the ladder back to the one's true self, but having climbed the mimetic rungs, the only thing left for the philosopher to do is jump and be carried by what catches him:

> Someone actually leaving all learning, up to then having been educated by instruction, settles in Beauty. Up to then he thinks, carried along in a way by the wave of the intellect, and in a way raised on high by it, puffed up in a way, he sees suddenly without seeing how. The spectacle fills his eyes with light, not making him see something else through it. The seeing was the light itself. For in the Good there is not one thing which is seen, and another thing that is its light; nor is there intellect and object of intellect, but the radiance, engendering these things later, lets them be beside itself. It itself is only the radiance engendering Intellect, without being extinguished in the act of generation, but remaining identical. Intellect comes about because the Good is. If the Good were not such, then Intellect would not have been made to exist. (*Enn.* 6.7.36)

The image that gave the soul definite existence perfectly aligns with its imageless archetype and renders itself null. But there remains an excess, an indefiniteness, or infinitude (ἀόριστος) beyond same and other.[39] The mimetic life has gone, even if the self is not completely void. As Charles Stang writes, "Even at the 'end of the journey,' final union with the One, there remains a hairline crack or difference between the two centers, self and One. It is a difference so subtle that we cannot even count the two centers as two because they exist prior to number, a gap so thin that there is no longer any internal 'otherness' wanting to reemerge."[40] That gap between being and being like, between the two kinds of likeness, never fully vanishes, even if alterity and the need to close it does.[41] Plotinus's union here is still participatory, but it moves beyond any recognizable form of a mimetic relationship. There is no more suturing the distance between image and archetype, no more hunger for union, no more chiseling in search of a more accurate imitation. Accurate imitation ultimately becomes no imitation at all.

Iamblichus

Plotinus's synthesis, internalization, and organization of Plato were the three legs on which much of later interpretations of Plato will stand. Even those who critiqued Plotinus argued within a system he built. For Plotinus, mimesis was a way to transcend the gap between the imitation and the true, a specific mode of separation to help overcome all separation, stitches that bring together image and reality but that must eventually dissolve to bring about the desired wholeness or union. The soul unites with the One through introspection and contemplation, internalizing and then cutting away all images, to achieve its rightful place beyond being. A little more than a generation later, Iamblichus questioned this belief in a soul that needs only to be cleansed to unite with the One, as well as the correlated practice of contemplation that would perform this reunion. His challenges reshaped the practice of philosophy in the late ancient world.

For Iamblichus, philosophy had lost the beat. In *On the Mysteries*,[42] he accused his teacher, Porphyry, himself a student of Plotinus, of placing theology over theurgy,[43] God-talk over the God-work that could make humans divine. Their "doctrine," Iamblichus warned, "constitutes the ruination of sacred ritual and theurgical communion of gods with men, by placing the presence of the superior beings outside the earth. They teach that the divine is set apart from the earthly realm, and that it does not mingle with humanity, and that this realm is bereft of divinity" (*Myst.* 1.8, trans. altered). In insisting that the soul does not descend all the way into matter and instead remains outside materiality with the gods, these Platonists, according to Iamblichus, suggested that the gods did not dwell in the world. These philosophers also, Iamblichus continued, pridefully placed their hopes in their own ability to rise above matter through contemplation.[44] That "the breach between divine and human souls" could be "bridged by the soul itself" drastically downplayed the soul's alienation.[45] "Even the perfect soul is incomplete," Iamblichus writes (*Myst.* 3.20). Embodied souls required the gods.

Plotinus saw the soul as already divine, only dirtied by its descent. "Each one's place is its very self and when it ascends (so to speak) the place it came from runs along with it, and it is not itself one thing and its place [χώρα] another" (*Enn.* 5.8.4). For Iamblichus, by contrast, the soul needs the liturgies to transform it—a changed place for a changed soul.[46] The gods provide the sacred place of the liturgies, which facilitate a transformation that humans, on their own, could not attain. The soul, for Iamblichus, did not already unknowingly contain the Intellect, as it did in Plotinus.[47] The philosopher's aim could, therefore, no longer be only to awaken what was present but asleep. For Iamblichus, the soul was distinct from and, thus, had no access to superior hypostases; it needed divine aid to make such a leap. Praying with these liturgies "gradually brings to perfection the capacity of our faculties for contact with the gods, until it leads us up to the highest level of consciousness (of which we are capable); also, it . . . augments divine love [θεῖον ἔρωτα συναύξει], [and] kindles the divine element in the soul" (*Myst.* 5.26). The images presented in the liturgies are not merely "human customs" or "conventions"; rather, "God is the initiator of these things" (*Myst.* 5.25). The actual place is not something to overcome or something that one already is;[48] it is a place of participation that takes the practitioner out of herself.

Mimesis stands at the center of Iamblichus's goal of theurgic union, and efficacious mimesis happens liturgically. Philosophy and theology, for Iamblichus, should enhance or deepen one's appreciation for what goes on in the rites and might even increase the capacity to remember what it is like to be taken out of oneself, but only theurgic ritual can transform split, traumatized humans into unified, creating gods.[49] The rituals allow practitioners to "take the shape of the gods" (*Myst.* 4.2, trans. altered).[50] Theurgy, and not contemplation, unlocked our "innate knowledge of the gods . . . [and] the essential desire [ἐφέσει] of the soul towards the Good" (*Myst.* 1.3, trans. altered; cf. *Enn.* 5.6.5). Theurgy facilitates a "contact" that achieves the goal of likeness to God.[51] "The task for every soul," Gregory Shaw writes, "was to partake in divine mimesis by creating a cosmos out of the initial chaos of its embodiment."[52] The work of ordering matter puts practitioners in direct imitation of the Demiurge, who both orders chaos and providentially provides the rituals as a way for its creatures to imitate its actions.[53] But this work cannot be done without the aid of the gods, who provided images to spur humans toward the Good.

Iamblichus does not deny that rituals involve some human work. Theurgy, he argues, is twofold. "On the one hand, it is performed by humans, and as such observes our natural rank in the universe" (*Myst.* 4.2, trans. altered). Seen in this way, theurgy invokes visions (φαντάσματα) that inspire the practitioners "to modes of imagination" beyond "normal human behavior" (*Myst.* 3.14). At this human level, Iamblichus insists on the need for long training and slow growth. Only fools believe that after "a mere hour" they "have caused some spirit to enter" (*Myst.* 3.13). Recalling Socrates's critique of mimetic art in the *Republic*, Iamblichus insists that true learning happens more slowly. On the other hand, theurgy "controls divine symbols, and in virtue of them it is raised up to union with the higher powers, and directs itself harmoniously in accordance with their dispensation, which enables it quite properly to assume the mantle of the gods" (*Myst.* 4.2). The human work of imitating the divine by positing and chasing after images is one, but only one, part of theurgy. "It is in virtue of this distinction," Iamblichus continues, that theurgy "both naturally invokes [καλεῖ] the powers from the universe as superiors, inasmuch as the invoker is human," and that theurgy "gives them orders, since it invests itself, by virtue of the ineffable symbols with the hieratic role of the gods" (*Myst.* 4.2, trans. altered).

I return to the role of the symbols shortly, but first I need to stress that this inspired mimesis is possible, for Iamblichus, because humans, while descended, retain an "innate knowledge" of the gods. Humans do not naturally have access to this knowledge, but it can be accessed by the work of the gods.[54] This knowledge—unlike other ways of knowing, which keep subjects and objects separate—puts practitioners directly in contact with the gods. Iamblichus puts it like this:

Indeed, to tell the truth, the contact with the divine is not knowledge [οὐδὲ γνῶσίς ἐστιν ἡ πρὸς τὸ θεῖον συναφή]. Knowledge, after all, is separated (from its object) by some degree of otherness.[55] But, prior to that act of knowing [γιγνωσκούσης] another as being, itself, "other," there exists a spontaneous [αὐτοφυής][56] ... uniform conjunction suspended from the gods [ἡ τῶν θεῶν ἐξηρτημένη μονοειδὴς συμπλοκή[57]]. We should not accept, then, that this is something that we can either grant or not grant ... for it is rather the case that we are enveloped [περιεχόμεθα] by the divine presence, and we are filled with it, and we possess our very essence by virtue of our knowledge that there are gods [ἐν τῷ τοὺς θεοὺς εἰδέναι ἔχομεν]. (*Myst.* 1.3, trans. altered)[58]

This is not Plotinus's contemplation. Philosophers are not returning to themselves. The gods here come to take over human knowing; liturgies move us behind our split ways of knowing to a prior, spontaneous unity.[59] And humans cannot achieve this unity on their own. "It is neither through faculties nor through organs that the gods receive into themselves our prayers, but rather they embrace within themselves the realizations of the words of good humans, and in particular of those which, by virtue of the sacred liturgy, are established within the gods and united to them; for in that case the divine is literally united with itself, and it is not in the way of one person addressing another that it participates in the thought expressed by the prayers" (*Myst.* 1.15, trans. altered). The gods, in the rituals, graft humans into a kind of frictionless space that joins heaven and earth, and in that grafting they awaken in deified humans a secret, divine self. "We are raised gradually to the level of the object of our supplication, and we gain likeness to it by virtue of our constant consorting with it, and starting from our own imperfection, we gradually take on the perfection of the divine" (*Myst.* 1.15). Praying with those rituals "bind[s] together a single continuity from top to bottom, and render[s] the communion of all things indivisible" (*Myst.* 1.5). This completion or perfection is an initiation into a kind of mystery or transcendence. When the analogous microcosms all harmoniously line up, when the soul looks like the cosmos, which looks like the heavens, which looks like the gods, when everything clicks into place, theurgists experience an "ecstatic release." Or better, "not even ecstasy pure and simple, but an exaltation and transference to what is superior" (*Myst.* 3.7). The rituals provide a place to which humans can transcend, to which they can be transferred.[60] This transfer point is where the Egyptian liturgies and the Chaldean Oracles, so helpfully studied by Crystal Addey, become crucial for Iamblichus.[61] Ritual language, like theurgic knowledge, does not function like other language.[62] The sacred names are the actual "bodies" of the gods that "should not be violated by translation."[63] Instead of "conjecture or opinion," these words do not provide knowledge like other knowledge; humans know them the same way the gods do. Iamblichus fields a question from a hypothetical critic, "surely all that matters is that the conception remains the same, whatever the kind of words used?" Iamblichus replies with an unequivocal "no":

For if the names were established by convention [κατὰ συνθήκην], then it would not matter whether some were used instead of others. But if they are dependent on the nature of real beings [τῇ φύσει συνήρτηται τῶν ὄντων], then those that are better adapted to this will be more precious to the gods. It is therefore evident from this that the language of sacred peoples is preferred to that of other men, and with good reason. For the names do not exactly preserve the same meaning when they are translated; rather there are certain idioms in every nation that are impossible to express in the language of another. Moreover, even if one were to translate them, this would not preserve their same power. For the barbarian names possess weightiness and great precision, participating in less ambiguity, variability and multiplicity of expression. (*Myst.* 7.5)

These names do not explain; they are what he calls "symbols" (σύμβολα). They inspire rather than inform, possess rather than teach.[64] "Those who are inspired," Iamblichus writes, "have no consciousness of themselves [οὐ παρακολουθοῦσιν ἑαυτοῖς ἐνθουσιῶντες]" (*Myst.* 3.4). Those who chant these symbols perform the same actions as the gods, not opposing some words for others, not trying to get some meaning across, but speaking the same unity as the gods.[65]

Their actions are in no way human because what is inaccessible becomes accessible under divine possession: they cast themselves into fire and they walk through fire and they walk over rivers like the priestess at Kastabala. From these examples it is clear that those who are inspired have no consciousness of themselves [οὐ παρακολουθοῦσιν ἑαυτοῖς ἐνθουσιῶντες], and they lead neither the life of a human being nor of a living animal so far as concerns sensation or appetite, but they exchange their life for another more divine life, by which they are inspired, and by which they are completely possessed. (*Myst.* 3.4)

They have given themselves completely over to the gods and become their vehicle (ὄχημα), pulled along by the gods themselves.[66]

These symbols push beyond what Plotinus described as the mimetic art that reaches beyond nature to the forms. Iamblichus amplifies Plotinus's insistence that art is not any more removed from reality than anything else in creation and carries something of the divine in it, perhaps to the point where these symbols become all the theurgist can hear. "The Egyptians," Iamblichus writes, "imitating nature of the universe and the demiurgic power of the gods, themselves make appear certain images of mystic and hidden and invariable thoughts through symbols, just as also the power of nature stamped out, in a certain way, the invisible principles in visible forms by means of symbols" (*Myst.* 7.1, trans. altered). For Iamblichus, these are not useful "imitations of reality [μίμημα τοῦ ὄντος]," or "phantasms [φαντάσματα]" that facilitate thought (*Myst.* 2.10), as they are in Plotinus.[67] The imitations are revelatory, not by revealing a "resemblance" or "likeness"; rather, "the names of the gods and the other types of divine symbols ... have the capacity of raising us up to the gods and are enabled to link [συνάπτειν] us to them" (*Myst.* 1.12).[68] These symbols themselves, rather than the human mind, do the lifting.[69] Mimesis here surpasses any relation between sign and referent, and gives way to an ontological union. "We preserve in their entirety the mystical and arcane images [μυστικὴν καὶ ἀπόρρητον εἰκόνα] of the gods in our soul" (*Myst.* 7.4). Practitioners join in that imitation of the demiurgic power of the gods, which also is the gods, by being connected (συνάπτειν) to it and making themselves into it. Iamblichus will refer to these symbols as images, but the line between imitation and reality seems to have disappeared.

The goal, then, is not the correction of thought in order to overcome division, but the ecstatic transformation of the self through prayer. In giving oneself over ecstatically to the symbols, the gods speak to the gods. Iamblichus writes,

> It is not pure thought that unites theurgists to the gods. Indeed what, then, would hinder those who are theoretical philosophers from enjoying a theurgic union with the gods? But the situation is not so: it is the accomplishment of acts not to be divulged and beyond all conception and the power of the unutterable symbols, understood solely by the gods, which establishes theurgic union. Hence we do not bring about these things by intellection alone; for thus their efficacy would be intellectual, and dependent upon us. But neither assumption is true. For even when we are not engaged in intellection, the symbols themselves, by themselves, perform their appropriate work, and the ineffable power of the gods, to whom these symbols relate, itself recognizes the proper images of itself, not through being

aroused by our thought. For it is not in the nature of things containing to be aroused by those contained in them, nor of things perfect by things imperfect, nor even of wholes by parts. Hence it is not even chiefly through our intellection that divine causes are called into actuality; but it is necessary for these and all the best conditions of the soul and our ritual purity to pre-exist as auxiliary causes; but the things which properly arouse the divine will are the actual divine symbols. And so the attention of the gods is awakened by themselves, receiving from no inferior being any principle for themselves of their characteristic activity. (*Myst.* 2.11)

If, for Plotinus, what mattered with the names is what goes on in one's mind, here the names have a power of their own. They act independent of human thought (and on human thought). The stability of these names, moreover, allows practitioners to join these rituals. Their fixity gives theurgists something to join that pulls them outside themselves in ecstatic release. In the names, gods unite with themselves; humans, therefore, must join in the names to unite with the gods.

These symbols become the connection point between heaven and earth in a representation that moves beyond all representation. Iamblichus writes that the sacred rite "imitates [μιμεῖται] the order of the gods, both intelligible and that in the heavens. It possesses eternal measures of what truly exists and wondrous tokens, such as have been sent down hither by the creator and father of all, by means of which unutterable truths are expressed through secret symbols, beings beyond form brought under the control of form, things superior to all image reproduced through images, and all things brought to completion through one single divine cause, which itself so far transcends passions that reason is not even capable of grasping it" (*Myst.* 1.21). These symbols are not to be transcended. They are given by the gods, and are the gods. In joining these reproduced images, the philosopher joins what is beyond form in the liturgies. These new names and new places offer new selves.

What we see in Iamblichus, then, is a different mode of transcendence achieved by different means. For Iamblichus, the aim of the philosophical life is the imitation of the divine, and this is achieved as theurgists perform ritual action that places them in a circuit through which the divine speaks to itself. This circuit is accessible through particular images or names, which are the very bodies of the gods, and the aim of the theurgist is to connect to those sacred sites in order to be opened to what only the gods can do: make humans divine.

Julian, Cappadocia, and a Theory of Everything

The increased focus on ritual in Iamblichus as well as the style of transcendence and transformation offered in his philosophy became widespread in the fourth century. Students flocked to Syria to study with Iamblichus, and his pedagogical training program became the basis for much of later Platonism. But his teaching and philosophy were still limited to local, private schools. It was not until his thought was disseminated more widely, largely through the emperor Julian, that it posed opportunities or challenges to early Christians.

This chapter so far has focused on how Plotinus and Iamblichus thought about Plato's two conceptions of mimesis. But its larger goal is to situate Gregory of Nyssa. Those who write about Gregory often make a contrast between the supposedly world-denying Neoplatonism, typified by Plotinus, and Gregory's incarnational theology, which insists that there is no location of the mind outside the body, and which sees care of the poor as a theological imperative.[70] But Iamblichus both historically and philosophically seems the better contextualizing philosopher. Quickly, I would like to show how Iamblichus's thought, especially after it was taken up by the emperor Julian, both filled the air the Cappadocians breathed and presented a challenge they faced.

Gregory's connection to Neoplatonism is not simply an intellectual connection of great minds speaking from one ivory tower to another.[71] It is difficult to know exactly what Gregory did or did not read, but Iamblichus's philosophy, from its beginnings in his school in Apamea, quickly spread across the empire. It made its way into its centers of power within his lifetime.[72] His influence became even more widespread when, less than a century after *On the Mysteries* was written, the emperor Julian—surrounded by a passel of philosophers, most notably Maximus of Ephesus—sought to bring about educational and religious reforms across the empire, and it was Iamblichus who stood at the center of those reforms.[73]

Iamblichus's system of education became the standard curricula of late ancient philosophy. His ritually oriented philosophy offered an attractive Hellenism for those seeking *paideia*. With the emperor Julian—who insisted that Iamblichus was his "source"[74]—Iamblichus's philosophy entered the philosophical air Gregory breathed. This air gets thicker when we recall that Julian, Basil, and Gregory of Nazianzus were in Athens at the same time; that they likely shared teachers, such as Prohaeresius and, perhaps, Himerius;[75] and that Julian also wrote to, and invited for a visit, Aetius, the teacher of Eunomius.[76] Gregory's family, friends, and rivals all traveled in the same circles, where this literature was common intellectual currency.

Attending to Julian's Iamblichus and Gregory, then, the contrast is not between world-lovers and world-deniers, but between two ways that embodied creatures relate to language and experience transcendence. For Iamblichus, "God uses [our bodies] as its organs [ὀργάνοις]" (*Myst.* 3.7, trans. altered).[77] As Proclus later writes, "The divine character penetrates even to the last terms of the participant series, but always through mediation of terms akin to itself. . . . The henad communicates even to the body an echo of its own quality: in this way the body becomes not only animate and intellective, but also divine."[78] Iamblichus, like Gregory, offers a theophanic universe, a world in which the divine dwells in and among bodies, as well as a complex set of mimetic practices that connect humans with the divine.

Iamblichus and Gregory participated in a shared intellectual sphere in which disagreement was possible. Gregory inherits Iamblichus's emphasis on the one *akolouthia* or "sequence" of a text as essential for understanding its aim (*skopos*).[79] Iamblichus makes divine mimesis central to his theory of theurgy in a way comparable to Gregory's defining Christianity as "mimesis of the divine nature." Both insist on a divine initiative into the mimetic life. The two share a conviction that humans can sense the essence of superior beings only through divine powers, which are known by divine activities.[80] And Iamblichus's account of the direct connection between divine names and the divine essence bears stylistic similarities to that of Gregory's so-called "Neo-Arian" rival Eunomius.[81] Gregory and Iamblichus, when they theorize mimesis, try to carve out a style or way of life within a shared world.

Iamblichus's influence alters the shape of late antique philosophy. It connects ritual and *paideia*, but more so, the insistence on the soul's descent entirely into matter and the gods' actions in it make coherent the emperor's tightening of the bond between the philosophical life and political action in the world. As Dominic O'Meara shows, Julian's circle did not see him as the philosopher-king of the *Republic*. "Instead they read that philosopher-king as analogous to the Demiurge in Plato's *Timaeus*; something they could do because the highest divine principle in Neoplatonism, the One, which the philosopher sought to emulate and to which he wished his soul to return, was also the Good."[82] Training, philosophical contemplation, ritual performance, and political engagement might cohere in a pure soul in imitation of the demiurge. The emperor saw himself imitating the gods who reached down to the world to pull up what was below them.[83] Iamblichus's system, moreover, allows philosophers fully to link heaven and earth; divine names and the Roman *oikoumene* were all part of the same ordered space with the divine presence active and available at every stage. As Susanna Elm demonstrates, what Julian accomplishes in his taking up of Iamblichus is "a consistent system that merged everything, from the Highest One to the selection of magistrates, from the issuing of laws to the celebration of festivals, from sacrifice and statues of the gods to the reduction of taxes and the conduct of war."[84] Heaven and earth might be organized in imitation of the demiurge—a relationship that transcended mimetic relations given in symbols and powers, and connected what was already divine in humans to the gods by giving them names to chant, spaces to worship, and characters to aspire to. Iamblichus provided Julian a way to account for everything.

With that gauntlet thrown, Christians needed their own theory of everything. For Elm, Gregory of Nazianzus's response to Julian is "why [he] was honored as Gregory the Theologian,"[85] but of course Gregory of Nazianzus is not the only Cappadocian responding to the emperor (whose influence could still be felt in Cappadocia long after his death). When Basil argues for his reforms to "care for the poor," for example, he does so in relation to Julian's poverty relief program.[86] The Theologian quite directly attacks Julian in a way that Basil's younger brother will not. But Gregory of Nyssa's explanation of mimetic names, spaces, and characters is his own way of providing Christians with a vision of the whole, a theory of everything. Debates about what to imitate, after all, are also debates over how to imitate. But before turning to that project directly, we need to see how mimesis functions in another, equally, if not more, influential realm, for Gregory, that of early Christianity.

CHAPTER 3

Early Christian Mimesis

> Because the reader has no use for a work written for him,
> what he wants is precisely an alien work in which he can
> discover something unknown, a different reality, a
> separate mind capable of transforming him and which he
> can transform into himself. . . . The fact is that other
> people do not want to hear their own voices; they want to
> hear someone else's voice, a voice that is real, profound,
> troubling like the truth.
>
> —Maurice Blanchot

In the twentieth century, Maurice Blanchot argued against literary theorists who assumed that readers were looking for themselves in literature. He insisted that literature must offer an alternative, something real and different, something "like the truth." Only in an encounter with difference can the reader paradoxically "transform into himself." Christians in late antiquity posed similar questions of sameness, alterity, and the role of mimesis in encountering the holy: can holiness be imitated, or does holiness defy, contest, or escape mimesis? Transforming into themselves could happen through striving toward ever greater sameness, or by recognizing a boundary past which they could not go.

Christians were never separable from their social, political, economic, religious, and cultural location, and their emphasis on mimesis is not unique to them either. We have already seen some of the invisible expectations and assumptions operative within Gregory of Nyssa's world. But Christianity inherited more than invisible expectations. The Christians with whom Gregory is most closely in contact walked down the streets of the Roman

Empire, looked at its statues, worshiped in its buildings, cheered at its games, and spoke its languages. Greco-Roman life, that is, was constitutive of Christianity, not something Christianity appropriated from without. Christianity grew up in the diverse Greco-Roman world that we saw, in its philosophical aspects, in the previous chapters, and was itself just as diverse. Christian literature, too, participated in and was modeled on wider literary leanings that were popular in the Empire. And, as with all imitations, Christians also resisted their models and developed their own styles.

Christianity's distinctiveness, even while participating in the larger Empire, requires us to narrow the scope of this study and to examine how Christians leading up to and contemporary with Gregory discussed mimesis. Gregory's thinking presumed Plato's, but his sermons more often unpacked Paul's writings or gathered listeners around martyr relics. Gregory cited Origen as inspiration for his own writing, and his theological debates put him more often and more immediately in contact with bishops than with, say, Aedesius the Cappadocian, who studied with Iamblichus, or Aedesius's disciple Eustathius of Cappadocia.[1]

One benefit of narrowing the scope for this chapter is that it gives us space to see how, in the first four centuries of the Common Era, far more than philosophers and educators concerned themselves with the role of mimesis. Plotinus understood imitation as a way to get beyond images, whereas, for Iamblichus, imitation placed theurgists in the presence of the divine. For both, imitation yields to a higher form of reverence or union. In this chapter, we will see that a productive, if sometimes contentious, tension around mimesis runs throughout much of early Christian life, organizing practices of moral formation, martyr devotion, asceticism, visual culture, and theology. The tension plays out in different ways in each of these domains, but runs roughly as follows: on the one hand, imitation is necessary for the formation of Christian virtue, and, on the other hand, many Christians insist, there is something *inimitable* about holiness. Some argued for a participatory relationship that surpasses imitation. They ask: How "set apart" is something holy if it is imitable?

This distinction is neatly summarized by Gregory when he writes that with respect to the names Paul gives to Christ, those seeking Christian perfection should *imitate* some and *worship* others. Those names "that we make room for, we imitate [χωροῦμεν, μιμούμεθα]," Gregory writes, "and those that our nature does not have room for in imitation, we revere and worship."[2] Chapter 4 examines the aims of Gregory's distinction. (In short, it is a distinction to be overcome.) This chapter, however, demonstrates how his distinction between imitation and worship found energy and became recognizable within a larger late ancient context. To that end, this chapter highlights how the tension between imitation and worship also organizes a range of early Christian discourses, sets of references with encoded values and norms that are stabilized and supplemented by repeated performance. Gregory's distinction, we will see, touches a hot topic in late antiquity: What can be imitated, and what is inimitable and, therefore, must only be worshiped? Or, asked differently: When does aesthetic mimesis need to give way to fuller participatory union that transcends mimesis?

This chapter moves more quickly than the others. Rather than the close readings in the previous chapters, my goal here is to demonstrate that, in a wide range of discourses, we can detect a pervasive concern among early Christians about the relationship between transcendence and Christian formation structured by imitation. I by no means name them all, but by seeing how pervasive these debates were, we will be better prepared to see the force of Gregory defining Christianity as "mimesis of the divine nature."

More specifically, while I move quickly through these areas, and some readers will surely want more, I selected the topics because they are relevant to the texts that I examine in the second half of the book. Gregory's writings deal with *scripture*, and especially the example of Paul (notably in the connection between *epektasis* and imitation in Philippians 3); *martyrdom* (especially in my Chapter 5, where I discuss Gregory's emphasis on the martyria and the saints); *asceticism* (e.g., in connection with Macrina in Chapter 6); *visual culture*, including relics and icons (the artist painting is a common metaphor for Gregory's discussion of mimesis, and relics become important at a key moment in *The Life of Macrina*); and *theology* (which pervades the final chapters). The range of this chapter, therefore, means that it will raise questions around mimesis, questions that I can answer only by turning to the specific example of Gregory in the second half of the book. Debates around mimesis were everywhere in early Christianity. Across theological, literary, and social history, we can see debates around what could be imitated and what should be worshiped. Gregory's work should be read with the philosophical and theological questions, as well as the literary and social questions, in mind.

Imitating Paul

A few years after Quintilian arrived in Rome, where he would instruct orators in the centrality of imitation in their formation, the apostle Paul exhorted nascent Christian communities to another mimetic relation: "Imitate me, as I imitate Christ" (1 Cor 11:1). To read Paul's account of mimesis requires a shift in focus. In the previous chapters, I scrutinized the philosophical accounts of various mimetic relationships; for Paul, the complexities of mimesis as both a philosophical concept and as an ascetic practice give way to a rather clear call: do as I do. "Do as I do" is never so simple, but with Paul, we are closer to Quintilian's rhetorical education than Plotinus's philosophical scaffolding. As with the discussion of rhetorical education, in Paul's letters, imitating Paul involved questions of what exactly someone should imitate, as well as what kind of loving or revering relationship could inspire a mimetic relationship. Even if it is, in Blossom Stefaniw's words, the "most pedestrian form of mimesis,"[3] it still constitutes Christian formation with the imperative to imitate Paul, the imitator of Christ. These imperatives to imitate Christ by imitating leaders establish an important piece of Christian discourse: that Christ can be revealed through Christian leaders.[4] When Paul writes, "Imitate me, as I imitate Christ," the intent may be to point readers to Christ, but the effect is also to make Christ in the image of Paul.

Implied in this call to "imitate me," as Elizabeth Castelli has argued, was a request to submit to Paul's authority (over and against others competing for status).[5] To perceive Paul as an image of a suffering Christ was also to be obedient to the gospel he put forth.[6] In the first letter to the Corinthians, for example, Paul cast himself as the "father" of the community and reminded the Corinthians that children ought to imitate their father.[7] "For though you might have ten thousand guardians in Christ, you do not have many fathers. Indeed, in Christ Jesus I became your father through the gospel. I appeal to you, then, be imitators of me" (1 Cor 4:15–16). Among all the competing images of Christ, it is the one Christ whom *Paul* preaches in word and in deed that demands imitation. Paul's sacrificial, paternal love not only shows his dedication to the cause of Christ; he is himself an image of Christ. In his letter to the Galatians, he writes, "I have been crucified with Christ; and it is no longer I who live, but Christ lives in me" (Gal 2:20). Christians were to see a crucified messiah in a suffering Paul.

Paul's call for imitation in his letter to the Philippians is notable for this study because it connects mimesis to the Greek word with which Gregory of Nyssa is most associated, epektasis. Here "epektasis" is not an ascent into the infinite as it will be in Gregory of Nyssa; instead, Paul discusses the dangers of those who would "mutilate the flesh" by demanding circumcision (Phil 3:2). He builds up his past as part of the tribe of Benjamin, a Pharisee, a persecutor of the Church, and a righteous follower of the law, only to dramatically let it all fall down: "Whatever gains I had, these I have come to regard as loss because of Christ" (Phil 3:7). All things are "rubbish" compared to "the surpassing value of knowing Christ Jesus my Lord" (Phil 3:8). He continues:

> I want to know Christ and the power of his resurrection and the sharing of his sufferings by becoming like him in his death, if somehow I may attain the resurrection from the dead. Not that I have already obtained this or have already reached the goal; but I press on to make it my own, because Christ Jesus has made me his own. Beloved, I do not consider that I have made it my own; but this one thing I do: forgetting what lies behind and straining forward [ἐπεκτεινόμενος] to what lies ahead, I press on toward the goal for the prize of the heavenly call of God in Christ Jesus. Let those of us then who are mature be of the same mind; and if you think differently about anything, this too God will reveal to you. Only let us hold fast to what we have attained.
>
> Brothers and sisters, join in imitating me [Συμμιμηταί μου γίνεσθε], and observe those who live according to the example you have in us. For many live as enemies of the cross of Christ; I have often told you of them, and now I tell you even with tears. Their end is destruction; their god is the belly; and their glory is in their shame; their minds are set on earthly things. But our citizenship is in heaven, and it is from there that we are expecting a Savior, the Lord Jesus Christ. He will transform the body of our humiliation that it may be conformed to the body of his glory, by the power that also enables him to make all things subject to himself. (Phil 3:10–21)

That work of "straining forward [ἐπεκτεινόμενος]" to a heavenly calling (Phil 3:13–14), counting all as "loss because of the surpassing value of knowing Christ Jesus" (Phil 3:8), becoming "like [Christ] in his death" (Phil 3:10), and claiming "citizenship in heaven" (Phil 3:20), is summed up for Paul in a call for the Philippians to imitate him in his willingness to walk away from his past and to suffer in hopes of glory. Either they will imitate Paul or they are enemies of Christ, one of those "evil workers" who trust in flesh and refuse to share in Christ's suffering.

This call to imitate Paul expands the so-called Christological hymn earlier in the letter. It begins: "Let the same mind be in you that was in Christ Jesus, who, though he was in the form of God, did not regard equality with God as something to be exploited, but emptied himself, taking the form of a slave, being born in human likeness. And being found in human form, he humbled himself and became obedient to the point of death—even death on a cross" (Phil 2:5–8). To imitate Paul, then, is also to be emptied (κενόω) and humbled, even to the point of death, and in so doing, to join Christ who is "highly exalted" (Phil 2:9). Paul, that is, places himself in this mimetic line, a co-sufferer with Christ, in whom the Philippians can find unity and a common love (Phil 2:2). By loving Paul, continuing to support him in prison, and loving each other they empty themselves and are poured into Paul who funnels them into Christ.

By imitating Paul, Christians also become representations of Christ. In 2 Corinthians Paul shows how Christians become imitations of the imitator. The Corinthians are to imitate Paul as Paul imitates Christ. But Paul also looks to them as a representation of Christ. "You yourself are our letter, written on our hearts, to be known and read by all; and you show that you are a letter of Christ, prepared by us, written not with ink but with the Spirit of the living God, not on tablets of stone but on tablets of human hearts" (2 Cor 3:2–3). Paul at once authors them, and they take on a force of their own that Paul can, in turn, imitate. They show both Paul and the world what Christ looks like. If Paul becomes another Christ by imitating Christ, those who follow his lead also make Christ legible as they become God's letter that is written on Paul even as he writes. Paul becomes a palimpsest with a new messianic hermeneutic.[8]

Across Paul's writings, then, we see that imitation governs Christian behavior. Mimesis calls for unity around the figure of Paul, a figure who represents Christ in his ability to suffer for the gospel. When the boundaries of Christian community begin to fragment, Paul reinforces them by holding himself up as a stable point that can center and solidify it. We also see that Christian leaders claim to represent Christ in their own lives or the lives they hold up as exemplary. Paul's readers can expect to find the presence of God "written on . . . human hearts" (2 Cor 3:2–3). The authority of Christian leaders, moreover, seems to hinge largely on their ability both to live in imitation of Christ and to put forth other models of Christ that their hearers might imitate.

Before moving to those other models, however, I should note what we do not see in the New Testament. There is little, if anything, by way of what in previous chapters I called ontological mimesis. Paul's calls for imitation are ethical, and assume an ontology, but do not theorize an ontological system or provide a philosophical account of participation in Christ. Nor do they posit a need to worship an inimitable Paul. Paul is to be respected; but when he calls for imitation, he assumes that imitation is, more or less, possible.

Over the next four centuries, however, Christ took on an increasingly inimitable quality that troubles Paul's relatively straightforward demands or calls for mimesis. By the second century, Christians explicitly engaged with more complex thinking around mimesis along the lines drawn in the previous chapters. Intellectuals such as Justin Martyr and Tatian joined ancient debates around aesthetic mimesis and argued that images are both didactic and deceptive.[9] The *Gospel of Thomas*, for example, teaches that humans have a "divine double" in Jesus, to whom they must mimetically connect to be their true self.[10] And *The Secret Revelation of John* crafts a narrative of "Christian theology, cosmology, and salvation,"[11] in which the god Yaldabaoth functions much like *Timaeus's* demiurge in creating the world. What I stress in the sections that follow are different areas in which we can see a tension or ambiguity between, on the one hand, calls for imitation, where exemplary lives held forth are attainable, and, on the other hand, calls for worship, where objects of reverence demand fear or awe rather than emulation. Perhaps nowhere is this more pressing than in reference to martyrs.

Mimetic Martyrs

The connection between martyrdom and imitation of Christ not only forged Christian subjectivity in its earliest years; it also attracted various "saint cults," which only became more important throughout late antiquity.[12] With the rise in popularity of martyr devotion, debates around the status of these

saints and how Christians should relate to them became urgent. Both bishops and monastic communities asked: Should Christians worship them or
imitate them? Even if feasts and festivals for the martyrs do not represent
the martyr's life, can they, nevertheless, inspire imitation? And if so, what is
at stake in this indirect persuasion? For clarity, I separate two connection
points that animate Christian martyr piety: one between the saint and
Christ, where the martyrs, in imitating Christ, become "other Christs";[13]
and the other between the larger Christian community and the saints.

Other Christs

Martyr texts fashioned an early Christian "collective memory" centered on
Christlike suffering.[14] Writing to the Romans on his way to death, for example, Ignatius evokes Paul's discussions in Philippians 2–3, writing of the
tension between the desire to be with God and the desire to serve God by
loving God's people. Ignatius pleads with his hearers that he should no longer have to "run my race,"[15] and wishes to be "be poured out as a libation for
God while an altar is still ready." Success for Ignatius would make him "an
imitator of the suffering of my God."[16] By late antiquity, Ignatius's letters
function as part of a larger literary project and create what Castelli calls a
"usable past."[17] The stories that were kept alive tell us as much about those
who repeated the stories as about the characters in the stories. They create
"ideology in narrative form."[18] Christians wrote, told, and, most importantly, repeated martyr stories, and in so doing, created their own history.[19]

The widespread claim that martyrs were "imitators of Christ" occurred
in the same dynamic relationship of archetype and image that we saw with
Paul; that is, martyrs were modeled on Christ, *and* Christ was modeled on the
martyrs.[20] As Candida Moss argues, martyr narratives often repeat specific
episodes from the gospels—most notably the crucifixion and resurrection—
such that the martyr is recognizable as holy because she follows a pattern set
forth by Christ. And Christians understood Christ's death and resurrection
by looking to those of the martyr. From the stoning of Stephen forward,
early Christians cast martyrs as "part of a mimetic chain, one that connects
the audience of the martyrdom to Christ himself."[21]

We see an example of the exhortative function of martyr texts in *The
Martyrdom of St. Polycarp*, which opens with a call to imitation: "For practi-
cally everything that had gone before took place that the Lord might show
us from heaven a witness in accordance with the Gospel. Just as the Lord did,

he [Polycarp] too waited that he might be delivered up, that we might become his imitators [ἵνα μιμηταὶ καὶ ἡμεῖς αὐτοῦ γενώμεθα], not thinking of ourselves alone, but of our neighbors as well. For it is a mark of true and solid love to desire not only one's own salvation but also that of all the brothers."[22] There is clearly a call to do what Polycarp does. Salvation for oneself and one's neighbors depends on Christians doing what Polycarp did, putting themselves on the same path toward heaven by aligning themselves with the martyr, and making themselves imitators of Christ by imitating Polycarp.

To emphasize what this imitation might look like, the text counters narratives that would see Polycarp's death as shameful. Like Christ's, Polycarp's death is not that of a weak person easily defeated by the Roman Empire; it is a victory, and those imitating him are fellow victors.[23] "He was not only a great teacher but also a conspicuous martyr, whose testimony, following the gospel of Christ, everyone desires to imitate [μιμεῖσθαι]. By his perseverance he overcame the unjust governor and so won the crown of immortality; and rejoicing with the apostles and all the blessed he gives glory to God the almighty Father and praise to our Lord Jesus Christ, the saviour of our souls, the pilot [κυβερνήτην] of our bodies, and the shepherd of the Catholic Church throughout the world."[24] Polycarp's death does more here than instruct; it stirs a desire to imitate as it reveals who Christ is.

Even within this call to imitate the martyrs, however, something resists imitation. The martyr's suffering is inimitable. It is set apart and should not be attempted. When the pyre was lit to burn Polycarp, "the flames, bellying out like a ship's sail in the wind, formed into the shape of a vault and thus surrounded the martyr's body as with a wall. And he was within it not as burning flesh but rather as bread being baked, or like gold and silver being purified in a smelting-furnace. And from it we perceived such a delightful fragrance as though it were smoking incense or some other costly perfume."[25] Those near Polycarp can delight in his smell, but they are not expected to become him. Unable to kill Polycarp with fire, the soldiers sent an executioner (confector) to stab him, and, now "purified," Polycarp dies, letting out enough blood to extinguish the flames.[26]

Polycarp's death, then, is miraculous, and the faithful around him do not rush out to die with him. Instead, they collect his bones and create for themselves a place to revere him. "Collecting the remains that were dearer to us than precious stones and finer than gold, we buried them in a fitting spot. Gathering here so far as we can, in joy and gladness, we will be allowed by the Lord to celebrate the anniversary day of his martyrdom."[27] Christians jostle to be buried next to the martyr and celebrate Eucharistic meals by his grave.[28] The martyrs' victories orient Christian practice, but do so by holding the martyrs at a distance.

Martyrs here do not inspire direct imitation. Sometimes they inspire a "spiritual martyrdom," by which they mean rejecting wealth or some kind of struggle for virtue.[29] But often the stories are meant to elicit adoration without hopes of imitation.[30] The martyrs' suffering is too great even to train for. Those who undergo it hold a special place in their devotees' hearts, which, at most, they aspire toward; here it is enough to want to be next to the martyr, to pick up his remains, and keep his story alive.

We get a sense of the power of these martyrs even within some of the stories themselves. Martyrs, here, not only imitate Christ, but also replace (or are replaced by) Christ. In *The Martyrs of Lyons* we read:

> Blandina was hung on a post and exposed as bait for the wild animals that were let loose on her. She seemed to hang there in the form of a cross, and by her fervent prayer she aroused intense enthusiasm in those who were undergoing their ordeal [πολλὴν προθυμίαν τοῖς ἀγωνιζομένοις ἐνεποίει], for in their torment with their physical eyes they saw in the person of their sister him who was crucified for them [διὰ τῆς ἀδελφῆς τὸν ὑπὲρ αὐτῶν ἐσταυρωμένον], that he might convince all who believe in him that all who suffer for Christ's glory will have eternal fellowship in the living God.[31]

Blandina's effect on her witnesses seeps through the page and allows readers to see her too as another Christ. Christians could understand Blandina's death as a repetition of Christ's, but they could also see Christ's crucifixion as an iteration of Blandina's.[32] She "aroused intense enthusiasm" in those around her as well as in readers, but readers are unlikely to seek out a beast to eat them. Their devotion will take other forms.

These stories are not interested in ontology. Language of *ousia* or *esse* rarely appears. But the lack of explicit engagement does not mean they avoid those questions. These martyrs repeat Christ's death, resurrection, and ascension, and begin to take on their own power, occasionally becoming nearly indistinguishable from Christ, carrying within themselves a salvific function, and joining the angels and sometimes even Christ in the great hierarchy of heaven.[33] This transposition of the martyr and Christ does not, moreover, happen only in these widely popular narratives. It organizes worship practices across much of the late ancient Christian landscape, especially in the rise of the cult of the saints. For us, the question this raises is: What relations ought Christians have to these saints?

Imitations and Inimitability

Peter Brown highlights a debate in late antiquity over the relationship Christians ought to have with the saints: do they participate in God by rejoicing in them with feasts or do they imitate them?[34] Augustine comes down clearly on one side: "through those festivals the congregation made up of members of Christ should be prompted to imitate the martyrs of Christ. That is the only use [*utilitas*] of a festival. There is no other."[35] Augustine takes such a stance precisely because of the rapidly multiplying sermons in which the saints were radically set apart.[36] The festival "was a showing of God." Seeing the martyr there "unleashed salvation."[37] The suffering of the martyr becomes "a *spectaculum* . . . in that the believers were drawn by the deeper imaginative logic of the occasion to *participate* in the glory of the martyrs rather than to imitate them."[38] Augustine will not deny "the majesty of God's presence in the martyrs," but, against the growing tendency of non-mimetic awe toward the saints, "he went out of his way to insist that the martyrs did not enjoy an outright monopoly of the overwhelming grace of God."[39]

These debates were not limited to Augustine's North Africa. Sermons from across the late ancient world show clashes over how to have relationships with the martyrs. Should Christians dwell in the saints' presence or imitate them in their lives? The question of imitability was not so straightforward. The martyrs were clearly special and set apart.[40] And yet saintly suffering was "*in*imitable," and that inimitability was essential to the role of the saint.[41] Christians, Brown argues, did not want "a frail bridge of imitation" between themselves and the saints. "For if sacred figures such as the saints were no longer seen as utterly, inimitably different from the profane, then the very life-force of the profane world, which depended on intermittent contact with the sacred, would wither away." To infuse the world with holiness and inspire reverence, saints needed to be too holy to imitate.[42]

Against this backdrop we can see some of the force behind Gregory of Nyssa's coupling of Christian formation through imitation of the saints and his insistence on incomparability of the sacred, including those humans who most perfectly imitate God. Gregory's writings, along with those of his brother, Basil of Caesarea, and of Gregory of Nazianzus, attest to the way "martyr piety permeated almost every aspect of Christian life."[43] Forming virtuous Christians who constantly strive for perfection often meant leading them to martyria and filling their lives with the presence of the saints.

While Augustine demanded that his hearers choose between imitation and worshipful participation, most bishops moved productively between these categories. Basil, in his *Homily on the Forty Martyrs*, writes, "It is clear that the one who welcomes noble men will not fall short of imitating them in similar circumstances. Bless the martyred sincerely, so that you become a martyr by choice."[44] But Basil then refuses to let the martyrs be too much like his audience. "What sermon, then, could hit on their worth? Not even forty tongues could suffice to hymn the virtue of so many men. In fact, if just one were to be praised, he would be sufficient to overthrow the force of words, let alone such a great crowd, a phalanx of soldiers, a corps hard to struggle against, as much unconquerable in battle as inaccessible by praise."[45] Imitation of the saints and reverence for them work together here. Recounting the narrative and pointing to the visual depictions of it, Basil continues, "the facts which the historical account presents by being listened to, the painting silently portrays by imitation. In this very way let us too remind those present of the men's virtue, and as it were by bringing their deeds to their gaze, let us motivate them to imitate those who are nobler and closer to them with respect to their course of life. I mean that this is the encomium of the martyrs: the exhortation of the congregation to virtue."[46] For Basil, praise at once demands respect for what is "inaccessible" about martyrs, while also rendering them present in speech, art, liturgy, or an ethical life.

His sermon concludes with a swell of desire, lifting hearers before their throne.

> O holy chorus! O hallowed battalion! O unbroken fighting order! O common guards of the human race! Good companions in times of anxiety, helpers in prayer, most powerful ambassadors, stars of the world, flowers of the churches. The earth does not hide you; instead, heaven accepts you. The gates of paradise have opened for you. The sight is worthy of the army of angels, worthy of patriarchs, prophets, [and] the just. . . . Becoming a spectacle for the world and for angels and human beings [1 Cor 4:9], they raised the fallen, they strengthened the ambivalent, they doubled the desire of the pious.[47]

Basil's sermon lifted his audience to the level of the angels, letting hearers peer into heaven, while also exhorting them to a life of virtue.

Farther north of Basil's Caesarea, Asterius of Amasea's ekphrasis of a painting of the trial, torture, vision, and death of Euphemia also shows how speech often collapses the distinction between a mimesis that provides a "representation of" a martyr, and the mimesis that calls hearers to "act like" the martyr. The rhetorical *energeia* or vividness produced an affective intensity that overflowed into imitation.[48] When, for example, Asterius wrote of executioners "cut[ting] out her teeth as if they were pearls" and drawing "drops of blood,"[49] Ruth Webb argues, "both viewer and listener can be made to feel 'as if' they were present; they may even lose sight of the fact that they are responding to an illusion and react as if they were indeed present."[50] His speech ends with an enigmatic call to "complete the description," perhaps asking viewers to see the martyr more clearly, or perhaps asking them to enter into the story and become another Euphemia.[51]

The presence of these martyrs, moreover, subtly challenged the way Christians thought about presence and absence. The martyrs provided examples of virtue, and yet they also provided an active force working in and through late ancient life. Christian representation—sometimes through the performance of virtue, sometimes through rhetorical techniques, sometimes through liturgy or visual art—intensified the presence of the martyrs precisely because, paradoxically, the martyrs transcended all possibility of imitation. The fear and mysteriousness of martyrs made it all the more important to tell stories about them that would usher in something powerful, sacred, and set apart.[52]

The martyrs' active presence in the lives of early Christians defined what it meant to be a Christian, providing both an object of veneration and an example to follow. But martyrs were only one of many sites where the tension between the imitation and worship in Christian life plays out. The martyr narratives become templates for other saints.[53] We turn next to those holy ascetics, and especially to Antony, who in his discipline "was daily a martyr in his conscience and a contender in the contests of the faith."[54]

Asceticism: Two Antonys

Ascetics, like martyrs, also bore this tension between worshipful participation and moral imitation. The rise of monasticism is a defining feature of late ancient Christian life. While it differed in size and style from region to region, some of the numbers reported in ancient sources give a sense of its cultural force. In his preface to *The Rule of Saint Pachomius*, Jerome reports that "nearly fifty thousand monks took part in the annual meeting of Pachomian monks." The *Historia Monachorum* boasts the presence of "twenty thousand virgins and ten thousand monks" in fifth-century Oxyrhynchus. Those numbers seem exaggerated, but the exaggeration speaks to their outsized influence in the popular social imagination.[55]

In this monastic movement, there was perhaps no more well-known figure than Antony, and no more well-known story than Athanasius's *The Life of Antony*. The Alexandrian bishop tells his readers that he wrote the *Life* "so that you also might lead yourselves in imitation of him."[56] Athanasius writes that "even in hearing, along with marveling at the man, you will want also to emulate his purpose, for Antony's way of life provides monks with a sufficient picture [ἱκανὸς χαρακτὴρ] for ascetic practice."[57] If Antony turned the desert into a city by attracting monks to the desert, Athanasius wanted to build the infrastructure that would organize and sustain that city.[58] By filling their minds with Antony's way of life, Athanasius gave order to monks'.

David Brakke argues that mimesis of Antony is the cynosure of the *Life*. "The primary social function of the Athanasian Antony is . . . to inspire imitation. The Church, in Athanasius's view, realized its unity through the formation of a shared πολιτεία ['way of life'] by individual imitation of the saints' πολιτεία; as individual Christians formed themselves into saints through imitation, they also formed the Church."[59] Athanasius's Antony is not only an example; he is also a teacher. And his pedagogy puts imitation at the center of *askesis*. Monks are "to repeat by heart [ἀποστηθίζειν] the instructions of the scriptures, and to remember the deeds of the saints, so that the soul, ever mindful of the commandments, might be educated by their ardor."[60] And monks, filled with the words of scripture, must "act as [the holy ones] acted and . . . imitate [μιμεῖσθα] their courage."[61] Like the Psalms, saints become a kind of "mirror" in which a monk can "acquire knowledge of his own life."[62]

Athanasius's Antony performs marvels, but he is quick to point out that the marvels are strictly "the Savior's work." Ascetics need only focus on the disciplined life. They must look to each other—and especially to Antony— for archetypes of ascetic perfection. "We ought not to boast about expelling demons, nor become proud on account of healings performed; we are not to marvel at him who casts out a demon, and treat with disdain him who does not. Let one learn well the discipline of each, and let him either copy and emulate it, or correct it [καὶ ἢ μιμείσθω καὶ ζηλούτω, ἢ διορθούσθω]. For the performance of signs does not belong to us—this is the Savior's work."[63] Antony's life, that is, is important first and foremost as one to emulate. Monastic *politia*, for Athanasius, checked any reverence for Antony, keeping it well within the bounds prescribed by imitation.

Athanasius's Antony, however important he is, is only one view of the saint. In other sources that report on Antony, imitating him is a part of a larger project. The stated goal of the *Apophthegmata* is "to inspire and instruct those who want to imitate their [the holy and blessed fathers'] holy lives, so that they may make progress on the way that leads to the kingdom of heaven."[64] But the kind of mimetic relation to the fathers is difficult to parse, often because the commands and prohibitions are less clear, and readers are given less sustained descriptions of the saints' lives. As the Greek suggests, these sayings are not so much to be read as they are to strike and reverberate through the body.

The monks, for example, are regularly encouraged to remain in their cells. When a brother approaches Antony asking "What ought I to do?" Antony replies: "Just as fish die if they stay too long out of water, so the monks who loiter outside their cells or pass their time with the men of the world lose the intensity of inner peace. So like a fish going towards the sea, we must hurry to reach our cell, for fear that if we delay outside we will lose our interior watchfulness."[65] In response to the question "What must one do in order to please God?" Antony replies: "Pay attention to what I tell you: whoever you may be, always have God before your eyes; whatever you do, do it according to the testimony of the holy Scriptures; in whatever place you live, do not easily leave it. Keep these three precepts and you will be saved."[66] The call to remain in the cell is clear, but moral formation happens less by imitating a model than by putting oneself in the presence of God and being transformed by God's presence.[67] Antony was the model of this life, but his followers were to look *through* him rather than *to* him to dwell in a larger presence.

Encountering Antony did not lead directly to becoming another Antony; instead, in Gregory of Nyssa's words, the goal was to "catch the halo" around the holy man.[68] The *Sayings*, for example, tell a story of three fathers who make an annual journey to see the saint. Two of them speak of spiritual things with Antony. Antony says to the third, "You often come here to see me but never ask me anything." The priest replies, "It is enough for me to see you, Abba."[69] The Antony of the *Sayings* is a spiritual force in the desert, providing and gathering pearls of wisdom. Viewers, however, are to sit at his feet, to listen, and to enjoy his sacred glow. They can be near him, but they need not be like him. Abba Sisoes, likewise, concedes that he himself would "become all flame" if he "had one of Abba Antony's thoughts."[70]

Saints other than Antony attract devotion as well. "When you see your brother," Abba Apollo says, "you see the Lord your God."[71] We get insight into how this might materialize from a painting in the Monastery of Apa Jeremiah at Saqqara. It depicts a monk prostrating himself before Abba Apollo. The monk, recognizing Abba Apollo's holiness, treats him as he would Christ. Elizabeth Bolman summarizes the effect of the image: "Apollo so successfully imitated Christ that he became one with Christ while still walking about in the world in his physical body."[72] Only after falling facedown before this Christ, therefore, would the monk attempt imitation.

In short, for Athanasius, Antony, like Christ, was close enough to mimic, even as he transcended human nature. His transcendence could be represented and repeated in text and in life. "The self-consciousness of asceticism itself embodies an act of self-creation that possesses its own aesthetics," Averil Cameron argued. "It transcends the natural and resembles an act of literary or artistic creation."[73] For Athanasius, mimesis also forged a sacred community, a "city in the desert" with its own governance and virtues.[74] Other depictions of Antony, however, see imitation as, at most, secondary. If these Antonys are works of art, they do not draw readers up a ladder to the beautiful with an increased desire for producing images in the presence of the beautiful; they instead leave monks in reverent silence. The presence of the holy man filled the monks with awe and sent them back to their cells in search of what Evagrius of Pontus called "imageless prayer."[75] By participating in the saint's life, they dwelt in holiness, and that encounter itself was life-giving—"it is enough for me to see you, Abba."

In ascetic and martyr texts, then, we see two popular ways that Christians learned what holiness looked like. We turn next to another way that was just as, if not more, important: the visual art that filled the buildings and minds of Christian life.[76] If, as Jaś Elsner writes, "to be Roman was to do the kinds of things repeatedly represented in Roman art," then so too was being Christian about doing the things repeatedly represented in Christian art.[77] But Christians, we will see, did not only provide art that instructed a way of life. Especially in the fourth century, the images moved beyond schooling action or highlighting important qualities; art inspired worship as well.

Visual Culture: Between Narratives and Portraits

Before the fourth century, Christians seemed particularly concerned not to produce a certain kind of image: the portrait, the image associated with traditional Roman gods and the Emperor.[78] Recent studies estimate that there was one portrait of Augustus for about every thousand inhabitants of the Empire (which is roughly the ratio of churches to people living in the United States today).[79] It was, therefore, counterintuitive that Christians, as they gained in numbers, did not add their own portraits of their God to the mix. Robin Jensen argues, "Early Christians seem to have known that the simple representation of Christ's or a saint's face, without any narrative context, had the potential to attract devotion or worship."[80] It was this devotion to images that these Christians sought to avoid.

Early Christians instead created narrative art. Images of Jesus as the good shepherd, for example, were not timeless portraits, "but a metaphor expressing the qualities of Jesus as a loving caretaker of souls."[81] The message was clear: Jesus lovingly took care of souls, and so should you. As politics and the theological imagination shifted in the fourth century, so too did the styles of art. While early Christian art remained primarily didactic, the fourth century witnessed a rise in portraits that "omitted specific narrative context" and instead offered themselves for reverence.[82] These portraits do not tell a story of doing anything imitable. They, like the Antony in the *Sayings*, draw worshipers into a sacred presence without giving them a clear sense of what it would mean to "go and do likewise."[83] These representations became sites of worship or adoration.

With these portraits we can see a broader transformation of the role of mimesis.[84] To encounter these images was not to enjoy the decoration of things belonging only to the spiritual realm.[85] Like the martyrs who were invisible and yet present, these images took on a power of their own as they mediated relations between heaven and earth. They led to Christ, but they also carried what James Francis describes as "a certain 'numinous' quality; they were not reduced to mere symbols to be deciphered in an intellectual process. They possessed immediacy, force, power."[86] Christians in the fourth century remain concerned—perhaps increasingly so—about the inimitability of the divine, but images were increasingly not a reflection that needed to be transcended to touch reality.[87] They were a force at work in early Christians' daily lives. Portraits sat next to narrative art in the homes, chapels, burial sites, and martyria of late ancient Christians. This visual world, then, both provided instruction for imitation and inspired worship.[88]

Basil of Caesarea instructs Gregory of Nazianzus to be like painters who by keeping their eye on their model "strive to transfer the expression of the original to their own artistry." To become perfect (τέλειος) in virtue, Basil instructs, the Christian "must gaze upon the lives of the saints as upon statues [ἀγάλματα], so to speak, that move and act, and must make their goodness his own through mimesis."[89] Basil then places an ensemble of saints before Gregory: be like Job to gain fortitude, Joseph for chastity, and so on. These saints are instructive models. And these moving, acting statues resonate with a broader late ancient movement of so-called magic statues or "telestic arts."[90] The statues are not simply examples; when Christians pray with these statues, Basil writes, they "become temples of God," housing these statues as they become "God's dwelling place [ἐνοίκησις]."[91] These statues should come alive in the souls of those who pray with them. Theurgists and philosophers such as Iamblichus and Maximus, who advised Emperor Julian, viewed statues of the gods as *symbolon*, not symbolic representations, but hot spots that could link people to the gods.[92] These statues were "receptacles" for the gods that are made out of elements "akin to them."[93] And, as Sarah Iles Johnston has argued, no single statue or *symbolon* was a sufficient vehicle for union.[94] As with the aspiring rhetoricians imitating multiple models to catch something of the ineffable style of their teacher, so the theurgists' and early Christians' rituals gathered a series of "receptacles" to compose "an integrated and pure receptacle" that links human and divine.[95] These "statues" for Basil, then, function as models to follow, but also could transform the Christian into a container of the divine, could link them to a life otherwise unattainable.

More than the content of the images, what changes in late antiquity, Elsner argues, are the habits of perception. That is, fourth-century Christians could look at the same image and see something quite different. A relic or portrait no longer only represented the sacred; to see it was to see holiness, to encounter the art was to be put in touch with a different realm. Late antique viewers, that is, came to question the classical period's understanding of art, which Elsner summarizes as having a fundamentally deceptive quality to it: "Since no mimetic representation can actually *be* that which it represents, the distinction between the two only becomes sharper the more closely the image resembles the model."[96] Against and alongside this understanding, late antique viewers developed what Elsner calls a tendency toward "mystic" or "sacred" viewing in which the binary between image and reality and between subject and object dissolves and a "genuine, nonmaterial reality [is] communicated through an image."[97] Put back in our categories of mimesis, ontological participation in these images here subsumes the distance needed for aesthetic representation. These new habits of perception allow for "mystic experience" that transcends "subject and object . . . and yet is simultaneously both."[98]

This immediacy appeared not only in the statues and paintings of the fourth century but also in ekphrases and in ritual objects of devotion, both of which aimed to make the listener "see" what was being described. Asterius's ekphrasis, discussed earlier, made the painting of Euphemia's martyrdom "seem almost alive" to his audience. The depicted drops of blood appeared to "really stream from her lips."[99] In ritual, for example, Jerome knew that by showing onlookers the relic of the prophet Samuel, his audience would experience it "as if they beheld a living prophet in their midst."[100] Whether in icons, relics, liturgical objects, or portraits, an ambiguity develops around the function of the image: is it a presence to participate in, or is it fuel for further imitation?

Visual culture, then, held a (by now familiar) tension between imitation and worship. As Christians developed new ways to represent Christ, they also perceived those representations differently, and with new modes of perception also came new representational practices. These new habits of representation encouraged Christians toward specific virtues, but these representations also became points of intensity, sacred spaces where God might put on paint, just as God put on flesh. Mosaics, sculptures, portraits, and images saturated Christians in their daily lives and, moreover, were in ongoing relationships with the theological claims that provided Christians with conceptual frameworks for perceiving images.

Theological Doctrine

Theological claims should not be thought of as abstract and uninteresting to the ordinary faithful. They formed some of the basic categories in which the laity understood their lives and the world around them. In an oft-cited passage in which Gregory of Nyssa describes the talk of the town just before the

Council of Constantinople in 381, we read: "Throughout the city everything is filled with these discussions: the alleyways, the marketplaces, the broad avenues and the city streets; the clothing hucksters, the money-changers, the food vendors. If you ask about small change, someone will philosophize to you about the Begotten and the Unbegotten. If you ask about the price of bread, the reply comes, 'the Father is greater and the Son is a dependent.' If you should inquire whether the bath is ready, someone will respond, 'the Son was created from not being.'"[101] This may be hyperbole, but the point is nevertheless clear: doctrinal talk is inseparable from the everyday acts of piety. The "elites" who engaged most directly in these doctrinal debates were not locked in libraries. They lived in same world as and spoke in the same languages with the same Christian communities we have seen throughout this chapter.[102] And it should not surprise us that similar tensions between aesthetic and ontological mimesis are visible across a wide variety of theological texts.

I focus on two key thinkers engaged in two theological disputes. First, I look at Origen of Alexandria, whose influence on Gregory of Nyssa is hard to overstate. Theologians, including Gregory, will adjust Origen's framework, but it serves, nevertheless, as a starting point for much of the theology that comes after him.[103] This framework, we will see, depends on imitative relations that can lead Christians to a participation beyond all representation. I then turn to Athanasius of Alexandria, the pugnacious bishop whom we encountered earlier in his *Life of Antony*, to examine the role of mimesis in his influential writings on Trinitarian debates. These Trinitarian debates are technical and change between Nicaea and Gregory's most active period,[104] but Athanasius provides for us a sense of how the language of mimesis became important in considering the Trinity and humanity's relationship to it: humans participate in God by imitating Christ, whereas Christ, as the Son of God, even though he is the "image of God," does not imitate God because he is God by nature.

Origen: Image and Likeness

To talk about Origen's view of mimesis, I need to tell a broad, metaphysical story that emerges from his magnum opus, *On First Principles*.[105] The story moves most quickly when told with categories Origen himself helps make familiar: creation, fall, return, consummation. For Origen, in the beginning, humans were created as minds who contemplated God. These minds are what Genesis 1:27 means by the "image of God"; and the aim of God's economy is to bring that image into a likeness, such that in the end, humans would be "the image and likeness of God" (Gen 1:27). These minds, however, instead of immediately becoming like God by contemplating God, were distracted and drifted away from God.[106]

If distraction is the problem, the solution, as Origen sees it, is to help focus these minds and bring them back to their rightful state as contemplators. God does this by providing bodies and materiality that would limit the mind. When that was not enough, Christ, who is the one mind that was not distracted, took on flesh to provide a model that could focus the mind back on God.[107] The incarnation, then, begins a long process of restoration. For, in the end, humans will retain their focus in an even more intense and sturdy way. Their return fully unites them to God as both the "image and likeness of God" in a way that surpasses any image-archetype relationship that humans experience in the body, an image and likeness that allows God to be "all in all" (1 Cor 15:28).

With this rough sketch in mind, we can focus in on the role of mimesis in Origen. As for Plotinus, for Origen, mimesis is both the way back to God and a way to get beyond mimesis.[108] First, it is how one advances in perfection. Origen writes, "Each one by his own voluntary choice either . . . make[s] progress through the imitation of God or . . . deteriorate[s] through negligence."[109] Humans can "progress through imitation" because of the incarnation, and they can move beyond the body because of the incarnation as well. Origen writes that "since he [the Son of God] is the invisible 'image' of the 'invisible God' (Col 1:15) he granted invisibly to all rational creatures whatsoever a participation in himself, in such a way that each obtained a degree of participation proportionate to the loving affection with which he had clung to him."[110] Participating in the Son of God, for Origen, is a matter of what one does with one's mind, as a "rational creature."

But to arrive at this invisible participation requires visibility. God, Origen insists, provides bodies that will shape the activities of the mind but refuses to touch the mind itself, which must remain free. By providing something to constrain, attract, and concentrate a wandering mind, the image of God "gradually and by degrees" transforms Christians back to their original state, and even makes them more stable than they were before.[111] The human "received the honour of God's image in his first creation, whereas the perfection of God's likeness was reserved for him at the consummation. The purpose of this was that the human should acquire it for himself by his own earnest efforts to imitate God, so that while the possibility of attaining perfection was given to him in the beginning through the honour of the 'image,' he should in the end through the accomplishment of these works obtain for himself the perfect 'likeness.'"[112] Mimesis is what moves humans from an indelible image to a perfected "likeness." And yet this likeness is unlike any human likeness: drawing on Jesus's words, "Father, I will that, where I am, these also may be with me," and "as you and I are one, so may they be one in us" (John 17:24, 21). Origen writes, "Here indeed the likeness [*similitude*] seems, if we may say so, to make an advance and from being something similar to become 'one thing' [*proficere et ex simili 'unum' iam fieri*]; for this reason undoubtedly, that in the consummation or end God is 'all in all.'"[113] Origen, that is, posits a mimetic relationship in order to transcend it and to make it possible to "become one thing" with God.[114]

Throughout this chapter we have been tracking a tension between a representational mimesis and an ontological one. And we have seen that some things Christians are to imitate; others they participate in by worshiping. We have seen along the way how imitations of Christ become objects of reverence themselves. We can see a similar tension in Origen as well, but to see it, we have to remember that for him, Christ's role was principally pedagogical. He taught Christians how to contemplate the invisible and immaterial God and that Christ was more a guide through the ontological maze than part of it himself. By looking to Christ, Christians cleared away false notions and prepared themselves for a more thorough transformation, when "progressing through imitation" will no longer be necessary.

ON READING, OR BECOMING ANOTHER CHRIST

Christ, for Origen, was most often a teacher to imitate, and all of creation was a kind of "lecture room or school for souls"[115] that trains the soul and the mind to focus on God. But within this larger school, scripture was a particularly intense space of education.[116] We can best see Origen's understanding of how to train for Christian perfection in his *Commentary on the Gospel according to John*. "Since the Savior has come, and has caused the gospel to be embodied in the gospel," Origen writes, "he has made all things gospel, as it were."[117] His *Commentary on John* shows the kind of transformation Origen hopes Christians achieve through their engagement with scripture. There he explains how to read the gospel well, and the connection between reading and Christian perfection.

Toward the beginning of the treatise, Origen pauses to explain to readers what kind of text they are engaging when they encounter a "gospel." "The gospel," he writes, "is either a discourse which contains the presence of a good for the believer, or a discourse which announces that an awaited good is present."[118] That is, a gospel either ushers in something or points toward it. The written gospel (i.e., the text of the Gospel of John) "teaches a shadow of the mysteries of Christ."[119] But that gospel points to something beyond itself, namely, the ideal form, "which John calls an eternal gospel," or "which would properly be called a spiritual gospel."[120] Just as the human body helps focus the mind for an encounter beyond the body, so the written Gospel points beyond itself. Origen's reading practices are meant to "translate the gospel perceptible to the senses into the spiritual gospel."[121] In this translation, they encounter the "symbols," which do not announce, but "contain" the truth that is invisible and eternal.[122]

The translation in language also translates the self. A spiritual reading does not boost readers into an empyreal hinterland; spiritual readers, for Origen, "become another John," because to understand John, readers must become him. Readers should internalize and identify with the author's words to the point where the distance between reader and author collapses.[123] Spiritual reading does not bring about an encounter with difference, with someone else; it lifts readers into a new life. This kind of reading, moreover, does not simply engage the words of another human; that human (John), to write what he wrote about Jesus, had to become another Jesus.

> We might dare say, then, that the Gospels are the firstfruits of all Scriptures, but that the firstfruits of the Gospels is that according to John, whose meaning no one can understand who has not leaned on Jesus' breast nor received Mary from Jesus to be his mother also. But he who would be another John must also become such as John, to be shown to be Jesus, so to speak. For if Mary had no son except Jesus, in accordance with those who hold a sound opinion of her, and Jesus says to his mother, "Behold your son," [Jn 19:26] and not, "Behold, this man also is your son," he has said equally, "Behold, this is Jesus whom you bore." For indeed everyone who has been perfected "no longer lives, but Christ lives in him [Gal 2:20]," and since "Christ lives" in him, it is said of him to Mary, "Behold your son," the Christ.[124]

In becoming another John, readers also become another Christ. They "have the mind of Christ," restoring readers to their true destiny as minds eternally contemplating God. For Origen, then, bodily representation becomes scenery for participation in and contemplation of God. But that stage should become so natural, so much a part of oneself that it fades to black leaving only a spotlight on the mind, the true self, and its participation in God.[125]

Athanasius: Mimesis in the Trinitarian Debates

If in Origen imitations are shadows of the truth but also breadcrumbs leading back to heaven, we see a different relationship between imitation and reality emerge in the Trinitarian debates of the fourth century. There is no simple way to characterize the Trinitarian debates, but, for Athanasius, it was imperative that the Son is an image of the Father and that the image is both of equal status and "of one substance [ὁμοούσιος] with the Father."

In a defense of the Council of Nicaea, Athanasius puts this in explicitly mimetic terms.

> The bishops . . . found it necessary again to gather together the sense of the Scriptures and to speak more clearly the things which they said before, and to write, "the Son is 'one in essence [ὁμοούσιον]' with the Father" in order to signify that the Son is not only like, but from the Father as the same in likeness [ταὐτὸν τῇ ὁμοιώσει], and in order to show that the likeness and inalterability of the Son [τὴν τοῦ υἱοῦ ὁμοίωσιν καὶ ἀτρεψίαν] is other than the mimesis [μίμησιν] that is ascribed to us and which we attain through virtue by keeping the commandments.[126]

Humans must imitate the divine, whereas the Son's likeness to the Father is not mimetic. Humans participate in and represent Christ and in doing so become what they are not, namely, divine. Christ, by contrast, is from the essence of God "by nature," and therefore does not move from what he is not when he is the image of God.[127] Unlike humans, who move from human to divine in Christ, the Son "was not a human being and later became God." Rather, "being God, he later became a human being in order that we may be divinized."[128]

When humans speak of bodily generation and sons as images of their fathers, the two are, Athanasius writes, "in some way separated and distant

from one another."[129] But within the Trinity, likeness did not require distance: "since the generation of the Son from the Father is other than that
which pertains to the nature of human beings he is not only like [ὅμοιος]
but also inseparable [ἀδιαίρετός] from the essence of the Father and he
and the Father are one, as he himself said [Jn 10:30] and the Word is always
in the Father and the Father in the Word [Jn 10:38], as is the radiance in relation to the light."[130]

In his third *Oration*, drawing on John 14:9–11, Athanasius provides an
illuminating example of the relationship between image and archetype that
occurs between the Son and the Father. He discusses the way that the image
of the emperor is a presence of equal vitality and authority as the emperor
himself.[131] The Son, as the image of the Father, Athanasius argues, is one
with the Father.

> And we may perceive this at once from the example of the Emperor's
> image [εἰκόνος]. For in the image is the shape and form [τὸ εἶδος καὶ
> ἡ μορφή] of the Emperor, and in the Emperor is that shape which is
> in the image. For the likeness of the Emperor in the image is indis-
> tinguishable [ἀπαράλλακτος], such that a person who looks at the
> image, sees in it the Emperor; and he again who sees the Emperor,
> recognizes that it is he who is in the image. And since the likeness
> does not at all differ, the image might say to one who, having seen the
> image, wished to view the Emperor, "I and the Emperor are one; for
> I am in him, and he in me; and what you see in me, that you behold
> in him, and what you have seen in him, that you hold in me." Ac-
> cordingly, he who worships the image, in it worships the Emperor
> also; for the image is his form and appearance [ἡ γὰρ ἐκείνου μορφὴ
> καὶ τὸ εἶδός ἐστιν ἡ εἰκών]. Since then the Son too is the Father's Im-
> age, it must necessarily be understood that the Godhead and propri-
> ety of the Father is the Being of the Son.[132]

Recalling what Elsner calls the "mystic view," which dissolves any distance
between subject and object or representation and reality, we see here how
shifts in mimesis also shape Trinitarian debates. Humans imitate God to
become virtuous, which by their nature they are not. And yet there is another
kind of relationship between representation and reality in which the representation is "indistinguishable" and, indeed, shares the same essence.[133] To
be an image here is in no way a diminishment or derivation of a more primal

truth. If the Word could become flesh, then the highest truth could be re-vealed in a body, even if it is not contained by that body. The Word's "natu-ral" connection to the Father connects the sacred and the body as well.

Origen's claim that in the incarnation, Christ "made all things gospel," takes on a different sense in Athanasius's theology. As with Origen, for Athanasius, Christ, in becoming human, became an image, and could turn wayward humans back to God and could allow them to participate in God. "For since the reason of humans had descended to sensible things, the Word submitted to being revealed through a body, in order that he might bring humans to himself as human and turn their senses to himself, and that thenceforth, although they saw him as a human, he might persuade them through the works he did that he was not merely a human but God, and the Word and Wisdom of the true God."[134] But there is an added dimension to Athanasius's Christ. The problem for Athanasius is that "humans, contemp-tuous of the better things and shirking from their apprehension sought rather what was *closer to themselves*—and what was closer to them was the body and its sensations."[135] And the solution must therefore be that Christ is not only a visible image for those who need something to see. Christ also must scoop down below and stretch beyond humans. Christ becomes closer to humans than they are to themselves.

> For the Word spread himself everywhere, above and below and in the depth and in the breadth: above, in creation; below, in the incar-nation; in the depth, in hell; in breadth, in the world. Everything is filled with the knowledge of God. For this reason, not as soon as he came did he complete the sacrifice on behalf of all and deliver his body to death, and resurrecting it make himself thereby invisible. But by means of it he rendered himself visible, remaining in it and completing such works and giving signs as made him known to be no longer a man but God the Word. For in two ways our Saviour had compassion through the incarnation: he both rid us of death and re-newed us; and also, although he is invisible and indiscernible, yet by his works he revealed and made himself known to be the Son of God and the Word of the Father, leader and king of the universe.[136]

The incarnation here works on two levels. Christ makes an ontological change in humanity, "renew[ing] us," while also providing a representation of the divine that can lead humans back to God. Only with both of these mimetic relations—ontological participation and aesthetic representation—working together can Christ bring about the necessary change in humanity. It is with respect to both of these changes that Athanasius can write his famous line: "He [the Word] became human that we might become divine [Αὐτὸς γὰρ ἐνηνθρώπησεν, ἵνα ἡμεῖς θεοποιηθῶμεν]."[137] The incarnation infuses creation with the divine presence, making it possible to participate in the divine and providing an image by which the Word is known.

Theological doctrine, then, operates within larger late ancient concerns around mimesis and how to participate in and represent the divine. With Origen and Athanasius, mimesis frames everything from hermeneutics and asceticism to soteriology and the Trinity. Relationships between image and archetype link heaven and earth, and do so in contradictory and contested ways.

Before turning explicitly to Gregory of Nyssa, we can also note one more connection in these doctrinal discussions around mimesis. For Origen, God is, at least functionally, finite. He writes, "For if the divine power were infinite, of necessity it could never understand itself, since the infinite is by nature incomprehensible."[138] The aim of contemplation of the divine, for Origen, assumes a finite and comprehensible God. Athanasius too, as we saw in his rendering of Antony, sees the divinization of humanity as a special holiness, but not as an endless journeying into an endless God. Antony is knowable and imitable, an image of a God who is unknown, but not infinite, and therefore, in some way, comprehensible. Origen and Athanasius acknowledge that humans may always be too feeble to fully face the divine glory, but God is, at least in theory, knowable. More to the point, as Anthony Meredith has argued, even in places where Origen and Athanasius claim that God is infinite,[139] their understanding of "infinite" differs from Gregory's.[140] For example, Origen discusses souls being "infinite," writing, "For souls are, as one may say, infinite, and their dispositions are infinite [Ἄπειροι γὰρ ἡμῖν, ὡς ἂν εἴποι τις, αἱ ψυχαί, καὶ ἄπειρα τὰ τούτων ἤθη]."[141] He simply means a lot; it would take a long time to count—like the number of sand grains on the beach—but there are actually a limited number of souls, and one day they will all be transformed. Athanasius, too, will use the language of infinity, but for Origen and Athanasius, divine incomparability is about the human mind being (currently) too weak to contemplate God. Gregory's discussions of divine incomparability make a stronger claim. For Gregory, even the greatest mind could not contemplate God because God is intrinsically limitless and therefore unknowable. Put starkly, Origen and Athanasius's unknowability is about humanity's nature; Gregory's is about God's nature. As we turn to Gregory, we will see how this stronger claim to divine incomparability complicates already complicated questions around the imitation of God.

*   *   *

Across a wide range of Christian discourse, we have seen a tension between what I have been calling the two sides of mimesis. These different discourses are not reducible to the broader intellectual and ascetic trends that we saw in Chapters 1 and 2, but they do partake in them. On the one hand, Christians represent Christ in a variety of ways. Paul holds himself up as an imitator of Christ; martyrs inspire courage and valorous suffering; ascetics become models for the life of perfection; visual art fills Christians' imaginations; and theologians understand Christ as an image of God. On the other hand, these representations can inspire something beyond or different from imitation. Martyrs have a power of their own that occasionally rivals Christ's; ascetics become sites of reverence; portraits stir desire for devotion; and, for Origen, the image of God, like the words of scripture, encourage Christians to move beyond the visible and the imitable to a point where God will be all in all.

Gregory sums up this tension when he writes, "those that we have room for, we imitate, and those that our nature does not have room for in imitation, we revere and worship."[142] And yet Gregory's refusal to separate imitation and worship is crucial for understanding his definition of Christian perfection as a constant straining forward. When Gregory writes that "Christianity is mimesis of the divine nature" and also insists that the divine nature is infinite, he can continue infinitely this dynamic relationship between representation and participation.

The second half of this book examines how Gregory reimagines mimetic relations of names, spaces, and characters.

CHAPTER 4

Mimetic Names

Names, too, are a kind of system.
—Anne Carson

The names we take into the soul.
—Gregory of Nyssa

Toward the end of his life, Gregory of Nyssa received a request from an old friend asking "how could anyone become perfect through a life of virtue."[1] Gregory, in response, offered a reading of the thirty-four names the apostle Paul gave to Christ. Those names provided targets for the life of virtue, and his reading sketched a practice of constellating the multiple scriptural names into the one name of Christ, the name that defines the Christian life. For Gregory, those names structured a system, an interlocking network, of reverence and imitation that produced what Gregory defined as perfection (τελειότης): an ever-renewing, ever-expanding participation in Christ, which happens by being constituted by those names.[2] This response, later titled *On Perfection*, forms some of his most succinct, Christological reflections on perfection as constant growth and also highlights Gregory's program of a mimetic life.

The treatise seemingly revolves around a distinction: those names "that we have room for, we imitate, and those that our nature does not have room for in imitation, we revere and worship."[3] This distinction, as we saw in the previous chapter, would have been familiar. What Gregory did with it, however, was not. He posited the distinction between imitation and worship in order to overcome it. Or rather, he showed how imitation and worship are not so much distinct as dialectic. For Gregory, mimesis should include the devotional longing associated with worship. Gregory's joining of the two sides of mimesis—ontological participation and aesthetic representation—involved an orientation toward that which Christians love and that which is the source of their existence, which, for him, was also what it meant to revere or worship it. The work of the treatise, therefore, involves getting his readers to see that relationship; imitation is a form of worship, and true worship involves imitation of the inimitable. The particular practices involved in imitating any name forged a larger project of honing desire for what is beyond imitation.

What Is in a Name?

It is no coincidence that Gregory focused on the names of Christ. In late antiquity, names condensed theologies and scaffolded ritual pieties. Philosophers' entire range of thought came to bear in their interpretations of Plato's most famous dialogue about names, *Cratylus*. With that text, they debated the nature of the relationships between minds, words, and essences.[4] Those debates seemed especially important in a world in which names were crucial to personal and communal piety. Philosophers, that is, theorized a widely shared practice. Even if few people could read, say, Iamblichus, most understood the ways names could reverberate in the soul and take on a force of their own. Worshipers chanted and even wore them. Amulets with specific names of God on them were "worn as magical objects for cure and protection, and were addressed not so much to the potential reading audience of the *literati* as to the still overwhelming majority of the semiliterate and those who could not read at all," Valentina Izmirlieva writes.[5] And as Peter Brown once quipped, "To be without an amulet in early Christian times, whatever one's religion, was as ill-advised as forgoing a flu shot or daily multivitamin today."[6] Names did more than label. Their signifying carried a charge. And the question for theorists was how people should relate to those live, powerful words.

This wider phenomenon shaped Gregory most directly when, a generation after the Council of Nicaea, a debate about what and how names signify became urgent. Mark DelCogliano described this as a debate over the "theology of theology."[7] What do Christians "name" when they name God? How should Christians relate to the names of God? Do names provide access to the essence of God? Are names aids for prayer that leads beyond names?

Does God speak with human words? If so, how? And if not, how else would humans receive God's revelations? How theological language functions, Gregory argues, speaks to larger issues of Christian practice, and especially to the role and function of imitation in the Christian life.

Susanna Elm has helpfully demonstrated how Gregory's chief theological rival, Eunomius of Cyzicus, owed much to the Neoplatonism inspired by Iamblichus.[8] "Sacred names of the gods," Iamblichus argued, "have the capacity of raising us up to the gods and are enabled to link [συνάπτειν] us to them."[9] Unlike "conjecture or opinion," these words do not provide knowledge like other knowledge; humans know them the same way the gods do: simple knowledge for simple beings.[10] These names or "symbols" do not explain; they inspire rather than inform, possess rather than teach. "It is essential," Iamblichus writes, "to remove all considerations of logic from the names of the gods, and to set aside natural representations [φυσικὰς ἀπεικασίας] of the spoken word to the physical things that exist in nature."[11]

Eunomius drew upon a similar logic to argue that the name "Unbegotten" (agennetos) announces God, not "only in name, in conforming with invention [κατ' ἐπίνοια]," but "in conformity with reality [κατ' ἀλήθειαν]." The name Unbegotten is not simply a good idea for God or a name that elucidates other names; it is the truth of God. "We do not understand his essence to be one thing and the meaning of the word which designates it to be something else. Rather, we take it that his substance is the very same as that which is signified by his name, granted that the designation applies properly to the essence."[12] Eunomius's theory of names draws heavily on Iamblichus's school of language, in that humans must know God the way God knows God. Socrates Scholasticus preserves a passage from Eunomius that takes this principle to its logical conclusion: "God does not know anything more about his own essence than we do, nor is that essence better known to him and less to us; rather, whatever we ourselves know about it is exactly what he knows, and, conversely, that which he knows is what you will find without change in us."[13]

The differences between Iamblichus and Eunomius also matter. Most important is Eunomius's concern with monotheism and the simplicity of God.[14] To know a simple God, Eunomius argued, Christians must have simple knowledge: they must know God as God knows God, and because God is one, God must have *one* name: unbegotten. To know what it is to be unbegotten is to know what it is to be God. This one name, therefore, is set on a different ontological plane, cut off from all other language. Humans have access to this name only because they have an "innate knowledge [φυσικὴν ἔννοιαν]," a special, given faculty that allows God's essence to be present to them in that name.[15]

For Gregory, the gift of scripture, and of language more broadly, delivers less and more than Eunomius's *agennetos*: less in that no name is the essence; more in that while the divine nature transcends humanity, it is not cut off from the world in the way that Eunomius's *agennetos* is "wholly other." Human finitude makes it clear that God is beyond all limits and spurs humans to move in and toward God. In his formative sparring with Eunomius, therefore, Gregory contends that no name can deliver the divine essence.[16] "Though many such things are said of the divine Nature, by which we learn what we must understand God to be," Gregory writes, "what in itself it [the divine essence] essentially is, the words do not teach us."[17] Even the words that "are in the divine scripture spoken personally by God" are accommodated.[18] This is not to suggest a rather low view of language. The words of Moses, for example, "are indications of the divine will, illuminating in one way or another the purity and intelligence of the saints with such share of the grace as their status merits."[19] To know the name Christ requires knowing more names while acknowledging that no name captures an infinite God.

> While avoiding every kind of concurrence [συνενεχθῆναι] with any wrong notion in our views about God, we make use of a great variety of names [ὄνομα περιληπτικὸν] for God, adapting our terminology to various concepts. Since no one title has been discovered to embrace the divine nature by applying directly to the subject, itself, we therefore use many titles, each person in accordance with various interests achieving some particular idea about him, to name the Divinity, as we hunt amid the pluriform variety of terms applying to him for sparks to light up our understanding of the object of our quest.[20]

Language does not transmit perfect descriptions of God, or even the exact words of God as God might think them if God thought in words, which God does not. Instead, these names flicker just long enough to allow Christians to move onward in their quest toward virtue and knowledge. Representation, that is, allows for continued participation in Christ; names conform to and expand the Christian's capacity to share in a God who remains unknown. Christians join in a conversation started and sustained by God, and through continuous engagement in it, are transformed, little by little. They take on new names as they take on new life.

Because Christ is *both* an image and reality,[21] Gregory needs to posit a different understanding of mimesis, one that can account for a God who is infinite—that is, who is closer to Christians than they are to themselves and yet always beyond their grasp. To do so, Gregory defines perfection not as the assimilation to a model, but as growth in it. Images that spur growth in participation, therefore, need not be lies. For Gregory, God can be present in these names even if they are not the bodies of the God. God can work through accommodated language in particularly powerful ways, but language exists "to suit the habits of humans [κατὰ τὸ ἀρέσκον ταῖς τῶν ἀνθρώπων συνηθείαις],"[22] not to be an essence abstracted from a divine encounter. God provides finite conventions that mediate relationships between humans and between heaven and earth, but these mediations allow for participation in God while also spurring Christians toward that which is beyond them. Mimesis is not about pulling away from reality; it is how Christians engage reality.

Susanna Elm has even argued that these theological positions and their implications turn on an understanding of mimesis. Eunomius argues that the Father's unbegottenness is inimitable, but "salvation was possible because the Son was of lesser divinity than the father and therefore closer to man than the unbegotten essence, so that man could share essential characteristics of the Son through *mimesis*."[23] Elm posits that "the central difference" between Eunomius and Gregory of Nazianzus is that Eunomius emphasizes that "mimesis implies that one shares commonalities with but never fully becomes what one imitates, whereas [Gregory of Nazianzus's emphasis on] *oikeiōsis pros theon* and *theon pioein* or *theopoiein* denote a greater degree of merging."[24] Elm forwards this distinction with respect to the Theologian, and yet it is precisely this distinction between "becoming divine" and "mimesis" that Gregory of Nyssa challenges in his theory of mimesis, which merges the two conceptualizations of mimesis—ontological and aesthetic—that I laid out in the opening chapters. Gregory's redefinition of mimesis as both participation and representation challenges both Eunomius's claim that a mimetic relationship with God requires the Son to be a lesser divinity, and Eunomius's claim that representations cannot link heaven and earth. We can see in *On Perfection*, therefore, the ascetic and theological implications of Gregory's understanding of names worked out in *Against Eunomius*. If no name reveals the divine nature, but Christians are to imitate the divine nature, then how does imitation of the names of Christ lead to Christian perfection?

Patterns and Perfection

The reading of the names Paul gave to Christ theorized a set of patterns and illustrations (τὰ ὑποδείγματα): how to pattern a life; how patterning words relate to performing those patterns; and how to theorize the gap between archetypal illustrations and mimetic performance.[25] Gregory opens the work noting that he can make "an accurate description" of this perfect life, but he is not himself "in tune with [συμφθεγγομένου] his words."[26] This atonality, however, has its blessings. While he cannot live the perfect life himself, his words form an image "painted on the heart [ἐνζωγραφεῖται τῇ καρδίᾳ]" with which and to which his readers must strive (ἐφ᾽ ὃ δεῖ συντεῖναι), if they are to become an "image of the invisible God."[27] His words reach beyond what he can show in his life.

This is more than a humble opening. Gregory must describe the transition from imperfection toward perfection, and to do so he writes about writing. Our two conceptions of mimesis come together here in Gregory in a complicated way. What Gregory describes as the mimetic practice of writing does not remove him another step from perfection (à la Plato's poets); it allows him to achieve or participate in what he does not know and cannot do. It does not pull him away from reality; it allows him to engage more fully in it. Writing, like perfection, is both an archetype and a practice. For Gregory, it stretches the writer toward perfection.[28] But if perfection is always on the move, how does one write this? What kinds of ascetic, reading, and representational practices can place and sustain a person on the journey of perfection? How can one live a life of perfection, when perfection is marked by excess?

Here begins Gregory's discussion of the names. Perfection, he writes, is about "understanding" and "showing through our lives" what the name "Christian" signifies; that is, what the "partnership [κοινωνίαν]" that "Jesus Christ bestowed . . . in his revered name [χαρισαμένου . . . τοῦ προσκυνουμένου ὀνόματος]" means for one whose life is marked by Christ.[29] Christians take their name from Christ (not those other names, which could define someone—family, wealth, business, or position), but what it means to share in or represent Christ does not become immediately clear from that one name.

The doubleness of archetypal name and mimetic practice continues in the opening, as the name of Christ structures the practice of prayer. Both name and practice require supplements—other names that are both extra and necessary to pray. The name of Christ gives rise to and directs prayer, but each name Paul gives to Christ, Gregory continues, aids the Christian in his "prayers"; Christians "call out" (προσκαλέω) the name of Christ, and these names help to give shape to that voice. The name Christ—and, in turn, Christian—is too large to be understood on its own. Christians find out what their name means by gathering different names, praying with them, and allowing them to shape their lives. The resonances between Paul's names form a kind of overtone, which is the name of Christ. Paul's names allow Christians to "be with [συνεῖναι] the notion [ἔννοιαν] that we are taking up into our souls [ταῖς ψυχαῖς ἡμῶν ἀναλαμβάνομεν]." And taking the notion of Christ into the soul provides "zeal for this way of life [τῆς περὶ τὸν βίον σπουδῆς]" that governs and propels Christians to continue calling out to the name beyond all names.[30]

Before listing and exegeting the names, Gregory explains why he suggests turning to Paul's names, rather than, say, the Gospel's. Paul is the "safest guide" in this journey because

> he, most of all, observed who Christ is [τί ἐστιν ὁ Χριστὸς κατενόησε], and he indicated by what he did the kind of person named [ἐπονομ αζόμενον] for him, imitating him so brilliantly [οὕτως ἐναργῶς αὐτὸν μιμησάμενος] that he displayed [δεῖξαι] his own Master in himself, the form of his own soul being transformed through accurate mimesis [διὰ τῆς ἀκριβεστάτης μιμήσεως μεταβληθέντος] of his prototype, so that Paul no longer seemed to be living and speaking, but Christ himself seemed to be living in him [Gal 2:20].[31]

Gregory highlights Paul here not only because of the names he offers, but because of how he displayed them. Paul, "the imitator of our Lord,"[32] participated in that which he displayed. He indicated what was beyond indication. He joined in his prayer that was too deep for words (Rom 8:26), and the constant stretching of his own soul through his mimetic life made him an "accurate image" of Christ.[33] In following Paul, readers are asked to do the same.[34] Imitating Paul, like writing, moves Christians toward perfection, establishing archetypes that can structure practices that expand the soul's capacity to imitate and participate in Christ—and all this happens through a system of names. Christians take these names into the soul and in so doing stretch themselves into an image of an uncontainable God.

Minotaurs, Dragons, and Christians: Counterfeits and True Mimesis

A fragile relationship between "becoming" and "imitating" emerges in *On Perfection*. And Gregory knew it would fall apart by considering them complete opposites. Christians do not live up to their name by "becoming" Christ by nature, Gregory argued. They "become" Christians through their imitation of the names they share with Christ. Just because names do not reveal the divine nature does not mean they are not true. The truth they display requires a larger system of virtue than simple knowledge—what Gregory argues Eunomius's *agennetos* claims to offer—could provide. The great fear of the text is that Christians would fail to move from word to flesh, fail to allow the words of scripture to reconstitute lives.[35] Words become "true" only when they are "taken into the soul" and lived. The letter, that is, assumes it is possible for people to call themselves Christians, even if their lives bear little resemblance to the title; they can be "imitators" as opposed to "real" Christians.[36] Gregory can define Christianity as mimesis of the divine nature, but mimesis continues to carry the risk of hypocrisy. How can one maintain a distance between the archetype and the image without lapsing into lies or cutting oneself off from the archetype? Even if there is no discernable archetype to which mimesis is anchored, these words must be able to pattern a life. Imitating infinity is not imitating anything. Gregory's letter searched for (and perhaps performed) a way to avoid the fakeness that can be implicit in mimicry while holding to the constitutive work that proper imitation can perform.

Before he attempts his answer, however, Gregory gives two figures of improper mimesis, two ways Christians "do not conduct imitation agreeable to archetype of nature [οὐ πρὸς τὸ τῆς φύσεως ἀρχέτυπον τὴν μίμησιν ἄγουσιν]."[37] The first is that of the Minotaur: those who appear to be living the good life but are "bull-headed in the belief in idolatry." The second are the centaurs or dragons who say the correct words only as a "façade" for their "bestial body."[38] Mimesis here is not only about appearances. Perfection can be derailed by either improper thinking or improper acting. Gregory did not conclude from this that mimesis is futile. Instead, he sought a different kind of mimesis. Gregory's mimesis "expands the soul," allowing those seeking perfection to demonstrate and live what cannot be said. By "taking on the names of Christ," their lives—in mind and body—form an image of an invisible God.[39]

Some We Imitate, Others We Revere and Worship?

The joining of participatory and representational aspects of mimesis structures Gregory's work, but in *On Perfection* a distinction surfaces between mimesis and worship. Mimesis and worship form the central heuristic or pedagogical distinction of the treatise. "The characteristics of a real Christian [χαρακτῆρες δὲ τοῦ ὄντως Χριστιανοῦ] are all those things we think about when we think about Christ [πάντα ἐκεῖνά ἐστιν, ὅσα περὶ τὸν Χριστὸν ἐνοήσαμεν]. Those that we have room for, we imitate, and those that our nature does not have room for in imitation, we revere and worship."[40] Christians are the impress (χαρακτήρ) of Christ, and they are defined by both what they imitate and what they worship. As the treatise continues, it becomes clear that there are not some names of Christ that are to be imitated and others to be worshiped, as if there were two different "stamps." Just as Christ makes himself known while not being "sealed in" by any name, so too the Christian takes on all the names of Christ without allowing them to end the epektatic life. Mimesis here carries within it the excess that calls for reverence, and reverence is never wholly without modes of representation and participation. Practices of representation require adaption both of one's life and of *how* the words signify.[41] Words will fail or even slip into silence, but this mimetic failure marks true of worship.[42] Running out of room in oneself begins the larger practice of running after God.

Gregory's theorization of mimesis as representation and participation constantly plays with a double movement of adapting and becoming.[43] Those honored with the name "Christian," he writes, must "make visible [καθορᾶσθαι] all the interpretations of these names [πάντα τὰ ἑρμηνευτικὰ τῆς τοιαύτης φωνῆς ὀνόματα], such that they are not pseudonyms, but that our lives might bear witness to them."[44] Gregory continues, "It is necessary for those calling themselves after Christ, first of all, to become what the name implies [βούλεται], and then to adapt themselves to the title [ἑαυτοῖς ἐφαρμόσαι τὴν κλῆσιν]." Becoming what a name implies is only the beginning of readapting to a new participatory reality.

Gregory presented the work of perfection as a matter of both putting on and adapting to the names. By performing the names, the names begin to take on new implications and form new connections to the other names by which the Christian is constituted. Mimesis expands mimetic possibilities. Conforming (συμμορφόομαι) to the name Christian is a process of gathering the names of Christ, learning what they mean, and then readapting oneself to those names.[45] Wisdom, for example, "is necessarily interwoven [συμπλέκεται] with power in connection with the definition of Christ."[46] These words are "yoked together [συζυγίας]," Gregory writes, because it is only

> when all these [names], being placed together with the others, each name contributing a thought [διανοίας] by itself for a demonstration of what is signified [εἰς ἔνδειξιν τοῦ σημαινομένου συνεισφερούσης], that they make a certain emphasis in the signification of the name of Christ, which as much as we make room for in the soul to contemplate [ἔμφασίν τινα τῆς σημασίας τοῦ κατὰ Χριστὸν ὀνόματος ἡμῖν ἐμποιεῖ, ὅσον χωροῦμεν τῇ ψυχῇ κατανοῆσαι], manifests the unspeakable greatness for us [τῆς ἀφράστου μεγαλειότητος ἡμῖν ἐνδεικνύμενα].[47]

As the different names come together in and expand a life, they stylize what cannot be represented but only revered. Participatory becoming contains within it a representation that calls forth further adaption. For while the order is never settled—to become first, then adapt or illustrate, then perform?[48]—this restlessness between participation and representation is built into the very infinite, virtuous life that Gregory asks his readers to take on, if they are to become "synonymous with Christ [ὁ τῷ Χριστῷ συνονομαζόμενος]."[49]

Gregory frames the treatise by noting that some names of Christ we imitate and others we worship. The text circles through the importance of mimesis as both bodily and spiritual and argues that to gain in virtue is to drive out evil. Gregory then returns to the promised exegetical project:

> Let us take up the original argument, namely that the one road to the pure and divine life for lovers of virtue [τοῖς φιλαρέτοις] is knowing what the name of Christ signifies [σημαίνει], in conformity with which we must shape our life [τὸν ἡμέτερον συμμορφωθῆναι βίον], attuning it to virtue through reflection on the remaining names [διὰ τῆς τῶν λοιπῶν ὀνομάτων ἐμφάσεως εἰς ἀρετὴν ῥυθμιζόμενον]. So in the introduction of the argument, we gathered the interpretation

[ἑρμηνευτικὰ] of the signs [σημασίας] of Christ, both the words and the names from the holy voice of Paul. Now, placing them before us in the appointed zeal, we shall make them the most unfailing guide for the life of virtue—imitating [μιμούμενοι] some, as we said before, and revering and worshiping others.[50]

The distinction here seems as obvious to modern readers as it did to ancient ones: some concepts we imitate, others we worship. We might expect it to break down along the lines of what John Behr calls "partitive exegesis," where some names define the human Christ and others the divine, or according to the tensions we saw in Chapter 3.[51] But for Gregory, sharing in Christ's name involves living out *all* the names of Christ, human *and* divine. Hans Boersma rightly notes that Gregory "is not simply advising Christians to follow the example of Jesus's humanity. For Nyssen, imitation of Christ is imitation of his divine virtues and is thus also imitation of and a participation in the life of God."[52] Gregory writes in his *Homilies on the Song of Songs* that "when [the soul] stretches herself out [ἑαυτὴν ἀνατείνη] from things below toward the knowledge of things on high, once she has grasped the marvels produced by God's working, she cannot for a while [τέως] progress further by her busy search for knowledge, but is filled with wonder and worships the One who is known to exist only through things that his activity brings about."[53] But after "a while" she catches her breath and continues "progressing toward the better." That is, "wonder" transforms and teaches her that "the ineffable Blessedness shall be apprehended in another fashion," which leads her to imitate her inimitable beloved anew.[54]

The repetition of the heuristic distinction—"imitating [μιμούμενοι] some . . . and revering and worshiping others"—emphasizes the connection between hermeneutics and way of life. That is, one must interpret well to live well, and vice versa. How Christians understand the names ought to determine the habits of their faith, and how they live creates their interpretive possibilities. Gregory therefore turns to Paul, insisting that the way to live as a Christian—the way to conform one's life to an infinite Christ[55]—is to look to a series of meditations taken from a worthy follower of Christ, from whose own mimetic activity readers can glimpse Christ.[56] The names Paul gives to Christ guide toward the perfect life. But this, for Gregory, does not make them penultimate, for they also constitute that perfect life. Mimesis is the goal and the way one comes to know the goal. Seeking the perfect life and living it are less clearly distinguished when perfection is defined as a pursuit, not a destination.

The Names We Take into the Soul

Assembling and imitating the names patterns a life, even if the names never fully synthesize into Christ himself. As they revere Paul's names for Christ, Christians gradually transform themselves into those names. For example, even though Christ is "the power of God and the wisdom of God" (1 Cor 1:24)—important categories in Gregory's Trinitarian debates[57]—the reverence of these names "is not useless or without benefit."[58] Christians also absorb those names toward which they reach in worship: "For, when someone prays, he draws to himself through prayer [πρὸς ἑαυτὸν διὰ τῆς εὐχῆς ἐπισπᾶται] what he is invoking and looking toward with the eye of his soul. Thus the person looking toward power (Christ is power) 'is strengthened with the power in [πρός] the inner human [Eph 3:16],' as the apostle says, and the person looking toward wisdom which the Lord knows of old becomes wise [σοφὸς γίνεται]."[59] Reverence and imitation are not quite conflated here, but they affect each other. A kind of feedback loop occurs, as revered names lead to prayer, and in prayer the soul draws into itself what it sees and is strengthened by it.

This, then, is the pattern of Gregory's argument: scripture[60] provides a series of names (ὄνομα) that the one striving for perfection "take[s] into the soul [χωροῦμεν τῇ ψυχῇ]."[61] Much hangs, therefore, on what it means to take a name—a name that signifies (σημαίνω), for example, an "inaccessible [ἀπρόσιτον]" and "infinite [ἀπερίγραπτον]" God[62]—into the soul. Gregory deploys a different verb for both iterations of this phrase. When "the concept [Christ] we take into the soul" first appears, the verb is ἀναλαμβάνω;[63] the second, "take [all the names Paul gives to Christ] into our souls," is a translation of χωρέω.[64] Though the two words can easily be taken to mean the same thing, the second iteration of this phrase is more important, as it situates the ascetic project Gregory prescribes. Χωρέω is the word Origen turns to when he discusses "becoming another John" in *Com. John* 1.23, which is a process of internalizing the words of John so deeply that one becomes another John, and from there through internalizing the words of Christ becomes another Christ.[65] Χώρα, as we saw in *Timaeus*, is a space, room, receptacle;[66] that "necessary" "third space" or placeless place in which the demiurge creates the world. The verb can mean both "to make room or give way" and "to go forward or make progress."⁶⁷ Gregory may even be punning on the word here, as the link between making room and making progress is important to Gregory's central image of the expanding, epektatic soul on the infinite journey toward God—the image with which the treatise will end. We could retranslate the passage to say that the names progress or advance the contemplation in the soul; or even that the names make possible contemplation in the soul (χωροῦμεν τῇ ψυχῇ κατανοῆσαι). The issue is less one of translation than of noting the connection between the stretching (συντείνω) that Gregory prescribes and the expansion (χωρέω) of the soul that happens through the mimesis and worship of the names of Christ.⁶⁸ Like the *khōra*, the soul is made and changed by that which is stamped on it, while remaining irreducible to any of those imprints. To be the image of God is to be made up of names that will dilate the soul. And the creation of this kind of epektatic space is performed through the twofold work of mimesis. Gregory calls those seeking perfection to *represent* Christ while participating in Christ, to make their lives a kind of art in which they become what they represent, and to *participate* in that which they worship. Good representations, Gregory argues, carry within them an excess that continues to draw the Christian toward an infinite perfection. They bring attention to the fact that they are fragments to be arranged and rearranged with an eye toward an image that is always out of reach. The more accurate the representation, the more clear it is that there is always more to represent; the more full the participation, the more acute the awareness that there is always more in which to participate.

Gregory, having set forth the goal of taking these names into the soul, pauses once more before performing his reading of the Christological names to provide the reader another negative example of it. He warns of the danger of separating ontology from representation, where the image-making activity does not also expand and transform the soul:

> If we distinguish a real human from an image [εἰκόνος] of him called by the same name in a picture by noting characteristic differences— for we call the human the living, logical, thinking thing [ζῷον λογικὸν διανοητικὸν] and the image a lifeless material which then takes on his form through mimesis [ὕλην ἄψυχον διὰ μιμήσεως ὑπελθοῦσαν τὸ εἶδος]—so too shall we adjudicate [ἐπιγνωσόμεθα] between the real Christian and the pretender [Χριστιανὸν τόν τε

ὄντως ὄντα καὶ τὸν δοκοῦντα] through what is displayed in their own characteristics [διὰ τῶν ἐπιφαινομένων τοῖς χαρακτῆρσιν ἰδιωμάτων].[69]

The still image is no random choice either. While it may seem odd that Gregory asks Christians to be an image of God and then takes as his example of someone unvirtuous the difference between an image of a human and a real human, Gregory here points to exactly the wrong kind of image: a static image that is not changed by what it takes on. Gregory worries that a Christian might become a "lifeless [ἄψυχον]" image, a coat of paint without a change in nature. The one seeking perfection participates in what she imitates. To see the difference between the human and the image, one cannot dig down to the true nature. Instead, one must discern if and how the image falls short of what is true through "what is displayed." If representation does not lead to deeper participation it is insufficient, and if participation does not "display" that in which it lives and moves and has its being it has failed its mimetic task.

Having commented, then, on what he wants with mimesis, Gregory turns to the marks of the true Christian. How does one tell the difference between the "true Christian" and the person only who "seems" like one? "Through what is displayed in their own characteristics [διὰ τῶν ἐπιφαινομένων τοῖς χαρακτῆρσιν ἰδιωμάτων]," Gregory says.

> The characteristics [χαρακτῆρες] of a real Christian are all those things we think about when we think about Christ. There are those for which we make room and those we imitate [ὅσα μὲν χωροῦμεν, μιμούμεθα]. And as much as our nature does not make room for imitation, we revere and worship. Therefore, it is necessary for the Christian life to illumine [ἐπιλάμπειν] every interpretive name signifying Christ [πάντα τὰ ἑρμηνευτικὰ τῆς τοῦ Χριστοῦ σημασίας ὀνόματα]—some through mimesis, others through worship [τὰ μὲν διὰ μιμήσεως, τὰ δὲ διὰ προσκυνήσεως], if the human of God [ὁ τοῦ θεοῦ ἄνθρωπος] is to be, as the apostle says, cut off from sin, completely without evil.[70]

Avoiding sin requires keeping representation and worship tethered, keeping the names that govern a life connected to an excess that allows perfection to be something the Christian constantly seeks even while performing it. Reverence and imitation define the Christian life, and *On Perfection* seeks

to dramatize and interpret the movement of these related but separate aspects. Both mimesis and worship elucidate and interpret the names of
Christ.[71] Worshipped names carry a sense of awe, continue to tug on the
Christian soul, and spark a desire for imitation. Worship provides a plastic
limit within which mimesis can be performed, and mimesis pushes at the
edges of this existence. The soul can contract around those names, and in
that contraction, the soul expands. The text provides little if any exposition of what worshiping with these names will look like aside from the
calling out of the names of Christ. What seems to be important, however,
is that the propelling awe of the names intensifies the need to understand
how the words attributed to Christ can be imitated by humans. His treatment of the name "rock" is typical: "When Christ is called 'a rock' [1 Cor
10:4], this word assists us in the firmness and permanence of our virtuous
life, that is, in the steadfastness of our endurance of suffering, and in our
soul's opposition and inaccessibility to the assaults of sin. Through these
and such things, we will also become a rock, imitating, as far as is possible in
our changing nature, the unchanging and permanent nature of the master
[μιμούμενοι, καθὼς ἐστι δυνατόν, ἐν τῇ τρεπτῇ φύσει τὸ ἄτρεπτον τοῦ
δεσπότου καὶ ἀμετάθετον]."[72] Christians revering Christ, the rock, are in
position first to be assisted by the name, and then to become it. The treatise
works to keep this motion going: worshiping Christ and then translating his
names into life, such that Christians become what they love.

By imitating these names that signify Christ, Christians take "the names
into the soul." Even the name "inaccessible" (ἀπρόσιτος) (1 Tim 6:16), which
seems beyond human attainment, is useful for Christians to revere and to
imitate, as it teaches Christians to clear their lives of all "falsehood." The inaccessible light of Christ makes Christians inaccessible to falsehood and darkness.[73] "By doing all things in the light, we become light itself, so that it 'shines'
before others."[74] In this act of making room (χωρέω), the Christian moves
from "soulless matter" to "true Christian," even as that successful mimesis is
constituted by a kind of failure, as every attempt at imitating the unchanging
God requires constant adaption for a finite creature. Successful imitation recognizes its own limits, which leads back to, or perhaps simply is, worship.

Limits, Cornerstones, and the Meeting Place of Body and Soul

To get at this expanded form of mimesis, it is important to see that perfection,
for Gregory, happens in faith, which Gregory describes as the "cornerstone,"

joining body and soul.[75] So far, I have been following Gregory's language in suggesting that the practice suited for the life of perfection in virtue involves taking the names given to Christ into the soul. But there is a parallel argument that runs through the text that requires not only internalizing the names but also "manifesting" and "elucidating" these names through one's life. And this requires bodily performance and representation. In this text, the ascent of the mind is not "useful" if it is separated from the body.[76] The difficulty, Gregory reminds his readers, involves taking the mind and body together; taking the names into the soul allows for transcendence, but not "illogically overstepping nature" by "fashioning something other than human, fabricating the impossible." Whatever Christian perfection looks like, for Gregory, "a person cannot accurately be called a Christian if he does not give assent to the faith with his mind, even if he conforms to it in other respects, or if his mind gives assent, but his body is not suited to his way of life, exhibiting the anger of dragons and the bestiality of serpents, or adding to his human character an equine madness for women. In such cases, a human becomes double-natured, a centaur made up of reason and passion."[77] Humans will imitate something, and a good check on the value of mimesis, Gregory argues, is if it can allow for human transcendence without denying either the body or the soul.

Gregory understands human plasticity as paramount to his anthropology.[78] Change is, for Gregory, the defining feature of human nature. Boundaries change, and Christians reaching perfection increase their capacity for participation, but this does not mean that Gregory has done away with limits altogether. As we will see further in Chapter 5, space and time will *change*, but they do not *disappear*. Limits allow for growth, and growth is the goal of the mimetic life. Gregory's most poignant comments around the role of limits in mimesis come in a string of names: "rock," "hope," and "image." This string begins in a passage I described above as typical of Gregory's exegetical method in the treatise. Gregory writes that to know Christ as "rock" is to know that Christ "assists us in the firmness and permanence of our virtuous life."[79] By shutting off "the assaults of sin," those seeking perfection "imitate, as much as possible, in our changing nature, the unchanging and permanent nature of the master [μιμούμενοι, καθώς ἐστι δυνατόν, ἐν τῇ τρεπτῇ φύσει τὸ ἄτρεπτον τοῦ δεσπότου καὶ ἀμετάθετον]."[80] What we have here is a discussion of limits. Christians are to reinforce their bodies and minds so that the assaults of sin do not penetrate. Performing mimesis of Christ's unchangingness, for Gregory, requires limits too. By closing off one boundary (that of sin), the Christian strives after the boundless one. "Overstepping" nature is about becoming "double natured," about what he calls centaur living, a disconnect between the Christian's "faith with his mind" and his "body [being] suited to his way of life."[81]

Gregory places the name "rock" next to the name "hope," which, he writes, "we know to be the same as the cornerstone toward which all things tend, if they are zealously pursued in virtue."[82] The solid point holding all things together, for Gregory, is also something to come. This cornerstone, which is Christ, holds the body and soul together and also pulls Christians onward.

> The beginning [ἡ ἀρχή] of this high "tower" [Luke 14:28] of life is our faith in Him, upon whom we build, putting down the principles of our life [τὰς ἀρχὰς τοῦ βίου] as a kind of foundation, and, through our daily achievements, we erect [νομοθετούντων] pure thoughts and actions upon it. Thus the cornerstone of all becomes our cornerstone [ἡ τοῦ παντὸς κεφαλὴ καὶ ἡμετέρα γίνεται κεφαλή], fitting Himself diagonally between the two walls of our life which are built out of our body and soul with elegance and correctness [δι᾽ εὐσχημοσύνης καὶ καθαρότητος ἐποικοδομουμένοις]. But if one part of the building is deficient, if the appearance of elegance [τὸ φαινόμενον εὐσχημοσύνης] is not built together with [συνοικοδομουμένης] the correctness of the soul, or if the soul's virtue does not join to the outward appearance [τῆς ψυχικῆς ἀρετῆς τῷ φαινομένῳ μὴ συμβαινούσης], then Christ, in fitting Himself to a single portion of a double structure, becomes the cornerstone of a half-completed life. For it is not possible for a cornerstone to exist if two walls do not join [συμβολῆς]. The beauty of the chief cornerstone sets off our building when our dualistic existence, straight and true, is harmoniously set up according to the right rule of life by the extended line of the virtues [τῇ τῶν ἀρετῶν σπάρτῳ ἀποταθῇ], having nothing in itself that is bent or crooked.[83]

A familiar movement appears here: the life of faith lays a foundation, and as Christians learn to live upon "principles of life," a new set of legislation is laid down (νομοθετέω[84]). Just as the movement of worship and mimesis establishes and expands the life of perfection, here faith provides both the foundational principles and the scaffolding of a towering life. The life of perfection is the life of daily building the space in which one lives, a space that is held together

by Christ. And again, we can see the two sides of mimesis: Christians represent Christ as they perform what the name means, and in that performance
they participate in the Christ who sustains them and gives them life.

This tower concerns both the life of the soul and the ability to show this
life in the body. As we will see in the next chapter, Christ's transcendence
does not negate spaces; it brings them out. But here we must emphasize that
splits between bodily actions and thoughts must be bound together in
Christ.[85] Extending (ἀποτείνω) the life of virtue happens as Christians participate in Christ, and the soul's extension manifests bodily. The correctness
of the soul and the elegance of the body are joined in faith by Christ to the
point where it is at least difficult to distinguish one from the other.

Imitating the Image of the Invisible

This string of names by which body and soul join in faith culminates in the
treatise's reading of the name "image of the invisible God." Only once it is
clear to readers that the body and the soul must work together to participate
in and represent Christ does it discuss this invisible image. The bodily practices of prayer that these names aid lead beyond all names, but that transcending makes it all the more important to have and become images of the
invisible. The passage is worth quoting in full:

> Paul names Christ the image of the invisible God [Col 1:15], namely
> the God over all and the great God (and with these words he pro-
> claims the greatness of the true master, saying "our great God and
> Savior Jesus Christ" [Titus 2:13] and the one from whom Christ is
> according to the flesh, who is over all things, God blessed [εὐλογητὸς]
> forever [Rom 9:5]). Saying these things, then, he teaches us what is
> the One existing forever. (It is that thing which only he knows [ὁ ὢν
> ἐπίσταται μόνος], which always in equal measure exceeds [ὑπερέκεινα]
> human comprehension, even if the one who always "minds the things
> which are above" [Col 3:2] approaches it in his progress [διὰ προκοπῆς
> προσεγγίζῃ]). He, who is above every knowledge and apprehension
> [ὁ ὑπερέκεινα πάσης γνώσεώς τε καὶ καταλήψεως], who is ineffable,
> unspeakable, and unexplainable, to make you anew as the "image of
> God," for the love of humanity [φιλανθρωπίας], he too became an
> "image of the invisible God," so that, in the very form that he took
> on, he would take shape in you [τῇ ἰδίᾳ μορφῇ, ἣν ἀνέλαβεν, ἐν σοὶ

μορφωθῆναι ἐν σοὶ μορφωθῆναι], so that, from the impress [πρὸς τὸν χαρακτῆρα[86]] of the archetypal beauty, you too again might be conformed [συσχηματισθῆναι, 1 Peter 1:14; Rom 12:1[87]] to him in order to become that which you were from the beginning. Therefore, if we ourselves must become also images of the invisible God [εἰκὼν θεοῦ τοῦ ἀοράτου], it is proper that the form of our life [τῆς ζωῆς ἡμῶν τὸ εἶδος] be stamped by the pattern of life [τοῦ βίου ὑπόδειγμα τυποῦσθαι] that is proposed to us [Jn 13:15]. And what is this pattern? That while living in the flesh, we not live according to the flesh. For the prototypical image of the invisible God, who came among us through the virgin, was tried in all things like human nature [καθ' ὁμοιότητα τῆς ἀνθρωπίνης φύσεως], but alone did not experience sin.[88]

In the string of names through which Gregory has walked his reader, the move to Christ as the image of God takes on a particular imperative. Christ at once makes visible what is invisible, makes known what is indescribable, and then calls for humans to allow that image to mark them like a stamp that expands and gives shape to metal as it is pressed on it. Christ is the *image* of the invisible, and Gregory emphasizes becoming an image of the *invisible*. Christians imitate an excess, imitate what is beyond imitation. In his reading of this name, Gregory also insists that Christ is "the God over all," the "ineffable," "unspeakable," and the "indescribable." That is, Gregory is quick to trouble what one can expect out of a "model" or "pattern" (ὑποδείγματα) because each image is tethered to an invisibility. The model (Christ) conforms himself to the Christian's position, which requires the Christian to be remodeled (συσχηματισθῆναι), and in that remodeling something beyond (ὑπερέκεινα) the previous model appears and calls for a different imitation.

Audience and Accommodation

The difference between Christ becoming the image of the invisible and the image Gregory exhorts his readers to become consists in this: Christ does not perform mimesis, at least not the way humans do. Christ accommodates and makes himself known, but as the prototype, Christ need not participate in or represent something beyond himself; rather Christ presents himself and in that presentation makes human representation possible. Christ's prototypical accommodation, therefore, becomes part of what it means to be an image. Proper mimesis requires not only participating in the God who becomes an image, but also becoming an image that will lead others to God. Just as Christ adapts to his audience without becoming less divine, so in Christ, the constant adaption of one's life does not make mimesis derivative or less worthy of pursuit, but a more accurate image of the divine.[89]

The ability to become a picture and to manifest what God looks like is coupled, then, with a question: For whom? Mimesis is not only imitation *of* something but also imitation *for* someone.[90] The work of representation, necessary for Christian perfection, involves others: representing Christ means representing Christ for others. By setting forth illustrations and creating patterns of holiness, one can glimpse the life given in the words. These names of Christ are given "for us."[91] That is, mimesis is as much about an audience (imitation for) as it is about an object (imitation of).[92]

Before beginning to think about the importance of accommodation in *On Perfection*, however, a summary of the argument so far may be helpful. I argue for the centrality of mimesis in Gregory's account of perfection. Perfection is an endless process of becoming what the name "Christian" implies, and this requires illuminating the various names of Christ in one's life by increasing one's capacity to contemplate, perform, and represent these names. Mimesis functions as both the way and the goal of a life of Christian perfection. Moreover, I have argued that the heuristic distinction in *On Perfection* between mimesis and worship is a distinction that is meant to be overcome. That is, one does not represent some names and worship others; worship and imitation work together, as Christ makes himself known as a target of imitation while at the same time transcending any name. Christ, who is virtue, is also the one worthy of reverence. Or to say that differently, when interpreted well, the names of Christ carry an excess such that the representation of them pushes subjects toward the unrepresentable.[93]

Keeping in mind that Gregory is answering a monk's question—how might anyone achieve perfection through a life of virtue?—Gregory's answer reminds his readers that perfection has to do not only with becoming like Christ in the virtues but also with showing this publicly. It demands both knowing who Christ is "for us" and how to demonstrate this transcendent truth. Christ's conformity to humanity allows humans to perform this same virtuous life, providing an image for others to see. To model one's life after Christ's is to make oneself a model for others—a recognizable image that leads beyond itself toward the infinite. Mimetic activity, then, is not a removal from reality but a way to bind one's life to the activity of God. Christ's conformity to the world, that is, is not something with which the Christian can ever be finished; instead it allows for new dimensions to be seen as subjects continue to be "corrected" and "reformed" (both of which are captured in the Greek συσχηματίζω) by their attachment to the image. The plasticity of the self requires a kind of feedback, where the mimetic life "illumines every interpretive name of Christ," and at the same time the one seeking perfection knows these names only by their "appearance."[94]

*   *   *

Paul is transformed by the mirroring he performs for his audience. Gregory, having noted that Christ is the image of God, and that in Christ humans can be as well, explains how humans go about this with the metaphor of a painter and an image. Recall, he has used the image before to contrast the "lifeless" image with the "real" thing. Having guided his reader to a different understanding of mimesis, he returns to it to make a different point. To represent Christ requires the proper media for representation—namely, the virtues, which are a series of colors with which a Christian becomes "the painter of his own life."[95] The two sides of mimesis come together here. Gregory writes,

> Just as when we are learning the art of painting, the teacher puts before us on a panel a beautifully executed model, and it is necessary for each student to imitate in his own panel the painting of that model in every way [ἔδει πάντως τὸ ἐκείνης κάλλος ἐπὶ τῆς ἰδίας ἕκαστον ζωγραφίας μιμήσασθαι], so that the panels of all will be made beautiful [καλλωπισθῆναι] in accordance with the example of the beauty set before them; in the same way, since every person is the painter of his own life, and choice is the craftsman of the work [τεχνίτης δὲ τῆς δημιουργίας ταύτης ἐστὶν ἡ προαίρεσις], and the virtues are the paints for executing the image, there is no small danger that the imitation [μίμησιν] may remodel [μεταχαράξαι] the prototype into a hateful and ugly person [ἄμορφον πρόσωπον] instead of reproducing the master form [δεσποτικοῦ εἴδους], if we sketch the character of evil with muddy colors. But, since it is possible, one must prepare the pure colors of the virtues, mixing them with each other according to some rule of art [κατά τινα τεχνικὴν] for the imitation of beauty [πρὸς τὴν τοῦ κάλλους μίμησιν], so that we become

an image of the image, having achieved the beauty of the prototype
through activity which is also a kind of imitation [δι' ἐνεργοῦς ὡς
οἷόν τε μιμήσεως], as did Paul, who became an "imitator of Christ,"
through his life of virtue [μιμητὴς τοῦ Χριστοῦ διὰ τοῦ κατ' ἀρετὴν
βίου γινόμενος].[96]

Christians should make their lives a work of art. By looking at the proper
model, and by "combining the pure colors of the virtues," they represent the
model and "become an image of the image." And this "image of the image,"
while echoing *Republic* 10's critique of mimesis as something three times
removed,[97] now carries a different sense: as Christ, who is the image, is equal
to the Father, so the one seeking perfection, by participating in and representing Christ, can also become an image of God that is not deficient.[98]
These names fashion a governing aesthetic by which one can make his life
beautiful (καλλωπίζω) as imitation of the beautiful one, Christ.

Becoming this image, however, is also about becoming the image for
others. An audience is constitutive, not accidental to the cultivation of the
life of perfection. Gregory emphasizes the pedagogy implicit in this passage
by turning to one of the few quotes he deploys from the gospels in this treatise about Christ. "Learn from me [Μάθετε . . . ἀπ' ἐμοῦ], for I am meek and
humble of heart."[99] The call is not only to "endure" meekness and humility,
but also to show it. "Being depicted [ζωγραφούμενος]" is part of the mimetic task.[100]

Layering Perfection

As Gregory's treatise comes to a close, he begins to layer images of perfection. Even in a text that has layered the names of Christ to fashion an image
of perfection, these diverse ideas and exhortations coming all in the final
pages form a startling ending to what Gregory tells his reader should be a
conclusion that is "easy" to understand.[101] To give a taste: "sequence," "examination," water from a stream to a jar, "purity," "struggle," "wings of
flight," and "never arriving too quickly" all appear in the final four pages.
This dense array of imagery to describe life in God is typical of Gregory's
linking of an ever-accelerated accumulation of ideas, exhortations, and ascetic practice. Growing in perfection requires the ability to take on and
manifest all the names of Christ.

Humanity's plasticity makes possible perpetual progress in the infinite life of God. Gregory concludes: "Let no one be grieved if he sees in his nature a penchant for change. Changing in everything for the better, let him exchange 'glory for glory' [2 Cor 3:18], becoming greater through daily increase, ever perfecting himself, and never arriving too quickly at the limit of perfection."[102] But before getting there, Gregory needs to fill out what this movement from glory to glory might look like.

Gregory begins his conclusion of the letter by asking: Why was it necessary to gather the names of Christ and form a particular appearance or emphasis (ἔμφασις) in a sequence (ἀκολουθία) that interprets (δειρμηνεύω) them so as to lead to the virtuous life?[103] Part of the answer to this question has to do with "memory," with keeping the names of Christ "in mind," which, as Peter Brown puts it, "was not to store away a fact: It was to assert a bond, it was to be loyal and to pay attention to somebody."[104] This bond directs perfection in what Gregory calls the three parts of Christian life: "action, word, thought." He continues, "For thought is the beginning of every word; second, after the thinking, is the word which reveals through the voice the thought coined in the soul; and action has the third rank after mind and thought, bringing what is thought to action."[105] At first, this appears to be a simple chain of causation. But as the treatise unfolds, the reader becomes aware that any of these three can be derailed by any other. One can be right in action and wrong in thought or vice versa.[106] Protecting the mind is no guarantee of perfect actions. But keeping the names of Christ in mind gives Christians something to strive with and toward. The sentence does not simply describe, but exhorts readers to reform so that thoughts, words, and actions align. Christ's accommodated action, word, and thought are to be mirrored, then, in human action, word, and thought. Gregory adds, "So, when the sequence of life [ἡ ἀκολουθία τοῦ βίου] brings us to any one of these [action, word, or thought], it is good to examine accurately [ἀκριβείας ἐπισκοπεῖσθαι] these divine ideas of every word, deed, and thought by which Christ is known and named [νοεῖται καὶ ὀνομάζεται], lest our deed or word or thought be carried outside [ἔξω] the power of those high terms."[107] Actions, words, and thoughts provide limits that orient Christian practice, focusing the self through Paul's writing, but they do not come "easily" before one has taken these names into the soul. They must be cultivated and examined. Gregory does note that making the distinction between what is and is not "at odds with Christ" is "very easy."[108] Yet this statement, coming at the end of a treatise that aims at the transformation of the self through a series of imitations and worship, teaches the reader that it is only the person who has learned to walk properly with Christ for whom this is easy. (Gregory, remember, can write this pattern, but cannot yet himself live up to it.)[109]

To stop with words, for Gregory, is to leave incomplete the power of Christ in one's life, as thoughts "become deeds through power," that is, through Christ, who is the power of God. By taking up these names of Christ, one strives to bring "agreement between the hidden and visible human," one that is brought about by "engaging in a reckoning with our opponent," by struggling (ἀγωνίζομαι) to achieve this perfection.[110] Perfection is here both a hermeneutic and an ascetic struggle, one that requires examination in mind and body. It delivers Christians into an endless growth that shows forth the power that animates them.

Gregory continues to describe the perfect participatory relationship with a telling image: that of a jar being filled with water from a stream. The image is not of a jar (body) with water (soul) but of the way God enters humanity. The water moves from the stream to the jar, but the nature of the water does not change. Read on its own, again, this is straightforward enough. But as this analogy is layered on the good news of the malleability of human nature, the reader notices something new: the jar containing the water is changed by the water in it—stretched, expanded, and taking the form of that which fills it. "For the purity in Christ and the purity seen in the one who has a share in him are the same, the one being the stream and the other drawn from it, bringing intellectual beauty to his life, so that there is agreement between the hidden and the visible human, since the decorum of our life coincides with our thoughts which are put into motion in accordance with Christ."[111] Fashioning Christian perfection requires both this sharing (κοινωνέω) and expanding (χωρέω).

Gregory then ends the treatise with two definitions of perfection that must be read together. The first asks Christians to participate in the names of Christ: "This, therefore, in my judgment, is perfection in the Christian life: the participation [κοινωνίαν] of one's soul and speech and way of life[112] in all the names by which Christ is signified [διασημαίνεται], so that the perfect holiness, according to Paul's good word [εὐλογίαν], is taken upon [ἀναδέξασθαι] oneself, in 'the whole body and soul and spirit' [1 Thes 5:23], continuously safeguarded against being mixed with evil."[113] Perfection requires participating in the names of Christ, which Paul, the "imitator of Christ" himself, provides. In this way, the "soul, speech, and way of life" become available to others seeking perfection.[114]

The second definition of perfection concludes the treatise. Here Gregory answers what seems to be the lurking question behind the mimetic exhortation: How does a changeable human imitate an unchanging God? Is this not the height of self-delusion or superciliousness?

> I do not think that it is a fearful thing (I mean that our nature is changeable [τρεπτὴν]). The word [λόγος[115]] shows that it would be a disadvantage for us not to be able to make a change for the better, as a kind of wing of flight to greater things. Therefore, let no one be grieved if he sees in his nature an inclination for change [τὸ πρὸς τὴν μεταβολὴν ἐπιτήδειον]. Changing [μεταμορφούμενος] in everything for the better, let him exchange "glory for glory," becoming greater through daily increase [καθ' ἡμέραν αὐξήσεως], ever perfecting himself, and never arriving too quickly at the limit of perfection. For this is truly perfection: never to stop growing toward what is better and never placing any limit on perfection.[116]

This is the payoff of a life of mimesis and worship. Christ, manifesting himself to humanity by taking on limits without allowing those limits to put an end to his infinite nature, allows endlessly changeable Christians to grow endlessly as they participate in his nature. Those seeking perfection need not rush past all representations to achieve an ontological union. (The very desire to "arrive too quickly" is, in fact, a mark of imperfection, the temptation being, as Plato worried, to imitate the imitation without participating in it.[117]) Instead, the perfect constantly reach toward and grow into these names of Christ. As Christians take the names of Christ into the soul, the names become containers for what is uncontainable, and what fills them expands and changes them into a new shape, a new name, a name that will facilitate more prayers that will continue to expand and advance the soul.

Epektatic Practice, Epektatic Life

Christians' exposure to and participation in the names of Christ make possible perfection in virtue. These names must be understood well if Christians are to orient their lives toward their proper ends. But understanding them does not imply mastery over them, as much as it puts the names to good use in spurring desire. The names are not divine but are accommodated for humans who constellate them into an ineffable image of Christ, an image that continually shifts as it entices Christians into an ever-greater perfection. As Christians grow, that is, so too does their understanding of what the names signify.

Gregory poses a heuristic distinction between imitation and worship that governs how Christians are to engage with these names, and then he complicates the distinction. It is not that some names are to be imitated and others worshiped, but that Christian imitation, for Gregory, must include within it a sense of awe and something that transcends any simple ability to imitate, even as worshipful participation in these Christological names must inspire Christians to make their life—body and soul—a work of art in imitation of them. For Gregory, Christian perfection requires taking the names into the soul, and therefore allowing those words to reconstitute the Christian. Like a jar that at once contains water from a stream, and is expanded by what fills it, taking names into the soul both gives shape to and expands the Christian. If this is the case, moreover, we may even have in this prescription a practice that places those seeking perfection ahead of themselves, an epektatic practice in hopes of an epektatic life. Taking these names into the soul expands and reshapes Christians as they imitate ever more accurately an infinite God. To appreciate more fully what Gregory is after in his image of a container of the uncontainable, we turn to how Gregory discusses space and place in the mimetic life.

CHAPTER 5

Mimetic Spaces

New Pilgrimages

Gregory of Nyssa was ambivalent about pilgrimage.[1] In *Letter* 3, he recalled his visit to Jerusalem in glowing terms: "When I saw and felt the sacred places [εἶδον μὲν καὶ αἰσθητῶς τοὺς ἁγίους τόπους], I became filled with such a great joy that words cannot describe it."[2] There he met "souls in whom such signs of the Lord's grace are so spiritually discernible [πνευματικῶς θεωρεῖται] that I am convinced that Bethlehem and Golgotha and Olivet and the *Anastasis* are truly in the heart of those who cling to God [ἐν τῇ καρδίᾳ ἐστὶ τοῦ τὸν θεὸν ἔχοντος]."[3] Places filled hearts. They marked a holy life. They attracted and could define those seeking Christian perfection, such that they became a place of God. Places, as we saw with names in Chapter 4, entered, expanded, and defined the soul. And places, like names, were represented by those who were properly shaped by them. Gregory, after journeying, could see Golgotha in those who had been crucified with Christ. These biblical places carried with them an intensity of affect and a sense of awe that inspired imitation. Those seeking perfection represented and participated in those places, as they participated in and represented God.[4]

Places have boundaries. So what kinds of places could imitate an unbounded God? The letter moves from a reflection on place to a discussion of how Christ takes on the boundaries of human life. Humanity finds its type in Mary, who, finite and bounded, becomes "the tabernacle" of the "infinite and immeasurable."[5] Human boundaries are "overshadowed [ἐπεσκίασε]"; they take on a luminous darkness, as Christ makes sensible (αἰσθητός) the signs (σημεῖα) of the holy places in the devoted ones.[6] The Holy Spirit, he writes, "came to be both in our soul, since it was fitting that it should come to be in the soul, and came also to be mingled with the body, so that our salvation might be wholly perfect in all respects."[7] The Spirit changes what is sensible, as she makes the body and soul the site of God's dwelling. Learning to take places into the soul and allowing the Spirit to mingle with the body such that it represents the place of Christ is what salvation looks like. It is how the infinite makes contact with humanity. Christ becomes a place, and salvation makes Christians into that place through the twofold work of mimesis: participation and representation.

In *Letter* 2, however, Gregory took a different tone. Jerusalem is not a sacred place (ἅγιος τόπος) or holy place (ἱερὸς τόπος); it is a place in which sin is "entrenched among those who dwell there."[8] He doubted both the utility of the destination[9] and the likelihood of the monks (especially female monastics under the care of Kensitor, the letter's recipient[10]) undertaking the journey without "contracting the infection" of vice.[11] The letter concludes by emphasizing that the Holy Spirit has come to humanity and is equally and infinitely present everywhere according to believers' faith, without any special preference for those living in Jerusalem. "The changing of one's place [τοπικὴ μετάστασις] does not bring about any greater nearness to God. No, God will come to you wherever you are, if the inn [καταγώγιον] of your soul is such that the Lord himself comes to dwell within you and walks with you."[12] Even as Gregory denied one kind of salvific place, he affirmed another: the soul must become the place where God dwells.

Becoming a place of God would require the same mimetic performance regardless of spatial location. For those in search of the contemplative life, seeing Jerusalem, though not necessarily harmful, held no added value. Gregory seemed to have loved his journey, and he was more sympathetic with those in the beginning of faith going on pilgrimage than with the monastics. He did not demand that those living in Jerusalem leave. But the dangers of exposure (especially for women[13]) were too risky for the momentary delight of seeing the holy land.[14]

Gregory wrote at length about journey and place because to misunderstand them was to misunderstand the Christ on offer in the life of perfection. Christians were to become an image of God by making themselves the place of God, but their archetype was not a physical place, at least not in any straightforward way. They were to pursue a different kind of presence, venture a different journey, become a difference place.

Gregory's own ambivalence about pilgrimage airs both the draw and danger of spaces in the quest for spiritual perfection, and also opens into other questions: What kinds of journeys and what kinds of places does Gregory ask his audiences to take on? And what is the relationship of place, journey, and perfection that ought to mark the Christian life? One reading of Gregory finds him ultimately uninterested in space, or "measurable, dia-stemic standards."[15] This chapter finds that a more nuanced view of space and place reveals a deeper connection between Gregory's insistence on mimesis as the defining work of the Christian life and the endless stretching of desire that marks Christian perfection. Like names, journeys and places at once give shape to and expand the Christian as she takes in and represents them in her life. The narration of the journey, I argue, serves as a map or *itinerarium* toward not the Holy Land but toward Christian perfection. And like any map, Gregory's is partial, creative, and reliant on improvised inter-pretation, even as it directs the journey.

The question of pilgrimage, then, seemed to have struck a nerve with Gregory because questions of journey and space were central to his theori-zation of the Christian life. What kinds of spaces exhibit an epektatic life of constant growth in God? And how can Christians participate in and repre-sent these spaces? This chapter shows how Gregory deployed mimetic activ-ity as a governing and propelling force in the journey of Christian life and how stylized places mark and guide this journey. Mimesis helps us answer two sets of questions: First, with an infinite God, present in all of creation, what kind of space can make sense of the progress Gregory asks of his reader? If there is no progress in Godself, what kind of space can allow for a mimetic relationship with the divine? Second, what kinds of images or points of intensity can shape this sense of progress? What are Gregory's representations of space (maps of the Christian life) and spaces of represen-tation (images that organize and give shape to the life on offer)?

This chapter, then, examines Gregory's treatment of mimetic space in two ways. First, it examines the creation of the space of the journey, how Gregory represents, organizes, and orients the space in which participation happens. The journey toward an unknown God, we will see, takes a rather structured path. Journey, that is, becomes space, a way to map the life of Christian perfection.[16] This map mirrors his reading practice.[17] His commit-ment to journey is modeled on God's providing an *akolouthia* (sequence) in scripture that is bound to the *skopos* (aim) of scripture. The goal and the way are inseparable when an endless movement forward defines perfection. Sec-ond, drawing on Jonathan Z. Smith's argument that imagined places—how cultures and individuals discuss and represent place—yield insight into their self-understanding, I examine Gregory's discourse around place as a way to analyze his self-understanding of the endless expansion of desire that at once constitutes and stretches the self.[18]

Space and Place

A bit more needs to be said about the two key terms of this chapter. Gregory will both "map" the Christian life, creating a *space* for it, and also provide images of *place* to mimic, places that at once define and stretch the self. This map making filled with particular points of intensity is helpfully categorized by Henri Lefebvre's *The Production of Space* as a "representation of space" and "spaces of representation" (*les spaces de representation*).[19] Lefebvre provides a threefold definition of space: lived, perceived, and conceived. First is what he calls "spatial practice" or the spaces to which a body grows accustomed (e.g., automatically pulling out a phone when waiting in line, walking a familiar route to work). Second, "representations of space" highlight the way space is ordered through verbal and visual representations (e.g., maps and charts). They provide a level of "control over the sheer givenness of space" to facilitate and encourage particular kinds of movements, expectations, and habits.[20] Gregory offered new kinds of maps for the life of Christian perfection to suit a world saturated by the divine, where "progress" was not defined by a "change of place," or by arrival. The organization of space, for Gregory, encouraged different relationships with God and different possibilities of transcendence according to the reader's ability. Third, these "representations of space" shape and are shaped by "spaces of representation"—imaginative or symbolic spaces that structure how humans virtually or affectively relate to space and how they theorize themselves through space (e.g., Augustine's "fields and vast mansions of memory [*campos et lata praetoria memoriae*]").[21] These can read as metaphors for an underlying reality, but these places constitute the imagination; they are "metaphors we live by."[22] They changed what Christians noticed, fantasized, and felt. The journey, for Gregory, spatialized the life of Christian perfection, and within the journey a self was organized and produced through mimetic relationships with these places that governed and propelled the epektatic self. If space provided a kind of map, a way to orient this life, then within this map, Gregory provided places along the journey. These places mediated encounters with God. For the sake of brevity, "representations of space" I call "space"; and "spaces of representation" I call "place." These places, we will see, are what Gregory called "containers of the Uncontainable."

As Christians became more accustomed to institutional forms of life, moreover, their relations to space and place changed. Gregory's organization and theorization of space, that is, was part of a larger practice of the later Roman Empire. Romans had long made organizing and ritualizing space a central focus of their imperial power.[23] Networks of temples and pilgrimages forged consensus through shared rituals, institutions, and habits.[24] Yet the fourth century saw an increase in not just holy places, but also in maps, pilgrim literature, and "hagiographical geography," which gave rise to what Scott Johnson has called "cartographical thinking."[25] This cartographical thinking was "part of a larger literary movement in Late Antiquity, that of the organization of knowledge, as well as of the related phenomenon of the sacralizing of specific holy places."[26] Specific places became holy as they were placed within a larger story or map. Gregory's *epektasis*, I argue, was part of this late antique trend of organizing and directing journeys through points of intensity within maps and narratives, a trend that emerged with the increased emphasis of the mysteriousness of the divine. Gregory, both following and inspiring this perspectival shift in how to orient oneself toward, and what one could expect from, the arrangement of space, created a Christian space in which the endless journey to God makes sense. His writings allowed late antique Christians to feel the force of these infinite spaces, to sense an infinite presence.

Paths of Reading: Origen, Pseudo-Dionysius, and Gregory

We can see how Gregory's texts function as *itinerarium* by quickly drawing contrasts with Origen, whom we met in Chapter 3, and with the sixth-century author writing under the pseudonym Dionysius the Areopagite. For all three, all of creation is an accommodated space leading back to God. Indeed, Gregory owes much to Origen, and Dionysius to both Gregory and Origen. But the connection between accommodated space and journey in Gregory marks something of a distinction with Origen and with Dionysius.

Origen's exegetical work tends to read more like a series of photographs that have some order to them, but could be rearranged, at least as long as one knows where the beginning and end are located and has a sense of the *skopos*.[27] "Stumbling blocks" exist all over scripture, and while Origen does posit the influential progression from Proverbs, to Ecclesiastes, to the Song of Songs, it is not clear that within these books there is a progression; rather the accumulated reading of scripture is meant to transform the reader in ways not quite reducible to a progressive "course" (ἀκολουθία). He will interpret the same passage multiple ways because he sees multiple paths available for reaching the "eternal gospel."[28] The text is a "veil" for the idea.[29]

Dionysius spatialized his reading in two ways. First, he arranged all of creation in a "holy order," that is, into "hierarchies" (a word he coined), one hierarchy for the Church and another for the angels. This sacred arrangement allows for "divine imitation [θεομίμητον]."[30] This aim of locking creation into this mimetic order forms, as Charles Stang has put it, a "circuit" through which Christ can move. Individual Christians can journey, but moments of transcendence happen less by changing place than by the rupture that happens when Christ moves through them as they properly occupy their rank.[31] They follow Christ from (πρόοδος) and back to (ἐπιστροφή) the divine source, but Christ is equally present (and absent) in every slot in the hierarchy. Second, Dionysius saw the names of God that Scripture reveals not as a progression, but as a set that forms a loop, or again a "circuit." Each name must be affirmed and negated.[32] Christians move no closer to God by knowing God as "Good" or "Light" than by knowing God as "drunk" or "worm." Instead, they meet God "beyond every denial and affirmation."[33] The arrangement of creation and of divine names makes possible moments of "ecstasy," but little sense of "progress."[34]

To sum up too roughly, then, Origen has a rather weak sense of arrangement, and Dionysius a weak sense of journey. For Gregory, by contrast, the journey within the text is itself accommodated. The sequence or narrative is inseparable from the goal. And those seeking perfection are to follow an *akolouthia*,[35] a progression, sequence, or course that parallels the progression in virtue, salvation, and the life of Christian perfection. The arranged space of exegesis—a dense site of mimetic activity—becomes the path for the journey to perfection.

The image of the journey is by no means unique to Gregory. Gregory's employment of it, however, is remarkable. While the image is easily associated with *The Life of Moses*, when reading across Gregory's work, one notices its near-ubiquity. Journeys may appear unremarkable in *On the Soul and the Resurrection* where, in a dialogue staged like Plato's *Phaedo*, Gregory aimed to show how the soul progresses endlessly toward God, who sustains and transcends all and continues to draw the soul even after death.[36] But it is hardly obvious, for example, that the Beatitudes would be likened to "rungs in a ladder" toward virtue,[37] which is how Gregory described them in his

Homilies on the Beatitudes, or that the Lord's Prayer recapitulates Moses leading the Israelites to the foot of Mt. Sinai.[38] By ascending the Beatitudes, Christians "follow" (ἀκολουθήσασιν) Christ, who "ascends the mountain";[39] the Lord's Prayer likewise proffers "the meaning of the ascent to God which is accomplished through a sublime way of life."[40] In short, Gregory's reading practice mirrored the aim of the treatise: just as the reader follows the sequence (ἀκολουθία) of a text, so the Christian follows (ἀκολουθέω) Christ, who has charted a course for the life of virtue.[41]

Even at the height of contemplation, new places emerge.[42] In the *Homilies on the Beatitudes*, for example, the journey does not end when, after encountering the words "Blessed are the pure in heart for they will see God," the reader summits the mountaintop and peers down "from the great height on the sea at the bottom." What Gregory calls "that slippery and precipitous rock which offers no foothold for rational thought" brings about a "vertigo of the soul [τὸν ἴλιγγον ᾧ ἡ ψυχή]."[43] But it does not cause the Christian to spin into the abyss. Instead, a new place emerges: the reader becomes like Peter who walks out "on firm and solid water," and the journey toward perfection continues.[44] This paradoxical play between the infinite and finite— where the infinite bursts through a text and provides new finite images that keep a reader moving through it—governs and propels life in God, providing new places for participation in God.[45] In *The Life of Moses*, Moses too enters "a place [τόπῳ]" to "see God" and then continues along the "sequence," because Christ is the "place [τόπος] for those who run" and "the 'way' of the course [ὁδὸς τοῦ δρόμου]."[46] Christ becomes the place in which participation happens and the one who leads those seeking perfection toward new places. Christ becomes both stable space and infinite progress.

The representation of a space, then, does not "encompass" desire or encourage harmony with a stable image; the space focuses and intensifies "desire for the Good," such that "by looking at what he can see, [he] rekindle[s] his desire to see more."[47] Places within this space draw readers ever forward to new places while remaining in the spatialized journey. On the journey to the hilltop, Gregory writes, God transforms humans as God "redraws [ἀναζωγραφῶν] the soul" in imitation (μίμησιν) of the only real blessedness.[48] The scriptures thus create an imaginative space oriented by the image of the journey. And, like names, growing into these places along the journey and being able to participate in and represent them is at the heart of Christian practice. In these places, Christians encounter and grow in the God who took on space for humanity.

By highlighting the journey, Gregory's texts created a map, that is, a representation (μίμησις) of space. The map includes different regions and challenges, but also carries a sense of the infinite life of virtue. The map has an order that must be followed, but within that order it invites different moments of transcendence, places that paradoxically break the literal surface by moving through it. The space establishes expectations for how to progress. And at the same time, as we will see, space leans on and is influenced by places that invite mimetic relationships, points of intensity (ἐπίτασις) within the space that give plastic boundaries to the epektatic life of Christian perfection.

Treatise on the Inscriptions of the Psalms

Sequenced Space

We see how journey becomes a stabilized and sequenced space most clearly in one of Gregory's least studied texts, his *Treatise on the Inscriptions of the Psalms*.[49] The text opens as a response to an unnamed recipient who seems to have asked Gregory how the Psalms can lead to virtue. Gregory eventually zeroes in on the inscriptions or "epigraphs" (ἐπιγραφαί),[50] but first he needs instead to examine "the Psalter in its totality" and to gain a sense of the necessary "approach [ἀκολούθου]" by which "the meaning [λόγος] will be made clear."[51] Not only do the Psalms, he says, provide a "total guidance" of the course of a human life,[52] but they are, in fact, a microcosm of human life: a bounded series of images directed toward and participating in God.[53] To chart how the Psalms lead Christians to virtue, Gregory writes, requires understanding both "the progression [ἀκολούθου]" and "the aim [σκοπός]" of the text. The progression is indicated "by the order [τάξις] of the psalms, which has been well arranged in relation to knowledge of the aim, and by the sections of the whole book which are defined by certain distinctive boundaries [ἰδίαις τισὶ περιγραφαῖς ὁριζόμενα]."[54] Reading well, like living well, requires seeing the whole and understanding its progression in relation to its aim.

Gregory divides the book into five parts, each of which takes the reader toward the goal of blessedness. The spatial stability allows readers to see the whole of human life reflected in the Psalms and how they are to advance through it. This mapping does not capture blessedness as much as it makes it recognizable. It condenses blessedness's unfathomable awe, makes readers aware of its own limits, and creates "sparks" just bright enough to reveal untraveled richness hidden within it. It shows the Psalms—which were central to Christian ritual—to be an epektatic space.[55] Whether reciting the Psalms in liturgies or carrying them in a liturgically formed soul, Christians' encounter with the Psalms, in Gregory's telling, should place them in a map toward ever-blessedness.[56]

The goal of the virtuous life to which the Psalms lead is "blessedness," Gregory writes, and "likeness to God . . . is a definition of human blessedness."[57] And because "the truly good, or that which is beyond the good [τὸ ἐπέκεινα τοῦ ἀγαθοῦ], in which everything that participates [μετέχον] becomes blessed is alone both blessed and desirable by nature," the scriptures set forth the way "through a skillful and natural sequence [διά τινος τεχνικῆς τε καὶ φυσικῆς ἀκολουθίας]." In "various and diverse forms," God provides "the method [τὴν μέθοδον[58]] for acquiring the blessing," and these forms are arranged such that participation is sequenced.[59] To live in likeness to what is "beyond the good," Gregory writes, God provides this *akolouthia* as a "technology" or "artistic rule" (τεχνολογοῦσα[60]) for life. Readers are immediately clued in that no single image functions on its own. The sequence of the text moves the reader.

The Psalms are representations (μίμησις) to be carved in the souls of those seeking divine likeness, as they follow (ἀκολουθέω) Christ by following the sequence (ἀκολουθία) of the Psalms.[61] Mimesis—both the representations set forth in scripture and the appropriate participatory responses to them—involves directionality. Readers are shown the map of the whole, but, as with names, where Christians can write perfection before they can attain it, here, they can map blessedness before they can complete the itinerary. The arrangement of sequenced space allows movement on this journey, but it does not negate the need to travel through it. Mimesis circumscribes a set of possible actions suitable in God's economy but calls for improvised action within it. To participate in and represent the divine is to move along a sequenced space, and along the way different possibilities of transcendence emerge in different places.

The treatise, then, is divided into two sections. The first is a methodological section on how the Psalms as a whole organize and demonstrate the progression toward (and in) a virtuous life. Having established a map of the Psalms, part two moves to "examine closely the subject matter," namely, the meaning of the inscriptions.[62] My reading examines how Gregory creates this map in the first section—looking to imagery from both parts to better understand this journey. For Gregory, space conditions relationships. It arranges the various mimetic relationships encouraged by the Psalms, teaching Christians what to strive toward and how to relate to obstacles thwarting those desires. And with this Christian space mapped, Gregory shows how, within it, different places allow for different modes of transcendence, or what he will later develop into epektasis. At every point in the journey, Christians find themselves in a place that allows them at once to participate in God and to move toward a new place within the space of the journey that God reveals in the Psalms.

Mapping the Journey: The Five Stages of Virtuous Living

The book of Psalms, Gregory explains, is divided into five parts, corresponding to five stages in the ascent of virtue toward the goal (τέλος) of blessedness (μακαριότης),[63] which is "likeness to God [ἡ πρὸς τὸ θεῖον ὁμοίωσις]."[64] The psalms form an itinerary, leading readers through specific places on their way to a goal of divine similitude. Like a good cartographer, Gregory here walks the path and then selects stopping points and stages to the journey. The first part of the treatise gives a sense of the different terrain pilgrims will travel on their journey to blessedness. He is selective, drawing attention to some spots more than others, encouraging readers to dwell in certain sections and rush past others. Readers might notice too that the book spends a good deal more time on the beginning stages than those at the end. From this, readers may assume that it will take a while to ward off the passions, but that once Christians begin this process, they gain momentum. Gregory's dwelling on the goal, then, spurs desire for the end. His mimesis of the final stage vivifies what might be too vague to orient a life. Humans will not become limitless as God is, but their likeness to God comes in following the course that God established for them. They imitate the infinite by moving through sequenced space offered by the Word, and within this space those seeking perfection find themselves in mimetic places where participating in and representing God is made possible.

The First Stage: The Stadium

The first step of this journey involves separation from evil, discerning between the good life and "the one that deserves reproach." Gregory elaborates on the distinction between the good and the reproachable life. On the one hand, there is a "joy of evil which delights our sense-perception, and on the other, that of virtue which brings joy to our soul."[65] Virtuous subjects are made by the cultivation of a certain kind of enjoyment, and thus readers are clued into the text's unit of analysis: "Longing [πόθος] is the road to plea-sure [εἰς ἡδονὴν]."[66] The text is a representation of desire that is meant to spur desire, and desire, as Sarah Coakley argues, is "the constelling cate-gory of selfhood."[67] Governing and directing desire remakes the self by pro-viding a series of stages on which the Christian life plays out.

A sense of place governs the first stage of the journey. Psalm 4 opens with the inscription "unto the end [εἰς τὸ τέλος],"[68] because the vision of the end, Gregory writes, "excites the desire [ἐπεγείρειν εἰς προθυμίαν] in those who are contending by means of virtues in the *stadium of life*."[69] Gregory places the first step of this journey in "the stadium," where "the common life of human beings" is marked by wrestling with evil. All humans begin the journey toward blessing by confronting the evil that constantly tries to trick contes-tants into desiring the wrong things, pinning them under their false desires.

The psalms act as a guide who leads Christians to victory. They do so by holding out a prize. "For when the crown is shown in advance to those wres-tling with one another in the stadiums it strengthens their zeal for victory even more, since the labors which they experience in the wrestling are dis-guised by the honor which is anticipated," and the crown draws attention toward the good in the midst of the battle over desire.[70] The psalms "lighten the labor in the contest" by providing hope. Staging participation in the good intensifies desire to resist evil, and draws readers to the next stage.[71]

The Second Stage: The Fountain

If the first step is wrestling with and separating from evil, the second as-sumes a victory, and looks to advance further, from the stadium to the foun-tain. Having won the battle, the one seeking blessing "imitates the deer in thirst, and is thirsty for the divine fountains." The fountains are "the divine nature." Commenting on the line "as the deer longs for the fountains of water, so my soul longs for you, O God," Gregory writes, "his soul eases the thirst which is sustained by desire, because it is eager to attain that for which it longs."[72] Drinking the divine nature is a mediated process, as this "foun-tain" gushes forth examples of holy living.[73] The prize that could before be seen only at a distance as encouragement is now in the water that fills Chris-tians with hope as they drink. "The examples drawn from lives produce a certain intensification of the disposition in the soul [ἐπίτασιν γάρ τινα τῆς ἐν τῇ ψυχῇ] and an obvious steadfastness [βεβαιότης], since hope attracts [ἐφελκομένης] the soul to honor which equals that of the best, and hostile comment on those who have been censured trains the soul to flee and avoid similar pursuits."[74] The first stage allowed Christians to know a good life from a bad one. For Gregory, the next step is where they stabilize (βεβαιότης) and stretch (ἐπίτασις) their lives toward virtue. This requires gathering examples to train (παιδοτριβεῖν) the soul.[75] The word *epitasis*, of course, shares the same root as *epektasis*. Both words can mean "stretch," but we get some clarification here when we read it with its related other meaning, "intensification."[76] The divine nature, here encountered by drinking sacred lives, expands desire while making virtue visceral. The saints stretch the traveler forward by making more vivid what the blessed life looks like. "Agape when intensified becomes eros [ἐπιτεταμένη γὰρ ἀγάπη ὁ ἔρως]," Gregory writes in his *Homilies on the Song of Songs*.[77] *Epitasis* even has a musical—notable as the Psalms were often sung—connotation: the tightening of a string on a musical instrument. Stretching and tightening desire should also tune the soul.[78] Drinking in these examples moves one from "entrance to the good," by the fact that he has separated from evil, to "participation in what is superior."[79]

Once this participation begins, Gregory explains, he "is no longer the kind of person who must be dragged away from his passionate attachment to evil by necessity and warning, and compelled to look to virtue. On the contrary, he has an excessive thirst for what is superior."[80] This second stage reactivates the intensity of desire (τὸ ἐπιτεταμένον τῆς ἐπιθυμία) that defines the quest for blessedness.[81] The soul's thirsting for virtue in God slowly merges with the place, so that the deer who thirsted becomes the fountain from which it drinks. "The divine fountain . . . come[s] into existence in and transforms" her, and she "is full of what [s]he desired." A different "physics" emerges: "For that which has become full is not again emptied on the model of physical satiety, nor does that which was drunk remain inactive in itself. In whomever the divine fountain has come into existence, it transforms [μεταποιεῖ] the one who has embraced it to itself, and imparts to this person a portion of its own power."[82] As we saw in the previous chapter with the jar that was reshaped by what it held, so here drinking from the fountain reshapes the drinker. Soaking in the subjects of desire that teach her how to pursue God while also being bound to God, the soul thirsts for the very thing that sustains and satisfies her.

The Third Stage: The Lookout Point

In the third stage, the Christian continues to move "through the course [δι' ἀκολούθου]" in such a way that "the one who adheres to God through hope and who has become one with him [ἓν πρὸς ἐκεῖνον γενόμενος] is in some way united [κολλώμενος] with him."[83] Union and progress (ἀκολουθία) come together here and stretch the reader forward.

The movement from the arena to the fountain of the holy now brings the Christian to a lookout point (σκοπιά) where he can strain to see "wherein the difference between evil and virtue lies."[84] This new setting allows for the perspective needed not only to contemplate but also to see the divine on earth. While "the majority of people" recognize the blessings of heaven, from this "look-out point" readers can say with Psalm 72, "What do I desire on earth besides you?"[85] Because, having moved through the first two stages, "he . . . has what he desired in himself," and he begins to be able to see his subject of desire, namely, "both the potentiality and the actuality of things which exist," which "is the unique propriety of the deity." By imitating God, virtue seekers become this lookout point; they make the potential present (παρόν) by being united to what is always already ahead of them, namely, the infinite God. Thus union with God has already happened in the third of five stages of ascent. But with "union," neither the path nor the ability to section space ends; space does not dissolve when one is joined to an infinite God. The Christian becomes the place of God and continues to move forward along the sequence in pursuit of perfection.[86]

The Fourth Stage: The Boundary

This union, being tied to the *akolouthia*, moves readers from the third to the fourth stage that the Psalms map. "In the third section . . . the person who has been taken up to such a height grasps again the intention of the step which lies beyond this one and surpasses himself and becomes better and more sublime [ἑαυτοῦ μείζων καὶ ὑψηλότερος]. Having passed through a third heaven, as it were, according to Paul, he becomes more sublime in the fourth part than in the previously attained heights. For the common person no longer receives these things, but the one who already adheres to God and has been united with God [ὁ προσκολληθεὶς ἤδη καὶ συνημμένος θεῷ]."[87] This passage can read much like the previous one: it is concerned with transcendence and with how one who is united with God continues to "receive" God. The third step, though, was one of "undistracted solitude," where the Christian acquires the discipline to "contemplate the invisible things." Now Moses, having taken on the discipline of solitude, "no longer needed to be led by law, but could himself become the author of a law for others."[88] Advancing in the journey toward blessedness requires representational activity, representing or even making oneself a law by which others can live.

Moses's movement is characterized by mimesis of the divine. And mimesis makes one a "boundary place"—united to and participating in God while also representing the divine for others.

> The person who has achieved this height stands as a kind of boundary place [μεθόριος τρόπον τινὰ] between the changeable and the unchangeable nature and mediates, as it is appropriate, between the two poles [μεσιτεύει καταλλήλως τοῖς ἄκροις]. He offers supplications to God on behalf of those who have been converted from sin, and he transmits the mercy of the supreme power to those who need mercy. We may learn from this that the more one has removed himself from things that are inferior and earthly, the more he is associated with that nature which transcends every mind. He imitates by beneficence the deity [μιμεῖται δι' εὐποιΐας τὸ θεῖον], by doing that which is the distinctive characteristic of the divine nature. Now I mean everything which needs kindness shows kindness, in so far as a need for beneficence exists.[89]

Mimesis transforms Christians into a kind of trope (τρόπος), a way, but also style, fashion, or way of life that holds together the changeable and the unchangeable, as they participate in God.[90] This "style" allows movement and stability to come together. Humans, for Gregory, never lose that movement, but by following the *akolouthia* their movement becomes unchanging. Union with God requires a constant performance of a mimetic relationship that intensifies desire, in which the ever-changing human nature participates in the unchanging God.[91] Advancing in participation in God and representation of "the distinctive characteristic of the divine nature" removes one from "earthly" concerns while desiring God and teaching the virtues on earth.

Gregory contrasts the exemplary life of Moses with the typical human life that chases after the lower things. Most chase after the spider's web of life, which is "unsubstantial [ἀνυπόστατός]."

> Life is unsubstantial and shadowy, like the thread of a spider's web. . . . For just as the thread is visible so long as chance may pre-

serve it, but if someone touches it with his hand it perishes immediately, wasted away by the touch of the fingers, so too that human life, which is always being woven from unsubstantial ambitions like so many ethereal threads, is weaving a non-existent web for itself. If someone assails this web with solid reasoning, the vain ambition escapes his grasp and disappears into nothing. For everything ambitiously pursued in this life is a fiction [οἴησίς], not reality [ὑπόστασις]. Honor is a fiction, as is also rank, family nobility, pride, pretension, wealth, and all those things in short that the spiders of life practice.[92]

The spider's web has neither direction nor substance—charges that could easily be leveled against mimesis. But Gregory suggests that the progression and transformation offered in the Psalms is a different kind of web: a series of examples entices Christians and inspires them to better imitate the divine. Each example builds a larger habitat, in which yearning for God becomes possible.

Moses's union with God moves him ever forward, and also represents (μιμέομαι) that movement. While very few people actually achieve this state, those few who do demonstrate "the fourth step in the ascent in the Psalms." Moses's "association" with the infinite does not remove him from his people. It "lifted the understanding of those ascending with him . . . by showing those who live vainly how the delusion of the material life, which is unsubstantial and like a spider's web, advances to no good goal."[93] In Moses, "the concern of the virtues, which is complex and manifold, becomes one work. And this work is the salvation of the one who performs it."[94] The one work unfolds over many forms, but remains "one" because it follows the one path, with the one goal: likeness to God. Moses's divine mimesis stylizes him as a boundary between the varied displays of beneficence and the singularity of God's path. (I return to the way Gregory deploys mimetic characters in the next chapter, but for now, it is important to keep the focus on space and place.)

The Fifth Stage: Through the Spider's Web

The final stage takes those who can follow to "the most sublime step of contemplation, as though it were a peak."[95] The Christian becomes strong and focused enough to pierce through the spiders' webs of the world. With the sharp eye of an "eagle," he "strains onward to the height [πρὸς τὸ ὕψος ἑαυτὸν συντείνων]." The momentum, "the wind alone," that he has gathered by this point on his flight easily cuts through the ephemeral web as he directs himself toward "the ray of light [πρὸς τὴν ἀκτῖνα τοῦ φωτὸς]."[96] Gregory, that is, has shown his reader a movement from stadium to soaring.

This gathered momentum toward the light prefaces what Gregory wants with this final stage, which is a "complete consummation and recapitulation of human salvation [συμπλήρωσίς τε καὶ ἀνακεφαλαίωσις τῆς ἀνθρωπίνης σωτηρίας ἐστίν]."[97] Not unlike Origen's account of salvation, the training and progression of the subject back to God, for Gregory, stabilizes focus. Here, though, rather than the gathering of focus leading to a kind of stasis, what one gathers is a *momentum* that propels the reader toward the light.

This momentum, however, never abandons the work of representation. Moses, Gregory's main character and exemplar in this methodical first part of the treatise, now "visually [ὑπ' ὄψιν]" brings the grace one has and continues to experience to the attention of those who have ascended to this peak. Another kind of visuality functions in a subject conditioned by what "is inexpressible, inconceivable, and better than all understanding, which eye has not seen, nor ear heard, nor has the human heart received."[98] To follow Moses toward the light in union with God precludes neither the work of imitation nor representation. It involves more fully learning to see as Moses sees, to move with Moses to the peak. The very act of stretching toward God is intensified by the production of words and images that draw and inspire others. "For [God] did not think it enough to intimate [παραδηλῶσαι] this grace in one way only, but in various ways he elaborates the events which we encountered in our propensity to evil. He also sets forth in many ways the assistance which we received from God for the good, as if to multiply the occasions for giving thanks by his account of the good things and of the thanksgiving which abounds to God."[99] Moses's ability to show the entirety of human life—as the Psalms do—is a mark of his true blessedness, and he does so through a multiplication of gratitude in the readers. That expansion lets them fly through the spider's web, "strain[ing] onward to the height"; that expansion makes them most like God.

*   *   *

For Gregory, the Psalms provided representations (μιμήσεις) that are "chiseled into the soul." But they are chiseled as readers moved through the mimetic sequence of the text. Gregory leads readers through various stages of a journey, providing stages on which the life of perfection could be performed, all the while propelling readers through each stage by allowing them a vision of the whole. Once placed on the journey, desire intensified with deeper engagement with and participation in mimetic relationships. The perspective and appreciation of the map would change depending on the stage—as it would for those who have traveled the journey and look back on the map—but the map nevertheless provided a path to follow and to guide others in the expansion and intensification of desire for God. *The Inscriptions of the Psalms* provided a model (the broad outline of the pursuit of Christian perfection) and method (creating a space for the pursuit and places that govern and propel it) that much of Gregory's writing followed throughout his life. I next look more closely at images of place in Gregory's *Homilies on the Song of Songs*, where Gregory both increases his focus on the incarnation and explicitly links these places to epektasis.

While epektasis is often described as "an advance into an ever-deepening darkness,"[100] darkness seems to be only one of the many places in which one meets God. If not only the mapped space of the journey but also the particular places within it establish relations between the human and divine, if they can figure, in Gregory's words, "the link between things of contrary nature,"[101] then by providing different places, Gregory shows readers different possibilities for this endless encounter with and striving after God. These places at once condition relations (e.g., one cannot see in the darkness) and provide an image of God (God is the very darkness in which one searches for God).

Hans Boersma has argued that Gregory's thought moves in one direction, from place to placelessness, "from the material to the spiritual, from this-worldly early existence to otherworldly, heavenly existence."[102] Gregory's vision of human beings here is ultimately "adiastemic";[103] that is, as Boersma writes, "Clearly, such anagogical progress implies that Gregory's moral theology is not concerned with measurable, diastemic standards ... and, instead ... [it] moves beyond this-worldly measurements by explaining that virtuous progress itself constitutes an advancing into the infinite, adiastemic life of God."[104] Advancing to the adiastemic life of God, Boersma claims, should lead beyond any spaces that would pull desire forward. The movement from material to immaterial, of course, is a consistent theme in Gregory's writings. And yet, that *movement* seems crucial. Without some sense of dividing up space and time, what does it mean to grow? Boersma's focus on "otherworldliness" seems to miss the importance of growth, desire, and mimesis, which are all central to Gregory's writing. Boersma argues that paradox is only necessary "once we leave behind the diastemic realities of earthly existence."[105] And yet Gregory argues just the opposite. In *Against Eunomius II*, he writes, "We humans live in total ignorance, in the first place about ourselves, and then about everything else. Who is in a position to understand his own soul? Who knows its inner being? . . . Not even in the physical being itself, in which the bodily qualities inhere, has so far been captured by clear comprehension; for if one mentally analyzes the phenomenon into its constituent parts and attempts to envisage the subject by itself, stripping it of its qualities, what will be left to reflect upon, I fail to see. . . . Someone then who does not know himself, how is he to get to know any thing beyond himself?"[106] Paradox and incomprehensibility can happen quite squarely on earth. Different temporalities and spatial intensities are at play, but that is hardly an argument for "leav[ing] behind the diastemic realities of this-worldly existence."

Boersma is a recent, if extreme, example of a broader debate within the study of Gregory's mysticism. Verna Harrison and Ann Conway-Jones have helpfully divided up scholarship into two camps: the "mystical" (those who emphasize a "sense of presence" or "union" with God) and the "theological" (who see "union" as impossible because of the ontological break between finite creatures and an infinite God).[107] My reading sees value in both sides of these debates.[108] *The Inscriptions of the Psalms* places "union" with God in the third of five stages. And even at the highest points of contemplation, new places emerge. Christians participate in a God whose essence is unknowable, and their participation opens them up to new possibilities of encounter with that unknown God.

*   *   *

Gregory offers specific places as privileged images for this "sense of presence." Conway-Jones concludes her study on temple imagery in *The Life of Moses* by arguing that, for Gregory, ascent is "to a place, not a person."[109] Is this distinction so clear? The Christ on offer seems to be a place where Christians can participate in and represent the divine. The kinds of places available, then, deserve a close look as they form Gregory's structuring images of desire and archetypes to be imitated. Mimetic places, moreover, are not only crucial for understanding how Gregory stylizes the pursuit of Christian perfection; they also are constitutive of the self on offer in it. In what follows, therefore, I examine the literary strategies and the kind of self that Gregory constructs through these places. These strategies affect Christians' understandings of the self and their place within the world. Like the names Christians take into the soul to form an image of God, these places create affective relations that establish a kind of common sense about Christ and about the self. They form the building blocks of a self and also teach Christians who they are. Smith writes, "It is through an understanding and symbolization of place that a society or individual creates itself. . . . It is by virtue of its view of its place that a society or an individual . . . takes place."[110] Paying attention to the places Gregory offers in his *Homilies on the Song of Songs*, then, should yield insight into not only the kind of life prescribed, but also the self assumed by this life.[111]

In short, if Gregory's conception of epektasis was part of a larger phenomenon of a "cartographical imagination," then what literary strategies did Gregory deploy to represent epektasis, where no final destination can be achieved? And what kind of self could be produced in an epektatic life?

Homilies on the Song of Songs

Epektatic Places

Around the time Gregory wrote *On Perfection*, he delivered a series of Lenten sermons on the Song of Songs.[112] These sermons were gathered, lightly edited, and delivered with a dedicatory letter to Olympias, a young, educated, ambitious, ascetic woman of noble descent living in Constantinople.[113] While some early Christians, such as Origen, were wary about discussing a text so erotically charged to wide audiences, Gregory saw no need to reserve it for "the advanced."[114] He tells his audience "the most intense of pleasurable activities (I mean, the passion of erotic love) is set as a figure at the very fore of the guidance that the teachings give." The text, in Gregory's reading, stages an erotic encounter between the bride (a sign of the soul) and the bridegroom (a sign of the Word) in order that "the mind may boil erotically [ἐρωτικῶς]."[115] This boiling happens through places that continually stage and shape the soul.

HOLY OF HOLIES: THE PLACE OF GOD AND THE PURSUIT OF GOD

Gregory draws readers' attention to place right away. The first homily opens by noting that the Song is "the Holy of Holies," the place where the infinite

God becomes present, a density of holiness even within the mapped space of the scriptures.[116] The Holy of Holies is at once an image for the Song as a whole and becomes the governing image of what is on offer in a place in the text: the life of Christian perfection.[117] Within the Holy of Holies, the text's conceit emerges: a bride being led "toward an incorporeal and spiritual and undefiled marriage with God."[118] The "intensity of holiness [ἐπίτασιν τῆς ἁγιότητος]" of the *place* leads to the *stretching* (ἐπέκτασις) of the soul toward God.[119] The message is clear: *the place where God is found is where pursuit of love takes place.*

The homily, then, signals for its audience what can be expected from places in these homilies and how this holy place teaches. The text, Gregory writes, "initiates the mind into the innermost divine sanctuary [τῶν θείων ἀδύτων μυσταγωγεῖ τὴν διάνοιαν]."[120] The Song "philosophizes by means of what cannot be said [δι' ἀπορρήτων φιλοσοφεῖ]," presenting, instead of words, "an image [εἰκὼν]" that "mediates our desire [ἐπιθυμία μεσιτεύει]."[121] Mimesis allows Christians access to places that can teach what propositions cannot. These places, moreover, become places of Christ, the Mediator; for Christ is both the way and the goal. Christ appears here as the character of the bridegroom who endlessly elicits desire, and, as the wedding scene, the Holy of Holies. To "be in love [ἐπάσθητι]," Gregory writes, is to join Christ in this place by participating in and representing it through the continuous stretching of desire.[122] With the Holy of Holies as the archetypal place for the epektatic life, Gregory, we will see, provides different places where the soul can, through mimesis, "stretch and expand" Christian desire.

EPEKTATIC FOUNTAINS

The entirety of the Song, therefore, is the place where the infinite God becomes ineffably present. But Gregory also highlights places that represent epektasis. In *Homily* 9, Gregory turns to a place we have seen from *The Inscriptions*, the fountain, here linking the image to resurrection and epektasis.[123] The homily, which will focus on Song 4:10–15, opens with the words of Colossians 3:1–4: "If you have been raised with Christ, set your minds on things above, not on things that are on earth. . . . For you have died . . . and your life is hidden with Christ in God." These words then become an interpretive principle. "Let us attend to today's passage as persons who are dead to the body and draw out no fleshly meaning from its words." Reading is here a practice of dying and rising with Christ. The practice is a microcosm for a larger aim: to read well for Gregory requires translating (μεταφέρω) the words of scripture into the images that shape the soul. Those who are "dead to passions and desires will transfer the meaning of the words [μετοίσει τὰς τῶν ῥημάτων ἐμφάσεις] into what is pure and undefiled, setting his mind on the 'things that are above.'"[124] Then the words of scripture "sustain a mood of loving" and show "the love with which [the bride and groom] desire each other."[125] To die and rise with Christ is to desire and represent what the scriptures offer; resurrection is mimetic and epektatic, an imitation of Christ that stretches Christians toward Christ.

Readers see the connection between place and this "resurrected" life as Gregory examines Song 4:12: "my sister bride is an enclosed garden, / a garden enclosed, a fountain sealed." The bride has been "made beautiful" and "perfumed" (Song 4:10–11), and Gregory links this beautiful scent to a place. As she learns to die with Christ, she becomes an "enclosed garden, a fountain sealed."[126] Gregory reads this closing off as part of an epektatic pattern of dying and rising. The soul before "gushes forth" wildly, but it "becomes properly ours only when it is going in the direction of what is beneficial for us and when it assists us in every way to possess what is good."[127] This pattern is now familiar: epektasis cannot be a mere "gushing forth"; wild longings render souls passive, subject to their "passions." Only after it is sealed can the soul truly desire, as opposed to being tossed by desires. The "sealing" of the fountain, therefore, is the necessary disciplining of "our soul's capacity for thinking [ἡ διανοητικὴ τῆς ψυχῆς ἡμῶν δύναμις]."[128] Those living the resurrected life must paradoxically become a bounded place if they are to imitate what is unbounded.

This gathering of stability, for Gregory, heightens a larger ascent. The place of God will look like a stable location that bursts forth. The bride mixes with the Word, but this sealing does not bring "to a halt in her stretching forward [ἐπεκτείνουσα] to higher things, nor does the Word cease to work together with her in her ascent." Becoming the fruitful, sealed garden transforms her into "a fountain that waters the gardens that stem from her."[129] Taking on the gifts of God transforms her into the place of God. Gregory links this to mimesis. The mixture of stability and desire now continues to stretch her, such that her disciplined desire makes her deepest longings a representation of her beloved. Participating in God makes her a "fountain," a living place of God.

And the most unbelievable thing of all is this: that of all the wells that contain a mass of water, only the Bride contains within herself

water that is in transit, so as to possess a well's depth, but at the same
time a river's unceasing motion.

Who could worthily attain to the wonderful things that are signified by the likeness that now attaches to the Bride? Perhaps she no
longer has anywhere further to be lifted up to, now that she has been
made like to [ὁμοιώσεως] the archetypal Beauty—for by the fountain, the Fount is exactly imitated [μεμίμηται]; by her life, the life; by
her water, the Water. The Word of God is living, and the soul that has
received the Word is alive. . . . And may we too, having taken possession of that well, become participants in that water, so that in accordance with Wisdom's injunction, we may drink not of strange water
but of the water that is ours in Jesus Christ our Lord.[130]

The images are places (*topoi*) in the rhetorical sense of a nonargumentative
mode of persuasion.[131] That is, the association of the bride with scriptural
images (water, fountain, life) lifts readers up with the bride, floating over
questions (e.g., why does she have nowhere to go when she is also in unceasing movement?) But it is more than rhetorical *topoi* on which Gregory depends. These places are storehouses of subjectivity. The bride is at once stable
and in "unceasing motion." As in the Holy of Holies, which at once houses
the divine and invites endless striving toward God, Christ here becomes the
fount, and the bride participates in it by representing it: the fountain, once
directed, becomes what the continual stretching forward looks like.

As a representational strategy, then, place figures the epektatic life in
two ways. First, the inability to secure any one image makes every image
both a promise and a threat. The fountain carries potential danger in that it
can spew aimlessly; when channeled, though, it becomes the place of Christ
and the source of the mimetic life. Second, that which sustains her (her participation in God) is inseparable from continuous motion in God. Disciplining desire constitutes a self that, while infinitely changing, moves in a
divine direction. The fountain showed the high stakes of directing desire,
and that the soul must stabilize desire to continually transcend herself.

WOUNDED CITIES, OR DWELLING PLACES THAT EXPAND

Homily 12 represents the soul as the juxtaposition of two places, "the city"
and "the wound."[132] How does this pair function as an image of epektasis?
The homily opens: "Think of people who are getting themselves ready for a
journey across the sea in the hope of finding riches." Reading scripture is

like making that journey. No matter how powerful the rudder of reason, readers depend on where the Holy Spirit blows as they set out on "the high seas in our search for insight." The map or order (ἀκολουθία) is clear, but in order to catch the wind needed to "find riches," the reader must become a certain kind of place, like a sail rightly set, capable of being moved by the Spirit.[133] Death has "no place [χώραν] of its own," but those dead to sin and alive in God become the "dwelling place of God [τὸ τοῦ θεοῦ οἰκητήριον]."[134] Song 5:7, Gregory says, shows what that place looks like, but it seems to be not one place, but two.

On their own, either the city or the wound could be a problem. When joined, however, they show the soul's epektatic journey and ever-renewing desire. The "city," Gregory clarifies, "is the soul, the dwelling place [οἰκητήριον] of God." He introduces "the city" with comments on the words "passed by" (Song 5:6). The Word "became unattainable for the one who desired him,"[135] and therefore the Word establishes a place in which the Word could be attained. For "he did not pass her by so as to leave the one he outpaced behind, but rather so as to draw her to himself."[136] Drawing the soul to himself creates a city in the soul. The Word stirs the soul to become a place where the Word can dwell, while the Word remains unattainable. A paradox emerges as the soul must become a place that makes attainable what surpasses all places. Gregory describes this place as plastic: holding shape, while morphing and expanding. The soul here also mirrors the Song, which is another kind of dwelling place, namely, the Holy of Holies. Mimicking the Song, this dwelling place cannot be only one place: it must hold what it cannot contain.

This "city" doubles as a "wound." Places *for* bodies (the city) and places *in* bodies (the wound) come together here. The city is something alive and bounded, and something formed by "the mark left in the depth [βάθει] of her being by the divine rod."[137] What exceeds the soul marks her, and that mark becomes a place unlike other places. "The place where he is found is outside every move to apprehend him."[138] God dwells in the place marked by the wound of love. This is why "it was not superficially that she felt the operation of the spiritual rod, so as to be ignorant of the place where it struck her."[139] The wound modifies the kind of place the one seeking perfection is to become. The point of contact between the bride and her beloved is this wound that at once brings her into being and intensifies her desire. The faithful city or dwelling place, then, gains greater depth (βάθος) as the wounds of desire mark and expand it. God's dwelling place, "the city," is one that is "wounded" by that which dwells in it. These reconciled images at once provide a place in which participation can happen and a representation of this contact, as the bride, like Paul, can say, "I bear on my body the marks of Christ." Participating in this wounded place where God opens the soul yokes to the need to show: the bride (and through the reader's mimetic relation with her, the reader) is called to "display . . . perfection in virtue."[140]

Summarizing the sermon, Gregory explicitly links the coupling of city and wound to imitating another place: "She imitates [μιμεῖται]" not Moses but "the rock of which the prophet said 'he smote the rock, and waters gushed out.'" With Paul, Gregory says, "The rock was Christ."[141] This is not just for her. She becomes this place, and from her "gush[es] forth, for those who are thirsty, the Word who poured water forth from his wound."[142] Participation in God and representation of God—the two sides of mimesis—are inseparable from the creation of places where God can dwell and others can find holiness.

The city and wound together show the soul to be a kind of epektatic place. Wounding without place is death, but when the wounding is in God's dwelling place—when dying is in Christ—a plastic place emerges. In this place, she "does not find any stopping place [στάσιν]," Gregory writes, but, by becoming this wounded city of God, she "advances toward the better."[143] This reconciliation of two images shows the dynamism involved in these dwelling places of God. The city, while bounded, is a dwelling place that is also a wound, a place sensitive to the spurs of desire that radiate beyond the point of contact.

Mimetic Place, Mimetic Self

Places stylize not only the movement of epektasis, but also a mimetic selfhood, which readers can best see in his final homily on the Song.[144] Gregory, as is his wont, works through the "sequence [ἀκλούθως]" of scripture to make his point. This homily on Song 6:1–9 begins with what Gregory will draw out as a parallel: the opening scene in the Gospel of John where Philip and Andrew are called to Christ, "the Lamb of God." As Andrew comes to Christ through listening to Philip, so the young maidens look to the bride, who has "been brought to perfection" in the virtues through her union with the groom, and they ask her, "Where has your kinsman gone, O beautiful among women?/Where has your kinsman turned his regard? And we shall seek him with you" (Song 6:1). Philip's injunction to "come and see" (Jn 1:46) is mirrored by the virtuous soul, who leads the virgins "toward comprehension of the One they seek [πρὸς τὴν τοῦ ζητουμένου κατάληψιν]."[145] To point others toward contemplation, however, she points not to her kinsman, but to a place. "She does not say, 'See,' but she points out the place [τὸ τόπον] where the One sought for is and where he is looking, for she says, 'My kinsman has descended into his garden, into bowls of spice' [Song 6:2]."[146] To look to the Word, here, is to look to "a place." And, as the passage continues, readers see that she points to this place precisely by becoming it mimetically. The self depicted in the homily becomes another Christ as she mimetically becomes the place of Christ.

TOWARD A REDEEMED PLACE

Having established the proper sequence for his readers on a journey and insisted on finding a proper place, Gregory begins his search for the mystical meaning in the text. The Song's discussion of "descent" and joining as "kin" signifies the incarnation, God's "coming down" to "the lowliness of our nature [ἐπὶ τὸ ταπεινὸν τῆς φύσεως ἡμῶν συγκατάβασιν]."[147] The homily then links the "garden" in Song 6:2 to Genesis 2 and offers a redemption story. "From the enigma of the garden . . . we learn that what the true Husbandman plants is we human beings (for according to Paul's statement, we are his field). Now he is the one who in the paradise at the beginning tended the human planting that the heavenly Father had planted. That is why, once the wild boar had ravaged the garden—which is to say, us—and ruined the divine field, he descended in order once again to make the desert, beautified by the planting of virtues, a garden and by the Word channeled the pure and divine spring waters of the teaching with the aim of fostering such plants."[148] When creation was as it ought to be, humans were the garden, the place where God dwelt. The trampled garden needs restoration, and God does this by planting virtues such that their germination will make a place of God again. Redemption is about the slow, orderly, "step by step" (διά τινος ἀκολουθίας καὶ τάξεως) work of becoming a garden of virtues.[149] The ordering of a place, then, emerges inseparably from the ordered growth of an epektatic self. God makes a place (τόπον ἑαυτῆς καὶ χώρημα ποιεῖται) where God will dwell, a self constituted by the virtues, and as God enters there, that place continues to expand.[150]

PORTRAITS OF PERFECTION

With the ideal of a restored place established, Gregory is in position to provide "the norm and definition of perfection in virtue [κανὼν καὶ ὅρος τῆς κατ' ἀρετήν ἐστι τελειότητος]."[151] Readers of Gregory should be prepared

for a paradox right away: measurement, boundary, and perfection come together in this place, yet the norm and boundary of perfection require a
"containing" of what is endlessly unbound. Gregory shows this in his reading of the passage "I am for my kinsman, and my kinsman is for me" (Song
6:3).[152] To "be for" requires becoming a "container of the Uncontained," to
find one's "being" in holding another who is constantly undoing, stretching,
and transcending that very being. To become this place is to become a self
that imitates the infinite.

The bride becomes, like Paul, an imitator of God, saying, "To me, to live
is Christ," and makes herself an image for others by "scrap[ing] off everything that is discerned as alien." She too can say, with Paul, "I have in me
nothing such as is not found in [Christ]."[153] The redemptive place stylizing
the mimetic self is recovered and redeemed, being transformed from a
trampled garden to God's dwelling place.[154]

Artists illustrate this place. In imitating the infinite, the bride is "in her
whole being" transformed and "makes of herself [ἀπεργάσασθαι] a supremely
vivid image of the prototypical beauty." The verb ἀπεργάζομαι[155] suggests a
painter finishing a picture, the completion or "perfection" of a sketching out
(ὑπογράψαι).[156] Having a sketch in mind from previous places, Christians
move toward perfection by filling them out, and then allow completed works
of art to become outlines for a more expansive perfection. To be "for my
kinsman," then, is to make oneself a work of art modeled on what one desires. Gregory's redemptive story continues:

> Thus the person who sees on the flat surface of a board a sketch that
> with precision [ἀκριβείας] takes the form [μεμορφωμένην] of a par-
> ticular prototype declares that the form of both is the same: he will
> say both that the beauty of the image is that of the prototype and that
> the original is palpably discerned in its copy [ἐναργῶς ἐν τῷ μιμήματι
> καθορᾶσθαι]. In the same way, she who says, "I am for my kinsman,
> and he is for me" asserts that she is conformed to Christ, that she has
> recovered her own beauty, the primordial blessedness of the human
> race, that is, to be arrayed in a beauty that conforms to the image and
> likeness of the first, the sole, and the true beauty.[157]

The self here is "recovered" as mimesis and place converge. By making herself into the place of the painting, the bride recovers her own beauty. She

must make herself an imitation of what she is not in order to become who she is.[158]

The bride becomes this redeemed place as she mirrors her beloved. To mirror God, Gregory will go on to say, is to become "in herself, the container of the Uncontained [ἡ γὰρ χωρήσασα ἐν ἑαυτῇ τὸν ἀχώρητον]."[159] This mirror absorbs and reflects more than it can hold. Selfhood is theorized here as a paradoxical place where the infinite is contained by the finite. Like the Holy of Holies, the mimetic Christian comes to be the place where God dwells, the place that "runs out to infinity."[160]

JOURNEY AND PLACE: THE CONTAINER OF THE UNCONTAINABLE

Mimesis brings together the movement of the journey with the creation of a place where God dwells. Being drawn up to God and becoming the city of God here perform the same movement. That is, the journey and the place of the journey, for Gregory, become increasingly indistinguishable as the bride's desires are marked by the same forms of beauty that mark the divine. Gregory continues this theme by commenting on Song 6:4: "You are beautiful, my close one, like goodwill [εὐδοκία], lovely, like Jerusalem, an object of terror, like serried ranks drawn up."[161] The Song figures the bride as "Jerusalem" and "goodwill," the place of Christ and that which Christ brings. In a lengthy, complex passage, Gregory writes,

> the soul, through the upward journey she has completed, has been exalted to the point where she is straining forward [ἐπεκτεῖναι] toward the wonders of the Lord and Master. For if God "in the highest," the One who is "in the bosom of the Father" (cf. John 1:18), has been mingled with flesh and blood because of his "goodwill toward his human creatures," so that "Peace" has come to be "on earth," then plainly the soul that has brought her own beauty into line with this "goodwill" [τὴν εὐδοκίαν] is imitating Christ by her righteous deeds [τὸ ἑαυτῆς ὁμοιώσασα κάλλος τὸν Χριστὸν μιμεῖται τοῖς κατορθώμασιν]; she is becoming toward others what Christ became for human nature [ἐκεῖνο γινομένη τοῖς ἄλλοις ὅπερ ὁ Χριστὸς τῇ φύσει τῶν ἀνθρώπων ἐγένετο].[162]

Just as Christ who is goodwill will come to be with humans, so the one straining toward God will reach down to fellow humans as well. In that way,

she becomes the place of Christ. As she travels toward Christ, she becomes
"lovely like Jerusalem."

> The very same quality of greatness is manifested by likening of the
> Bride's comeliness to Jerusalem—the Jerusalem that is above, to be
> sure, the Jerusalem that is free and the mother that is free, the city
> that we have learned from the words of the Lord and Master to be-
> long to the Great King; for the soul that contains the Uncontained [ἡ
> γὰρ χωρήσασα ἐν ἑαυτῇ τὸν ἀχώρητον], so that God dwells and tar-
> ries within her, has been beautified by the comeliness of the One who
> indwells her and becomes the heavenly Jerusalem because she has
> taken its beauty to herself. The beauty and comeliness of the King's
> city, though, are surely that of the King himself, for according to the
> language of the psalm, the beauty and comeliness are his to whom
> the prophecy says, "By your comeliness and by your beauty, gather
> yourself, and prosper, and reign, for the sake of truth and gentleness
> and justice [Ps 44:4–5]." For it is by these marks that the divine
> beauty is recognized—by truth, I mean, and justice and gentleness.
> Therefore, the soul that is shaped by such marks of beauty as these
> becomes comely like Jerusalem, rendered beautiful [καλλωπισθεῖσα]
> by the graceful charm of the King.[163]

There is more in these passages than can be accounted for here, but from the
first sentence we see that mimesis, journey, place, and epektasis entwine.
The bride aligns her beauty with the beauty that Christ has brought to earth
in "goodwill" (εὐδοκία[164]) by her "upward journey," by a direction propelled
by imitation of Christ. This makes her the city of Jerusalem. In bringing this
directed space and place together, she imitates Christ and becomes "toward
others what Christ became for the human race."[165] In the connection of
journey and place that happens as Christians progress in participating in
and representing Christ, Christians become containers of the Uncontainable. And they take on the characteristics of that which dwelled in the
bride—truth, justice, and gentleness—becoming the place where others can
find truth, justice, and gentleness.

The homily, then, has moved from the trampled garden in Genesis 2 to
the heavenly Jerusalem, and at every step, places mark the soul on its journey. Gregory emphasizes that the important things about this journey and
place are both how it comes into being (by participating in that which tran-

scends it) and how it is recognized by others (its representational value). When someone looks to the soul seeking perfection with God, they see what they see when they see God.

A Different Journey

The images of space and place that constitute the aim of Christian perfection are mimetic, that is, concerned with participation and representation. Space and place provide a sense of who Christians are and allow them to stretch beyond themselves. Places "mediate desire [ἐπιθυμία μεσιτεύει]," and in so doing constitute a self. And the mediator, for Gregory, is Christ. Christ is those bounded places that burst forward into new places along the mapped space. The homilies call for imitation of angels, prophets, and saints, as well as the fountain, the Holy of Holies, and Jerusalem. The places, Conway-Jones writes, provide "symbolic meaning; but [they are] also a theophany, and [reveal] a new name for Christ."[166] And in becoming these places Christians find Christ, and find new ways to make themselves recognizably true, just, and gentle. They participate in and represent Christ, the place of God, and thus become a container of the Uncontainable.

This chapter opened with an ambivalent journey, but Gregory had many enthusiastic ones as well. Cappadocian piety is almost unimaginable without journeys to martyria.[167] When building a martyria, Gregory insisted that it be cruciform, as "the cross might itself become a theologian [γένηται ... θεολόγος ὁ σταυρὸς]."[168] God was omnipresent, but it was in places that people felt holiness. These places were the wounded city about which Gregory speaks in his twelfth *Homily on the Song of Songs* or a container of the Uncontainable about which he speaks in the final homily.

These places rendered the holy ones present. Gregory preached, "Somebody coming to a place like this one, where we are gathering today, where the memory of the just is kept alive and his holy remains preserved, is in the first place attracted by the magnificence of what they see."[169] The architecture and especially the art intensify the desire for the holy one. "For even though it remains silent, a painting can speak on the wall and be of the greatest profit." It is "like a temple of God," attracting people with its beauty to a powerful presence inside. "When you look at the place," Gregory wrote of the martyrium in Sebaste, "it tells that it is the martyr's stadium."[170] The story lives in the walls, and those inside can more easily imagine themselves in that narrative that starts in the stadium and reaches to the heavens. "On the basis of what we can perceive, we believe in invisible things and because of what we experience in the world, we believe in the promise of future things."[171]

As beloved as the holy places were, however, it was often the holy martyrs who stood out from the sea of humanity. These saints structured a religious world. They punctured the soul with a feeling of awe and made tangible what it was to imitate the infinite. Theodore, Gregory's "invisible friend [ἀόρατος φίλος]," lives in the memory of those who gather at his martyrium. To touch his relic "is much-desired." And when the "friends of the martyr . . . approach it with all the senses, they pour tears out over it from piety and emotion [τῆς εὐλαβείας καὶ . . . τοῦ πάθους]."[172] Their bodies are not like other bodies.

Theodore's story is one of suffering, but his sacred presence infuses the place, blurring any clear boundary between the martyr and the martyria. The site of suffering becomes a "hospital for the most diverse diseases, a harbor for those suffering from the storms of life, a well-filled warehouse for the needy, a convenient resting-place for those who are travelling, a never-ending feast for those who are celebrating," Gregory preached.[173] Theodore's holiness, when it becomes a place, opens a world in which participation is possible. For "coming to a place" like Theodore's martyrium intensifies the desire to "emulate [ζηλώσατε]" the saint, as the place demonstrates the "fruit of piety."[174] Seeing the martyria and the art therein, "one longs for the rest."[175] Like "ants," Christians rush to the feast of the martyr, "craving" him and his "benefactions."[176] The relics continued to spur desire to see the holy one. Seeing Theodore's remains and dwelling place could at once usher in an experience of holiness that imprints Theodore's narratives on the soul and invite a mimetic relationship with the martyr. The story of his life was powerful enough to invite participation and concrete enough to orient emulation. Theodore, however, was only one of many invisible friends whose holiness fills the lives of the faithful. The next chapter turns to the role of these mimetic characters.

CHAPTER 6

Mimetic Characters

In theatrical performances, even though it is the same
actors who take the parts assigned them in the drama
[ἰστορίαν], nevertheless different persons seem to appear
in different instances as the actors alter their look by
changing their masks, and one who appears now as a slave
or an ordinary citizen is shortly seen as a valorous man
and a soldier, and again putting off the look of a subject,
takes on the appearance of one fitted for command or even
assumes the aspect of a king. In the same way, where
progress in virtue is concerned, those who are being
transformed from glory to glory because of their desire for
higher things do not always persist in the very same
character [χαρακτῆρι]. Rather, in proportion to the
perfection that each has attained for the moment through
good things, some special character [χαρακτὴρ] illumines
his manner of life, one such appearing and succeeding to
another by reason of his increase in good things.

In *On What It Means to Call Oneself a Christian*, Gregory of Nyssa noted
that hypocrites wear different masks but never change their nature. They
imitate change while still falling victim to the same temptations and suc-
cumbing to the same passions.[1] And yet, as we have seen, Gregory did not
contrast perfection with mimesis. Perfection required imitation. Mimesis
and divine infinitude come together to form the centerpiece of his theological project: "Christianity is mimesis of the divine nature."[2] The critique of
the hypocrites was not that they wore masks; it was that they removed their

masks at exactly the moment when they needed to stay in character. A mask could provide the courage and freedom to reach toward a life that was still ahead of them and yet was the truest thing about them.

In the opening passage of this chapter, those seeking Christian perfection enter into a mimetic relationship with God by assuming new masks, new characters, characters made as an "image [μίμημα] of the divine nature."[3] Gregory turned to the theater to make his point.[4] While bishops such as John Chrysostom railed against the theater, it was indispensable to the Roman world, so much so that Chrysostom's complaint against the theater was that it was not enjoyable enough: "Do those spectacles contain some pleasure? Not as much as [ours]."[5] Bishops complained that their congregations flocked to the theater but daydreamed through sermons. They yawned during discussion of doctrine, but "everyone gets excited and argues knowledgably for the merits of a favorite dancer or actor."[6] Libanius sensed that the dancer does not "imitate [μιμούμενος], but makes present [παριστάς] in himself the divinities he plays."[7] Gregory of Nazianzus even compared theology to a theatrical presentation. Only his theological rival Eunomians, he argued, would confuse theater with reality. And yet, knowing that all language will fall short of God, he argued that his words were a way of "contemplating spiritual realities, here presented on a stage [σκηνῆς]."[8] Christians needed stages on which they could imagine a God who transcends all stages. For Gregory of Nyssa, learning to play a series of roles within a larger drama of God—rather than assimilating to a single image—directed perfection. Over the course of a lifetime, Christians should progress "from glory to glory," and that transformation required taking on new characters and characteristics. In these characters, virtues and dispositions imprint (χαρακτηρίζω) on the soul and directed and expanded desire for God. Humans, for Gregory, were made of characters, just as they were made of names and places.

Characters are perhaps the most expected mimetic relationship for Gregory to encourage. "Imitation," Proclus wrote, "is primarily the creation of characters [ἠθοποιός]."[9] From Plato to Quintilian to Athanasius to Libanius, imitation of exemplars had been indispensable to ethical formation, and for each of them the mimetic relationship contained something excessive that spurred a change in the imitator. Throughout antiquity, moreover, the line dividing actors and orators was often blurred. They studied each other's arts, and both required mimesis and captivating an audience. Assuming personae, moreover, was a primary tactic of Roman education's effort to turn the student into an elite man.[10] While these exercises of impersonation (ἠθοποιός) aimed at taking on distinct, historical, or stock characters,[11] they added up to more than any persona; they stamped onto the souls of its best students Rome's deepest values, prized habits, recognized forms of speech, and a range of affections.[12]

Gregory's production of characters participated in and challenged this cornerstone of Roman pedagogy.[13] Basil, Macrina, Gregory Thaumaturgus, Paul, and Moses, to name a few, all filled similar roles that they had played in previous practices of moral formation. For Gregory, however, imitation of characters was not a stepping-stone to a larger goal; Christians never mastered or got beyond mimesis. Imitation was a way of life, a set of relationships that shape the soul as they deepen and expand over time. Imitation, moreover, was how God worked in the world, and how change happened. "Every kind of pursuit originates with one individual and is passed on to many," he writes. "When one individual has made something his business, that form of activity makes its way into the stream of our life by mimesis [κατὰ μίμησιν εἰς τὸν βίον τὸ ἐπιτήδευμα]."[14] Imitation was both the source and aim of transformation. The new ways of life reshaped what participation in God looked like. New modes of holy living became possible not only because one individual performed it, but also because this life had been put in the "living water," flowed into common sense.

Gregory described this process in aesthetic terms, too. Like an artist "applying the chisel with blows to the carving of letters," the Holy Spirit, "by means of continuous repetition," engraves characters into the memories of those seeking perfection. "The goal of the economy of the Holy Spirit [πρὸς τοῦτο γὰρ οἶμαι τὴν τοῦ ἁγίου πνεύματος οἰκονομίαν ὁρᾶν] is to set forth the previous accomplishments of holy ones for guidance for the life after these accomplishments, the representation leading us forward to good which is equal and similar [πρὸς τὸ ἴσον τε καὶ ὅμοιον ἀγαθὸν προαγούσης ἡμᾶς τῆς μιμήσεως]."[15] God's economy, the saving work of the Spirit, makes humans into the image of God. And it does so mimetically, like an artist crafting characters that are "carved into the soul."

This work of engraving and creating characters calls for a quick clarification before moving through the chapter. The Greek word χαρακτήρ most often signified less a "character" in a play and more an engraving, impress, or seal—a way of marking something moldable that signifies possession (as in the image of the emperor on a coin) or that provides a distinctive mark by which it is set apart. As we saw above, Gregory will turn to theatrical images. But the dual meaning of the word suggests how these mimetic relationships form: characters (in the theatrical sense) become characters (impresses) on the soul. Mimesis in the Christian life imprinted sacred lives, and in that impression the soul expanded and took a particular shape.

Gregory's writings most interested in the infinitude of God and in human desire for the infinite are also the writings most concentrated with and reliant on imitating characters. That is, the increased emphasis on divine incomparability intensified the production of mimetic characters.[16] What I suggest as importantly distinctive in Gregory, then, is his link between epektasis and mimesis. Incomparability was part of ethical formation. Ethical examples for formation were not so separable from theology when "God is absolute virtue,"[17] and virtuous subjects represented the divine as they participated in God. Christians were to model their lives in accordance with the divine, but the reverse was also true: imitators of God stylized the divine for others. In these varied saints, who all imitate an infinite God, readers found "sparks to light up our understanding of the object of our quest," namely, the presence of God.[18]

This chapter, then, examines two of the most important mimetic characters in Gregory's writings: Moses and Macrina.[19] If Gregory of Nazianzus saw theology as a kind of stage, Gregory of Nyssa put characters on stage to provide something with which Christians could identify and in which they could participate. While they were human characters, they were also images of an infinite God. Examining Gregory's readings of Moses and Macrina focuses this chapter's main questions: How did mimetic characters make possible participation in and representation of the divine? And how did their "perfect" mimesis heighten the contrast between human and divine while also inviting participation into that shared life?

We will see Gregory deploy different literary techniques that both demonstrated how Christian perfection could heighten the sense of divine incomparability as Christians deepened their participation in God and represented the ineffable. Moses dramatized Gregory's understanding of epektasis as the life of perfection in virtue. But Moses's distance from contemporary Christian life required Gregory to bend history toward the life of virtue to show Moses as an image of God. Macrina, by contrast, taught what mimesis of God looks like in the present. Telling their stories, and imitating them in life, required different practices of mimesis.

Imitation of these characters, we will see, became the access point to the life of Christian perfection, a crossing of infinitude, virtue, and humanity. "The purpose of theology [τοῖς περὶ θεοῦ λόγοις]," Gregory wrote, "is not to think up resounding and harmonious verbal beauty, but to identify a reverent notion by which what befits the thought of God may be kept intact."[20] The "reverent notion" was not limited to divine names or epektatic places. As these holy men and women became more glorious, more worthy of reverence, the call to imitate them grew louder.

Biographies and Saints in Late Ancient Christianity

Gregory wrote at a time when the relationship between the Christian and the saint was contested. Chapter 3 highlighted how late ancient Christians debated the role of the saints in the pursuit of virtue. Were the saints to be worshiped or imitated? Gregory, I have been arguing, wanted to hold onto both impulses rushing through Christian discourse around the saints. His understanding of mimesis makes imitation and inimitability not opposites as much as conditions of possibility for one another. Michael Williams argues that early Christian biographies "functioned not in the imperative but rather in the *indicative*. They represented a proposition about the world in which their readers lived."[21] If we examine what Williams calls the "proposition" that the subjects of biography offer, however, we will see that in the lives Gregory represented and called readers to imitate, the line between imperative and indicative is at least hazy. Or rather, these characters represented reality, but "reality" had a pull to it. Gregory hitched reality to an endless participation in God.[22]

Françoise Meltzer and Jaś Elsner write, "The holy man or woman provides a space in which to think differently, to think against and outside socially normative patterns.... The saint is a figure of mediation who by definition enacts or suggests 'vertical' access to a supernatural power or higher dimension of being. As such, the saint is a point of intensification and cannot help but therefore be a source of seduction."[23] For Gregory, mimetic characters could not be imitated by simply doing what they did. Imitating them required engagement with and seduction by the inimitable God who was enacted or evoked by these characters. Inimitable characters, Gregory might have said, were the only ones worth imitating. Only they had a seductive force strong enough to pull Christians out from the mud of sin and delusion and into the life of virtue. We see this first in Moses.

Moses: Infinitude and Virtue, or Imitation in the Dark

Written at the end of Gregory's life, likely for a group of monks, *The Life of Moses* is a book about virtue. Some manuscripts circulated with the title *On the Virtues,* and at least one as *On the Perfection of Virtue in Which the Life of Moses Is Examined* [ἱστορεῖται].[24] The connection between virtue and Moses would be clear enough (archetype and image, ideal and example) if virtue were a mere human activity. But God is "absolute virtue [παντελὴς ἀρετή],"[25] and "whoever pursues true virtue participates in nothing other than God, because God is absolute virtue."[26] Because God is "absolute virtue" and there can be no containing God, there can be no containing perfection in virtue. There is no endpoint on which the ladder of virtue can rest, no archetypical goal toward which one can strive. "In the case of virtue," Gregory writes, "its one limit of perfection is the fact that it has no limit."[27] Moses, virtue, and infinity are at the center of Gregory's ascetic and theological project, and they come together around mimesis.

The Life of Moses worries over and is motivated by mimetic relationships—relationships between readers and Moses, between Moses and God, and between readers and God. Mimesis defines the reader's relation to God, to Moses, and to the text; it gives rise to both the aim and the reading practices it employs toward that aim. To read Moses correctly, one must be able to imitate him as the image of God. The role of mimesis in the treatise, in short, is paramount to understanding Gregory's project.

Why, then, in this treatise concerned with the infinitude of God who is absolute virtue, did Gregory present readers with a mimetic character? The question goes to the heart of how Gregory sees God expanding the soul in love. But the question is so obvious that most commentaries do not bother to try to answer it.[28] Hans Boersma is an exception in that he deals directly with the question of Moses's role in the treatise. Moses, Boersma rightly argues, is not one of many "external examples—with the Christian following the example of Moses, who in turn follows the example of Christ (and of God)."[29] Moses is to be imitated because his life is constituted by participation in Christ. As Moses grows in virtue, he grows in the same God in whom contemporary Christians participate, and therefore imitation of Moses becomes a way of participating in the same God as Moses.[30] Imitating Moses involves imitating the infinite God in whom Moses participates, and, for Gregory, the contact between finite and infinite "sparks" and lights up the path toward virtue. The mimetic names, spaces, and characters—those standards that attract Moses and that he, in turn, becomes—remain exposed to the God who always exceeds them.

Writing Infinity

The famous turn to "epektasis" is often seen as a question of participating in the infinite,[31] which it is; but seeing participation and representation work together clarifies Gregory's emphasis on biography, the representation of a life, a character, meant to aid the life of perfection. Said differently, epektasis is best understood as a working out of these combined discourses of mimetic relationships.

Gregory likens his treatise to fans who "participate in the race with their eyes, thinking to incite the charioteer to keener effort, at the same time urging the horses on while leaning forward and flailing the air with their outstretched hands instead of with a whip."[32] His writing, that is, imitates the actions of those racers who are "straining [συντεινομένου] for the prize of the heavenly calling."[33] In so doing he spurs his readers "to increase your speed."[34] This writing does not primarily provide an accurate image; it intensifies desire, which is how readers achieve perfection. Gregory writes to cheer on his readers. He holds up a mirror in which they can see themselves as an image of God. Readers here are defined by that which transcends them. They find themselves in relation to the prize, the God who is revealed but always beyond the edge of comprehension.

With this analogy in place, Gregory notes that his treatise responds to a request to "trace in outline . . . what the perfect life is."[35] He does not point immediately to Moses. Instead he draws attention to questions of representation that will also pattern the participatory relationship between human and divine. "It is beyond my power to encompass perfection in my treatise or to show in my life the insights of the treatise," he writes.[36] The troubles of representation—the limited nature of words, language's constant reaching for something beyond its ken—become the problems of participation. The impossibility of literary realism—of representing the divine as it is—coincides with the impossibility of arriving at perfection. Gregory can write beyond what he can live, and while that writing remains inadequate, it still pushes him toward God.

This impossible mode of showing perfection gives way to another: "the perfection of human nature consists perhaps in its very growth in goodness."[37] With this model of perfection in place, readers meet their main character. Moses imitates God by desiring with a desire that "necessarily has no stopping place but stretches out with the limitless."[38] Watching Moses grow in participation, for Gregory, provides the best sketch of perfection because he represents to readers what limitlessness looks like and at the same time makes the contrast between himself and God sharper.[39] A less virtuous life could leave the reader thinking that a perfect resemblance is possible, if not yet attained. Moses's life, however, reveals an unspeakable beauty that surpasses even those who most perfectly imitate it. By the end of the text, readers are left with twin convictions: that Moses "has truly come to be in the image of God . . . bear[ing] in himself . . . the distinguishing marks [of the divine character]"; and that "none of those things known by human comprehension is to be ascribed to [God]."[40] Moses's life, for Gregory, represents divine infinitude: his endless changing likens him to God (in its endlessness) while magnifying the creator/creation distinction (in its "changing").

What Do You Imitate When You Imitate Moses?

What, then, is Moses's role in the treatise? "God," not Moses, is "our guide [καθηγεμόνα] in our treatise [λόγου],"[41] Gregory writes. But "by imitating those earlier examples of success [προκατορθωκότων] those who follow them may direct [ἀπευθύνοιτο] their lives to the good."[42] Moses is such an example. "The memory" of him provides "a beacon light . . . amid the storms of life," and shows how "we can bring our soul to the sheltered harbor of virtue."[43] But the treatise repeatedly asks: What kind of an example figures the infinite? What do you imitate when you imitate Moses?

Williams rightfully points out that the subjects of early Christian biographies, the characters, do not simply provide something to aspire to; they reveal something about reality.[44] These characters stand in for the deepest truths of their world. As Williams reads it, however, *The Life of Moses* emerges from a concession: because "virtue is impossible to attain," readers are to turn to the next best thing, namely, a Christian success story. The answer to how Moses's life can govern (ἀπευθύνω) and grow in Christian perfection, Williams argues, lies in looking toward another character in the text: Basil, who functions as a contemporary Moses. Basil reenacts the biblical hero, and Christians are to imitate the new Moses if they are to attain Christian perfection.[45] Williams's account, that is, sees the "reality" that Gregory represents as a social order with Moses as the ideal episcopal figure. Once readers find someone more contemporary, imitation becomes a simple, do-as-I-do imitation.

Gregory was certainly concerned with episcopal control even into his late age, but the mimetic relationship with Moses is first and foremost a mimetic relationship with God. Moses is worthy of imitation because he participates in and represents God. "The fact that Moses did attain the perfection which was possible"[46] leads Gregory to reflect on the relationship between Moses, infinitude, and mimesis. The reality Moses represents is at least as much the divine as it is ecclesial, which is not to deny the role of the Church as much as it is to point to where the text draws its readers' attention. Moses, moreover, is an image of the incarnate Christ, though in a particular way: he is an image of an infinite Christ who is both present and always ahead, and, therefore, he proleptically imitates what is to come.[47] My reading of The Life of Moses builds upon Williams's and asks: How does one imitate an infinite reality?[48] Whatever Moses is, imitating him requires a more complex mimetic relationship than a straightforward, do-as-he-does relationship. A more contemporary archetype alone will not solve Gregory's problem.

Mimetic relations in The Life of Moses run up against two problems that imperfectly mirror each other. The first is what I might call the infinitude problem. God, as we saw, is "absolute virtue," which means that virtue is limitless and thus any finite image of virtue around which the mind can contract is necessarily incomplete. The second is the history problem. How does one imitate the past or another material life? "Everyone knows," Gregory writes, "that anything placed in a world of change never remains the same but is always passing from one state to another."[49] There can be no pure repetitions in this life. Gregory anticipates a hypothetical reader interjecting, "I was not nourished by the daughter of the Egyptian." What does "my life" have to do with "the ancients?" Or "How shall I place myself in the same rank with one of them, when I do not know how to imitate anyone so far removed from me by the circumstances of his life?"[50] The inimitability of God and of Moses both, in Gregory's telling, should lead readers to question their conceptions of mimesis. Imitating Moses's life requires a "subtlety of

understanding and keenness of vision," both because Moses's life is inseparable from that of the infinite God and because repeating the force of Moses's actions requires doing so in a different time and place, which troubles
any simple claims about doing what Moses did.[51]

We see this first in the structure of the text. *The Life of Moses* is famously
divided into two parts—an "obvious" historical reading that "amplified the
account as to bring out its intention,"[52] and a contemplative reading of the
narrative that invites participation and representation. The relationship between the two parts is difficult to pin down exactly. Calling them a literal
and then a spiritual reading does not quite capture the complexity of the
first part, which is not "literal." Gregory does not simply quote Exodus and
Numbers the way he will interpret the Beatitudes or Ecclesiastes. He boils
the scriptural account down to biography, and then, "so that we might gain
some benefit for the virtuous life," he "adapt[s] [ἐφαρμόσαι] the life . . . to
the aim [σκοπὸν] we have proposed for our study [λόγου]."[53] As he informs
readers in the second part, "if the events require dropping from the literal
account anything written which is foreign to the sequence of elevated understanding [ἔξω τοῦ εἱρμοῦ τῆς ἀνηγμένης διανοίας], we pass over this on
the grounds that it is useless and unprofitable to our purpose [σκοπὸν
ἀλυσιτελὲς καὶ ἀνόνητον]."[54] Representation of history, like representation
of God, requires adaption if it is to be profitable.

What is often dubbed his "spiritual" or "allegorical" reading, then, turns
on the possibility of mimetic relation. Only in a mimetic relationship can
one move from the "literal events" to perfection in virtue.[55] It is "impossible
to imitate the marvels of these blessed men in these exact events," Gregory
acknowledges. Mimesis happens when readers "substitute a moral teaching
[ἠθικὴν διδασκαλίαν] for the material sequence [ὑλικῆς ἀκολουθίας]."[56]
Much hangs, then, on how we read this "moral teaching." It is not a way of
substituting the "moral of the story" for the story itself. Nor is it Aristotle's
moral virtue as opposed to intellectual (διανοητικός) virtue.[57] We should
see it, rather, as an instance of the popular distinction in ancient biographical literature between acts (πρᾶξις) and character (ἦθος). Patricia Cox Miller
has shown how history, from Plutarch to Xenophon forward, often concerns
itself with *praxeis*, whereas biography is about *ēthos*.[58] The binary does not
always hold, but it was one that late ancient readers could recognize. In examining the *ēthos*, biographers "laid bare the soul" of their subjects, drawing on history.[59] It may even link back to the *Republic*'s emphasis on mimesis
creating a particular "disposition [ἤθει] of the soul."[60]

Proper imitation of Moses requires repeating the "intention [ὑπόθεσιν]" of the text, which requires an intimacy and an understanding of the purpose of the story, the attainment of perfection in virtue.[61] In fact, the word ὑπόθεσις, in addition to its more common meaning, can have a theatrical association, as in the "role" (ὑπόθεσις) of an actor following a "script" (ἱστορία).[62] Successful actors must understand their character's (ὑπόθεσις) character (ἔθος) if they are to represent them on life's stage, which is precisely what the second part of the text offers. Readers must first know the story and then, like Moses, after "a long time,"[63] they can find deeper truths in it.

For Gregory, to understand Moses requires looking at his soul and what is imprinted on it: his character (χαρακτήρ), the image of God. Christians are to "copy the imprint [χαρακτῆρα] of the beauty which has been shown to us by imitating [μιμήσεως] [Moses's] way of life."[64] To see Moses as participating in and constituted by God is to see him showing forth a God beyond understanding. In this imitation a connection point appears at the crossing of Moses, God, and the reader. "Rather than seeking to stand in for what's 'really' there," Rowan Williams writes, "a representation is the 'thereness' of the object in relation to the perceiver."[65] Moses is not an obstacle that humans must get past to see God; he is the God on offer, the Christic image in whom readers can participate.[66]

Moses's Mimetic Desire

Gregory's most sustained treatment of epektasis is framed as the solution to an exegetical problem: How is it that Moses at once sees God "face to face, as a man speaks with his friend" and also "that God appear[ed] to him, as though he who is always visible had not yet been seen, as though Moses had not yet attained what Scripture testifies he had indeed attained?"[67] Not only is the larger frame here one of a mimetic relationship (what does it mean to imitate God through Moses in the present?), but Moses's own paradox is mimetic. Moses asks to see God "not in mirrors and reflections, but face to face," and yet the paradox only heightens as readers learn that a mimetic relationship keeps God's presence and reflecting mirrors tethered. The phrase "not in mirrors and reflections, but face to face" of course immediately brings Paul's words to the Corinthians to mind,[68] but it also taps into the mimetic discourse that goes back to the *Republic*'s critique of the poets. If Socrates's chief accusation against the poets was that they seduced people into giving in to their most base desires, Gregory's reading tells Christians that what they see in Moses should inspire their loftiest. Socrates argued that poets tell lies that people desperately want to believe and so are nearly incapable of resisting; Gregory shows in Moses a truth that Christians should want to believe and so must grow into. Moses challenges this distinction between "mirrors" and presence in that the images seen in mirrors spur desire for what is beyond them even as that excess conjures more images.[69] Moses wants to stretch mimesis into reality, and in that longing, he more fully imitates the ineffable. The inadequacy of representation shows the way to grow in participation in God. Moses's desire constantly expands his participation in God and also leads him to ever more representations of God.

Keeping representation and participation entwined here is key to how Moses grows. "Hope always draws the soul from the beauty which is seen to what is beyond, always kindles the desire for the hidden through what is constantly perceived. Therefore, the ardent lover of beauty, although receiving what is always visible as an image of what he desires, yet longs to be filled with the very stamp of the archetype [αὐτοῦ τοῦ χαρακτῆρος τοῦ ἀρχετύπου ἐμφορηθῆναι ἐπιποθεῖ]."[70] The images that pull Moses more fully into God change as Moses attaches to different representations and then advances past them. But the images also structure the way he desires. As Moses takes in images of desire, he is exposed to ever greater images that further draw his desire. He is "granted what is requested in what was denied."[71] Images of God stretch Moses ahead of himself, leaving him longing for more.

In the stretching, Moses at once becomes most like God and contrasts with God more sharply. Gregory writes, "What Moses yearned for is satisfied by the very things which leave his desire unsatisfied" because the boundary that makes God visible evokes "with that boundary what is beyond it."[72] God allows Moses to grasp what is visible, but in that grasping, something new breaks open. "Every desire for the Good which is attracted to that ascent constantly expands as one progresses in pressing on to the Good. This truly is the vision of God: never to be satisfied in the desire to see him. But one must always, by looking at what he can see, rekindle his desire to see more. Thus, no limit would interrupt growth in the ascent to God, since no limit to the Good can be found nor is the increasing desire for the Good brought to an end because it is satisfied."[73] Readers learn of God here, not by examining God straight on, but by watching Moses, whose desire imitates the infinite. Taking in what is visible "as an image of what he desires," he finds that the more he grasps, the more there is to grasp. Moses becomes in this mimetic reading the God that appears, the place of intensity that carries more than it can hold; and like Moses himself, readers are to see in him that which surpasses him.

Mimesis in the Dark

This endless growth eventually leads Moses into "the darkness," a place that should void any representation. The darkness, however, becomes another place to participate in the divine. There is no ontological fusing that swallows difference. Rather, Moses continues to advance even when he bumps against (and thus transforms) ontological limits. He imitates what he finds in the darkness. What is impossible ontologically can still be achieved mimetically.

Moses's entrance into the mysterious darkness dramatizes a larger late ancient Christian representational practice. The Christian "redefinition of the holy," Elsner argues, "lies in its passage into a hidden space of the mysterious (even mystic) secrecy whose existence was announced and access to which was enabled through material framing and visual representation."[74] As a gemmed box might hold a precious, secret, mysterious relic, so Moses's life holds the sacred.[75] In him comes an intensity of holiness that glows even in the darkness. He contains more than he can hold, and his holiness makes the holiness of God all the more vibrant.

Moses figures unknowability. His continued participation in God also displays something of God, even—or especially—to those who lose sight of him. In Gregory's historical reading, Moses becomes invisible as he joins company with the invisible God. In the contemplative reading, Moses fades into "darkness" as he "comes to apprehend reality [τῆς τῶν ὄντων κατανοήσεως]."[76] When "Moses entered the darkness and then saw God in it," all readers see of Moses is his progression in "yearning" (πολυπραγμοσύνη). "That which is sought transcends all knowledge, being separated on all sides by incomprehensibility as by a kind of darkness."[77] That densely sacred luminous darkness shows how participation in God brings about representations of God that make clear the difference between humanity and divinity. All readers can see are spinning, paradoxical images—such as "the luminous darkness"[78]—that represent an infinite desire for the infinite. And yet Moses, in the darkness, is shown a tabernacle and is told to "represent [μιμήσασθαι] in material construction that immaterial creation."[79] In his stretching, a space for participation appears. Moses is led to the darkness, "to the place where his intelligence lets him slip in where God is." And "when he arrives there, he shows it to others by a material representation [διὰ τῆς ὑλικῆς μιμήσεως]."[80] This then is the key movement to the treatise: Moses, the image of God, fades into the darkness and reappears through mimesis. Names, spaces, and characters all fall short, but through them Christians can keep moving. Infinity and virtue come together in mimesis.

Like the names of God, Moses must stretch and at a certain point fade out to allow readers an image of the divine. And, like the names of God, Moses will reappear to show new mimetic possibilities. Moses does not attain the divine essence there, but in representing what is revealed in the darkness, new places of participation are opened. In short, what is taken away ontologically reappears mimetically.

I now turn to another character and another literary technique designed to spur imitation of the infinite.

Macrina: Teaching Character

"She was for us a teacher of how to live [τοῦ βίου διδάσκαλος]," Gregory writes of his beloved sister.[81] Macrina was one of many teachers for Gregory. Basil, Paul, Moses, Gregory Thaumaturgus, Theodore, Solomon, David, and the bride from the Song of Songs all come to mind quickly. But in Macrina especially we see how Gregory taught Christian perfection through characters.

Morwenna Ludlow has called Gregory the "archetypal pupil" of late antiquity,[82] and in late antiquity student-teacher relationships were primarily mimetic. Desire and imitation were inseparable as great teachers of antiquity seduce, and their seduction heated the souls of the students to fit their teacher's mold.[83] Students became not only what they were taught, but the one who taught them. As Macrina drew Gregory to herself, Gregory drew readers to his teacher, and that pull revealed in her and those around her an image of God. Gregory presents himself as Macrina's faithful student in his ability both to remember and to imitate her, the two qualities Libanius looked for in a potential pupil.[84] He preserved her memory in his representation of her.

Learning how to imitate, however, was always about more than imitating what Cicero called the "the obvious" things (dress, gestures, etc.). What mattered in imitation was imitation of "the form" (*formam*) or, Cicero turned to Greek to be more precise, the "character" (χαρακτὴρ), the distinctive, often ineffable style of the teacher.[85] Gregory, then, also showed readers, though his writing, what mimesis should look like. While her body passed away, mimesis of her, in writing and in life, revealed an infinite image, the true "character," in which he and the other characters around her participate.

The story shows his sister growing from a young girl of noble birth to a monastic organizer and near angel. Through denial and cultivation of desire for God, she made "manifest to those then present that pure, divine love [ἔρωτα] of the unseen bridegroom."[86] Divine love became present love, and in writing her story, the pupil became the teacher. Writing, that is, both kept Gregory bound to his teacher and allowed him to continue her work of straining toward God and moving others toward God, so that they might "have in themselves plenty of room [εὐρυχωρίαν] for faith."[87] By drawing readers into the saint's life, *The Life of Macrina* and its companion text, written later,[88] *On the Soul and the Resurrection*, offered a point of transcendence, not only in philosophical acuity, but also in the life of his great teacher,[89] and with him they too can learn to glimpse the infinite in her.

My reading highlights two ways Gregory presents Macrina as the mimesis of God (and thus also the God on offer in her), which instructs as it expands. First, she shows forth the invisible as she transcends the prescribed roles of a Roman noblewoman. Her changing "characters" perform the paradox we saw at the opening of the chapter, where the multiplication of characters reveals a sacred glow illuminating the holy life. Learning the life of perfection from Macrina requires watching her multiply and, behind that multiplication, seeing the God who stretches her.[90] Second, she forms a *community* in the image of God. For Gregory, the "true image" of God is not any one individual, but all of humanity together. In the formation of a community imitating Macrina's indiscrete image, Gregory presents an image of the ineffable.

Genre and Gender

To see how Gregory will offer points of contact with the divine through mimesis in *The Life of Macrina* requires some understanding of the genre and thinking about the role of gender. (The two are of course related. Gregory, along with many of the late ancient Christian biographers, never doubts that a woman could signify the holy, but the way that holiness is revealed is gendered.)[91] Even if Elsner is right that in Byzantium, "every event, text and image could be read as an exegesis of the one fundamental and real event—namely, the Incarnation as represented by the narrative of Christ's life and Passion,"[92] that Macrina can be a reading or repetition of Christ's life requires some understanding of how Christ reappears in the *Life*. Where is Christ here? And how does one learn to recognize Christ?

The *Life* defines itself as a "letter" that has grown into a narrative,[93] bringing it quite close to a biography, an attempt to write the truth of a life through a few powerful episodes.[94] In those punctuating moments, readers can see sparks of the divine. Unlike with Moses, however, with Macrina, Gregory does not need to perform a "contemplative" reading.[95] Representing their "*charactēr*" happens differently. If Gregory was concerned with both the history and the infinity problems there, the problems do not entirely go away, but they must be addressed differently. Macrina still cannot be approached directly; her *Life* is still accommodated for its readers, and thus how her life mimetically relates to the divine differs as well.

If part of showing readers Christ in *The Life of Moses* involved bringing him closer, showing readers Christ in Macrina involved defamiliarizing her. In *Letter* 19, which is something of a first sketch of what will become *The Life of Macrina*, Gregory describes Macrina in terms recognizable to readers of the *Life*. She lived with a "choir of virgins whom she had brought forth by her spiritual labor pains." Her community sang the Psalms day and night. She had attuned her ears "to divine things," lived with a boldness and freedom (παρρησία), and taught others to do the same. Gregory asks, "how indeed could one bring before the eyes a reality that transcends description in words?"[96] The letter's broader aim was to demonstrate to "a certain John" in Antioch that while Gregory had recently undergone hardships, he was still a capable, orthodox Bishop. But when Gregory sat down to write the *Life*, that question continued to haunt him. What container could hold her uncontainable life? To show readers Christ in Macrina, it would not be enough to make the declarative statements. God would appear through a series of transformations, by taking a seemingly typical Roman woman and showing readers what a transformation into the life of perfection would look like.

Telling this story involved more than holding up a mirror to Macrina's life. Gregory gave it shape, put it into a recognizable genre, which he could transform.[97] Perhaps most importantly, Macrina's *Life* is staged as Plato's *Phaedo*, with clear connections to the *Symposium*, casting her as a Socrates or Diotima.[98] For both, the rapidly approaching death of the great teacher intensifies discussions of the soul and desire. Gregory's recasting, though, is more than swapping names in set scripts.[99] The staging, for one, shifts, as the "prayer space" (φροντιστήριον)[100] has replaced the jail cell. But, most importantly for our purposes, the way the characters represent the Good differs. Socrates's famously ugly body shows a beautiful soul; his ironic body speaks to a different kind of beauty. Macrina by contrast is so beautiful that no painter could capture her beauty, and her family needs to protect her from the "great swarm of suitors."[101] The word imitation (μίμησις), in fact, appears for the first time in the treatise in a discussion of her overwhelming beauty. The challenge for Gregory as a writer and for anyone who would imitate her in their life is to find the right organization or structures of desire for imitating a beauty too great for words.[102] We see not necessarily two different teaching styles, but different ways of viewing the teachers, of finding the "charactēr." To use Elsner's distinction, Socrates deconstructs beauty; Macrina symbolizes Christ's beauty, "naturally" becoming a container of the uncontainable.[103] Readers need not cut through layers of irony to see her truth; they are drawn closer, and the closer they get the more they are exposed to what they cannot comprehend.

Macrina's "biography" is not a search for the historical Macrina.[104] Her character performs a theological function, stylizing the divine, becoming a way to "conceptualize" the unknown, a way that, as Gregory writes elsewhere, "we find out things we do not know, using what is connected and consequent upon our first idea of a subject to discover what lies beyond."[105] Gender is not immune to this "symbolic" treatment. It moves in and out of focus, at once the most obvious thing about the saint and something she transcends. Macrina "rose above nature" as she imitated and rushed toward God,[106] and yet she "transcended" gender not so much in removing it as by multiplying it. Her taking on multiple characters over the course of the treatise troubles any stable understanding of gender and shows readers what holiness looks like.[107]

We should be careful, then, not to reduce Macrina to a purely symbolic figure. Late ancient biographical literature values both literal "truthfulness" and spiritual content.[108] Gregory, learning from his teacher, holds back from telling more stories of her because she so exceeds the "yardstick" of most people's experience that they are liable to "have no respect" for it, "suspecting it is false and outside of the truth."[109] He has to compress her life to fit within the small faith of his readers, so that once inside, it might expand them. But he also impresses on the reader that he knew her and that their intimacy authorizes him to speak. His training under her lets him teach.[110]

Gregory's twin imperatives—to present Macrina accurately and to show the divine in her—requires a kind of literary distortion necessary to reflect and render present the divine. Truthfulness and literary stylization or symbolism are not mutually exclusive.[111] In Macrina's biography, staged as a deathbed scene of a famous teacher, readers "come into contact with the divine nature [τῆς θείας φύσεως ἐφαπτομένη]"[112] and learn how to imitate God more fully.

Macrina and Her Pedagogical Images

Gregory provides some hints as to how to read Macrina. In *On the Soul and the Resurrection*, written about three years after the *Life*, Macrina's theorization of the soul helps readers see hers as an image of God.

> It [the soul] imitates the superior life [τὴν ὑπερέχουσαν μιμεῖται ζωὴν], being conformed to the properties of the divine Nature, so that nothing else is left to it but the disposition of love, as it becomes attached in its nature to the beautiful [τῆς ἀγαπητικῆς διαθέσεως, φυσικῶς τῷ καλῷ προσφυομένη] .... So when the soul that has become a simple and uniform and accurate image of God finds that truly simple and immaterial good, the one thing which is really lovable and desirable [τι ἀγαπητὸν καὶ ἐράσμιον], it attaches itself to it and combines with it through the movement and operation of love [διὰ τῆς ἀγαπητῆς κινήσεώς τε καὶ ἐνεργείας]. It conforms itself to that which is always being grasped and found and comes into being through its likeness to the good, that is, it is the nature of that in which it participates [ὅπερ ἡ τοῦ μετεχομένου φύσις ἐστίν].[113]

Her teaching forms a larger "way of life" of participating in and representing the divine. The constant expansion leaves nothing but a "disposition of love." Her soul, however, does not become "simple and uniform" through a gradual stilling, but through "the movement and operation of love [διὰ τῆς ἀγαπητῆς κινήσεώς τε καὶ ἐνεργείας]." Her "erotic disposition"[114] creates an "accurate image" precisely because it opens new ways of loving, and her progression in love provides new images to be "grasped and found." In her, readers see that "the accurate likeness of the divine consists in our soul's mimesis [μιμεῖσθαί] of the superior nature."[115] Her soul longs for God who defines the soul, and marks it as different. The more accurate her representation, the clearer it is that archetype transcends the image and will require more images.

Multiplying Characters

Gregory narrates a slow peeling away of expected norms of upper-class female virtue that results in Macrina's ability to show the "invisible presence" of God. Readers see not a radical conversion from one way of life to another that could then congeal into one archetypal life, but a slow growth in God that gradually accelerates as an increasing set of paradoxical characters are held together across the saint's life. As Susanna Elm argues, Gregory narrates her life around a series of turning points that each require different characters.[116] Each scene slowly finds its focus and stills for just long enough to dramatize a defining characteristic, and then the story propels forward toward a new character, a new role.

At the opening, Macrina is a devout, if conventional, daughter. She knows the scriptures, especially the Psalms, and remains uncorrupted by pagan literature. She begins to break the mold when her fiancé dies. She tells her parents that because he is still alive in Christ, she ought not marry another. In her role as widow-virgin, she takes on household work, dresses plainly, dedicates herself to the liturgies, and helps her mother, Emmelia, manage her estate.

Macrina's fidelity to God and to her family is only strengthened when her father dies, and her life of perfection advances more quickly. She serves her mother, but more, Gregory adds, "by the example of her own life she provided great guidance to her mother towards the same goal, namely that of philosophy, drawing her on little by little to the immaterial, more perfect life."[117] The mother-daughter relationship does not dissolve, but it stretches. Perfection reshapes their relationship, and daughter now leads mother. They give up "their rather ostentatious life-style" to "share a common life with all her maids, making them sisters and equals instead of slaves and servants."[118] This equalizing goes hand-in-hand with what Gregory describes as a "freedom" or "boldness" (παρρησία), which also defined Adam in the garden.[119]

Gregory stresses that Macrina's love of asceticism transforms the entire family.[120] She inspires "the great Basil," "swiftly" turning him from rhetoric to the life of virtue "and the subsequent activities for which he became famous."[121] Gregory hammers home the point: after converting Basil, the great monastic organizer, to the holy life, it is again Macrina who founds a community in "imitation of the life of the angels." Living the "life of the angels" and the transformation of her familial roles only multiplies the parts she can play. Instructing readers in how she raises her brother Peter, Gregory writes, "She became everything for the child, father, teacher, guide, mother, counsellor in every good, and she perfected him in such a way that before he left childhood, while he was still blossoming at the tender stage of adolescent youth, he was lifted up towards the sublime goal of philosophy."[122] Under her training, he was "of no less repute than the great Basil."[123] Her philosophical way of life allows her to move easily between roles and leads others to Christ, as they too take up her Christian philosophy.[124]

She again changes from philosopher to athlete as she wards off attacks of grief from her mother's and brother's deaths and "reveal[s] the authentic and undebased nature of her soul [ἀναδειχθῆναι τὸ τῆς ψυχῆς ἀκιβδήλευτόν τε καὶ ἀταπείνωτον]."[125] The conquering of the passions in the face of death demonstrates just how different Macrina was from expected gender norms. These paradoxical roles prepare the reader for an even more intense encounter.

Joining the Teacher

Having spoken of her from a distance, Gregory enters the story, both heightening the importance of the scene and modeling how to learn from the great teacher. Just before he approaches "the holy place"[126] where Macrina dwelled, he shapes his readers' expectations by sharing a vision he has of her. In a dream, he holds relics of the martyrs (among whom Gregory has just characterized Macrina by calling her an "athlete"), and from them comes "a bright gleam of light, as from a flawless mirror which had been placed to face the sun, so that my eyes were blinded by the brilliance of the gleam."[127] That blinding brilliance—a brilliance the narrator has to put into inadequate words—does not stop Gregory; the awe ushers him into Macrina's presence and lets readers know that if they had not seen her as an image of the infinite before, they soon will.

If Moses's life becomes imitable in Gregory's contemplative reading, here the narration shows (rather than tells) what imitation of God should look like. Macrina, dwelling in the "holy place," recounts the story of her life as a thanks offering (εὐχαριστία) to God.[128] This eucharistic representation continues her participation in God and invites others into her life. As Derek

Krueger writes, "Macrina gives license to Gregory's act of narration by giving biography an explicitly religious purpose. She teaches him how to do Christian biography by providing him, in her own narration, a model to imitate."[129] In telling her narrative, she "makes her flesh logos," and Gregory, "like a priest presiding over the eucharist . . . repeats the offering of Macrina's logos for the nourishment of others."[130] Storytelling itself accelerates her movement toward her beloved, and the vortex of her upward ascent sweeps readers into that love.

Her autobiographical narration merges with her "contemplation of beauty," and in those final hours, "it was as if an angel had providentially assumed human form, an angel in whom there was no affinity for, nor attachment to, the life of the flesh." This lack of attachment to the flesh, though, makes her only more pedagogically effective: "For this reason, she seemed to me to be making manifest to those then present that pure, divine love of the unseen bridegroom, which she had nourished secretly in the most intimate depths of her soul [ἐν τοῖς τῆς ψυχῆς ἀπορρήτοις], and she seemed to transmit the desire which was in her heart to rush to the one she longed for, so that freed from the fetters of the body, she might swiftly be with him. For it was really towards her beloved that she ran, and no other of life's pleasures ever turned her eye to itself away from her beloved."[131] Readers sense, without quite seeing, that secret center of deepest desire, her longing for the bridegroom as it shapes her in his image.[132] Her body shines out that most intimate, ineffable (ἀπόρρητος) part of her soul. Finding herself in the one she loves, her soul reflects and refracts in her body the God who became flesh.

In Macrina we see the broader late ancient assumption that matter itself was unstable but could, with training, strain, stabilize, and ascend to God. *On the Soul and the Resurrection* emphasizes that the human body is constantly remade in this life and will continue to in the resurrection. Not simply a container or form but a kind of code that endlessly reassembles, the body's only stability is its ability to change, even enduring radical changes like seeds that become plants.[133] Mirroring God rematerializes Macrina's body and dramatizes the possibilities of even more change to come. As she lies dying, however, Macrina's body mirrors her soul in the sense that the body inverts the soul: her body stills as her soul races. And yet Gregory is able to perceive that flight. Just as the push toward the immaterial stretched her relationship with her mother, here the infinite on offer in her *Life* is not a flight from, nor even the ascent beyond, the body, but a sacrament (εὐχαριστία), an intimate connection between flesh and spirit that mirrors and transforms this world.[134]

Just as God condescended to make visible what was by nature invisible, so participation in God joins that action of drawing creation back to its maker and attracting others to the infinite. A "sacramental perception" allows readers to see her as both human and divine.[135]

Macrina's *aristeia* culminates in a prayer in which reverence and imitation come together: "Remember me also in your kingdom, for I too have been crucified with you, for I have nailed my flesh out of reverence for you and have feared your judgments."[136] She traces the sign of the cross on her eyes, mouth, and heart, and "little by little" her body gives out. Her throat dries and hands stiffen as she moves toward death, and yet even in that crucified body "she realized her desire in her heart and in the movement of her hands."[137] Macrina's holiness and her growth in perfection find character in continued prayer. "Her voice was wavering and only by the parting of her lips and the movement of her hands did we recognize that she was praying." Her passionate love keeps disciplined, as "When she had completed the prayer of thanksgiving and, by bringing her hand to her face for the sign of the cross, had indicated that she had finished her prayer, she took a strong, deep breath, and with that she died."[138] That silent prayer nevertheless crystalizes her life: a single focus directed by liturgy overseen by the Church, which shows God to others. The woman who had been so many things, in the end, becomes another Christ.[139]

"The Thing Like God": Communal Characters

It is not only Macrina's life, though, that forms an infinite image. As her body moves to burial, Gregory continues assembling ever larger relationships. Readers have seen widening concentric circles from the mother-daughter dyad, to the brothers, to former slaves in Macrina's house, to a group beyond the walls of the original household-turned-institution, and at her funeral the local public will join as well.[140] There is an energy in each of these relations that seems to burst forward into a new, larger circle. "Her remote dwelling was packed tight with the crowds of people flooding in," Gregory notes.[141] More and more people throughout the treatise participate in Macrina's life, binding themselves to her as she races to the bridegroom. Through Gregory's telling, readers too are invited to join the crowd.

For Gregory, when the scriptures speak of humanity being made "in the image of God" (Gen 1:27), they speak not of any one human being but of the whole lump of humanity.[142] In the roughly contemporary *On the Making of*

Humanity, he writes, "Humanity was made in the image of God; that is, the universal nature, the thing like God [θεοείκελον χρῆμα]. It was made by the omnipotent wisdom not as part of the whole, but all the fullness of the nature all together."[143] Salvation, too, is dependent on human interconnectivity. Gregory likens the incarnation to "when some accident happens to the tip of a nail," where banging a nail through one's hand shoots through the whole body. "Because of the connection between the parts of our body, the effect is extended to the sufferer's whole body as the sensation runs through it. So he who is joined to our nature makes our sufferings his own."[144] Humanity's interconnectedness is assumed in its original and redeemed role as the image of God. Macrina too becomes a puncture wound radiating throughout the whole body of humanity. Readers join her family and community in the suffering desire that her life produces. A line from Gregory of Nazianzus's letter to Gregory of Nyssa even hints at how this union happens: "the act of yearning [ὁ πόθος] makes everything shared between us [πάντα . . . κοινοποιεῖ τὰ ἡμέτερα]."[145] By desiring with Macrina, readers share in her life, even as she travels on toward God.

Gregory points to Macrina's community in Annesi as particularly inspiring. They formed "a community whose way of life lay at the boundaries between human nature and the nature which is without body." He elaborates, "although they lived in the flesh, by virtue of their affinity with the incorporeal powers they were not weighed down by the attractive pull of the body, but their lives were borne upwards, poised on high and they took their souls' flight in concert with the heavenly powers."[146] Macrina might be the guide and glue of the community, but they, as a whole, imitate the divine as well. Drafting Macrina, the entire community obeys her, follows her, loves her, and imitates her.

In her funeral, the community continues on in Macrina's way of life after her death as well. They become, like the psalms they sing, a microcosm of "the universal nature" made in God's image. The community, governed by the bishop and tuned to the memory of the holy woman, is lifted, as it "listens to the singing of the heavens by transcending and being above the faculties of sense-perception that belong to our flesh."[147] Macrina's "band of angels" plays on as it remembers and imitates her, and in so doing they invite others into the imitation of the divine.[148] As with that other teacher whose absent body continues to make manifest the infinite God, through mimesis, Gregory's great teacher continues to pull readers forward even in her absence.

Changing Characters

In *Letter* 19, that first draft of what will become Macrina's *Life*, Gregory comments that some artists, trying to honor their "uglier friends," make them a little more beautiful than they are in life. The intention is kindness, but the "improvement" only makes visible what the painter thinks needs improving. The implicit critique stings. It forces the painted friends to recognize how the artist sees them and to rethink their relationship. Gregory warns that the "improved imitation" often erases the friend, or replaces the real friend with projected values.[149] But Gregory also hints that, with care, art can sometimes inspire new, better possibilities. A still small voice can creep in: maybe the artist is right? Maybe the image shows me something I didn't know was there? Maybe they see the real me? Some imitations are fakes. But others open into new possibilities of participation. Gregory reminds the letter's recipient, "a certain John,"[150] of a Proverb suggesting that self-knowledge requires outside forces: "they come to recognize themselves who are willing to know themselves according to the word from without [κατὰ τὸν ἔξωθεν λόγον]."[151] Knowing oneself is not a matter of cutting off all images and looking within as much as it is taking on the right words and images that can mediate a relationship within the self. An artist's imitation might prompt subjects to simulate or fantasize a new self. The imitation cracks the self-image, awakens desire for a new reality, and provides an image to guide that desire. Gregory's discussion of the artists then leads into his outline of Macrina's life. Macrina, in the *Life*, is recognizable to herself and to her community as a reflection of the Word made flesh. Moses likewise becomes a mirror in which readers can see themselves, and in finding themselves in these characters they too are spurred into deeper participation in the infinite.

Holy though they are, none of the characters manifests all of the divine. Each remains exposed to the divine excess (and all the more so in their most holy moments). But having examined Gregory's treatment of Moses and Macrina as images of God, let me conclude by returning to the chapter's opening passage. In it, Gregory likens Christian perfection to playing a series of roles in a play. Theology, here, requires producing parts to play. These are not characters outside a participatory relationship. They are not "external examples." Those seeking perfection find themselves in the lives of those who have participated in and therefore represented the divine, and with them continue stretching their desire for God. Like names and spaces, characters fill human souls, both framing and stretching them toward an unknown God.

Different moments require different characters. We see this within the characters Gregory deploys. In Chapter 4, we saw that Paul both reveres and imitates the thirty-four names of Christ. In this chapter, Moses finds himself assuming different roles (student, prophet, architect, priest, and so on), and Macrina is a daughter, fiancée, sister, "father, teacher, pedagogue, mother, and counselor in every good."[152] Across Gregory's texts the ideal Christian will be figured as multiple characters (Abraham becomes Moses, who becomes Paul, who becomes the bride in the Song, who becomes Adam, who becomes Paul, who becomes Christ). Through the constant changing of roles, humans and humanity reveal incomparable images of an incomparable God. This mystery, then, is heightened and refined by the constant flow of characters channeled together in a story that moves from glory to glory.

At the opening of this chapter, I noted that late antiquity saw a rapid increase in *Lives*, and with this new literature questions arose about what a proper relationship to saints looked like. Gregory participated in this debate and forwarded his own view in it. The saint's holiness led to an intensification of desire that drew imitation and then made it necessary to move on to the next character, to search out something different in the divine and to find some other way of exploring the mysteries of God. He refused to choose between imitation and reverence, but instead used the friction between them to spark desire for an unknown God, whom the saints fashion as they imitate what exceeds imitation.

CONCLUSION
_____

Mimesis and Mystery

> Ethics requires us to risk ourselves precisely at moments of
> unknowingness, when what forms us diverges from what
> lies before us, when our willingness to become undone in
> relation to others constitutes our chance of becoming
> human. To be undone by another is a primary necessity, an
> anguish, to be sure, but also a chance—to be addressed,
> claimed, bound to what is not me, but also to be moved, to
> be prompted to act, to address myself elsewhere, and so to
> vacate the self-sufficient "I" as a kind of possession. If we
> speak and try to give an account from this place, we will
> not be irresponsible, or, if we are, we will surely be forgiven.
> —Judith Butler

This study may prompt readers to ponder the "undoing" that Judith Butler centers in her ethical and political project of rethinking the modern self. Any account of an "I," Butler argues, must include things that are not me but that make up who "I" am. My language(s), my positions in social relations, and the ways I am addressed are, at once, beyond and constitutive of "me." And this formative excess makes "me" never fully available to myself or others. "The social parameters of address, the norms through which the 'I' becomes intelligible, the non-narratable or even unspeakable dimensions of the unconscious . . . persist as an enabling foreignness at the heart of my desire," Butler writes.[1] I am made by and, knowingly or unknowingly, drawn toward forces I cannot control.[2] And so when I am addressed or named, it overwhelms; Butler calls it a "trauma" that "can be experienced only belatedly through a *second* occurrence."[3] I am changed by and repeat this trauma, and yet I must repeat it with the words, images, and desires available to me.

This "I" who is never fully "my" own must in some way be responsible, must respond to others, and must be accountable to them, even if "giving an account of oneself" is always partial, fragmented, and subject to outside forces. Amia Srinivasan, commenting on Butler's account of how the names we are given frame our sense of self, argues that ethics requires us to "embrace a practice of naming that makes people's passage through the world more bearable." But at best, Srinivasan continues, naming points to a more important shift: "that we see the other, just as we see ourselves, as ultimately beyond names and categories. Each of us exists, finally, beyond the reach of mere words. We all know this instinctively in our own case: that feeling of exceeding, bursting beyond, all the words that can be truly applied to us." Srinivasan leaves her readers with a question: "What does it take for us to recognise that this is true, too, of everyone else: of him and her, of them, of you?"[4] One thing it may "take" is a reflection on history about the limits of language and the religious disciplines involved in remaining responsible to a mysterious other.

Gregory was not some proto-Butler, but Butler and Srinivasan help us see some of the stakes of Gregory's understanding of mimesis. How does the formation of the subject, who is constituted by forces they can never fully control, imply "a framework for understanding ethical response and a theory of responsibility"?[5] Gregory, moreover, may also help his readers fathom the questions that Butler asks of hers, as he thickens the descriptions of those moments "when what forms us diverges from what lies before us." The concepts we take into our souls, for Gregory, constantly bump up against that luminous darkness, and in those moments new possibilities emerge.[6] Gregory's account of mimesis, however, does not end with undoing; it attempts to shape those new possibilities.

So much of Gregory's program of Christian life happens in the mirror.[7] This is no Socratic insult or marker of inauthentic copying. To say that Christian perfection was mimetic, Gregory argued, did not assume a self that only later learned to imitate; from nothingness, rather, the mimetic life began with imitation, with participation in God's reality and with imperfect representations of it. In the mirror, the light of Christ finds a surface onto which it condenses into an image with depth and shadows and reflects back something previously nonexistent, which, in turn, calls for more imitation.[8] Mirrors, moreover, were not simply private matters; those reflective surfaces and what appeared in them pervaded Gregory's theorization of Christian perfection. Gregory's writing constellated a series of images that produced common sense, and, through what Butler calls the "ritualized repetition of norms," they "materialized" Christians.[9] Christians developed new instincts, thinking and feeling their way toward the infinity they mirrored. The names, spaces, and characters at once constituted Christians as the image of God and also carried an excess that attracted Christians participating in them.

Imitating an incomparable God, Gregory argued, makes the imitator incomprehensible. This is both an ontological and an aesthetic claim. For Gregory, humans being an "image [μίμημα] of the divine nature"[10] was both a statement about the deepest truth of humanity and a statement about the art of living. "Since one of the things we contemplate in the Divine nature is the incomprehensibility of the essence [τὸ ἀκατάληπτον τῆς οὐσίας]," he writes, "it is absolutely necessary that, in this way, the image must have a mimetic relationship with the archetype [τὴν εἰκόνα πρὸς τὸ ἀρχέτυπον ἔχειν τὴν μίμησιν]."[11] Being created by and as an image of an unknown God means that humans can no more comprehend their own nature than we can comprehend God's. "We humans," Gregory writes, "live in total ignorance, in the first place about ourselves, and then about everything else."[12] This ignorance of essences does not leave Christians forever staring into the abyss (though there is a place for that); it also underpins Gregory's ethical and theological project. To know the nature of God, oneself, another person, or any part of creation, for Gregory, is to gain a sense of mastery over them and to stop watching how they act (*energeia*) in the world and how those acts continue to make and remake them. Love of oneself, one's neighbor, and one's God begin where knowledge of essences ends. Only those who cannot be grasped can be truly loved and imitated.

Gregory's mimesis was both conceptual and practical; it organized the world and provided exercises for growth in virtue. Names, spaces, and characters invited intimacy and solidarity while also protecting human unfathomability. Concepts and categories limit what we can know of one another, and of God, and they must be "undone" if we are to be fully human; but "undoing" is complicated. As Butler argues, we also need them to recognize each other and to make relationships possible.[13] For Gregory, and perhaps for his best readers, it was not enough to say that people do not fit neatly into categories and then, without creating new ones, assume the old are gone for good. Part of maturing into perfection involved remaking the categories that rendered oneself and others recognizable with increasing awareness of an underlying mystery. It involved imagining, habituating, and forging consensus around new names, spaces, and characters. Otherwise, even an emphasis on "transcending" categories could end up reinforcing them. Learning how to hold frameworks of intelligibility up to the "luminous darkness" in order to stretch them required practice. Becoming "undone" was surely a chance to live otherwise, but without practice it could just as often lead to defensiveness or retreating back into people's worst impulses. Gregory's mimesis modeled how to have categories that help outgrow those very categories. His names, spaces, and characters provided something to aspire to and also performed how to transform those models to become more aware of deeper mysteries.

Gregory does not provide straightforward answers for modern subjects, but he can help readers see the stakes of the names, spaces, and characters that religious leaders, politicians, corporations, artists, and activists ask participants to inhabit, imitate, and love. Gregory radicalized earlier claims of divine incomparability by locating it not in human ignorance but in divine infinity. His calls for humility before others, therefore, suggest more than a claim that we humans should be aware of our limits. Humility was more than draining desire; his call responded to a heightened awareness of the incomparability in others who are made in the image of an incomparable God. To maintain a posture of studied ignorance—to insist that we do not fully know ourselves or our neighbors even as we attend to them carefully—is an ethical commitment that requires intellectual malleability and ascetic discipline, a retraining of the mind and body, what Gregory called "instruction through practice [ἡ διὰ τῶν ἔργων . . . ὑφήγησις]."[14] The conviction that others are essentially incomprehensible is a starting point that demands more attentiveness and fuller imaginations developed in community through practices. New names, spaces, and characters can make recognizable and outline the possibilities of care for those whom we can never fully know and yet are called to love.

In Gregory's earliest treatise, he suggested that Christian perfection is like learning a language: "One who wants to learn a foreign language is not a competent instructor of himself; he gets himself taught by experts, and can then talk with foreigners."[15] Christians, he argued, cannot learn this new language without exposure to someone or something beyond themselves. Like language instruction, the names, spaces, and characters, at once, offered something specific enough to practice (repeat this word, memorize that paradigm), and opened a world that learners never knew they never knew.[16] By learning this language, Christians learned to speak in ways they never thought possible, and also to participate in a world that once seemed distant and foreign.

This learning, however, never led to mastery. Any commonsense under-standing of how to imitate Christ, for Gregory, bumped into a Christ who was intimately known and utterly incomprehensible. He pointed to the saints, who let out a "perfume," the very "odors of Christ," that at once "sat-urate [ἀναπίμπλασθαι]" followers and give them something to "track."[17] The young, he says, should "refrain from laying down for themselves their future course in this profession."[18] Christians must remain exposed to this life of perfection without quite knowing where it will lead. Because they "have not lacked examples of holy lives,"[19] and because "saintliness flowered and ha-bituates [ἤνθησε καὶ ἐπιχωριάζει] our life,"[20] Gregory's program allows the one who "follows such footsteps in his daily rounds" to "catch this halo."[21] He advises those being formed to surround themselves with examples of holiness—to see, hear, touch, smell the holy ones—so that by participating in their world, they may continue to spur Christian desire. Holy lives are all around, as Gregory sees it, but to catch the halo requires a willingness to enter a world Christians do not fully understand, to be undone and then remade through practices of imitation.

A mimetic life, for Gregory, also included theological practices, but it suggested that, as important as doctrine was—and it was important—getting the words right was part of a larger process of formation. Learning to speak of God required habituated patterns of desire. Taking those names, spaces, and characters into the soul instilled an "erotic disposition" (διάθεσις ἐρωτικῆς).[22] Imitation, therefore, could never be as straightforward as mouthing a creed or copying a role model. It coupled with a desire that could lead to unexpected, "spiritual" meanings, which were often found in a "luminous darkness," a place only those confident in their ingrained prac-tices could enter.

*   *   *

How does one imitate the infinite? What "likeness" can be found between an unbound creator and its bounded creatures, who—in their expanding desire—constantly push up against boundaries? *Imitations of Infinity* has argued that the mingling of Plato's two conceptions of mimesis—ontological participation and aesthetic representation—form the conceptual context for

Gregory of Nyssa's claim that humans imitate an infinite God by infinitely stretching toward God. When Gregory wrote that "Christianity is mimesis of the divine nature," he joined and transformed a lively late ancient discourse. His theological claim that the divine is "infinite" troubled previously established rules of mimetic relationships and made recognizable another mode of relationship. Desire, for Gregory, would not only motivate imitation; imitation and desire became mutually constitutive, reinforcing, and expanding.

Gregory was neither the first nor the last to wrestle with problems of mimesis and mystery. Despite histories that tend to jump from antiquity to the Renaissance without attention to the medieval and byzantine worlds, rhetoricians, Neoplatonist pagans, and other Christians—not to mention Jewish and, later, Muslim authors—would all struggle to theorize mimesis as it reached for the inimitable. The fifth-century philosopher Proclus continued to ask how the ontological and aesthetic were related. The meaning of "infinity" was a central concern in the sixth-century Christian philosopher John Philoponus's *Against Proclus*.[23] And mystical theologians such as Pseudo-Dionysius the Areopagite argued that the heavenly and ecclesial worlds were arranged in a "hierarchy" so that humans could be "lifted up analogically in divine imitation [θεομίμητον]."[24] Mystery and mimesis continued to sit side by side as Dionysius asked how God could be "beyond all" and the "inimitable imitation of what is beyond deity and beyond the good, by which we are deified and made good [τὸ ἀμίμητον μίμημα τοῦ ὑπερθέου καὶ ὑπεραγάθου, καθ' ὃ θεούμεθα καὶ ἀγαθυνόμεθα]."[25] Dionysius too would have to theorize the names, spaces, and characters of his divine imitation. Questions of representation and of how to join in what exceeds imitation continue to confront and inspire writers well beyond the scope of this book and into the present.

Augustine of Hippo asked, "What do I love when I love my God?" Bringing together Plato's two concepts of mimesis while also insisting that Christians imitate an infinite God compelled Gregory to ask: What do I imitate when I imitate my God? Saying that they imitate "Christ" would only move the question back one step. For Gregory, humans were made and unmade in a constellating series of mimetic names, spaces, and characters that can remain unknown even as they govern and propel a dilating desire for an infinite God. In that desire, Christians could imitate what they did not know. Mimesis allowed Christians to inhabit and then stretch out the names, spaces, and characters that bound heaven and earth, even as they challenged any simple understanding of what it was to be bound, to desire, or even to imitate.

ABBREVIATIONS

I have largely followed the abbreviations in the *Brill Dictionary of Gregory of Nyssa.*

An. et Res.	Gregory of Nyssa, *On the Soul and the Resurrection*
BDGN	*Brill Dictionary of Gregory of Nyssa*
Cant.	Gregory of Nyssa, *Homilies on the Song of Songs*
CD	Pseudo-Dionysius the Areopagite, *Corpus Dionysiacum*
CE 1	Gregory of Nyssa, *Contra Eunomium I*
CE 2	Gregory of Nyssa, *Contra Eunomium II*
CE 3	Gregory of Nyssa, *Contra Eunomium III*
CG	Athanasius, *Contra Gentes*
Com. John	Origen, *Commentary on John*
Com. Rep.	Proclus, *Commentary on the Republic*
Com. Rom.	Origen, *Commentary on Romans*
De decretis	Athanasius, *On the Council of Nicaea*
Enn.	Plotinus, *Enneads*
GNO	*Gregorii Nysseni Opera Online*
Hom. Beat.	*Homilies on the Beatitudes*
In illud tunc	Gregory of Nyssa, *In illud: tunc et ipse filius*
Inc.	Athanasius, *De Incarnatione*
IP	Gregory of Nyssa, *Treatise on the Inscriptions of the Psalms*
Letter	Gregory of Nyssa, *Letters*
Lib. Ap.	Eunomius, *Liber Apologeticus: The Apology*
Mac.	Gregory of Nyssa, *The Life of Saint Macrina*
Mos.	Gregory of Nyssa, *The Life of Moses*
Myst.	Iamblichus, *On the Mysteries*
NPNF	Nicene and Post-Nicene Fathers
NRSV	New Revised Standard Version
Op. Hom.	Gregory of Nyssa, *On the Making of Man*
Or. Cat.	Gregory of Nyssa, *Address on Religious Instruction*
Or. Dom.	Gregory of Nyssa, *Homilies on the Lord's Prayer*
PG	*Patrologiae cursus completus, Series Graeca*, ed. J. P. Migne
PL	*Patrologia Latina*
Princ.	Origen, *On First Principles*
Perf.	Gregory of Nyssa, *On Perfection*
Phaedrus	Plato, *Phaedrus*

Prof.	Gregory of Nyssa, *On What It Means to Call Oneself a Christian*
Ref.	Gregory of Nyssa, *Refutation of the Views of Apolinarius*
Rep.	Plato, *Republic*
Symp.	Plato, *Symposium*
Theod.	Gregory of Nyssa, *Homily on Theodore the Recruit*
Timaeus	Plato, *Timaeus*
VA	Athanasius, *Life of Antony*
Virg.	Gregory of Nyssa, *On Virginity*

NOTES

Introduction

1. *Prof.*, 85; *GNO* 29.136. Translations of *Prof.* are mine, but I refer often to Callahan; for ease of reference and to acknowledge my debt, I provide page numbers for both Callahan's translations and *GNO*. Unless noted otherwise, all of Gregory of Nyssa's Greek is from *GNO*, and all translations in this book are from editions cited in the bibliography.

2. See Halliwell, *The Aesthetics of Mimesis*, 13–14; Burrow, *Imitating Authors*, 2; and Stefaniw, *Christian Reading*, 205.

3. *Perf.*, 122; *GNO* 30.213–14, trans. Callahan.

4. In *BDGN*, s.v. "Imitation," 504, Lucas Francisco Mateo-Seco describes the mimetic relationship between humanity and Christ as "the fundamental question of Gregory's theology." Walther Völker also notes that mimesis is at the heart of the Christian life in his *Gregor von Nyssa als mystiker*, 269–74. And yet, as far as I can tell, there has been no dissertation or book-length study on this "fundamental question." Mateo-Seco's article "Imitación y seguimiento" and dictionary entry are important starting points for this work.

5. *Rep.* 400d.

6. Hadot, *Philosophy as a Way of Life*. My reading, then, while tracing a different history, largely agrees with Burrow's *Imitating Authors*.

7. Here my work is especially indebted to Whitmarsh, *Greek Literature and the Roman Empire*; Cribiore, *Gymnastics of the Mind*; and Halliwell, *The Aesthetics of Mimesis*.

8. I more broadly examine this distinction between what and how to imitate in Motia, "Three Ways to Imitate Paul."

9. *Prof.*, 81; *GNO* 29.129. Whether Harmonius actually asked the question is unimportant for this study. It is common for ancient authors to pose the treatise as the response to a request, not unlike politicians today restating a question so that they can answer the question they want asked. While I refer to *Prof.* as a "letter," I see no hard line between "letter" and "treatise."

10. *Prof.*, 82; *GNO* 29.131.

11. See Mattern, *The Prince of Medicine*.

12. This question became even more pressing at a time when calling oneself a Christian increasingly could gain someone prestige and opportunity.

13. *Prof.*, 82–83; *GNO* 29.132–33. For Lucian's original, see *The Dead Come to Life, or The Fisherman* 36.

14. *Prof.*, 83; *GNO* 29.133.

15. For Gregory's contrast of virtuous mimesis and those wearing "soulless masks [προσωπεῖον ἄψυχον]," see *Prof.*, 85; *GNO* 30.135.

16. *CE* 3.9.54.

17. *CE* 2.117.

18. *Imitations of Infinity*, therefore, attempts to fill a gap identified by Morwenna Ludlow in *Gregory of Nyssa: Ancient and (Post)modern*, 231–59. Theological accounts tend to emphasize either Gregory's representational practices (typified by Scot Douglass) or his ontology (typified by John Milbank). Gregory's understanding of mimesis, I argue, requires both.

19. *Prof.*, 85; *GNO* 29.136.

20. *Prof.*, 84; *GNO* 29.134–35.

21. *Prof.*, 84; *GNO* 29.134.

22. *Prof.*, 85; *GNO* 29.136.

23. *Prof.*, 85; *GNO* 29.136.

24. *Prof.*, 85; *GNO* 29.136.

25. *Prof.*, 85; *GNO* 29.136.

26. *Prof.*, 85–86; *GNO* 29.137.

27. *Cant.* 5, 158. All translations of *Cant.* come from Norris. I cite the sermon number and then the Greek page from *GNO* 24, which Norris follows.

28. *Prof.*, 86–87; *GNO* 29.138.

29. *Prof.*, 87; *GNO* 29.138.

30. Ps 138:8–10 (LXX), trans. mine. Gregory continues later, writing, "Because the divine is equally present in all things, and, in like manner, it pervades all creation and it does not exist separated from being, but the divine nature touches each element of being with equal honor, encompassing all things within itself" (*Prof.*, 87; *GNO* 29.138).

31. *Prof.*, 87; *GNO* 29.138.

32. *Prof.*, 87; *GNO* 29.138.

33. *Prof.*, 88; *GNO* 29.140–41.

34. The closest Gregory gets to this is in answering another rhetorical question: "What activities of ours are like the activities of God." He answers: "those [actions] that are free from all evil, purifying themselves as far as possible in deed and word and thought from all vileness. This is truly the imitation of the divine and of the perfection concerning the God of heaven" (*Prof.*, 87; *GNO* 29.138).

35. *Prof.*, 82; *GNO* 29.129. For Gregory's critique of money lending, see *On the Love of the Poor*, trans. in Holman, *The Hungry Are Dying*, 193–206; *GNO* 35.

36. *Prof.*, 89; *GNO* 29.141.

37. E.g., Brown, *The Cult of the Saints*, 60; and Mathews, *The Dawn of Christian Art*, esp. 21–24, 131–52.

38. Stefaniw, *Christian Reading*.

39. For overviews, see Brown, *The World of Late Antiquity*, and *Through the Eye of the Needle*; Cameron, *Christianity and the Rhetoric of Empire*; Inglebert, "Late Antique Conceptions of Late Antiquity"; and Jacobs, *Epiphanius*, 1–13, 255–78.

40. Gregory of Nazianzus, *Orat.* 43.5, trans. mine; see also *Mac.*, 22; *GNO* 32.393.

41. For Gregory's biography, see Silvas, *The Letters*, 1–57.

42. Changing understandings of mimesis may also be part of a larger shift, highlighted by Andrea Giardina, in Roman views on dependency (see Giardina, "The Transition to Late Antiquity," 743–68, esp. 766). Whereas first-century philosophers such as Cicero saw the aim of philosophy as autonomy and saw labor as demeaning because of the way selling work subjects people to markets, the slow revolution of the fourth century shifted the emphasis such

that "dependency" carried no social, ethical, or cultural humiliation. It was a virtue. Mimetic relations required at once submitting to an archetype, while also forging an image from it. This understanding of artistic work and moral formation is especially clear in the monastic practices set forth by Gregory's brother Basil of Caesarea, who analogizes the Christian life to a smith making an axe. The smith must be "constantly mindful of him who gave him the charge." He creates the axe by keeping in mind the intention of the "master." "He directs the service of his hands to this end so that the form of the work fits the mind and will of him who enjoined it." Christians, too, "ought to direct every effort (and all diligence) whether small or great, to God's intention, at the same time, both accurately completing his action and safeguarding the intention of him who gave the order" (*The Longer Responses* 87–91, trans. Silvas, in *The Asketikon of St. Basil the Great*, 176–77). There is no presumption here of moving beyond mimesis. The more one looks to the archetype, the better the product will become. And for the monk, whose life is the work of art, this process never finds completion. Gregory theorizes the importance of mimesis and submission (ὑποταγή) in *In illud tunc* (e.g., GNO 11.16). My work here draws also on Michel Foucault's, who points to Christianity's emphasis on obedience as an end in itself. See "Technologies of the Self," 39–49.

43. Examples of this are legion. E.g., Colin Burrow's *Imitating Authors* moves from Plato to Roman rhetorical schools and then jumps into the Renaissance and early modern readings of Cicero and Quintilian. The study wonderfully demonstrates how debates over *imitatio* shaped the rhetorical schools and more modern literary practices and theories, but the jump leads the book to ignore the rich history of late ancient theorists of mimesis. For example, in discussing Erasmus's debates with the Ciceronians, Burrow raises the question, "How could a belief in the ethically instructive value of literature from the past survive the notion that everything—vocabulary, social mores, ethical priorities—changed, that Cicero today would not be as he once had been?" (192). An important question, but hardly a new one. The question occupied much of Christian exegesis of scripture. (I say more about this in Chapter 6.) Halliwell's *The Aesthetics of Mimesis* is another exemplary study of aesthetics, and a canonical chronicle. His story skips from Plato to Aristotle to the Stoics to the Neoplatonists, gives "some tangential attention" (334) to the iconoclast controversy, and then jumps to the Renaissance and eventually to Derrida. He spends about six pages of the 424-page book on the controversy or religious history more generally and then argues that mimesis "disappears" in medieval aesthetics (*The Aesthetics of Mimesis*, 340). Gunter Gebauer and Christoph Wulf's *Mimesis: Culture, Art, Society* tells the more typical version: Plato to Aristotle to the Renaissance and onward to Derrida. Similar issues appear in an influential and otherwise excellent essay by William Schweiker, "Beyond Imitation," and in Potolsky, *Mimesis*.

44. See Meredith, *Gregory of Nyssa*, 13.

45. Gregory's focus on how mimesis stretches out toward the infinite, moreover, troubles a helpful, but perhaps overly neat, dichotomy that governs much of the study of mimesis: Stephen Halliwell's distinction between a "world-reflecting" model of mimesis and a "world-simulating" or "world-creating" model (*The Aesthetics of Mimesis*, 23; Halliwell's schemata is meant to be heuristic, not an attempt to "simplify the history of mimeticism"). World-reflecting models assume a reality outside the realm of representation to which representations can correspond. World-creating models, by contrast, conjure "fictional coherence"; they have an internal consistency but need not relate directly to a reality outside their own world. For Gregory, however, the distinction breaks down: positing a "fictional" series of names, spaces, and characters is a way to engage reality; the words and images used to discuss

God aid humans' understanding of how God transcends them. Not only, therefore, does Gregory's "aesthetics of mimesis" trouble typical stories of the concept, but it also urges readers to think about ontological participation alongside the aesthetics. A mimetic life, for Gregory, holds together a self that is at once given and made. Christians participate in a reality that is never fully their own; and yet that participation requires representations of a God who transcends all understanding of "reality."

46. Asad, "Thinking about Religion, Belief, and Politics," 37.

47. More broadly, see Tannous, *The Making of the Medieval Middle East,* 11–81.

48. E.g., Bourdieu, *The Logic of Practice,* 52–80; and Hollywood, "Performativity, Citationality, Ritualization."

49. Foucault, "On the Genealogy of Ethics," 350.

50. E.g., Butler, *Giving an Account,* 136, which I discuss in the Conclusion.

51. Robert Orsi, "The Problem of the Holy," 99–102, and the secondary literature cited therein.

52. E.g., Carlson, *The Indiscrete Image,* esp. 74–117; and Keller, *Cloud of the Impossible,* esp. 50–86, 215–36.

53. More sharply, one question these theorists ask is: What must escape systemization in order for the system to work? Looking to Gregory helps us ask the question differently: How do systems organize themselves around what cannot be systematized?

54. Halliwell, *The Aesthetics of Mimesis,* 314.

55. Elm, *Sons of Hellenism,* 335.

56. 1 Cor 11:1.

57. Moss, *The Other Christs.*

58. In *Art and the Roman Viewer,* Jaś Elsner draws attention to a shift in basic habits of perception with respect to mimetic relations from the ancient world to those we see in, for example, Origen or Iamblichus. Elsner describes this as a shift from the realist to the symbolic. If Plato (realist) framed encounters with art with a viewer looking from a distance at an object, Plotinus's (symbolic) encounter with the One left no distance between viewer and viewed. For Plato, the closer a representation was to reality, the more sharply a viewer could see the contrast between image and reality. Representations always point to realities. But in late antiquity, we see a mode of perception arise wherein images are ends in themselves. In visual culture, ancient viewers looked at an image of a sheep and imagined a scene with a sacrificial animal; late ancient Christians looked at the same image and saw Christ. Symbols for Iamblichus activated something in humans that they could not sense themselves. To see the martyr, for Christians, was to see Christ in him. The sacred space of the church "does what it represents" by collapsing time and eternity on its walls (233). For Origen of Alexandria, only a lack of faith could allow someone to look at the scriptures and see only one possible world and not a whole symbolic universe. "Symbols," then, for Iamblichus and many early Christians, paradoxically contain more than they can hold, and viewers were asked to enter and to participate in them to find a truth condensed in them that can be accessed only from the inside. For Gregory, God's infinitude becomes only more mysterious as it is more clearly seen, and it is more clearly seen as Christians participate in and represent it. Gregory, that is, slips through the cracks of Elsner's dichotomy, seeming to take something from both modes of perception. A misfiring between representation and represented fuels desire, and yet, for Gregory, representations must exist by participating in the reality they seek.

59. See *CE* 2.70; and *An Answer to Ablabius*, trans. Richardson, 256–67; and *GNO* 5.37–57.

60. *Perf.*, 99; *GNO* 30.178, trans. altered from Callahan.

61. *Perf.*, 122; *GNO* 30.213–14, trans. Callahan.

62. *Cant.* 15, 444.

Chapter 1

1. *Com. Rep.*, 61, K70. Unless noted otherwise, the Greek and all translations are Lamberton's from *Proclus the Successor*, cited as *Com. Rep.*, page, Kpage.

2. *Com. Rep.*, 3, K42.

3. *Com. Rep.*, 3, K42.

4. *Com. Rep.*, 235–37, K165–66.

5. *Com. Rep.*, 291, K196, trans. altered.

6. *Com. Rep.*, 7, K44.

7. *Com. Rep.*, 259, K178.

8. *Com. Rep.*, 261, K179.

9. *Com. Rep.*, 78–79, K80.

10. *Com. Rep.*, 261, K179.

11. E.g., *Com. Rep.*, 77–81, K80–81. I largely agree with Halliwell's argument that the two essays may not be as divergent as they first seem (*The Aesthetics of Mimesis*, 329–32).

12. *Com. Rep.*, 257, K177.

13. *Com. Rep.*, 259–61, K179, trans. altered.

14. *Com. Rep.*, 301, K201–2.

15. *Com. Rep.*, 305, K204.

16. *Com. Rep.*, 259, K178–79. See *Phaedrus* 245a. See also *Com. Rep.*, 299, K201.

17. See Rappe, *Reading Neoplatonism*, e.g., 20–21.

18. *Com. Rep.*, 295, K198.

19. Halliwell, *The Aesthetics of Mimesis*, 329.

20. *Com. Rep.*, 55, K69; see *Timaeus* 36c.

21. Rappe, *Reading Neoplatonism*, 12.

22. Rappe, *Reading Neoplatonism*, 192.

23. Struck, "Allegory and Ascent in Neoplatonism," 68.

24. See Halliwell, *The Aesthetics of Mimesis*, 15–22 and the secondary literature therein.

25. For a helpful starting point and some of the work that has most influenced my reading of Plato and mimesis, see Burnyeat, "Culture and Society"; Nehamas, "Imitation"; Ferrari, "Plato on Poetry"; Lorenz, *The Brute Within*, 59–73; and Halliwell, *Between Ecstasy and Truth*, 155–206, 327–67.

26. For Plato's positive view of art, see Corrigan and Glazov-Corrigan, *Plato's Dialectic*, 215–20. See also Zuckert, *Plato's Philosophers*, on which my reading draws heavily. Unless noted otherwise, translations of the *Republic* are by Allan Bloom; all Greek for Plato comes from J. Burnet, *Platonis Opera* and is cited in text according to Greek line numbers.

27. See Lorenz, *The Brute Within*, 59–73; and Zuckert, *Plato's Philosophers*, 420–81.

28. *Com. Rep.*, 31, K57.

29. Plato, *Statesman*, 277d, trans. altered from Fowler and Lamb.

30. Clark, "Imitation: Theory and Practice in Roman Rhetoric," 13; and Halliwell, *The Aesthetics of Mimesis*, 37–39.

31. See Burnyeat, "Culture and Society," esp. 280: "What you imitate regularly is what you become, so from childhood the Guards must imitate appropriate models of courage, temperance, and other virtues."

32. Halliwell describes this as "the psychology of imaginative self-assimilation" (*The Aesthetics of Mimesis*, 25).

33. Halliwell, *The Aesthetics of Mimesis*, 25.

34. See Moss, "What Is Imitative Poetry and Why Is It Bad?" 415–44. In Book 10, "realistic painting, painting that looks like what it represents, must in a deeper sense *misrepresent* its subjects. . . . If [a painter] tries to paint the men as they are and not as they appear, his painting will be 'unrealistic': it will not *look like* what it represents" (421). Mimesis requires distortion; it is a question not of *if* that mirror will be bent but of *how* to bend the mirror to best reflect reality.

35. This is, perhaps, in line with Socrates's critique of the rhapsodies in Plato's *Ion*, wherein Homer's words are not interpreted as much as they are channeled. *Ion*, despite being much shorter than the *Republic*, adds a third critique to the "two tracks" model I am heuristically deploying. Readers see that Ion's ability as a rhapsode is due to his ability to ecstatically connect with the text. As in *Phaedrus* 244, Socrates critiques what might be Ion's greatest strength. Ion does not take in the content of the text; a "power divine" moves him. The words here are not representations that one stands outside of; the rhapsode is inhabited by them. See Muckelbauer, "Imitation and Invention in Antiquity," esp. 86.

36. Nehamas, "Plato on Imitation," 252.

37. On why Socrates keeps painting while rejecting poetry, see Nehamas, "Plato on Imitation," 264–69.

38. We can see the connection between mimesis and the immortality of the soul too as Gregory of Nyssa tethers mimesis and epektasis, in opposition to this less positive mimetic view and transmigration.

39. This ability to imitate what one knows not will become quite important for Gregory of Nyssa.

40. See *Rep.* 604d–605a.

41. See Halliwell, *The Aesthetics of Mimesis*, 133–42.

42. See also *Rep.* 514a–520a.

43. Plato, *Critias* 107b, trans. altered from R. B. Bury.

44. See esp. Klein, *A Commentary on Plato's* Meno, 112–25; and Bloom's interpretive essay in *Republic* 464n39.

45. On the divided line (*Rep.* 509d–511e), see Klein's most helpful reading, *A Commentary on Plato's* Meno, 115–16.

46. Unless noted otherwise, translations are by Lamb. Dealing with the speech without the rest of the dialogue is of course a shortcoming, but both for the sake of space, and because of the prevalence of the ladder of love image in late ancient texts, I pull out this passage to illustrate how, in Plato's writings, mimesis can have a kind of direction to it.

47. For connections between the *Republic* and the *Symposium*, see Corrigan, *Plato's Dialectic*, esp. 123–25.

48. Carson, *Eros the Bittersweet*, 15, 68.

49. See Halperin, "Platonic Erôs and What Men Call Love," esp. 188–89.

50. Corrigan, *Plato's Dialectic*, 164.

51. See Corrigan, *Plato's Dialectic*, 164, 212.

52. Especially in Diotima's speech it is clear that the line between aesthetic and ontological becomes quite blurred. My distinction is more meant to highlight two different areas of concern than to posit that there are actually two easily separable modes of mimesis in Plato's writings. As mentioned above, the form of the dialogue means that none of these writings are actually aimed at completing an entire system any more than, for example, Shakespeare's plays form one entire system. There is something to be gained in comparing them, but the literary quality of the dialogues resists systematization.

53. Recall that mimesis is what leads the city to war in *Republic* 373b–c.

54. Unless noted otherwise, translations of *Timaeus* are from Bury, with reference to Zeyl's and Kalkavage's translations.

55. My reading here largely follows Zuckert's analysis in *Plato's Philosophers*, 420–81, which emphasizes a subtle but important difference in mimetic relationships in *Timaeus* and *Republic*. On parallels in the literary openings of *Timaeus* and the *Symposium*, see Schoos's "Timaeus' Banquet," 97–107; see also Zuckert, *Plato's Philosophers*, 428.

56. Kalkavage, introduction to *Timaeus*, 16.

57. Halliwell, *The Aesthetics of Mimesis*, 333.

58. James, *The Principles of Psychology*, 1:488.

59. Aristotle, *Metaphysics* 987b.

60. While my translation fails to render this in English, it is no coincidence that Timaeus constructs the speech in such a way that participation (μετασχόντες) is in apposition to imitation (μιμούμενοι): ἐκμαθόντες δὲ καὶ λογισμῶν κατὰ φύσιν ὀρθότητος μετασχόντες, μιμούμενοι τὰς τοῦ θεοῦ πάντως ἀπλανεῖς οὔσας.

61. *Timaeus* 52d, trans. altered: "Being and space, and becoming, three distinct things, were existing even before the Heavens came into being." While I translate χώρα here as "space," *khōra* is not a "blank space." It is not "empty" or measurable. It is itself not anything, and thus quite difficult to discuss. Kalkavage suggests "field" for associations such as "field of play," "field of battle," or "agricultural field" needing to be tilled (introduction to *Timaeus*, 30).

62. Despite the excitement generated by Jacques Derrida, Julia Kristeva, John D. Caputo, Catherine Keller, and others, in thinking about *khōra* much work remains to be done in tracing how early Christians transform and adapt this "third thing" in their own creation theologies. See, e.g., Burrus, *Ancient Christian Ecopoetics*, 27–76.

63. Zuckert, *Plato's Philosophers*, 450.

64. The soul, for Timaeus, exists in connection with the body. Cf. Socrates in the Myth of Er.

65. When Aristotle describes a similar movement, he insists that God's activity (ἐνέργεια)—which is what humans experience of the maker—is the realization of an essence brought to perfection in activity. Humans join in that perfected activity of the maker while never moving toward it. See Tollefsen, *Activity and Participation*, 15–20.

66. Zuckert, *Plato's Philosophers*, 466–67.

67. In the *Phaedrus*, the best life is that of "the philosopher or lover of beauty or a musical and erotic person [φιλοσόφου ἢ φιλοκάλου ἢ μουσικοῦ τινος καὶ ἐρωτικοῦ]" (248d). All these are inspired by the "divine madness" that Proclus highlights. And at the same time, poetry is nearly always the lowest form of divine madness (see Corrigan, *Plato's Dialectic*, 220).

68. Zuckert, *Plato's Philosophers*, 465. See also Fletcher, "*Aisthēsis*, Reason and Appetite in the *Timaeus*." Fletcher argues that in *Timaeus* there are two modes of *aisthēsis*, one that causes a disturbance in the soul, and another that can restore the soul to its proper balance

(405; see *Timaeus* 45a–46). This second kind of *aisthēsis* makes it possible for representations to restore the soul to its natural state.

69. Zuckert, *Plato's Philosophers*, 39. Zuckert traces this distinction to the construction of the soul, in that for Timaeus the soul does not exist without the body, whereas Socrates insists that it does. Perhaps more than that, though, there are two visions of the good at work. For Timaeus goodness is equated with intelligibility, whereas for Socrates it is linked to justice and beauty (*Plato's Philosophers*, 459). Zuckert makes this distinction in part as a refute to Gordon, *Plato's Erotic World*.

70. Zuckert, *Plato's Philosophers*, 466.

71. For more, see Kalkavage, introduction to *Timaeus*, 8–9.

72. See McKeon, "Literary Criticism and the Concept of Imitation in Antiquity," 1–35; Fantham, "Imitation and Evolution," 1–16; for a helpful overview, on which I draw heavily, see Burrow, *Imitating Authors*, 62–135.

73. Xenophon, *Memorabilia* 1.2.3–4, trans. Marchant and Todd.

74. See Aristotle, *Poetics* 144b. For Aristotle on mimetic art, see Halliwell, *The Aesthetics of Mimesis*, 151–259.

75. See George A. Kennedy, *Classical Rhetoric*, esp. 132–35; despite criticisms, Burnyeat's "Aristotle on Learning to Be Good" remains a valuable introduction to habituation in the *Nicomachean Ethics*.

76. Isocrates, "Against the Sophists (*Orat.* 13)" 17–18, trans. altered from Norlin and Laure Van Hook; see Fantham, "Imitation and Evolution," 12.

77. Whitmarsh, *Greek Literature and the Roman Empire*, 1–130. With respect to Cicero, see Fantham, *The Roman World of Cicero's* De Oratore, 78–101, 240–41.

78. Whitmarsh, *Greek Literature and the Roman Empire*, 92–93.

79. Quintilian, *The Orator's Education* 1.3.1; all translations follow Russell. Quintilian may have been working with Dionysius of Halicarnassus's *On Imitation*, which survives only in fragments. See Richard Hunter, *Critical Moments in Classical Literature*, Chapter 4, "The Ugly Peasant and the Naked Virgins," 107–27.

80. Cicero, *On the Oratore* 2.22; all translations follow Sutton and Rackham. See Fantham, "Imitation and Evolution."

81. Libanius, *Ep.* 1261.2 (XI.339), cited in Brown, *Power and Persuasion*, 7n5.

82. On debates within Roman rhetorical theory, see Burrow, *Imitating Authors*, 71–105.

83. [Cicero], *Ad Herennium*, 1.2, trans. altered from Caplan. Scholarly consensus no longer accepts that Cicero wrote *Ad Herennium*.

84. *Ad Herennium* 1.1, trans. Caplan.

85. Burrow, *Imitating Authors*, 73.

86. Dionysius of Halicarnassus, *On Imitation*, fr. VI, pp 203–4 U.-R. = pp. 31–32 Aujac, cited in Hunter, *Critical Moments in Classical Literature*, 109–110.

87. Burrow, *Imitating Authors*, 72.

88. Burrow, *Imitating Authors*, 68.

89. Quintilian, *The Orator's Education* 10.2.10.

90. Quintilian, *The Orator's Education* 10.2.26.

91. As Raffaella Cribiore notes, "the reality was a far cry from that ideal," *Gymnastics of the Mind*, 236. Students often struggle to imitate even one master; beautifully combining styles is an aspiration. But that hope is nevertheless important. Difference here is produced by a goal of likeness. Providing many models allows for both a variety of students and a variety of examples.

92. Seneca, *Ad Lucilium Epistulae Morales* 84.6, trans. Richard M. Gummere.

93. Russell, *Greek Declamation*, 12; Penella, ed., *Rhetorical Exercises from Late Antiquity*, 9. See also Bloomer, "Schooling in Persona," 57–78. For more, see Brightbill, "Roman Declamation" and the secondary literature cited therein, esp. 1–26; Langlands, "Roman *Exempla* and Situation Ethics," esp. 115; and Van der Poel, "Use of *exempla* in Roman Declamation."

94. Penella, introduction to *Choricius of Gaza*, 10; for more, see the literature in my Chapter 6; Haskins, "*Mimesis* Between Poetics and Rhetoric"; Cribiore, *Gymnastics of the Mind*, 160–244; Whitmarsh, *Greek Literature and the Roman Empire*, 90–141.

95. See Habinek, *Ancient Rhetoric and Oratory*, esp. 60–78; on performativity, ritualization, and mimesis in Roman speech and song, see Habinek, *The World of Roman Song*, esp. 58–157.

96. Burrow, *Imitating Authors*, 65.

97. Cribiore, *The School of Libanius*, 139; see also Fox, *Augustine*, 61–79.

98. Quintilian, *The Orator's Education* 2.9.2. Note the triangulation of desire here. See also *Symp.* 219c–d.

99. Cicero, *On the Oratore* 2.22, 91, trans. altered.

100. Cicero, *On the Oratore* 2.11, 36; see Burrow, *Imitating Authors*, 82.

101. Burrow, *Imitating Authors*, 7.

102. Gregory inherits this rich tradition of education and places it at the forefront of his call to Christian perfection. Jaeger, in *Early Christianity and Greek Paideia*, 86–87, sees in Gregory of Nyssa's emphasis on the plasticity of human nature a mark of his inheritance of Greek education. See also Watts, *City and School*, esp. 48–78.

103. Burrow, *Imitating Authors*, 106.

104. Burrow, *Imitating Authors*, 100.

Chapter 2

1. For an important study on some of those intervening years, see Dillon, *The Middle Platonists*. See Tarrant, "Platonism Before Plotinus," 98, which notes that Platonists during the first two centuries of the common era "seems to be in general agreement that Plato's moral goal has been best expressed in the phrase 'assimilation to god insofar as is possible' (*Theaetetus* 176b)." See also Gerson, *Aristotle and Other Platonists*; and *From Plato to Platonism*. For the confluence between Philo and Gregory of Nyssa, see Geljon, "Divine Infinity in Gregory of Nyssa and Philo of Alexandria." For contrasts between Plato and the Platonists with respect to their understanding of epistemology and ontology, see Rappe, *Reading Neoplatonism*, esp. 27, 113.

2. Brown, *Power and Persuasion*, 36.

3. Brown, *Power and Persuasion*, 41. On shared organizational strategies in the third century, see Marx-Wolf, *Spiritual Taxonomies and Ritual Authority*. Scholarship around the complex networks of friendship and cultural capital formed by *paideia* is immense. See, e.g., Watts, *City and School*; Urbano, *The Philosophical Life*; Chin and Vidas, eds., *Late Ancient Knowing*; and Storin, *Self-Portrait in Three Colors*, esp. 1–28, 101–45.

4. For Longinus's comments on Plotinus, see Porphyry, *The Life of Plotinus* 14, in *The Enneads*, ed. Gerson, trans. Boys-Stones et al. *Enneads* are cited as *Enn.* book.chapter.paragraph marker; Greek in Henry and Schwyzer, *Plotini Opera*. Translations are from Gerson unless noted otherwise. I have also referred to Armstrong's translations. Plotinus famously showed little interest in literary production or form, but composed some treatises based on his lectures and, at the encouragement of Porphyry (if Porphyry is to be believed), eventually wrote

enough for Porphyry to arrange and disseminate his writings. The structure Porphyry gave to the treatises has lasted from late antiquity to the present.

5. Halliwell, *The Aesthetics of Mimesis*, 315.

6. See the introduction to Iamblichus, *On the Mysteries*, trans. Clarke et al. (hereafter cited as *Myst.* book.paragraph). All translations follow Clarke et al. unless noted otherwise. See also Addey, *Divination and Theurgy*, and the secondary literature therein.

7. Tanaseanu-Döbler, *Theurgy in Late Antiquity*, 278–90, has shown how Iamblichus's theory works with an existing set of practices, but that his theorization of theurgy is primarily "ritual in ink," a creation of a tradition through writing.

8. Johnston, "Animating Statues," 462–63.

9. See, e.g., Layne, "Cosmic Etiology and Demiurgic Mimesis," 134–63; and Timotin, "La Théorie de la Prière chez Jamblique," and the secondary material therein.

10. See O'Meara, *Platonopolis*, 40–115. For Julian's relation to Iamblichus and religion, see *Platonopolis*, 120–31.

11. Elm, *Sons of Hellenism*.

12. O'Meara, *Platonopolis*, 71; see also Elm, *Sons of Hellenism*, esp. 327–35; Dingeldein, "Julian's Philosophy and His Religious Program," 119–29; Remes, *Plotinus on Self*, 238; and Teitler, *The Last Pagan Emperor*, 9–11.

13. Halliwell, *The Aesthetics of Mimesis*, 314.

14. For some of the most important overviews of Plotinus, see Emilsson, *Plotinus*, and the secondary literature therein, including Hadot, *Plotinus or the Simplicity of Vision*; O'Meara, *Plotinus*; Reale, *A History of Ancient Philosophy*, 4:325–400; Gerson, *Plotinus*; Gerson, ed., *Cambridge Companion to Plotinus*; Beierwaltes, *Das wahre Selbst*; and Clark, *Plotinus*.

15. Stang, *Our Divine Double*, 188. See also, e.g., *Enn.* 5.4.2. Stang's work here is in conversation with Rist, "The Indefinite Dyad."

16. See Rappe, *Reading Neoplatonism*, 27: "Precisely because intellectual knowledge is infallible due to intellect's inherent self-reflexivity (intellect is its objects), for Plotinus, philosophical activity operates beyond the constraints of epistemology." Epistemology and ontology are not separable spheres in Neoplatonist philosophy because there is no gap between epistemology and ontology in the Intellect, even if philosophers could emphasize one more than another. Plotinus will occasionally refer to this kind of image as a "natural image [φύσει εἰκών]" as opposed to an image that is the product of art (τέχνῃ γενομένης τῆς εἰκόνος). The natural image exists "as long as its archetype is there."

17. See Rappe, *Reading Neoplatonism*, 19–20.

18. Humans are the determined "effect" of that in which they participate, which is their cause. For a brief discussion of the so-called "doctrine" of double causation, see Tollefsen, *Activity and Participation*, 21–31.

19. This claim is largely based on Plato, *Timaeus* 41d–42d. See also *Enn.* 5.7.1 and 6.5.8.

20. The soul's status as an image gives it what Charles Stang and Pauliina Remes describe as doubling. For more, see Schroeder, "Plotinus and Language," 336–55, which notes the distinction between two senses of "likeness" in Plotinus—symmetrical and asymmetrical relationships. The symmetrical relationship finds its model in the portrait (*Enn.* 6.3.15–31). We can judge a kind of likeness (yes, his nose does look like that, or no, it does not). The asymmetrical relationship, however, is indexed to a "different kind of likeness." The colors and shapes that make up the picture of Socrates are not Socrates, but representations of his visible

form. While language and art cannot "disclose" the One, there is a kind of binding or holding toward (ἔχειν) that language can perform (*Enn.* 5.3.14).

21. See Rappe, *Reading Neoplatonism*, 108–14, 231–43.

22. These two likenesses mimic those between the One and the Intellect. See *Enn.* 5.1.7.

23. See Schroeder, "Plotinus and Language," 338.

24. See Stang, *Our Divine Double*, 212.

25. See, e.g., *Enn.* 6.4.2.

26. Rappe, *Reading Neoplatonism*, 27–28. Rappe continues: "The locus of the representational gap has migrated in the philosophy of Plotinus."

27. See *Enn.* 5.3.1 and 4.6.2.

28. For Plotinus the Intellect does *not* simply receive impressions (τύπος). "If we were merely taking in impressions of what we see, it will not be possible to view the actual objects that we are seeing, but only reflections and shadows of those objects, so that the actual things themselves will be one thing, another objects of sight another" (*Enn.* 4.6.1). For Plotinus, overcoming this gap is what philosophy trains us to do. It is a "power" that allows for seeing and seen to be one. It sees "from the inside." See, e.g., Clark, *Plotinus*, 194–208.

29. Stephen Halliwell, *The Aesthetics of Mimesis*, 316–23, rightly highlights this passage and passages like this to point to the possibility of a way in which art itself can become valuable or lead to disinterested contemplation of beauty. A stone in and of itself, Plotinus says, is not art. Some stones just sit there, but others, having been "mastered by art," can be "turned into a statue of a god or of a man." How a stone becomes a piece of art, though, happens through a rather specific process (*Enn.* 5.8.1, 9–11, trans. altered). Because the stone cannot turn itself into art, it is through a series of participations that art manifests itself: (1) the stone is touched by a man, who (2) had the image in his mind, because (3) he was participating in art (μετεῖχε τῆς τέχνης). At every step of dissemination—from the form of art, to the image in the mind, to the chiseled object—there is a weakening, but enough of a trace remains (for those with eyes to see) to see that the object points away from itself.

30. Cicero, *On the Orator* 2.11, 36; see Burrow, *Imitating Authors*, 82.

31. *Enn.* 4.3.11; *Enn.* 5.8.4; and Halliwell, *The Aesthetics of Mimesis*, 317.

32. Stang, *Our Divine Double*, 213, citing Mazur, "Mystical Self-Reversion."

33. We might rewrite the passage quoted above about Phidias (*Enn.* 5.8.1) by saying that by working on our statue, we too "run back up to the forming principles"; but "also we do a great deal by [our]selves, and, since [we] possess beauty, [we] make up what is defective in us."

34. See Chapter 1 and the importance of ἐξαίφνης in the *Republic*. Those images, Plotinus writes in *Enn.* 1.6.7, provide the jolt needed to ascend.

35. *Enn.* 6.4.2, trans. altered: "Certainly there is both the true All and the imitation of the All [Ἔστι δὴ τὸ μὲν ἀληθινὸν πᾶν, τὸ δὲ τοῦ παντὸς μίμημα], that is, the nature of this visible universe. The really All is in nothing [Τὸ μὲν οὖν ὄντως πᾶν ἐν οὐδενί ἐστιν], for there is nothing prior to it."

36. Plotinus might even be playing off the abusive relationship of poetry in *Rep.* 607e–608b, though the abused there is a man.

37. See Gerson, *Plotinus*, 293n50.

38. This translation follows Mazur, "Mystical Self-Reversion," 34.

39. See Plato, *Timaeus* 36c.

40. Stang, *Our Divine Double*, 230.

41. Even calling this union "being" is a mistake because being exists only as far as the Intellect, whereas the One is beyond being.

42. Or perhaps the more accurate title, *The Reply of the Master Abamon to the Letter of Porphyry to Anebo, and the Solutions to the Questions It Contains*. For more on the history of text, including Iamblichus's authoring the text under the pseudonym Abamon, see the introduction, esp. xxvi–lii.

43. "Theurgy" was coined by the authors of the Chaldean Oracles about a century before Iamblichus. Iamblichus provides very little description of what these rituals actually looked like. It was knowledge he assumed his audience already possessed. For an example of theurgy, see Fowden, *The Egyptian Hermes*, 116–41.

44. *Myst.* 3.27. For Proclus's report of Iamblichus's critique of Plotinus's undescended soul, see his *Commentary on Timaeus* 4, fr. 87, trans. Dillon, in *Iamblichi Chalcidensis*, 198–201.

45. Shaw, *Theurgy and the Soul*, 103.

46. See Plato's *Laws* 713c–d.

47. Shaw, *Theurgy and the Soul*, 269.

48. Cf. Plotinus, *Enn.* 5.8.4.

49. Shaw, "The Soul's Innate Gnosis of the Gods," 129. See Hadot, "Théologie, exégèse, révélation, écriture dans la philosophie grecque," 13–34, where Hadot defines theurgy as "a technique revealed by the gods themselves in order to allow the human to enter into contact with them" (27, trans. mine). See Addey, *Divination and Theurgy*, 220.

50. See Shaw, "Taking the Shape of the Gods."

51. See *Myst.* 1.15: "And indeed, if any degree of kinship and likeness, whether near or remote, is present, this is sufficient for the contact of which we are now speaking. For nothing enters, even to a minimal extent, into likeness with the gods, to which the gods are not straightway present and united. It is not then, as with beings which are possessed of sense-perception and souls, but in accordance with the divine forms themselves and with the gods themselves, that contact (resulting from these offerings), so far as possible, comes about."

52. Shaw, *Theurgy and the Soul*, 17.

53. Shaw, *Theurgy and the Soul*, 25.

54. See Shaw, "The Soul's Innate Gnosis of the Gods," 117–29.

55. See *Enn.* 5.3.

56. There is a break in the text here.

57. See Lampe, *A Patristic Greek Lexicon*, s.v. "συμπλοκή" for the "union of natures in Christ."

58. My changes to the translation in part follow Shaw's in *Theurgy and the Soul*, 136.

59. Iamblichus calls this "another principle of the soul superior to all nature and generation" (*Myst.* 8.7). See also Digeser, "The Power of Religious Rituals," 81–92.

60. See Shaw, "The Role of *Aesthesis* in Theurgy," 93. Iamblichus writes of ecstasy in two illuminating passages, *Myst.* 1.5 and *Myst.* 3.25.

61. Addey, *Divination and Theurgy*, esp. 127–282.

62. E.g., *Myst.* 7.2.

63. Shaw, *Theurgy and the Soul*, 204.

64. This is not unique to Neoplatonism. For remarkable similarities between Iamblichus and Origen on magical divine names, see Dillon, "The Magical Power of Names." Origen's theory of names there is not so different from Eunomius's *Apology* 8, 12. See my brief analysis in Chapter 4. While there is a real overlap here, the contrast is telling as well. For Iamblichus

there could be no single language or word because that would give "universal power to a particular *qua* particular" (Shaw, *Theurgy and the Soul*, 205). The connection is that the names of the gods are determined by the gods. It is this claim that Gregory of Nyssa never grows tired of critiquing in *Against Eunomius*.

65. See *Myst.* 2.11: "It is the accomplishment of the acts not to be divulged and beyond all conception, and the power of the unutterable symbols, understood solely by the gods, which establishes theurgic union." For a more full discussion beyond Rappe's *Reading Neoplatonism*, see Coulter, *Literary Microcosm*, esp. 32–72; Dillon, "Image, Symbol, and Analogy"; and Struck, *Birth of the Symbol*, esp. 226.

66. See Iamblichus, *In Timaeum*, Book 3, fr. 49.1, in *Iamblichi Chalcidensis*, 152–55: "Our vehicle is made spherical, and is moved in a circle, whenever the Soul is especially assimilated to Mind."

67. See *Enn.* 5.6.5 above.

68. See Struck, *Birth of the Symbol*, 223–25; and *Myst.* 7.4.

69. See Addey, *Divination and Theurgy*, 221.

70. See, e.g., Corrigan, *Evagrius and Gregory*, 155; and Holman, *The Hungry Are Dying*.

71. For the connection between Julian, Iamblichus's philosophical influence, and Cappadocia, see Elm, *Sons of Hellenism*, esp. 88–143. Elm points in particular to the importance of Julian's teacher and leading theurgist of his day, Maximus of Ephesus; for more on Julian's career and turn away from Christianity, see Teitler, *The Last Pagan Emperor*, esp. 7–16, 49–70; more broadly, see Edwards, *Religions of the Constantinian Empire*.

For the spread of Iamblichus through his own letters and then the letters' subsequent interest, see Dillon, "The Letters of Iamblichus," 51–62.

72. This is especially true of Iamblichus's *Pythagorean Sequence*, esp. his *On the Pythagorean Life* and *Exhortation to Philosophy*. See Dillon, "The Letters of Iamblichus"; and Dillon and Polleichtner, eds., *Iamblichus of Chalcis: The Letters*; and more broadly on protreptic literature, Collins, *Exhortations to Philosophy*.

73. See, e.g., Athanassiadi, "Apamea and the Chaldaean Oracles"; Bowersock, *Julian the Apostate*; Bowersock, *Hellenism in Late Antiquity*; and Wiemer, *Libanios und Julian*. For a helpful overview of the secondary material, see Banchich's review of Smith, *Julian's Gods*; more recently, see Watts, *The Final Pagan Generation*, 109–15; and Teitler, *The Last Pagan Emperor*, esp. 49–70.

74. Julian, *Hymn to the King Helios* (*Orat.* 4) 157d, trans. Wright.

75. Socrates, *Church History* 4.26; Sozomen, *Ecclesiastical History* 6.17; and Julian, *Letters* 14 and 69.

76. Julian, *Letters* 15.

77. See Shaw, "The Role of *Aesthesis* in Theurgy," 98.

78. Proclus, *Elements of Theology* 129, trans. Dodd, 115.

79. For the overlap in exegesis in Julian's writing, see, e.g., Julian's *Hymn to the Mother of the Gods* (*Orat.* 5) 7.217c-d: "The more improbable [παράδοξόν] and wondrous the riddle, the more it seems to implore [us] not merely to believe what is being said, but to strive for the hidden and not to desist until, revealed with the guidance of the gods, it fills us with reason, or rather fulfills reason," cited in Elm, *Sons of Hellenism*, 113–14.

80. See Iamblichus, preserved in Proclus's *Commentary on Alcibiades* 85.14–16, fr. 4, in *Iamblichi Chalcidensis*, 74–75: "A power is median between an essence and an activity, put forth from the essence on the one hand and itself generating the activity on the other." See

Elm, *Sons of Hellenism*, 295–96; and Barnes, *The Power of God*. Barnes shows that "The continuity that Eunomius thought to find in the relation between activity and product Gregory locates in the relation between power and being. Gregory says that the activity does not reveal the nature of itself or its origin, but he will accept that activity makes known (in the sense of indicating the fact of the existence of) the originating being" (*The Power of God*, 280).

81. I say more about this resemblance in Chapter 4. Eunomius, of course, is not Iamblichus. (If nothing else, real problems arise when trying to map Eunomius's rigorous monotheism onto Iamblichus's many gods.) Mark DelCogliano argues in his *Basil of Caesarea's Anti-Eunomian Theory of Names* that Eunomius's theory of names bears only a "superficial similarity" (80) to those of Iamblichus or other Neoplatonists. For an important distinction between a general theory of names and a theory of divine names, see DelCogliano, *Basil of Caesarea's Anti-Eunomian Theory of Names*, 25–27. Eunomius's (and Aetius's) close ties to Julian and his court may suggest some kind of affinity between Julian's ritual and philosophical sensibilities and those of Eunomius. See Vaggione, *Eunomius of Cyzicus and the Nicene Revolution*, 14–26, 35.

82. Elm, *Sons of Hellenism*, 104, summarizing O'Meara, *Platonopolis*, 40–115. The philosopher-demiurge, here, is still set apart. His ability to perform the correct rituals puts him in position to create for those under him. As Elm points out, this is at odds with the Cappadocian Christian claim that "all could become God if they followed the ethical demands of the Trinity as taught them by their divinely inspired mediators, such as Gregory [of Nazianzus]" (485). See also Layne, "Cosmic Etiology and Demiurgic Mimesis."

83. See, e.g., Julian, *Hymn to the Mother of the Gods* 163d–65d; and Mayer, "Antioch and the Intersection Between Religious Factionalism, Place, and Power in Late Antiquity." On the role of ritual and space, see Falcasantos, *Constantinople*.

84. Elm, *Sons of Hellenism*, 335. For the universalism in Iamblichus's thought compared with previous philosophers, see also Fowden, *The Egyptian Hermes*, 131–41.

85. Elm, *Sons of Hellenism*, 335.

86. See, e.g., Watts, *The Final Pagan Generation*, 112; Holman, *The Hungry Are Dying*, esp. 56–57, 83, 154, 182; and Brown, *Poverty and Leadership*, 32–34, 40–41, 92–94. Julian's reforms, including programs of care for the poor, magnified the importance for the bishops of the Church being the locus of care. This required building physical spaces (e.g., hospitals, leprosaria, poor houses, and more), but also forming theological and liturgical imagination that made this kind of care central to Christian life. Indeed, the construction of these physical spaces and the theology enacted in, with, and through them are inseparable, and is a project I hope to take on in the future. While this coincidence of thought and space is well studied in theoretical material and in the early Roman Empire, there is more work to be done in late antiquity. I begin to address some of this material in Chapter 5.

Chapter 3

Note to epigraph: Blanchot, "Literature and the Right to Death," 306–7.

1. Eunapius, *Lives of the Philosophers*, trans. Wright, 376–79, 390–419.

2. *Perf.*, 99; *GNO* 30.178, trans. altered.

3. Stefaniw, "A Disciplined Mind," 242.

4. See Wendt, *At the Temple Gates*, 146–89.

5. My reading here owes much to Castelli, *Imitating Paul*.

6. In the authentic letters, see 1 Cor 4:16, 11:1; Phil 3:17; 1 Thes 1:6, 2:14; 2 Thes 3:7, 3:9. Unless noted otherwise, Biblical translations are from the NRSV. Greek is from *Nestle-Aland* 28. For mimesis in letters that many early Christians considered to be written by Paul, see Heb 6:12, 13:7; Eph 5:1.

7. On the father and child relationship as the model for imitation, see Seneca, *Ep.* 84.8: "I would have you resemble him as a child resembles its father not as a picture resembles its original, for a picture is a dead thing."

8. Beyond this command to imitate, we see another important way Christ is represented in the New Testament: typology or allegory. Paul frames the Christian life as a recapitulation of stories from the Hebrew Bible. Paul describes this reading practice as a "change in tone [ἀλλάξαι τὴν φωνήν]," or an "allegory [ἀλληγορούμενα]" (Gal 4:24). For our purpose, the nuances of the reading are less important than the mimetic imagination at work here. Paul sees contemporary Christians as living out iterations of sacred stories. See Young, *Biblical Exegesis.*

9. Nasrallah, *Christian Responses to Roman Art and Architecture*, esp. 144.

10. Stang, *Our Divine Double.*

11. King, *The Secret Revelation of John*, 2; for connection with Plato's *Timaeus*, see 111–15, 145, 158, 162, 185, 202–3.

12. See, e.g., Brown, *The Cult of the Saints*; Davis, *The Cult of Saint Thecla*; and Shoemaker, *Mary in Early Christian Faith and Devotion.*

13. Moss, *The Other Christs.*

14. Castelli, *Martyrdom and Memory*; and Perkins, *The Suffering Self.*

15. For echoes of Paul, see Phil 3:13–14; 1 Cor 9:24; 2 Tim 4:7.

16. Ignatius, *Epistle to the Romans* 2.2, 6, trans. Schoedel. For dating of Ignatius's letters to the Ephesians and to the Romans, see Moss, *Ancient Christian Martyrdom*, 54–55. See also Ignatius, *Epistle to the Ephesians* 10.3.

17. Castelli, *Martyrdom and Memory*, e.g., 8, 32, 135–39.

18. Lincoln, *Theorizing Myth*, cited in Castelli, *Martyrdom and Memory*, 31.

19. Different stories—and different iterations of those stories—took root in different regions, each holding up different characters and characteristics as the ideal martyr. On the importance of visual images of the martyrs, see Grig, *Making Martyrs*, 1, 111–35.

20. The point here has more to do with imitation than with Paul specifically. The relationship between imitation and archetype is dynamic. See Moss, *The Other Christs*, 46. Moss also draws heavily on Castelli's *Martyrdom and Memory.*

21. Moss, *The Other Christs*, 46; see Acts 6:8–7:60. Moss argues that the parallel between Stephen's asking God to forgive his stoners and Jesus's "forgive them for they know not what they do" is not the case of Stephen following Jesus's lead, but of Luke, under the influence of martyr texts, placing these words in both their mouths (*The Other Christs*, 56).

22. *The Martyrdom of St. Polycarp* 1. All translations follow Musurillo, in *Acts of the Christian Martyrs.*

23. On the development of the martyrdom genre and possible dating, see Moss, "On the Dating of Polycarp."

24. *The Martyrdom of St. Polycarp* 19.

25. *The Martyrdom of St. Polycarp* 15.

26. *The Martyrdom of St. Polycarp* 16.

27. *The Martyrdom of St. Polycarp* 18.

28. Stewart-Sykes, *The Life of Polycarp*, 4–22, 74–84; and, more broadly, see Mayer's introduction to John Chrysostom, *The Cult of the Saints*, 11–19.

29. See Origen, *Exhortation to Martyrdom*, in *Origen* 15, 37, trans. Greer; Greek in *Origenes Werke*, vol. 1. Origen calls these spiritual martyrdoms "different sorts of racks [ποικίλοις στρεβλωτηρίοις]."

30. The martyr's death becomes an anchor for Christian piety (if they died, can you not even perform these basic acts?). Their story becomes a touchstone for many other aspects of piety.

31. *The Martyrs of Lyons* 1.41, ed. and trans. Musurillo, 75.

32. See Castelli, *Martyrdom and Memory*, 104–33, esp. 126.

33. See Moss, *The Other Christs*, 113–76, esp. 164.

34. Brown, "Enjoying the Saints," 1–24.

35. Augustine, *Sermon* 325.1; *Patrologia Latina* 38:1447, quoted in Brown, "Enjoying the Saints," 4, trans. altered.

36. Brown, "Enjoying the Saints," 9.

37. Brown, "Enjoying the Saints," 9.

38. Brown, "Enjoying the Saints," 9, italics original.

39. Brown, "Enjoying the Saints," 10.

40. Brown, "Enjoying the Saints," 16.

41. In "Enjoying the Saints," Brown corrects his original *patroni* model—where saints functioned analogously to the late Roman aristocracy as protectors and intercessors—because it cannot explain the importance of the heavenly hierarchy *imperfectly* mirroring the earthly Roman world, e.g., Brown, *The Cult of the Saints*.

42. Brown, "Enjoying the Saints," 16–17. See also Cazelles, *Le corps de sainteté*; and Moss, *The Other Christs*, 146.

43. Limberis, *Architects of Piety*, 52.

44. Basil of Caesarea, *Forty Martyrs*, trans. Allen, 68–69; *PG* 31.508. All translations follow Allen.

45. Basil of Caesarea, *Forty Martyrs*, 68; *PG* 31.508.

46. Basil of Caesarea, *Forty Martyrs*, 68–69; *PG* 31.508.

47. Basil of Caesarea, *Forty Martyrs*, 76; *PG* 31.524–25.

48. James and Webb, "'To Understand Ultimate Things,'" esp. 9–11; and Nelson, "To Say and to See," 143–68.

49. See Asterius of Amasea, *Ecphrasis on the Holy Martyr Euphemia* 4, trans. Dehandschutter, 176.

50. Webb, "Accomplishing the Picture: Ekphrasis, Mimesis, and Martyrdom," 23. Webb also points to Basil's *Homily on the Forty Martyrs of Sebaste* as another example of mimesis intensifying the presence of a martyr to inspire imitation of the martyr.

51. Asterius of Amasea, *Ecphrasis on the Holy Martyr Euphemia* 4, trans. Dehandschutter, 176.

52. Miller, *The Corporeal Imagination*, 100.

53. See Brakke, *Demons and the Making of the Monk*, 23–47.

54. *VA* 47. All translations are from Gregg; Greek in *Vie d'Antoine*, ed. Bartelink. See 2 Cor 1:12.

55. Vivian, "St. Antony the Great and the Monastery of St. Antony," 5; Rufinas, *Inquiry About the Monks in Egypt* 5.3, trans. Cain, 99. After providing the evidence from Jerome and

the *Historia Monachorum*, Vivian suggests "as many as four thousand male and female monastics." David Brakke and Andrew Crislip suggest that about one thousand were under Shenoute's leadership (*Selected Discourses of Shenoute the Great*, 5n11).

56. *VA* introduction.

57. *VA* introduction.

58. *VA* 14.

59. Brakke, *Athanasius and Asceticism*, 258.

60. *VA* 55, trans. altered.

61. *VA* 27, trans. altered. See Brakke, *Athanasius and Asceticism*, 258. It is also worth noting the ambivalence around imitation here as the devil "undertook one night to assume the form of a woman and to imitate [μιμεῖσθα] her every gesture, in order that he might beguile Antony" (*VA* 5).

62. *VA* 7. See Athanasius's *Letter to Marcellinus* 10–12, trans. Gregg.

63. *VA* 38.

64. Ward, ed., *Sayings*, prologue, xxxv.

65. Ward, *Sayings*, 3. For a similar tendency within the letters of Antony, see Stefaniw, "The Oblique Ethics of the Letters of Antony," 169–85.

66. Ward, *Sayings*, 2.

67. See also Ward, *Sayings*, 2. While Bolman in "Mimesis, Metamorphosis, and Representation" helpfully argues that these cells were often filled with representations of saints, it is not clear to me that monks always took those images as imitations to follow. It seems more that these images were meant to focus the mind to see the sacred beyond them. (See my discussion of Origen below.)

68. *Virg.* 24; *GNO* 31.337, trans. slightly altered from Moore and Wilson.

69. Ward, *Sayings*, 7.

70. Ward, *Sayings*, 214.

71. Ward, *Sayings*, 37.

72. Bolman, "Mimesis, Metamorphosis and Representation," 69; and for the image, see Plate 3.

73. Cameron, "Ascetic Closure and the End of Antiquity," 153. See also Harpham's "Asceticism and the Compensations of Art," in *Asceticism*, 357–68.

74. Brakke, *Athanasius and Asceticism*, 266.

75. See Stewart, "Imageless Prayer," esp. 201.

76. Though we should not underestimate the power of words and literature (literacy rates barely cracked double digits), the role of visual culture is even more important than it is often credited. Current work on literacy rests on the foundation of Harris, *Ancient Literacy*.

77. Elsner, *Imperial Rome and Christian Triumph*, 27.

78. Jensen, *Face to Face*, 1–34.

79. Peppard, "Was the Presence of Christ in Statues?" in *The Art of Empire*, ed. Jefferson and Jensen, 232. The entire book provides a helpful entry point to recent discussions of Christian art and its relation to the Roman Empire. The book as a whole is a reevaluation of Mathews's *The Clash of Gods*. Peppard draws the ratio from Zanker, *The Power of Images*; and from Pfanner, "Über das Herstellen von Porträts," 178; the analogy to churches in the US is Peppard's.

80. Jensen, *Face to Face*, 23.

81. Jensen, *Face to Face*, 23.

82. Jensen, *Face to Face*, 23. For a comparison with the rise and fall of statues of Christ in the fourth century, see Peppard, "Was the Presence of Christ in Statues?," 225–70.

83. The work of turning oneself into a statue as an image of holiness is one we saw in Plotinus in the previous chapter, but is one that runs through much of late ancient ascetic literature. On Christian concerns about the power of statues, not unlike the power of portraits, see James, "'Pray Not to Fall into Temptation and Be on Your Guard,'" 12–20.

84. Jensen, *Face to Face*, 67–68.

85. See, e.g., Brown, "The Glow of Byzantium."

86. Francis, "Living Icons," 586.

87. Francis, "Living Icons," 586; Jensen, *Face to Face*, 68.

88. Importantly, we need to see this not as a replacement, but as another possible mode of viewing. For Basil of Caesarea, while the saints do have a special presence about them, they could also be shown as a way to cultivate virtue. Mimetic practices such as painting, ekphrasis, and energeia could vivify the saints, but that did not negate them as models of virtue. In his *Letter* 2.3, to Gregory of Nazianzus, Basil suggests that the ability to be virtuous is helped by holding up biblical characters as "divinely inspired statues," whom Gregory can imitate in his pursuit of Christian perfection.

89. Basil, *Ep.* 2.3, trans. altered from Deferrari and McGuire, 17.

90. For more context, see Johnston, "Animating Statues."

91. Basil, *Ep.* 2.3, trans. altered from Deferrari, 19.

92. Eunapius, *Lives of the Sophists*, trans. Wright, 475.

93. *Myst.* 5.23.

94. Johnston, "Animating Statues," 469.

95. *Myst.* 5.23–24.

96. Francis, "Living Icons," 589–90, referring to Elsner, *Art and the Roman Viewer*, 18–22. This distinction for Elsner is not one about a shift in formal style as much as it is about what Roland Barthes called a "History of Looking" in his *Camera Lucida*, 9–12. For Elsner, "the key to an understanding of the transformation of Roman art—its shift from illusionistic verisimilitude to abstraction—is not in the observable formalism alone but also in the underlying conceptions, views and ideologies of the people who commissioned, who made and who looked at the works of art" (*Art and the Roman Viewer*, 124).

97. Francis, "Living Icons," 590.

98. Elsner, *Art and the Roman Viewer*, 90. Elsner here takes Plotinus's *hypernoesis* as representative of late ancient viewing.

99. Asterius of Amasea, *Ecphrasis* 4, trans. Dehandschutter, 176.

100. Jerome, *Against Vigilantius* 5, in *NPNF* 6, 419, trans. Fremantle et al. See Frank, *Memory of the Eyes*, 176.

101. Gregory of Nyssa, *De deitate filii et spiritus sancti*, GNO 57.120–21, trans. altered from Elsner, *Imperial Rome and Christian Triumph*, 221–22.

102. For an analysis of how "ordinary Christians" might have engaged in doctrine, see Tannous, *The Making of the Medieval Middle East*, esp. 29–31; and Cassin, "*De deitate filii et spiritus sancti et in Abraham*," 287–88.

103. E.g., Gregory cites his reading practices as foundational for his own. See Gregory's preface to his *Homilies on the Song of Songs*; see also Gregory of Nyssa, *Life of Gregory the Wonderworker*, 2.22; GNO 49.13, trans. Slusser.

104. For an overview of these debates, see Ayres, *Nicaea and Its Legacy*; for Gregory's own role, see Radde-Gallwitz, *Gregory of Nyssa's Doctrinal Works*.

105. Origen, *On First Principles*. I consulted Behr's edition and translation of *On First Principles*, but translations follow Butterworth, whose translation is based on *De Principiis*, ed. Koetschau (hereafter cited as *Princ.* book.chapter.section).

106. See *Princ.* 2.8.3: Origen, to describe this fall, provides a false etymology, explaining that soul (ψυχή) is derived from the verb "to cool" (ψύχεσθαι). As minds drift from God who is "fire," they become "cold." To guard against this cold, minds took on material "either fine in substance or grosser" in proportion to how far they had drifted from God. Portions of the text are disputed. See Behr's translation and commentary in *On First Principles*, vol. 1–2, 1: xcvii–xcviii, 2:223–35. The legitimacy of authorship, for this chapter, is less important than the likelihood that the ideas ascribed to Origen were a live option for many Christians.

107. E.g., *Princ.* 3.5.6. See Giulea, "*Simpliciores, Eruditi*."

108. Cf. Stefaniw, "A Disciplined Mind," esp. 244–48. Stefaniw's bringing together of Origen, Iamblichus, and Athanasius demonstrates a heightened emphasis on mimesis in late antiquity. My goal in this book, however, is to highlight the *different* work mimesis does in different philosophical and theological programs. Mimesis is controversial because it can organize and govern so many aspects of religious life.

109. *Princ.* 2.9.6.

110. *Princ.* 2.6.3. For Origen's discussion of "image," see 1.2.6–8.

111. *Princ.* 3.6.6.

112. *Princ.* 3.6.1.

113. *Princ.* 3.6.1.

114. *Princ.* 3.6.1. We might imagine how this looked in practice by turning to Methodius's *Symposium* 10.4, in which Domnina argues that unlike the other tools God provided to lead people back to God (e.g., laws), the devil could make deceptive imitations of virginity. The inimitability of virginity is the mark of its truth: it is not an external law to obey or archetype to imitate, but a stability in the soul beyond imitation. Virtue, and specifically chastity, transcends mimesis and weds the Christian to God.

115. *Princ.* 2.11.6.

116. The Church, too, is a particularly intense kind of schoolroom within creation (e.g., *Princ.* 2.11.6).

117. *Com. John* 1.33. All translations are from Heine. Greek from *Commentaire sur saint Jean*, ed. Blanc.

118. *Com. John* 1.27.

119. *Com. John* 1.39.

120. *Com. John* 1.40.

121. *Com. John* 1.45.

122. *Com. John* 1.39–40. On the power of words, especially names, in Origen, much like in what we saw in Iamblichus and Proclus, see Dillon, "The Magical Power of Names."

123. As we saw in Plotinus, there can be no gap between epistemology and ontology.

124. *Com. John* 1.23.

125. The impossibility of representation is due to materiality, which is at odds with God's nature. Human limitation is the only thing that prevents humans from fully contemplating God, and thus as bodily limits fade so too does the problem. A fuller participation is possible as

images fall away, and therefore, participatory mimesis sublimates representational mimesis. To anticipate a contrast, we can say that, for Gregory, representation and participation work together differently. For Origen, divine power is finite (see *Princ.* 2.9.1). The infinitude of God makes any representation fail and keeps Christians in constant need of finding new representational practices to continue participating in God. Mimesis holds both of these discourses together.

126. *De decretis* 20.3, trans. altered from Anatolios, *Athanasius*, 197–98. All translations follow Anatolios. Greek in *Athanasius Werke*, ed. Opitz.

127. *De decretis* 20.5, *Athanasius*, 197–98; and *De decretis* 22.5, *Athanasius*, 200.

128. *Orations Against the Arians* 1.39; *Athanasius*, 96–97, commenting on Phil 2:5–11.

129. *De decretis* 20.5, *Athanasius*, 198.

130. *De decretis* 20.5, *Athanasius*, 198. See Anatolios, *Retrieving Nicaea*, 106.

131. Jensen, *Face to Face*, 52.

132. Athanasius, *Oration* 3.5, in *NPNF* 4, 396, trans. altered from Atkinson and Robertson.

133. See Francis, "Living Icons," 558.

134. *Inc.* 16, trans. altered from Thomson. All Greek and translations from *Inc.* and *CG* follow Thomson.

135. *CG* 3, trans. altered. See Anatolios, *Athanasius: The Coherence of His Thought*, esp. 63–67.

136. *Inc.* 16.

137. *Inc.* 54.

138. *Princ.* 2.9.1.

139. E.g., *Princ.* 3.1.14; and *Inc.* 1.3.

140. See Meredith, *Gregory of Nyssa*, 13.

141. *Princ.* 2.9.1, trans. altered.

142. *Perf.*, 99; *GNO* 30.178, trans. altered.

Chapter 4

Notes to epigraphs: Carson, introduction to Euripides, *Hippolytos*, in *Grief Lessons*, 168; *Perf.*, 97, *GNO* 30.176.

1. *Perf.*, 95; *GNO* 30.173. I have frequently altered Callahan's translations, but I provide her page numbers as well as the *GNO* reference throughout. Both the recipient and the dating of *On Perfection* are unclear. The letter is likely written to the monk Olympius, the same monk to whom *The Life of Macrina* is addressed, and is typically dated in the final years of Gregory's life. See Daniélou's dating in "La chronologie des oeuvres de Grégoire de Nysse"; cf. May, who places *On Perfection* between 370 and 379 in "Die Chronologie des Lebens und der Werke des Gregor von Nyssa," 56.

2. *Perf.*, 122; *GNO* 30.213–14.

3. *Perf.*, 99; *GNO* 30.178.

4. See Elm, *Sons of Hellenism*, 247–49, and the secondary literature therein. For Gregory on the Cratylus, see Radde-Gallwitz, *Gregory of Nyssa's Doctrinal Works*, 143–46.

5. Izmirlieva, *All the Names of the Lord*, 144. For more, see Edmonds, *Drawing Down the Moon*, esp. 133–48. And for an up-to-date survey, see Frankfurter, ed., *Guide to the Study of Ancient Magic*.

6. Brown, "A World Winking with Messages."

7. DelCogliano, *Basil of Caesarea's Anti-Eunomian Theory of Names*, 1. See also Douglass, "The Combinatory Detour," 82–105; and Radde-Gallwitz, *Transformation of Divine Simplicity*, esp. 87–112.

8. Elm, *Sons of Hellenism*, 245–65. For perfection in Eunomius's teacher and mentor Aetius, see Aetius, *Syntagmation* 9–10, in Wickham, "The Syntagmation of Aetius the Ano-mean," esp. 541; and Radde-Gallwitz, *Transformation of Divine Simplicity*, 212–20. For Eunomius, perfection requires a simplicity that does not allow for change. Gregory's call for perfection here counters that definition, locating perfection in the endless change toward the better.

9. *Myst.* 1.12. See also Dillon, "The Magical Power of Names," 203–16.

10. Anatolios, *Retrieving Nicaea*, 158–215, esp. 159.

11. *Myst.* 7.4. For my more detailed analysis, see Motia, "Gregory of Nyssa."

12. *Lib. Ap.* 12. All Greek and translations of Eunomius are from *Eunomius: The Extant Works*, ed. and trans. Vaggione.

13. Eunomius, *Frag.* 2, in *Eunomius*, 178–79. See Vaggione, *Eunomius* 167–70; and *Eunomius of Cyzicus and the Nicene Revolution*, 253–54.

14. See Radde-Gallwitz, *Transformation of Divine Simplicity*, 81–86; and DelCogliano, *Basil of Caesarea's Anti-Eunomian Theory of Names*, 49–95.

15. *Lib. Ap.* 7.

16. Gregory's theorization of divine infinity, while novel, had antecedents. See Weedman, "Polemical Context of Gregory of Nyssa's Doctrine of Divine Infinity."

17. *CE* 2.144.

18. *CE* 2.238.

19. *CE* 2.260. Radde-Gallwitz, *Transformation of Divine Simplicity*, esp. 182–85.

20. *CE* 2.144–45. For more on this passage, see Douglass, "The Combinatory Detour," 93–94.

21. E.g., *CE* 2.215; see also Vasiliu, *Eikôn*, 11–298, esp. 115–28.

22. *CE* 2.281–83, trans. altered.

23. Elm, *Sons of Hellenism*, 263.

24. Elm, *Sons of Hellenism*, 263n176.

25. While "illustration" is a "performance" in the sense of a speech act, I use "perfor-mance" here to signify a way of living that includes both the interiority of a mimetic life of perfection and the necessary representational part of it. In this way "performance" is not just an external phenomenon with no bearing on an inner life but would include a way of training both. Ritual studies can fall into the distinction that I am trying to overcome here. See, e.g., Seligman et al., *Ritual and Its Consequences*, esp. 3–42. Their claim that the subjective and sincere are antithetical turns affect into something necessarily expressive instead of some-thing that can also be performativity shaped. "The whole issue of our internal states is often irrelevant," Seligman writes, "What you *are* is what you *are in the doing*, which is of course an external act" (24). Gregory, however, sees ritual and the pursuit of Christian perfection as a larger practice of joining the inner and outer. "What you are in the doing" includes affective or internal states even if it is not reducible for them.

26. *Perf.*, 95; *GNO* 30.173.

27. *Ref.* 14; *GNO* 2.318; *Perf.*, 95; *GNO* 30.173; *Perf.*, 111; *GNO* 30.191.

28. Stang, "Writing," 252–63.

29. *Perf.*, 95; *GNO* 30.173–74.

30. *Perf.*, 96; *GNO* 30.174; see Phil 2:9.

31. *Perf.*, 96; *GNO* 30.174–75.

32. *CE* 2.259; see also *In illud tunc*, *GNO* 11.3.

33. More broadly, see Vasiliu, *Eikôn*, esp. 115–28. Vasiliu describes a shift that happens in Gregory—as well as in Basil and Gregory of Nazianzus—from images being transparent and open (like a book) to the image as more mirror-like. She argues that to be an image of God, for Gregory, is not to achieve any "likeness" or "resemblance" but to become a kind of "vertical relay [*relais vertical*]." Unlike earlier versions of this "relay"-thesis, the Cappadocian's is not an abstract principle, but an individualized, incarnate "truth" in act.

34. For an analysis of Gregory's understanding of how to imitate Paul compared with John Chrysostom's and Pseudo-Dionysius's, see Motia, "Three Ways to Imitate Paul."

35. *Perf.*, 98; *GNO* 30.177–78.

36. Alternative manuscript titles for the treatise include "On What is Necessary to be a Christian [ον χρὴ εἶναι τὸν χριστιανόν]" and "A letter quite useful for Characterizing a Real Christian [ἐπιστολὴ χρήσιμος πάνυ χαρακτηρίζουσα τὸν ὄντως χριστιανόν]" (*GNO* 30.173); see Callahan's introduction to *Perf.*, 93.

37. *Perf.*, 99; *GNO* 30.179.

38. *Perf.*, 99; *GNO* 30.179–80.

39. *Perf.*, 99; *GNO* 30.179–80.

40. *Perf.*, 99; *GNO* 30.178. There is a Christological import to this, as Christ carries the "character" or "impress" of the father, and this "character" signifies the "equality [ἰσοστάσιον]" of the son with the father (*Perf.*, 106; *GNO* 30.188–89). This, in typical Nicene and post-Nicene rhetoric, does not decrease the size of the father, but "shows the greatness of God through the form shown [τὸ μέγεθος τοῦ θεοῦ διὰ τῆς μορφῆς ἐνδεικνύμενος]" (see *Perf.*, 113–14; *GNO* 30.200). See Ayres, *Nicaea and Its Legacy*, esp. 278–94.

41. Perhaps this excess that calls for imitation is most clear in knowing Christ as "light inaccessible [ἀπρόσιτον]" (*Perf.*, 96–97; *GNO* 30.175; 1 Tim 6:16). I comment on this below, but for now it is worth noting how Gregory shifts the title. Paul calls Christ, among other things, "light inaccessible" (1 Tim 6:16), yet when he comments on this name he writes, "Knowing Christ as 'the true light' [Jn 1:9], 'inaccessible' to falsehood, we learn this: that it is necessary for our lives to be illuminated by the rays of true light [φῶς δὲ ἀληθινὸν καὶ τῷ ψεύδει ἀπρόσιτον νοήσαντες τὸν Χριστὸν τοῦτο μανθάνομεν, ὅτι χρὴ καὶ τὸν ἡμέτερον βίον ταῖς τοῦ ἀληθινοῦ φωτὸς ἀκτῖσι καταφωτίζεσθαι]" (*Perf.*, 103; *GNO* 30.184). Gregory is not denying Christ as "inaccessible light," but in the adaption or association (προσοικειόω) of the names into life, there is endless interpretive work to be done.

42. The language of "failure," while inspired by Gregory, is largely mine. Gregory will use the language of façade, counterfeit, falsehood, and derivative, words that derive from Plato's concerns (see Chapter 1). I use "failure" here in ways akin to Halberstam's *The Queer Art of Failure*: to make out the way "failure" can be productive, even reverent or holy.

43. Both askesis and theology require both ontology and representation. Part of the ascetic life requires making oneself a representation, and the work of theological representation, for Gregory, is part of the ascetic life, pushing him toward perfection.

44. *Perf.*, 98; *GNO* 30.178.

45. *Perf.*, 101; *GNO* 30.181.

46. *Perf.*, 101; *GNO* 30.182.

47. *Perf.*, 97; *GNO* 30.176.

48. *Perf.*, 98; *GNO* 30.178; *Perf.*, 95; *GNO* 30.173.

49. *Perf.*, 102; *GNO* 30.183.

50. *Perf.*, 101; *GNO* 30.181–82.

51. See Behr, *The Nicene Faith*, e.g., 210–15; 475–81. "Fundamental to [Athanasius's, Basil's, Gregory of Nazianzus's, and Gregory of Nyssa's] exegetical work of understanding Christ is the distinction made between what Scripture says of Christ as divine and what it says of him as human, what has been called 'partitive exegesis'" (476). In *To Theophilus*, Gregory writes, "because of the intimate union between the flesh that was assumed and the Godhead that assumed, the names can be exchanged, so that the human can be called divine and the divine human" (267 [M. 1277]; *GNO* 9.127, trans. Orton).

52. Boersma, *Embodiment and Virtue*, 224–25. The comment is on *To Call Oneself a Christian*, but it also serves as his introduction to *On Perfection*.

53. *Cant.* 11, 334.

54. *Cant.* 11, 336; *Cant.* 12, 367.

55. For Christ as infinite, see *Perf.*, 106; *GNO* 30.190.

56. The artistic metaphor is explicit in *Perf.*, 110–11; *GNO* 30.195–96, quoted below. More broadly, see Webb, "Rhetorical and Theatrical Fictions," 107–24.

57. For the role of "the power of God" in Gregory, especially in connection with Eunomius, see Barnes, *The Power of God*, 1–20, 260–307.

58. *Perf.*, 102; *GNO* 30.182.

59. *Perf.*, 102; *GNO* 30.183.

60. While this treatise is structured around Paul's names for Christ, Gregory does occasionally reach outside Paul's writings into the Gospels.

61. *Perf.*, 97; *GNO* 30.176.

62. *Perf.*, 96–97; *GNO* 30.175–76; 1 Tm 6:16; Lk 1:33. On the importance of shared names between the Father and Son in pro-Nicene theologies, see Anatolios, *Retrieving Nicaea*. Gregory draws on a similar logic when he comments on Christ being the "power of God and the wisdom of God," that "through this description of Christ, we derive, first of all, notions befitting the divine, notions that make the name an object of reverence for us" (*Perf.*, 101; *GNO* 30.182).

63. *Perf.*, 96; *GNO* 30.174.

64. *Perf.*, 97; *GNO* 30.176.

65. For Origen, χωρέω is primarily a move toward internalization. He gives the example of Peter and Paul being Jews outwardly "for the salvation of many" and internally, for the same reason, being Christians (*Com. John* 1.41). Origen notably uses χωρέω in the run-up to describing the "eternal gospel" (*Com. John* 1.40): "The forerunners of Christ have visited them—words with good reason called 'pedagogues' because they are suited to souls which are called children—but the Son himself, who glorified himself as the Word who is God [Jn 1:1], has not yet visited them, because he awaits the preparation which must take place in men of God who are about to receive [χωρεῖν] his divinity" (*Com. John* 1.38). For Origen's connection between the names of Christ and virtues, see Origen, *Com. Rom.* 9.34.

66. See, e.g., *Timaeus* 47–48.

67. See Liddell and Scott, *LSJ*, and Lampe, *A Patristic Greek Lexicon*, s.v. "χωρέω." With an infinitive, the verb can mean "to be capable of doing." It also appears in Gen 13:6 LXX, where because the land could not contain (ἐχώει) him, Abraham goes forth. Gregory will make much of this passage in *CE* 2.84–96. And it appears in Matthew 19:11: "Not everyone can accept this teaching, but only those to whom it is given [Οὐ πάντες χωροῦσιν τὸν λόγον (τοῦτον), ἀλλ' οἷς δέδοται]."

68. *Perf.*, 95; *GNO* 30.173; *Perf.*, 97; *GNO* 30.176.

69. *Perf.*, 98; *GNO* 30.178.

70. *Perf.*, 99; *GNO* 30.178. Χαρακτήρ primarily means a minting, impressing, or stamping coins, and it thus takes on a sense of a distinctive mark, characteristic, character, type, image, or even style. I have tried to translate it according to context. I translate χωρέω here as "make" rather than "have" room to emphasize the point above about Gregory's linking human capacity to human growth.

71. For different views, see, e.g., Mateo-Seco, "Imitación y seguimiento"; and his entry "Imitation, μίμησις" in *BDGN*, 502–5.

72. *Perf.*, 108; *GNO* 30.192. For more examples of this kind of treatment, see below, esp. *Perf.*, 109–10; *GNO* 30.194–95.

73. *Perf.*, 103; *GNO* 30.184.

74. *Perf.*, 103; *GNO* 30.185.

75. *Perf.*, 109; *GNO* 30.193. For a broader view of faith across Gregory of Nyssa's writings, see Laird, *Gregory of Nyssa and the Grasp of Faith*, esp. 62–99.

76. See also *Or. Cat.* 37, trans. Richardson, 318–19; *GNO* 28.40–89. Gregory argues that the soul is united by faith by participating in God, and "the body comes into intimate union with its Saviour" by eating and drinking the bread and the water and wine in the Eucharist.

77. *Perf.*, 99; *GNO* 30.178–79.

78. See von Balthasar, *Presence and Thought*, 37–45; Daley, "Divine Transcendence and Human Transformation," esp. 69–72; and Douglass, *Theology of the Gap*, 36–37, 222–23, 267–68.

79. *Perf.*, 108; *GNO* 30.192.

80. *Perf.*, 108; *GNO* 30.192.

81. *Perf.*, 99; *GNO* 30.179. "As with the human body," Gregory writes, "the Christian ought to be recognized in his entirety [δι' ὅλου γνωρίζοιτο], as it is in every way befitting of those good considerations [νοουμένων] of Christ that the characteristics [χαρακτῆρας] are signified [ἐνσημαίνεσθαι] by his life" (*Perf.*, 99, *GNO* 30.179–80). Gregory refuses a bodiless transformation or a linking of the Christian life to an entirely soul-focused matter, as part of mimesis requires signifying with his life, body and soul.

82. *Perf.*, 109; *GNO* 30.193.

83. *Perf.*, 109; *GNO* 30.193–94.

84. The doubleness in νομοθετέω between lawgiving and construction here gets at both the analogy Gregory is working with from Luke 14:28 and the ways in which as one acquires more names in this life of faith, new forms of life become part of one's dwelling place.

85. See Maspero, *Trinity and Man*, 95–147, esp. 125–33.

86. The "stamp," "impress," or "mark" seems to be what the word χαρακτήρ is after here. The "picture" of the archetypal beauty has to do with representing by means of having an image impressed upon oneself. It is tied up with being a trustworthy image. The proper human mimetic activity is to become an image sanctioned by God as a representation of God. Gregory will use the analogy of the coin with Caesar's image on it.

87. 1 Peter 1:14 and Rom 12:2 are the only times the word συσχηματίζω appears in the New Testament. 1 Peter associates it with a change in desire: "Like obedient children, do not be conformed [συσχηματιζόμενοι] to the desires [ἐπιθυμίαις] that you formerly had in ignorance" (1 Pet 1:14). Romans links it with being "transformed by the renwing of your minds."

88. *Perf.*, 109–110; *GNO* 30.194–95.

89. For an explicit connection between mimesis and the incomprehensibility of the image of God, see *Op. Hom.* 11.2–4; *PG* 44.156.

90. Potolsky, *Mimesis*, 47–70.

91. *Perf.*, 96; *GNO* 30.175.

92. Gregory follows Paul, who follows God in providing accommodated speech for the one seeking perfection. Gregory's accommodated words provide a space that the one seeking can inhabit. And by dwelling in those words, readers too can be transformed. Through a reading of Paul's names for Christ, the Christian can glean this perfect life and, more, can join in this life. But because the life of Christ is itself infinite—both present and elusive—the life on offer must always conform to the virtues in one's capacities. The pattern can be a new path or a path forward, but it must be recognizable as a path if it is to lead to perfection. This accommodation requires speech to have an audience such that the true speech and the speech that leads to the virtues in God are not fully separable.

93. The line between imitation and worship is quite blurry here, as accurate imitation spills over into greater worship, and worship provides a necessary starting point to animate imitation.

94. Gregory's theory of the self involves struggle both against others and itself (*Perf.*, 102–3; *GNO* 30.184). For a broader account of selfhood and individuality in late antiquity, see Torrance and Zachhuber, eds., *Individuality in Late Antiquity*; and Brakke, Satlow, and Weitzman, eds., *Religion and the Self*.

95. *Perf.*, 110; *GNO* 30.195–97.

96. Gregory of Nyssa, *Perf.*, 110–11; *GNO* 30.195–96. Gregory's understanding of an endless desire coupled with mimesis seems to draw on, while differing from, Origen. They agree that as Christians learn more, they are also more prepared to learn. We can see a contrast in that just before it, Origen writes that "we have not received this longing from God on the condition that it should not or could not ever be satisfied; for in that case the 'love of truth' would appear to have been implanted in our mind by God the Creator to no purpose, if its gratification is never to be accomplished" (*Princ.* 2.11.4). But the parallels, as the passagge continues, are striking:

> When even in this life men devote themselves with great labour to sacred and religious studies, although they obtain only some small fragments out of the immeasurable treasures of divine knowledge, yet [they gain this advantage,] that they occupy their mind and understanding with these questions and press onward in their eager desire. Moreover they derive much assistance from the fact that by turning their mind to the study and love of truth they render themselves more capable of receiving instruction in the future. For when a man wishes to paint a picture, if he first sketches with the faint touch of a light pencil the outlines of the proposed figure and inserts suitable marks to indicate features afterwards to be added, this preliminary drawing with its faint outline undoubtedly renders the canvas more prepared to receive the true colors. So it will be with us, if only that faint form and outline is inscribed "on the tablets of our heart" by the pencil of our Lord Jesus Christ.

97. E.g., Plato, *Republic* 603b.

98. Avoiding those "heretical assumptions" makes a "contribution [συντελοῦντα] to our ethical life." Contemplating the non-heretical interpretation demands that doctrine and askesis remain tethered. See *Perf.*, 113; *GNO* 30.200: τὰ πρὸς τὸν ἠθικὸν βίον διὰ τούτων ἡμῖν

συντελοῦντα κατανοήσωμεν. Conforming oneself to an image, representing that image, and participating in that image are not antithetical, but anagogical; they mark an endless maturity and perfection (τέλειος). Anagogy carries a rather broad range for Gregory—broader than the well-known medieval definition. For the linking of virtue and anagogy, see Boersma, *Embodiment and Virtue*, 4.

99. *Perf.*, 111; *GNO* 30.196; Mt 11:29.

100. *Perf.*, 111; *GNO* 30.197.

101. *Perf.*, 120; *GNO* 30.211.

102. *Perf.*, 122; *GNO* 30.214.

103. *Perf.*, 119; *GNO* 30.209.

104. Brown, *The Ransom of the Soul*, 39.

105. *Perf.*, 120; *GNO* 30.210.

106. *Perf.*, 99; *GNO* 30.179–80.

107. *Perf.*, 120; *GNO* 30.210.

108. *Perf.*, 120; *GNO* 30.211.

109. Gregory also follows much of ancient medical literature (especially that of Galen). See, e.g., Sorabji, "The Mind-Body Relation in the Wake of Plato's *Timaeus*," 152–62; and Gill, *The Structured Self*, 238–322; or more broadly, see Gill, Whitmarsh, and Wilkins, eds., *Galen and the World of Knowledge*.

110. *Perf.*, 101; *GNO* 30.182; *Perf.*, 121–22; *GNO* 30.213. It appears here that the "opponent" is both a promise and threat; if "τὸ τρεπτὸν" is the enemy, it is also the solution, as this change is what allows humans to change for the better. Gregory here is answering the question: "What if someone should say that the good is difficult to achieve, since only the Lord of creation is immutable [ἄτρεπτος], whereas human nature is unstable [τρεπτή] and subject to change [πρὸς τὰς μεταβολὰς ἐπιτηδείως]." In Gregory's language from before, what is on offer is not an "overstepping" or "destruction" of nature, but a transformation of it.

111. *Perf.*, 121; *GNO* 30.212.

112. See *Perf.*, 120; *GNO* 30.212. On κοινωνέω or κοινωνία as participation in Gregory, see Balàs, *Μετουσία Θεοῦ*; Balàs, "Participation in the Specific Nature," 1079–85; and Balàs, *BDGN*, s.v. "Participation," 581–87.

113. *Perf.*, 121; *GNO* 30.212–13.

114. Paul's authority here, combined with the emphasis on actions and models, leads to questions about what it means to be a living model. How, if at all, does scripture function differently from another person who is so in tune with the words of scripture that her words and the words of scripture become indistinguishable?

115. While, especially in this Christological text, the connection between λόγος and Christ cannot be overstated, the word could mean the "treatise" or "the logic behind what I just laid out." See *Perf.*, 95; *GNO* 30.173; *Perf.*, 110–11; *GNO* 30.195–96; *Perf.*, 119; *GNO* 30.209; *Perf.*, 120; *GNO* 30.210; and *Perf.*, 121; *GNO* 30.212–13. The logic of the treatise shows that through mimesis and worship one can constantly change toward the better.

116. *Perf.*, 122; *GNO* 30.213–14.

117. See Chapter 1 for my comments on Plato's *Republic* 394e–395d.

Chapter 5

1. *Letters* 2–3; all translations follow Silvas; *Mac.*, trans. Corrigan, 21; *GNO* 32.370; *Ref.*, 225 [M 1240]; *GNO* 10.212, trans. Orton. The issue is well studied. See, e.g., Bitton-Ashkelony,

Encountering the Sacred, esp. 49–57; more broadly, see Casson, *Travel in the Ancient World*; Leyerle, "Mobility and the Traces of Empire," 110–23; Frank, *The Memory of the Eyes*; Elsner and Rutherford, eds., *Pilgrimage in Graeco-Roman and Early Christian Antiquity*; Johnson, *Literary Territories*; and Jacob, *The Sovereign Map*.

2. *Letter* 3.3; *GNO* 33.20, trans. altered.

3. *Letter* 3.1; *GNO* 33.20, trans. altered. Importantly, these are not only biblical sites; they are also Constantinian Churches. On the connection between pilgrimage and contemplation, see Nightingale, "The Philosopher at the Festival," 151–80.

4. See my discussion of "place" and "space" below. My reading of Gregory owes much to David Harvey, who argues that space "can be said to exist only insofar as it contains and represents within itself relationships to other objects" (Harvey, "Space as a Key Word," 121). The different spaces—e.g., Bethlehem and Golgotha—take on meaning for Gregory in a network of narratives, guiding the Christian toward God.

5. *Letter* 3.20; *GNO* 33.25.

6. *Letter* 3.3; *GNO* 33.20.

7. *Letter* 3.22; *GNO* 33.26.

8. *Letter* 2.10; *GNO* 33.16.

9. *Letter* 2.8–10; *GNO* 33.15–16; he goes on to say that his own trip's only benefit was that he "came to know by comparison that our own places are far holier than those abroad" (*Letter* 2.15; *GNO* 33.17–18).

10. See Silvas's introduction to *Letter* 2, p. 115.

11. *Letter* 2.7; *GNO* 33.15; and *Letter* 2.18a–b; *GNO* 33.18.

12. *Letter* 2.16; *GNO* 33.16, trans. altered. See *Letter* 2.16–18; *GNO* 33.16–19; and Frank, *The Memory of the Eyes*, 88–91.

13. More broadly, see Brakke, *Athanasius and Asceticism*, 17–79; and Cooper, *The Virgin and the Bride*, esp. 68–115.

14. See Silvas, *Letters*, 123–24. *Letter* 3 is written to female ascetics whom Gregory met in Jerusalem and is tied up in the Apollinarian controversies. His critique of pilgrimage is not just a critique of the Apollinarian community and influence in the city, though; Gregory's critique of the role of space is tied into the same Christological concerns. If Christ takes on and invites Christians to become places where God is manifest, then how that happens is a matter of Christology as well as ascetic practice. Later in *Letter* 2.18c, Gregory notes that only before the Holy Spirit dwelt on the apostles did Christ command them to "remain in the one place [Acts 2:1]." Once the Spirit has come, however, living in Jerusalem makes you no more present to "Golgotha or on the Mount of Olives" or any other place of which the Gospels speak than in Cappadocia (*Letter* 2.15, 17; *GNO* 33.20). What matters is that "the Lord himself comes to dwell within you and walk with you" (*Letter* 2.16; *GNO* 33.18; Jn 14:23; 2 Cor 6:16). Only then will Christians become those sacred places. He does not condemn the city, but does emphasize that it holds no more holiness than anywhere else. It is certainly not more holy than Macrina's school of virtue or the Cappadocian pilgrimage sites. (*Mac.*, 34; *GNO* 32.410; *Letter* 2.15; *GNO* 33.18). Gregory's ambivalence, therefore, has something to do with audience. Brouria Bitton-Ashkelony has rightly pointed to the polemical nature of Gregory's *Letter* 2, which was "perhaps directed against the views of Cyril, the bishop of Jerusalem, on the role of the *culte de mémoire* and sacred geography" (*Encountering the Sacred*, 53).

15. Boersma, *Embodiment and Virtue*, 245.

16. On maps in late antiquity, see Johnson, "Travel, Cartography, and Cosmology," esp. 568.

17. See Young's distinction between "ikonic" and "symbolic" mimesis in her *Biblical Exegesis*, esp. 21–27, 162, 175, 209–13. As with most binaries, though, many things slip through the cracks. Gregory is interested in both styles of mimesis. He will often show how a symbol represents some coded reality that breaks the "surface coherence of the text" (*Biblical Exegesis*, 162). But he is also committed to a σκοπός (aim, goal) achieved through an ἀκολουθία (path, sequence) that governs and guides the reading. Narrative and symbolic reading come together here, as texts work by both sequence and symbol, paths marked by charged places.

18. Smith, *To Take Place*, esp. 45; and his essay "The Influence of Symbols," 143–44.

19. See Lefebvre, *The Production of Space*, 33–46, esp. 41–42. (Some translations render *les spaces de representation* as representational spaces.) Any serious comparison of late ancient space with Lefebvre's definition must account for different modes of production in differing times—a worthy project, but not mine here. For connection between capital and mimesis, see Greenblatt, *Marvels*, 6–7. For recent work on late antiquity and space, see Shepardson, *Controlling Contested Places*.

20. Jungkeit, *Spaces of Modern Theology*, 16.

21. Augustine, *Confessions* 10.8.12–13.

22. Lakoff and Johnson, *Metaphors We Live By*, esp. 25–32. For more on memory and space, see Carruthers, *The Craft of Thought*, 7–24, where she discusses "locational memory." Ancient rhetoricians and Christian monastics crafted memory through "the images in which those memories were carried and conducted" (10). Those imagined places were mnemonic devices, which helped students memorize long and varied passages, but also shaped the *intentio* or affective disposition they brought to those memories. By setting images in difference places, they took on a different "color."

23. Gargola, *The Shape of the Roman Order*.

24. Padilla Peralta, *Divine Institutions*.

25. Johnson, *Literary Territories*, esp. 1–16, 41–44.

26. Johnson, *Literary Territories*, 28.

27. See, e.g., Miller, "Pleasure of the Text, Text of Pleasure," 241–53; and Young, *Biblical Exegesis*, 21–27, 209.

28. *Com. John* 1.40.

29. For more, see Young, *Biblical Exegesis*, 27. Origen does have places where he will say that the order of the text matters. But it is not a constant principle of interpretation the way it is for Gregory. See Heine, in *BDGN*, s.v. "Epinoiai," 94; Ludlow, "Anatomy"; and Norris's introduction to Gregory's *Homilies on the Song of Songs*, and the secondary material cited therein.

30. Ps.-Dionysius, *Celestial Hierarchy* 3.1. Greek in *CD*; translations of Dionysius are modified from Parker, *The Works of Dionysius the Areopagite*.

31. Stang, "'Being Neither Oneself Nor Someone Else,'" 61.

32. Ps.-Dionysius, *Mystical Theology* 1.2, in *CD*.

33. Ps.-Dionysius, *Mystical Theology* 1.2, in *CD*.

34. For a more expanded discussion, see Motia, "Three Ways to Imitate Paul."

35. Ἀκολουθία becomes a technical term (owing much to Iamblichus) in Gregory's *Treatise on the Inscriptions of the Psalms* and remains so for the rest of Gregory's career. See Daniélou, "Akolouthia chez Grégoire de Nysse," 219–49; and Heine's introduction to *IP*, 9, as well as the literature cited in *IP*, 9n23. Unless noted otherwise, translations of *Treatise on the Inscriptions of the Psalms* are cited Book.Section, Page; *GNO*. I have changed British spellings to American (e.g., labour to labor).

36. See *An. et Res.*; *GNO* 15. Sarah Coakley, "Gregory of Nyssa," in *The Spiritual Senses*, 36–55, locates a major shift in Gregory's thought, where Gregory slowly turns from Origen's view of the resurrected body toward what he lays out in *On the Soul and the Resurrection*. "Gregory's work moves over time from a predominant emphasis on the more 'Platonic' disjunctive approach in his earlier work to a more consistently purgative and transformative approach in his later work" (43). For shifts in relations to the body over Gregory's career, see Cadenhead, *The Body and Desire.*

37. *Hom. Beat.* 2.1; *GNO* 27.89–90. Unless noted otherwise, translations follow Hall. Ambrose of Milan, likely drawing on Gregory, will also read the Beatitudes in this progressive way.

38. *Or. Dom.*, Sermon 2.1, trans. Graf, 35.

39. *Hom. Beat.* 1.1; *GNO* 27.78.

40. *Or. Dom.*, Sermon 2, trans. Graf, 36.

41. I want to be careful not to read "epektasis" too deeply into Gregory's early work, even if it is noticeable that he does not need to radically rethink his reading practices for either *Homilies on the Song of Songs* or *The Life of Moses.*

42. See *Hom. Beat.* 2.1–2; *GNO* 27.89–90. On the trope of "the place of God" in early Christian literature, especially monastic understandings of prayer (e.g., Evagrius and Cassian), see Douglas Burton-Christie, "Early Monasticism," esp. 51–58.

43. *Hom. Beat.* 6.1; *GNO* 27.137, trans. Graef, 143.

44. *Hom. Beat.* 6.1; *GNO* 27.138.

45. For an alternate view, see Boersma, *Embodiment and Virtue*, 245–46.

46. *Mos.* 2.219–20, 249. See Certeau, "A Variant," 281: "The organization of the space through which the saint passes folds and unfolds in order to display a truth which is a place."

47. *Mos.* 2.238–39.

48. *Hom. Beat.* 1.6; *GNO* 27.82–83, trans. altered.

49. For more on the Psalms and the inscriptions in earlier Christian writings, see Heine's introduction, 2–5; Daley, "Finding the Right Key," 189–205; Collins, "The Psalms and the Origins of Christology," 113–23; and Taft, "Christian Liturgical Psalmody," 7–32.

50. The epigraphs are the short statements at the beginning of a Psalm such as "a prayer of David," or "for them that shall be changed," or "unto the end."

51. *IP* 1.pref, 2; *GNO* 21.24, trans. altered.

52. *IP* 1.2, 9; *GNO* 21.27.

53. *IP* 1.3, 17–20; *GNO* 21.29–31.

54. *IP* 1.pref, 3; *GNO* 21.24–25, trans. altered.

55. *IP* 1.pref, 3–4; *GNO* 21.25; *IP* 1.2, 12–15; *GNO* 21.27–28.

56. On the importance of the Psalms in ritual life, see, e.g., *Mac.*, 23; *GNO* 32.373, where Gregory highlights Macrina's holiness by noting that even as a child she "recited the Psalms [ψαλμῳδουμένης]" at the appropriate time every day (see also *Letter* 19.8–9; *GNO* 33.64–65). Singing the Psalms is also central to the proper reaction to Macrina's death and at her funeral (*Mac.*, 42, 50; *GNO* 32.401, 407). On the connection between ritual and doctrine, see Radde-Gallwitz, *Gregory of Nyssa's Doctrinal Works*, e.g., 8–9. Basil in his *Homily Psalm* 1 emphasizes how the pleasure of singing the Psalms imprints their teachings even more fully on souls (*Exegetic Homilies*, trans. Way, 151–64; *PG* 29:209–28). For a broader look at the Psalms in early Christian discourse, see Heine's introduction to *IP*, 20–29. Basil's analysis of the Psalms echoes Athanasius's *Letter to Marcellinus* 8 (*PG* 27.20), which notes that the book of Psalms

has a "certain grace of its own [τινὰ πάλιν χάριν ἰδίαν]" for Christians because the book "contains even the emotions [κίνηματα] of each soul, and it has the changes and rectifications of these delineated and regulated in itself" (trans. Gregg). Derek Krueger describes Athanasius's *Letter* as "a sort of liturgical guidebook on how to chant the Psalms" in *Liturgical Subjects*, 17. The *Letter* is the starting point for Krueger's analysis of the Byzantine "Penitential Self" (see *Liturgical Subjects*, 17–23). For the *Letter* and spatial memory, see Frank, "The Memory Palace."

57. *IP* 1.1, 6; *GNO* 21.26.

58. I have stuck with Heine's translation, but μέθοδος should not be confused with a kind of scientific method. The word here nuances the claim that the Psalter "shows the way [ὁδὸν ὑποδείκνυσιν]" through the "sequence [ἀκολουθίας]."

59. *IP* 1.1, 7; *GNO* 21.26.

60. See Iamblichus's use of the term in his *Protrepticus* 120. For more, see Heine's introduction, esp. 40–49; and, more broadly, Jordan, "Ancient Philosophical Protreptic," 309–33. Jordan notes that Iamblichus persuades through an ordering of "verbal icons, in which the end is . . . removed from view" (327).

61. See *IP* 2.16, 261; *GNO* 21.166; and *IP* 2.11, 135; *GNO* 21.116–17. The inverse is true as well: divine likeness requires not static images, but representations that are always on a path. I discuss this more below.

62. *IP* 2.1, 1; *GNO* 21.69.

63. While the treatise takes the inscriptions as its aim, the treatise does break roughly into the order of the Psalms (stage one is roughly Ps 1–40 and stage two begins with 41). But the text ends not with the final Psalm but with Psalm 56 because one needs to read not for the historical order but for the spiritual one. Heine notes that this seems to cut against his methodology, but the final topics of the Psalms deal with the meaning of διάψαλμα and why some Psalms diverge from the historical sequence (*IP*, 20).

64. *IP* 1.1, 5–6; *GNO* 21.25–26. Gregory lays out the five stages in two steps. First he paints three broad strokes (separation from evil, contemplation of sublime things, and likeness to God). Readers then receive the five stages that will frame the course when Gregory begins a "more precise [ἀκριβέστερον]" teaching about how the "Word instructs us [about the virtues] through the total guidance of the psalm" (*IP* 1.2, 9; *GNO* 21.27, trans. altered); *IP* 1.1, 8; *GNO* 21.26.

65. *IP* 1.2, 11; *GNO* 21.27.

66. *IP* 1.2, 15; *GNO* 21.28.

67. Coakley, *God, Sexuality, and the Self*, 26.

68. Readers must wait for part two and his engagement with "the subject matter [λόγος]" to see that this journey begins with a glimpse of the end. The phrase "unto the end" occurs as something of a signpost, occurring in the titles of fifty-five different Psalms, beginning with Psalm 4 and ending with Psalm 139. See Heine's note on *IP* 2.2, 14; *GNO* 21.72n10.

69. *IP* 2.2, 15; *GNO* 21.73, trans. altered.

70. *IP* 2.2, 15; *GNO* 21.73.

71. *IP* 2.2, 15; *GNO* 21.72.

72. *IP* 2.12, 160–61; *GNO* 21.125; Ps 41:2–3.

73. The second step involves a topic that will be taken up again (and more extensively) in the following chapter, namely, gathering a set of characters to which a subject can turn as an example and a way to increase desire for the virtuous life.

74. *IP* 1.2, 12; *GNO* 21.27–28.

75. The incarnation, Gregory notes, challenges what kinds of space and "materiality" are required for virtue. See also *Mos.* 2.136, 243–44.

76. In the preface to the treatise, Gregory notes that he hopes his treatise will work to intensify (ἐπίτασις) the recipient's zeal for virtue (*IP* 1.pref, 1; *GNO* 21.24).

77. *Cant.* 13, 383, trans. altered.

78. *IP* 1.3, 19–20; *GNO* 21.30–31.

79. *IP* 1.5, 39; *GNO* 21.39.

80. *IP* 1.5, 40; *GNO* 21.39.

81. Moreover, the desires that were poisonous in the first stage now become sweet and sustaining (*IP* 1.5, 40; *GNO* 21.39–40). For classical and early Christian sources on this transformation of poison, see Heine's note on this passage (n. 49). For more on the importance of mimetic characters, see my Chapter 5.

82. *IP* 1.5, 41; *GNO* 21.40. While Gregory's understanding of epektasis in his later work is not the central focus of this treatise, there are certainly seeds of it already in this early work of his.

83. *IP* 1.6, 49; *GNO* 21.43, trans. altered.

84. *IP* 1.6, 44; *GNO* 21.41.

85. *IP* 1.6, 44, 49; *GNO* 21.41, 43.

86. On the connection between union and participation, see Harrison, *Grace and Human Freedom*; and Balàs, *Μετουσία Θεοῦ*.

87. *IP* 1.7, 50; *GNO* 21.43, trans. altered.

88. *IP* 1.7, 51; *GNO* 21.43.

89. *IP* 1.7, 57; *GNO* 21.45, trans. altered.

90. See, e.g., *IP* 1.7, 58; *GNO* 21.46. This "style" also seems to motivate *Letter* 2 (above).

91. *IP* 1.7, 58; *GNO* 21.46.

92. See *IP* 1.7, 67; *GNO* 21.48–49, trans. altered.

93. *IP* 1.7, 75; *GNO* 21.51.

94. *IP* 1.7, 74; *GNO* 21.51.

95. *IP* 1.8, 76; *GNO* 21.52.

96. *IP* 1.8, 76; *GNO* 21.52.

97. *IP* 1.8, 77; *GNO* 21.52.

98. *IP* 1.9, 123; *GNO* 21.69.

99. *IP* 1.8, 78; *GNO* 21.53.

100. Louth, "Apophatic and Cataphatic Theology," 138; and Daniélou, *From Glory to Glory*, 46. Martin Laird, in *Gregory of Nyssa and the Grasp of Faith*, esp. 174–204, rightly highlights how, for Gregory, the "light of union" and the "dazzling darkness" can signify "the profoundest of divine-human encounters." This important corrective, nevertheless, keeps the guiding images of *epektasis*—darkness and light—in place.

101. *CE* 2.76.

102. Boersma, *Embodiment and Virtue*, 12.

103. Boersma, *Embodiment and Virtue*, 13.

104. Boersma, *Embodiment and Virtue*, 245.

105. Boersma, *Embodiment and Virtue*, 246.

106. *CE* 2.106–17, trans. altered for spelling.

107. Harrison, *Grace and Human Freedom*, 62–79; and Conway-Jones, *Gregory of Nyssa's Tabernacle Imagery*, 12–15.

108. For more analysis of scholarship on Gregory's mysticism and theology, see Ludlow, *Gregory of Nyssa: Ancient and (Post)modern*, esp. 125–34, 231–78.

109. Conway-Jones, *Gregory of Nyssa's Tabernacle Imagery*, 96–115; her work also draws on Douglass, *Theology of the Gap*.

110. Smith, "The Influence of Symbols," 143–44.

111. On "selfhood" in (late) antiquity (rather than a modern invention), see Brakke et al., eds., *Religion and the Self*. In *The Corporeal Imagination*, moreover, Patricia Cox Miller describes a shift in self-understanding from the third century's "touch of transcendence," where the soul is the point of analysis for transformation, to the fifth century's "touch of the real," where material places become the place of transformation. In Gregory we see a transition point, as place and soul come together: people mimetically become places. Souls, which come into being with the body, become different places of transcendence such that those places become real as they are mimetically participated in and portrayed.

112. See *Cant.* preface, and Norris's introduction, xxi.

113. I use female pronouns in reference to a generic human or Christian while discussing Gregory's *Homilies on the Song of Songs* because it is likely that the text was addressed to Olympias. The consistency of pronouns is an attempt at clarity, but it comes at a cost. It would probably be more accurate to try to perform the shifting gender that Gregory himself performs. As Virginia Burrus argues, there is much fluidity between the bride and the bridegroom. See, e.g., Burrus, "Queer Father," 147–62; Burrus, "Is Macrina a Woman?"; and Coakley, "The Eschatological Body," 61–73. For an overview of debate on sex, gender, and embodiment in Gregory, see Ludlow, *Gregory of Nyssa: Ancient and (Post)modern*, 163–227.

114. Gregory does warn his audience that a certain amount of maturity might be needed to ascend "the spiritual mountain" (*Cant.* 1, 25), but his preaching this to a lay audience should give us pause about how "advanced" the hearers need to be for this text. On broader shifts in sexual norms in late antiquity, see Harper, *From Shame to Sin*.

115. *Cant.* 1, 27.

116. *Cant.* 1, 26.

117. On Christians as the "temple of God," see Gregory of Nyssa, *Homilies on Ecclesiastes*, *GNO* 21.384–85. See also Douglass, *Theology of the Gap*, 184–85.

118. *Cant.* 1, 15.

119. *Cant.* 1, 26.

120. *Cant.* 1, 22, trans. altered.

121. *Cant.* 1, 23.

122. *Cant.* 1, 23.

123. E.g., *IP* 1.5, 41; *GNO* 21.40. This image of the continually flowing fountain may even have special significance with the memory (and threat) of drought still resonant with many of his readers. See, e.g., Holman, *The Hungry Are Dying*; and Brown, *Poverty and Leadership*, esp. 6, 39.

124. *Cant.* 9, 262, trans. altered; and Col 3:2.

125. *Cant.* 9, 264.

126. *Cant.* 9, 261; see Harvey, *Scenting Salvation*, esp. 120–22, 230–31.

127. *Cant.* 9, 275–76.

128. *Cant.* 9, 277, trans. altered.

129. *Cant.* 9, 291.

130. *Cant.* 9, 293.

131. Aristotle, *Art of Rhetoric* 2.24.

132. *Cant.* 12, 359–66.

133. *Cant.* 12, 340–42; Norris's translation includes a note that Gregory may have borrowed the image from Methodius, *Symposium* 7.1, trans. Musurillo, 96.

134. *Cant.* 12, 349, 364.

135. *Cant.* 12, 363.

136. *Cant.* 12, 363.

137. *Cant.* 12, 365.

138. *Cant.* 12, 357.

139. *Cant.* 12, 365.

140. *Cant.* 12, 365–66.

141. *Cant.* 5, 162–64; 1 Cor 10:4. See also, e.g., *Mos.* 2.136, 225, 243–45.

142. *Cant.* 12, 367–68.

143. *Cant.* 12, 367, trans. altered.

144. For questions about the status of the final homily within the text, see Dörries, "Griechentum und Christentum bei Gregor von Nyssa," 582–92; Dünzl, "Formen der Kirchenväterrezeption"; and Norris's introduction to the *Homilies*, xxii–xxiii.

145. *Cant.* 15, 435.

146. *Cant.* 15, 435; Song 6:2.

147. *Cant.* 15, 436.

148. *Cant.* 15, 436–37.

149. *Cant.* 15, 458.

150. *Cant.* 15, 438.

151. *Cant.* 15, 439.

152. See *Cant.* 15, 439.

153. *Cant.* 15, 440–41.

154. Gregory writes that the bride regains her own beauty and "in her own form has taken on the beauty of her Beloved [δεξαμένη τοῦ ἀγαπηθέντος τὸ κάλλος ἐν τῇ ἰδίᾳ μορφῇ]" (*Cant.* 15, 442). For the importance of the "primordial beauty" as not any individual but "the whole lump of humanity," see Chapter 6.

155. Plato uses the same verb often in Book 10 of *Republic*; see 597c, 589b, 600c, 603a, and 616e.

156. This artistic work is constituted in a cleansing of "every material act and thought [παντὸς ὑλικοῦ πράγματός τε καὶ νοήματος]." And when "she is entirely, in her whole being, transposed [μετατεθεῖσαν] into the intelligible and immaterial realm," she "makes of herself a supremely vivid image of the prototypical beauty" (*Cant.* 15, 439).

157. *Cant.* 15, 439, trans. altered.

158. *Cant.* 15, 440–41. It is not only one's representational work but also the soul's formation and transformation that happens in this mirroring. Gregory's note on Paul's "echoing" or "representation" of Song 6:3 with his words "to me, to live is Christ" (Phil 1:21) shows how mimesis happens at multiple levels. First, it shows Paul performing the same action as the bride, supplementing and deepening what the reader can see in her words. Second, it shows mimesis working not only at the level of dispositions but also at a textual and representational one. Paul's mimesis of the Song echoes Gregory's, situating a place for contemplation and transformation.

159. *Cant.* 15, 440. Participation and representation come together here, as the mirror is not an external object, but is the soul.

160. *Cant.* 5, 157.

161. *Cant.* 15, 442.

162. *Cant.* 15, 443–44, trans. altered.

163. *Cant.* 15, 444–45.

164. Εὐδοκία can mean both goodwill toward as in Luke 2:14, "goodwill toward humans," and the object of desire, LXX 144:16, "You open your hand and satisfy the desire of every living thing [ἐμπιπλᾷς πᾶν ζῷον εὐδοκίας]."

165. See Phil 2:7; 3:13.

166. Conway-Jones, *Gregory of Nyssa's Tabernacle Imagery*, 232.

167. Limberis, *Architects of Piety*, 9.

168. Gregory of Nyssa, *On the Three-Day Period of the Resurrection of our Lord Jesus Christ*, GNO 41.303, trans. altered from Hall. See also *Letter* 25; GNO 33.79–83.

169. *Theod.*, trans. Leemans, 85; GNO 50.62. All translations follow Leemans. On the connection between "seeing" and "touching," see Nelson, "To Say and to See," 153; and an important corrective in Betancourt, *Sight, Touch, and Imagination*, esp. 1–89.

170. *Forty Martyrs of Sebaste* 1a, trans. Leemans, 96; GNO 51.141.

171. *Theod.*, 86; GNO 50.64.

172. *Theod.*, 85; GNO 50.63.

173. *Theod.*, 90; GNO 50.69. For more on hospitals in late ancient Cappadocia, see Horden, "The Earliest Hospitals," 361–89; and Holman, *The Hungry Are Dying*, esp. 74–77.

174. *Theod.*, 84; GNO 50.62.

175. *Theod.*, 85; GNO 50.63.

176. *Theod.*, 90; GNO 50.70.

Chapter 6

Note to epigraph: *Cant.* 6, 185–86. For a parallel where God puts on masks, see *CE* 2.419.

1. *Prof.*, 85; GNO 29.133.

2. *Prof.*, 85; GNO 29.136.

3. *Or. Cat.*, 21; trans. Richardson, 297; GNO 16.55.

4. For more on late ancient theater, see, e.g., Leyerle, *Theatrical Shows*, esp. 12–41; Webb, *Demons and Dancers*, esp. 139–216; and Lieber, "Setting the Stage."

5. John Chrysostom, "A Homily on the Martyrs," 117, trans. altered from Mayer; *PG* 50.645.

6. Leyerle, *Theatrical Shows*, 27, referring to John Chrysostom, *Hom. in Matt.* 2.5 (*PG* 57.30); *Sal. Prisc.* (*PG* 51.188); *Hom. in Jo.* 17.4 (*PG* 59.112); and *Hom. in Coloss.* 9.2 (*PG* 62.362).

7. Libanius, *Reply to Aristides* (*Orat.* 64.116), cited in Webb, *Demons and Dancers*, 77. For broader discussion of the power of mimesis in dance, see *Demons and Dancers*, esp. 157–60.

8. Gregory of Nazianzus, *Oration* 31.11; *On God and Christ*, trans. Wickham, 125.

9. *Com. Rep.*, 25, K53.

10. See my discussion of declamation in Chapter 1, and the secondary literature cited therein.

11. See Cribiore, *Gymnastics of the Mind*, 228–29.

12. See, e.g., Brightbill, "Roman Declamation," 27–72, 76, 125; and Bloomer, "Schooling in Persona."

13. This production of characters who will stylize Christian perfection is among Gregory's most consistent literary practices. His accounts of his sister Macrina and the third-century

bishop Gregory Thaumaturgus, along with his homilies on Basil and local martyrs, were among his most widely circulated works.

We know remarkably little about Gregory of Nyssa, especially when compared to Basil or to Gregory of Nazianzus. This surely has something to do with the history of reception, but it also suggests something of his own writing practice, and perhaps something of his literary persona. We find almost none of the self-revelation found in Gregory of Nazianzus's *Autobiographical Poems*. And even when he appears in the stories of his siblings, he seems to find himself in them, rather than exploring himself. This is not to deny Gregory a sense of interiority, as much as it suggests how that inner life is formed, namely, through a series of mimetic names, spaces, and (especially) characters. For the importance of texts in Gregory's pedagogy, see Ludlow, "Texts, Teachers and Pupils," esp. 102.

On the importance of biographies in early Christian and Neoplatonist literature, see, e.g., Cox (Miller), *Biography in Late Antiquity*; Hägg and Rousseau, eds., *Greek Biography and Panegyric*; Krueger, *Writing and Holiness*; and Urbano, *The Philosophical Life*, 245–72.

14. *Cant.* 15, 453, trans. altered.

15. *IP* 2.15, 247; *GNO* 21.160–61, trans. altered.

16. In part because all these characters are mediated through texts, mimetic relationships also feed back onto and animate a style of reading and writing. Writing becomes part of a larger ascetic program of representing what transcends the self. Gregory, we will see, will write his way toward virtue, catching up to a perfection he can compose before he can understand, and that will always remain both intimate and elusive. See Krueger, *Writing and Holiness*, esp. 125.

17. *Mos.* 1.7.

18. See *CE* 2.145.

19. For a comparison of Gregory's modes of imitating Paul with those of John Chrysostom and Pseudo-Dionysius, see Motia, "Three Ways to Imitate Paul."

20. *CE* 2.136.

21. Williams, *Authorised Lives*, 183. Williams refers here to Auerbach's *Mimesis*. But Williams's larger project is set against accounts such as Cox (Miller)'s *Biography in Late Antiquity*, which argues that "Biographical writing is evocative, not descriptive" (xiii).

22. For the divine as reality or real "Being," see, e.g., Gregory of Nyssa, *Mos.* 2.23.

23. Meltzer and Elsner, *Saints: Faith Without Boarders*, ix.

24. For the transmission history, see Daniélou, *La Vie de Moïse*, 38–42. Greek text is cited from Daniélou's edition, with consolation to the *GNO* edition. For alternative titles, see Daniélou's critical apparatus and *GNO* 25.1.

Though this text is likely written to what Williams describes as "the more ascetically inclined," Gregory deploys Moses as an exemplar widely. While there are different ways in which Moses becomes an exemplar, Williams might exaggerate the connection between Moses and the "the most spiritually expert" (e.g., *Authorised Lives*, 82). Andrea Sterk and Claudia Rapp both rightfully note that *The Life of Moses* theorizes the episcopate, and presents the episcopal life as reconcilable with the ascetic ideal. There is merit to this argument, but *The Life of Moses* is surely more than that. See Sterk, *Renouncing the World Yet Leading the Church*, 78, 95–118; and Rapp, *Holy Bishops*, 125–52.

25. *Mos.* 1.7. See also 2.166.

26. *Mos.* 1.7, trans. altered.

27. *Mos.* 1.5.

28. See, e.g., Malherbe and Ferguson's introduction to *The Life of Moses*, which helpfully notes that Gregory comes in a line of interpreters of Moses's life (they highlight Philo, Clement, and Origen), but they see Moses as rather peripheral to the theological and spiritual concerns of the text.

29. Boersma, *Embodiment and Virtue*, 242. See Chapter 5 for my critiques of undertheorized notion of imitation and participation.

30. See, e.g., *CE* 2.106–17.

31. See *BDGN*, s.v. "Epektasis," 263–68.

32. *Mos.* 1.1.

33. *Mos.* 1.1; Phil 3:14, trans. altered.

34. *Mos.* 1.1. This spurring happens in both the English sense of spur and the German sense of "track" by providing both an impetus and a direction.

35. *Mos.* 1.3. The "request" is a late ancient trope. I only point it out as a framing device.

36. *Mos.* 1.3.

37. *Mos.* 1.10.

38. *Mos.* 1.7.

39. Recall my discussion in Chapter 3 of what Elsner describes as a shift in perception in *Art and the Roman Viewer*, 1–14.

40. *Mos.* 2.318; 2.166.

41. *Mos.* 1.3.

42. *Mos.* 1.13–14, trans. altered. On Moses as the guide when he approaches and enters the darkness, see *Mos.* 2.153.

43. *Mos.* 1.13–14, trans. altered.

44. Williams, *Authorised Lives*, 183.

45. Williams, *Authorised Lives*, 62.

46. *Mos.* 2.319.

47. *Mos.* 2.173–78; see Conway-Jones, *Gregory of Nyssa's Tabernacle Imagery*, 109–10; see also Douglass, *Theology of the Gap*, 132.

48. For God as infinite reality, see *Mos.* 2.318.

49. *Mos.* 2.2.

50. *Mos.* 1.14, trans. altered.

51. *Mos.* 1.14. If Moses's life helps guide readers to virtue, Gregory must "harmonize the order of the history with the anagogical sense [τῆς ἱστορίας τάξιν τῇ ἀναγωγῇ προσαρμόσαι τὸ νόημα]" (*Mos.* 2.153, trans. altered). The "keenness of vision" should bring about a harmonization with the anagogical meaning. This harmonization is one that Moses himself seems to perform: Moses purifies his clothing and his body such that his body mirrors the purity of his soul. Gregory writes, "No one would say that a visible spot on the garments hinders the progress of those ascending to God, but I think that the outward pursuits of life are well named the 'garment [περιβολὴν]'" (*Mos.* 2.155). The Greek word περιβολὴ can mean both clothing and circumference, but also in rhetoric the word has a sense of "expansion" or "amplification." The doubleness here seems important. The body, enclosed, is also the way to expand the pursuit of the divine.

52. *Mos.* 1.77.

53. *Mos.* 1.77.

54. *Mos.* 2.50.

55. For Gregory, the lives of the holy set forth a "pattern of virtue for those who come after them" (*Mos.* 2.48).

56. *Mos.* 2.49, trans. altered. Gregory can show this only by performing a reading of Moses's life, fashioning the life of perfection without allowing the "description of its perfection [to] hinder its progress" (2.306). The "ineffable and mysterious illumination which came to Moses" (2.19) also attracted Moses—for we are attracted to and desire to become what is beautiful—and so transforms him that in him we see an "image of God" (2.318).

57. Aristotle, *Nicomachean Ethics* 2.1, 1103a.

58. See Cox (Miller), *Biography in Late Antiquity*, xi, xv, 8–16.

59. Cox (Miller), *Biography in Late Antiquity*, xi. See also Gray, "Mimesis in Greek Historical Theory." While Aristotle distinguishes between poetry and history as mimetic and non-mimetic literature, by the first century, history too was often considered mimetic.

60. See Chapter 1.

61. *Mos.* 2.2. Malherbe and Ferguson's translation makes the short, ambiguous sentence clearer than it is. "The narrative is to be understood according to its real intention [Νοείσθω δὲ καθ' ὑπόθεσιν]."

62. *LSJ*, s.v. "ὑπόθεσις." See, e.g., Iamblichus, *De vita Pythagorica* 8.39.

63. E.g., *Mos.* 2.43, 2.56, 2.98.

64. *Mos.* 2.319, trans. altered.

65. Williams, *The Edge of Words*, 191.

66. Moses's continual growth, we should also note, is represented here, not with an extended analogy, but with his own life—or better, his life takes on a mimetic quality into which readers can enter. In part 2, Moses's life does not disappear; it is deepened especially as Gregory introduces those most mystical moments. The text often spirals, moving back through the story to gain momentum needed to advance further. To imitate Moses is to see these events as the ladder that he "continually climbed to the step above and never ceased to rise higher, because he always found a step higher than the one he had attained" (*Mos.* 2.227). The acts or history never disappear from the text, but they are arranged or placed in an *akolouthia* that shows a deeper truth, which links imitation and epektasis. Representing his life intensifies the reality in which readers participate. Each instance provides a kind of traction, propelling Moses to the next, such that as new representations of God are revealed his participation (μετέχω) deepens and his capacity to share in God is expanded. His participation makes clearer the distinction between himself and the divine, which leads him once again into new practices of imitation. Macrina's recounting of her own life (see below) functions similarly to these recaps, where by circling back through Moses's life readers are propelled forward to the unknown God.

67. *Mos.* 2.219. The word πρόσωπον, usually translated as "face," can also carry the sense of "character," which is how Gregory uses it in *On What It Means to Call Oneself a Christian*, 82; *GNO* 30.130. The tension between presence and character, that is, runs through much of Gregory's writing.

68. See 1 Cor 13:12; and 2 Cor 3:18.

69. *Mos.* 2.233; Ex 33:20.

70. *Mos.* 2.231.

71. *Mos.* 2.232.

72. *Mos.* 2.235–36.

73. *Mos.* 2.238–39.

74. Elsner, "Relic, Icon, and Architecture," 13.

75. *Mos.* 2.160.

76. *Mos.* 2.162. See also *Mos.* 2.163. It is noteworthy that readers see this scene twice. In the historical reading, Moses becomes invisible as he joins company with the invisible God. And yet even in his invisibility, "he teaches." His absence has a pedagogical effect. "By the things he did," readers learn that "the one who is going to associate intimately with God must go beyond all that is visible and (lifting up his own mind, as to a mountaintop, to the invisible and incomprehensible) believe that the divine is there where the understanding does not reach" (*Mos.* 1.46). The darkness, for Gregory, is not only something that happens in contemplation. It appears also in history, even if to understand and repeat it requires *theoria*.

77. *Mos.* 2.163.

78. *Mos.* 2.163.

79. *Mos.* 1.49, trans. altered.

80. *Mos.* 2.169, trans. altered.

81. *Letter* 19.6; *GNO* 33.64.

82. Ludlow, "Texts, Teachers and Pupils," 83.

83. See Chapter 1 and the literature cited therein, esp. Cribiore, *The School of Libanius*, 172.

84. Cribiore, *The School of Libanius*, 172; Libanius likely inherits this from Quintilian, *The Orator's Education* 1.3.1, 2.8.1–3.

85. Cicero, *On the Orator* 2.11.36; on this passage, see Burrow, *Imitating Authors*, 83: "*Imitatio* was a process by which charisma might be transmitted from person to person and across the generations."

86. *Mac.*, trans. Corrigan, 40; *GNO* 32.396. All translations follow Corrigan. On the importance of texts and teaching, see Ludlow, "Texts, Teachers and Pupils," 102.

87. *Mac.*, 54; *GNO* 32.414, trans. altered; on εὐρυχωρία, see esp. Gregory's *Homilies on Ecclesiastes*, trans. Hall, 107; *GNO* 23.385; and Douglass, *Theology of the Gap*, 184.

88. Anna Silvas places the text between 383 and 384 in her introductory biography to *The Letters*, 51; Terrieux's *Grégoire de Nysse, Sur l'âme et la résurrection*, 12, dates it between 381 and 383.

89. I do mean "in" here. Whereas *The Life of Plotinus* shows its readers Plotinus in order to transcend him, Gregory's Macrina seems to offer something more. Macrina's contact with the divine stages an encounter for the reader as well. Readers are to become another Macrina, to be sure, but Gregory provides a host of other characters who are also trying to imitate her, not least Gregory himself.

90. *CE* 2.476.

91. See, e.g., Clark, "The Lady Vanishes"; Brakke, "The Lady Appears"; Krueger, *Writing and Holiness*, 110–32; Burrus, *The Sex Lives of Saints*, 69–76, and "Is Macrina a Woman?"; and Muehlberger, "Salvage."

92. Elsner, *Art and the Roman Viewer*, 124; for Elsner this process is not complete until the sixth century, but his examples often include Gregory's *The Life of Moses* and *Homilies on the Song of Songs*.

93. Gregory did write a brief letter (*Letter* 19) that contains many of the themes that move through the *Life*, though that does not seem to be the point of the opening.

94. Cox (Miller), *Biography in Late Antiquity*, xi. See also Rapp, "Storytelling as Spiritual Communication."

95. This seems to be more a function of time than of gender. E.g., in his *Life of Gregory the Wonderworker* there is no "contemplative" reading either.

96. *Letter* 19.6–9.

97. These questions of genre have occupied much recent scholarship on Macrina. Elizabeth Clark has argued that the focus on the private sphere rather than on public activities makes it more similar to the ancient novel than the biography ("The Lady Vanishes," 16). Georgia Frank's "Macrina's Scar" draws attention to the parallels with the *Odyssey*. Derek Krueger has highlighted the way "a saint's vita constitutes an image of a lived liturgy" (*Writing and Holiness*, 125). Macrina's life becomes a repeatable, shared ritual that opens to God as it reenacts the incarnation. Arthur Urbano compares Gregory's and Eunapius's *vitae* (*The Philosophical Life*, esp. 258). Ellen Muehlberger's "Salvage" highlights how staging the *On the Soul and the Resurrection* "reclaims" Greek philosophy after Julian's educational reforms linked religious identity to reading material.

98. Burrus, "Is Macrina a Woman?" Cf. Boersma, *Embodiment and Virtue*, 110n95.

99. On swapping types and its effect, see Clark, "The Lady Vanishes," 27; and Muehlberger, "Salvage," esp. 295–97.

100. *GNO* 32.410; *LSJ*, s.v. "φροντιστήριον" can mean anything from a meditation or prayer space to a school or a monastic community. The word later also becomes identified with Socrates's school (see Aristophanes, *Nubes* 94–96).

101. Moses too, Gregory notes, is quite beautiful. His beauty "caused his parents to draw back from having such a child destroyed by death" (*Mos.* 1.16).

102. *Mac.*, 24; *GNO* 32.374.

103. Elsner, *Art and the Roman Viewer*, 9.

104. Since at least David Halperin's now classic essay "Why is Diotima a Woman?" modern readers of Macrina are rightly aware of the multiple levels on which Gregory's rendition of his sister works. See e.g., Burrus, "Gender, Eros, and Pedagogy," 168.

105. *CE* 2.182.

106. *Mac.*, 29; *GNO* 32.381. As we will see, Macrina being a woman highlights that for Gregory, there is no sexual division in the image of God, in whom "there is no male and female" (Gregory of Nyssa, *Op. Hom.* 16; *PG* 44.181, 185). See also his *Mos.* 1.11–12, where Abraham serves as the archetype for virtuous men and Sarah for Godly women, but Moses seems to serve for both, even if "the material and passionate disposition" is often gendered as female with "the austerity and intensity of virtue" as male (*Mos.* 2.2).

107. Virginia Burrus can even memorably ask: "Is Macrina a Woman?" Sarah Coakley argues that, for Gregory, there may be no male or female in God, and yet, gender, in Gregory's writings, does not disappear in union with God: all of humanity is to take on a "female soul in pursuit of God," desiring God by becoming an "active recipient" of the divine (*Powers and Submissions*, 166). See also Harrison, "Gender, Generation, and Virginity."

108. Turner, *Truthfulness, Realism, Historicity*, esp. 3, 12, 40–44.

109. *Mac.*, 24, 54; *GNO* 32.372, 413.

110. *Mac.*, 21; *GNO* 32.370–71; while Socrates makes a similar claim about Diotima in the *Symposium* 201d, the specificity of Gregory's emphasis on his family and her ascetic community, as I see it, changes the force of this claim.

111. Johnson, *Literary Territories*, 15–16: late antique communities of readers "self-reflectively recognized the impossibility of literary realism and allowed, in a manner previously considered gauche (if considered at all), the form to mix with the subject in creative ways."

112. *CE* 2.419, trans. altered.

113. *An. et Res.*, trans. altered from Roth, 79–80; *GNO* 15.69. All translations are from Roth unless noted otherwise.

114. Gregory seems to use *eros* and *agape* interchangeably. E.g., for "erotic disposition" (διάθεσις ἐρωτικὰς), see his *Mos.* 2.231; and *Cant.* 15, 461; for "loving disposition" (διαθέσεως αγαπητικῆς), see *On the Soul and the Resurrection*, 84; *GNO* 15.69; and *Cant.* 1, 38.

115. *An. et Res.*, 78; *GNO* 15.67, trans. altered.

116. Elm, *Virgins of God*, 87.

117. *Mac.*, 26; *GNO* 32.378. Recall that the philosophical life in late antiquity was often also considered the "most erotic" life, and that what is "most erotic tunes . . . the soul itself to the best tuning (or mode) through which the soul becomes a thing capable of setting all human matters in order and of perfectly singing the praises of the divine, imitating the leader of the Muses himself." See, e.g., Proclus, *Com. Rep.*, 31, K57, trans. altered.

118. *Mac.*, 26–27; *GNO* 32.378; for Gregory's argument against slavery, written around the time of *Mac.*, see *Homilies on Ecclesiastes, Hom* 4, 72–84; *GNO* 23.334–43.

119. Silvas, *Letters*, 176n282, commenting on Gregory's *Letter* 19.6, writes that *parrēsia* is "the deep freedom of someone who has paid the interior cost through a life of self-denial, prayer and great love." Her willingness to sacrifice the small pleasures expected by women of her status gave her a boldness (παρρησία) toward God unshakable even in the midst of pain. See Cooper, *Band of Angels*, 180.

120. See, e.g., Elm, *Virgins of God*, esp. 86–88; Rousseau, "The Pious Household and the Virgin Chorus"; Van Dam, *Families and Friends*, 99–113, esp. 103–9; Burrus, "Gender, Eros, and Pedagogy"; and Cooper, *Band of Angels*, esp. 180.

121. *Mac.*, 26; *GNO* 32.378.

122. *Mac.*, 31; *GNO* 32.383. This may be an allusion to Paul's becoming "all things to all people" (1 Cor 9:22).

123. *Mac.*, 31; *GNO* 32.383.

124. Rubenson, "Philosophy and Simplicity."

125. *Mac.*, 33; *GNO* 32.386.

126. *Mac.*, 34; *GNO* 32.388.

127. *Mac.*, 33–34; *GNO* 32.373. On the importance of light (in addition to darkness) in figuring divine incomparability, see Martin Laird's discussion of "mysticism of light" in *Gregory of Nyssa and the Grasp of Faith*, 174–204.

128. *Mac.*, 38; *GNO* 32.393.

129. Krueger, *Writing and Holiness*, 124.

130. Krueger, *Writing and Holiness*, 117.

131. *Mac.*, 40; *GNO* 32.396.

132. See Elsner, "Relic, Icon, and Architecture," 40.

133. *An. et Res.*, 115–16; *GNO* 15.120–21. See also 99; *GNO* 15.92–94.

134. Burrus, "Macrina's Tattoo," 103–18. "Flesh is not transformed into spirit, it is not even redeemed by (or simply 'married to') spirit. . . . Flesh is itself the mirroring of spirit, the stigmatization of the spirit," Burrus argues. "By the same logic, spirit itself is the reflection of the mark (the sign), of the flesh" (111).

135. Francis, "Visual and Verbal Representation," 302; and Frank, "Taste and See," 621.

136. *Mac.*, 42; *GNO* 32.398; Gal 2:19; Ps 118:120 LXX. While Frank does not compare this scene to an *aristeia*, for other Homeric illusions in *Mac.*, see Frank, "Macrina's Scar."

137. *Mac.*, 43; *GNO* 32.399.

138. *Mac.*, 43; *GNO* 32.399.

139. Macrina dies with dignity and confidence and, not unlike Christ, in her death, she only intensifies as a site of the holy. The prefigured relic now appears as "she [Macrina] shone even in the dark mantle; God's power, I think, added even such grace to her body that, exactly as in the vision I had while dreaming, rays of light seemed to shine out from her beauty" (*Mac.*, 48–49; *GNO* 32.406). This imitation, clearly, is not her own. "A sure sign of God's presence in the body is for the flesh to be kept uncorrupted after death," Gregory writes in *Refutation of the Views of Apolinarius*, trans. Orton, 245 [M 1257]; *GNO* 10.224.

140. See Elm, *Virgins of God*, 93.

141. *Mac.*, 49; *GNO* 32.407.

142. See esp. *Op. Hom.* 16.5–7, 22.4; *PG* 44.177, 204; and *In illud tunc*, *GNO* 11.16. The discussion of the whole of humanity as the image of God is well studied especially in literature on Gregory and gender, e.g., Rosemary Radford Ruether's extensive work, including "Imago Dei"; Børresen, "God's Image, Man's Image?"; Coakley, *Powers and Submissions*, 55–68, 153–67; Behr, "The Rational Animal"; Hart, "The 'Whole Humanity'"; and Chapter 2 of Vasiliu, *Eikôn*. For a broader view on the question of individuality or the self in late antiquity, see Torrance, "Individuality and Identity-formation in Late Antique Monasticism"; and Brakke et al., eds., *Religion and the Self in Antiquity*.

143. *Op. Hom.* 22.4; *PG* 44.204, trans. altered.

144. *Ref.*, 138 [M 1165]; *GNO* 10.160.

145. Gregory of Nazianzus, *Letter* 74, trans. Storin, 101, Greek from Gallay, ed., *Saint Grégoire de Nazianze. Lettres.*

146. *Mac.*, 30; *GNO* 32.382.

147. *IP* 1.3, 19; *GNO* 21.31. At her funeral, Gregory, stepping into Macrina's role, "gets from [the choirs] . . . a rhythmical, harmonious unity in their singing of the psalms" (*Mac.*, 49; *GNO* 32.408). See Harvey, *Song and Memory*, and "Revisiting the Daughters of the Covenant"; and Münz-Manor and Arentzen, "Soundscapes of Salvation."

148. Cooper, *Band of Angels*.

149. *Letter* 19.1, 2b.

150. Silvas, in her introduction to the letter, written in 379, floats the unlikely possibility that the addressee ("a certain John") may in fact be a young John Chrysostom (*Letter*, 173).

151. *Letter* 19.3b. Silvas notes that this is Gregory's rather idiosyncratic combination of Proverbs 13:10 and the Delphic imperative "know thyself." Proverbs 13:10 reads, "those who discern themselves are wise [οἱ δε ἑαυτῶν ἐπιγνώμονες σοσφολί]" (*Letter*, 176n278).

152. Gregory of Nyssa, *Mac.*, 31; *GNO* 32.383, trans. altered.

Conclusion

Note to epigraph: Butler, *Giving an Account*, 136.

1. Butler, *Giving an Account*, 135.

2. Butler, *Giving an Account*, 84.

3. Butler, *Giving an Account*, 84.

4. Srinivasan, "He, She, One, They, Ho, Hus, Hum, Ita."

5. Butler, *Giving an Account*, 135.

6. That new possibilities emerge, moreover, does not make this unknowingness painless—Gregory, like Butler, compares it to wounding—but it is necessary to become human.

7. Hart, "The Mirror of the Infinite," 117–21. On ancient mirrors, see Clark, *Plotinus*, 83–87.

8. Hart, "The Mirror of the Infinite," 117. See e.g., *Cant.* 3, 90; and *CE* 2.215.

9. Butler, *Bodies That Matter*, ix.

10. E.g., *Or. Cat.*, 21; trans. Richardson, 297; *GNO* 16.55.

11. *Op. Hom.* 11.3; *PG* 44.156, trans. altered from Wilson.

12. *CE* 2.106.

13. Butler, *Giving an Account*, 134.

14. *Virg.* 23; *GNO* trans. altered from Moore and Wilson. All citations follow Moore and Wilson; *GNO* 31.333

15. *Virg.* 23; *GNO* 31.333.

16. Todd Berzon calls this production of Christian "culture" a kind of "world making" in *Classifying Christians*, 255n41; he follows here a line of thinking about early Christianity as creating a "collective memory" begun by Castelli, *Martyrdom and Memory*. See also Cameron, *Christianity and the Rhetoric of Empire*.

17. *Virg.* 24, trans. altered; *GNO* 31.338.

18. *Virg.* 24; see text-critical notes on *GNO* 31.338. The division into chapter 24 appears in the English translation but not the Greek; the English chapter 24 begins at 23.5.

19. *Virg.* 24, trans. altered; *GNO* 31.338.

20. *Virg.* 24, trans. altered; *GNO* 31.388. See *LSJ*, s.v. "ἐπιχωριάζω." Within this metaphor ἐπιχωριάζει can mean, broadly: to become customary or in fashion in a place, or even to acquire the local character (hence my translation of "habituate"). Recall, too, that the root (χώρα) also provides Gregory with a word for growth. See Chapter 4.

21. *Virg.* 24; *GNO* 31.388. A humbler translator might have rendered μετασχεῖν τὸν τοῖς τοιούτοις as "participate in this," but Moore and Wilson's "catch this halo" captures Gregory's meaning.

22. *Mos.* 2.231; *Cant.* 15, 46.

23. Philoponus, *Against Proclus* 1.3, trans. Share.

24. Pseudo-Dionysius, *Celestial Hierarchy* 3.1, trans. mine from *Corpus Dionysiacum*.

25. Pseudo-Dionysius, *Letter* 2, trans. mine. For a comparison of Dionysius and Gregory, see Motia, "Three Ways to Imitate Paul."

BIBLIOGRAPHY

Gregory of Nyssa

GREEK TEXTS

Gregory of Nyssa. *De hominis opificio. PG* 44. 124–256.

———. *Gregorii Nysseni Opera Online.* Ed. Ekkehard Mühlenberg and Giulio Maspero. Leiden: Brill. https://referenceworks.brillonline.com/browse/gregorii-nysseni-opera. Based on *Gregorii Nysseni Opera*, ed. Werner Jaeger et al. Leiden: Brill, 1952–.

———. *La Vie de Moïse, ou Traité de la Perfection en Matière de Vertu*, 3rd ed. Ed. and trans. Jean Daniélou. Paris: Les Éditions du Cerf, 2007.

TRANSLATIONS

Gregory of Nyssa. *An Address on Religious Instruction.* Trans. Cyril C. Richardson. In *Christology of the Later Fathers*, ed. Edward R. Hardy, 268–325. Philadelphia: Westminster Press, 1954.

———. "An Answer to Ablabius: That We Should Not Think of Saying There Are Three Gods." Trans. Cyril C. Richardson. In *Christology of The Later Fathers*, ed. Edward R. Hardy, 256–67. Philadelphia: Westminster Press, 1954.

———. *Ascetical Works.* Trans. Virginia Woods Callahan. Washington, DC: The Catholic University of America Press, 1967.

———. *The Biographical Works of Gregory of Nyssa: Proceedings of the Fifth International Colloquium on Gregory of Nyssa (Mainz, 6–10 September 1982).* Ed. Andreas Spira. Cambridge, MA: Philadelphia Patristic Foundation, 1984.

———. *Contra Eunomium I.* In *El "Contra Eunomium I" En La Produccion Literaria de Gregorio de Nisa: VI Coloquio Internacional sobre Gregorio de Nisa*, ed. Lucas F. Mateo-Seco and Juan L. Bastero, trans. Stuart G. Hall. Pamplona: Ediciones Universidad de Navarra, 1988.

———. *Contra Eunomium II: An English Version with Supporting Studies. Proceedings of the 10th International Colloquium on Gregory of Nyssa (Olomouc, September 15–18, 2004).* Ed. Lenka Karfíková, Scot Douglass, and Johannes Zachhuber. Trans. Stuart G. Hall. Leiden: Brill, 2007.

———. *Contra Eunomium III: An English Translation with Commentary and Supporting Studies. Proceedings of the 12th International Colloquium on Gregory of Nyssa (Leuven, 14–17 September 2010).* Ed. Johan Leemans and Matthieu Cassian. Trans. Stuart G. Hall. Leiden: Brill, 2014.

———. *De deitate filii et spiritus sancti et in Abraham.* Trans. Ernestus Rhein. In *Gregory of Nyssa: The Minor Treatises on Trinitarian Theology and Apollinarism: Proceedings of the*

11th International Colloquium on Gregory of Nyssa (Tübingen, 17–20 September 2008), ed. Volker Henning Drecoll and Margitta Berghaus, 71–86. Leiden: Brill, 2011.

———. *The Easter Sermons of Gregory of Nyssa: Translation and Commentary*. Ed. Andreas Spira and Christoph Klock. Trans. Stuart G. Hall. Cambridge, MA: The Philadelphia Patristic Foundation, 1981.

———. *Encomium of Saint Gregory, Bishop of Nyssa on His Brother, Saint Basil Archbishop of Cappadocian Caesarea*. Trans. Sister James Aloysius Stein. Washington, DC: The Catholic University of America Press, 1926.

———. *First Homily on the Forty Martyrs of Sebaste*. Trans. Johan Leemans. In *"Let Us Die That We May Live,"* ed. Johan Leemans et al., 93–110.

———. *Homilies on the Beatitudes*. Trans. Stuart G. Hall. In *Homilies on the Beatitudes: An English Version with Supporting Studies. Proceedings of the Eighth International Colloquium on Gregory of Nyssa (Paderborn, 14–18 September 1998)*, ed. Hubertus R. Drobner and Albert Viciano, 21–90. Leiden: Brill, 2000.

———. *Homilies on Ecclesiastes: An English Version with Supporting Studies. Proceedings of the Seventh International Colloquium on Gregory of Nyssa (Paderborn, 14–18 September 1998)*. Ed. and trans. Stuart G. Hall. Berlin: Walter de Gruyter & Co., 1993.

———. *Gregory of Nyssa: Homilies on the Song of Songs*. Trans. Richard A. Norris Jr. Atlanta: Society of Biblical Literature Press, 2012.

———. *A Homily on Theodore the Recruit*. Trans. Johan Leemans. In *"Let Us Die That We May Live,"* ed. Johan Leemans et al., 82–90.

———. *In illud: tunc et ipse filius*. Trans. Brother Casmir, O. S. O. In "When (the Father) Will Subject All Things to (the Son), Then (the Son) Himself Will Be Subjected to Him (the Father) Who Subjects All Things to Him (the Son): A Treatise on First Corinthians 15:28 by Saint Gregory of Nyssa." *The Greek Orthodox Theological Review* 28, no. 1 (1983): 1–25.

———. *Gregory of Nyssa: The Letters: Introduction, Translation and Commentary*. Ed. and trans. Anna M. Silvas. Leiden: Brill, 2007.

———. *Life of Gregory the Wonderworker*. In Saint Gregory Thaumaturgus, *Life and Works*, trans. Michael Slusser, 41–87. Washington, DC: The Catholic University of America Press, 1998.

———. *The Life of Moses*. Trans. Abraham J. Malherbe and Everett Ferguson. New York: Paulist Press, 1978.

———. *The Life of Saint Macrina*. In *Ascetical Works*, trans. Virginia Woods Callahan, 163–97.

———. *The Life of Saint Macrina*. Trans. Kevin Corrigan. Eugene, OR: Wipf and Stock, 2001.

———. *The Lord's Prayer, The Beatitudes*. Trans. Hilda C. Graef. New York: Paulist Press, 1954.

———. *On the Baptism of Christ*. Trans. Henry Austin Wilson. In *NPNF* 5, 518–24.

———. *On the Christian Mode of Life*. In *Ascetical Works*, trans. Virginia Woods Callahan, 127–59.

———. *On the Love of the Poor 1–2*. In *The Hungry Are Dying*, trans. Susan Holman, 193–206.

———. *On the Making of Man*. Trans. Henry Austin Wilson. In *NPNF* 5, 387–427.

———. *On Perfection*. In *Ascetical Works*, trans. Virginia Woods Callahan, 95–122.

———. *On the Soul and the Resurrection*. Trans. Catherine P. Roth. Crestwood, NY: St. Vladimir Press, 1993.

———. *On the Three-Day Period of the Resurrection of our Lord Jesus Christ*. Trans. Stuart Hall. In *The Easter Sermons of Gregory of Nyssa*, ed. Andreas Spira and Christoph Klock.

———. *On Virginity*. Trans. William Moore and Henry Austin Wilson. In *NPNF* 5, 343–71.

———. *On What It Means to Call Oneself a Christian*. In *Ascetical Works*, trans. Virginia Woods Callahan, 81–89.

———. *Refutation of the Views of Apolinarius*. In *St. Gregory of Nyssa: Anti-Apollinarian Writings*, trans. Robin Orton, 91–258.

———. *To Theophilus, Against the Apollinarians*. In *St. Gregory of Nyssa: Anti-Apollinarian Writings*, trans. Robin Orton, 259–68.

———. *Treatise on the Inscriptions of the Psalms*. Trans. Ronald E. Heine. Oxford: Clarendon Press, 1995.

Ancient Sources

Greek in ancient sources comes from the *Thesaurus Linguae Graecae*.

Aetius. *Syntagmation 9–10*. In L. R. Wickham, "The Syntagmation of Aetius the Anomean." *Journal of Theological Studies* 19 (October 1968): 532–69.

Aristophanes. *Nubes*. Ed. N. G. Wilson. In *Aristophanis Fabulae*, 137–202. Oxford: Oxford University Press, 2007.

Aristotle. *Art of Rhetoric*. Trans. J. H. Freese. Cambridge, MA: Harvard University Press, 1926.

———. *Metaphysics*. Ed. W. D. Ross. 2 vols. Oxford: Clarendon Press, 1924.

———. *The Nicomachean Ethics*. Ed. Lesley Brown. Trans. David Ross. Oxford: Oxford University Press, 2009. Greek: *Aristotelis Ethica Nicomachea*. Trans. Ingram Bywater. Oxford: Clarendon Press, 1894 (repr. 1962).

———. *Poetics*. Trans. Stephen Halliwell. In *Aristotle* XXII, 28–141. Cambridge, MA: Harvard University Press, 1995.

Asterius of Amasea. *Ecphrasis on the Holy Martyr Euphemia*. Trans. B. Dehandschutter. In *"Let Us Die That We May Live,"* ed. Johan Leemans et al., 173–75.

Athanasius. *Athanasius Werke*. Ed. H. G. Opitz et al. 3 vols. Berlin: De Gruyter, 1905–.

———. *Contra Gentes and De Incarnatione*. Ed. and trans. Robert W. Thomson. Oxford: Clarendon Press, 1971.

———. *Epistola encyclical*. In *NPNF* 4. Trans. M. Atkinson and Archibald Robertson, 92–96.

———. *Letter to Marcellinus*. Trans. Robert C. Gregg, 101–29. Mahwah, NJ: Paulist Press, 1980. Greek: *PG* 27.1857–66.

———. *The Life of Antony*. Trans. Robert C. Gregg, 29–99. Mahwah, NJ: Paulist Press, 1980. Greek: G. J. M. Bartelink, ed. *Athanase d'Alexandrie, Vie d'Antoine*. Paris: Éditions du Cerf, 2004.

———. *On the Council of Nicaea (De decretis)*. In Khaled Anatolios, *Athanasius*, 178–209.

———. *Oration 3*. In *NPNF* 4. Trans. M. Atkinson and Archibald Robertson, 393–431.

———. *Orations Against the Arians*. In Khaled Anatolios, *Athanasius*, 87–175.

Augustine. *Confessions*, 2nd ed. Trans. Maria Boulding. Brooklyn: New City Press, 2012. Latin: James J. O'Donnell, ed. Oxford: Oxford University Press, 1992.

———. *Sermon 325*. Latin: *PL* 39. Quoted in Brown, "Enjoying the Saints."

Basil of Caesarea. *Against Eunomius*, books 1–3. Trans. Mark DelCogliano and Andrew Radde-Gallwitz. Washington, DC: The Catholic University of America Press, 2011.

———. *The Asketikon of St. Basil the Great*. Trans. Anna M. Silvas. Oxford: Oxford University Press, 2005.

———. *Hexaemeron*. In *Saint Basil: Exegetic Homilies*, trans. Agnes Clare Way, 3–150. Washington, DC: The Catholic University of America Press, 1963.

———. *A Homily on the Forty Martyrs of Sebaste*. Trans. Pauline Allen. In *"Let Us Die That We May Live,"* ed. Johan Leemans et al., 68–76. Greek: *PG* 31.508–52.

———. *Homily on Psalm 1*. In *Saint Basil: Exegetic Homilies*, trans. Agnes Clare Way, 151–64. Washington, DC: The Catholic University of America Press, 1963. Greek: *PG* 29:209–28.

———. *Saint Basil, The Letters*. Trans. Roy Joseph Deferrari and Martin R. P. McGuire. 4 vols. Cambridge, MA: Harvard University Press, 1934.

Choricius of Gaza. *Rhetorical Exercises from Late Antiquity: A Translation of Choricius of Gaza's Preliminary Talks and Declamations*. Ed. Robert J. Penella. Trans. Robert J. Penella et al. Cambridge: Cambridge University Press, 2009.

Cicero. *De Oratore, On the Oratore*. Trans. E. W. Sutton and H. Rackham. Cambridge, MA: Harvard University Press, 1942.

[Cicero]. *Ad Herennium*. Trans. Harry Caplan. Cambridge, MA: Harvard University Press, 1954.

Clement of Alexandria. *Stromata Liber 4*. Ed. Annewies van den Hoek. Paris: Éditions du Cerf, 2001.

Codex Theodosianus. http://ancientrome.ru/ius/library/codex/theod/liber16.htm#1.

Dionysius of Halicarnassus. *Critical Essays*, vols. 1–2. Trans. Stephen Usher. Cambridge, MA: Harvard University Press, 1974, 1985. Greek: *De imitation (fragmenta)*. In *Dionysii Halicarnasei quae exstant*, vol. 6, ed. L. Radermacher and H. Usener, 202–16. Leipzig: Teubner, 1929.

———. *On Imitation*. In Richard Hunter, *Critical Moments in Classical Literature*, 107–28. Cambridge: Cambridge University Press, 2009.

Eunapius. *Lives of the Sophists*. In *Eunapius: Lives of the Philosophers and Sophists*, trans. Wilber C. Wright. Cambridge, MA: Harvard University Press, 1921.

Eunomius. *Eunomius: The Extant Works*. Trans. Richard Paul Vaggione. Oxford: Oxford University Press, 1987.

Evagrius of Pontus. *Evagrius of Pontus: The Greek Ascetic Corpus*. Trans. Robert E. Sinkewicz. Oxford: Oxford University Press, 2003.

Gregory of Nazianzus. *Autobiographical Poems*. Trans. Carolinne White. Cambridge: Cambridge University Press, 1996.

———. *Gregory of Nazianzus's Letter Collection*. Trans. Bradley K. Storin. Oakland: University of California Press, 2019. Greek: Paul Gallay, ed. *Saint Grégoire de Nazianze. Lettres*. 2 vols. Paris: Les Belles Lettres, 1946–1967.

———. *On God and Christ: The Five Theological Oration and Two Letters to Cledonius*. Trans. Lionel Wickham. Crestwood, NY: SVS Press, 2002. Greek: Joseph Barbel, ed. *Gregor von Nazianz. Die fünf theologischen Reden*, 218–76. Düsseldorf: Patmos-Verlag, 1963.

———. *Oration 43*. In *NPNF* 7. Trans. Charles Gordon Browne and James Edward Swallow. Greek: F. Boulenger, ed. *Grégoire de Nazianze. Discours funèbres en l'honneur de son frère Césaire et de Basile de Césarée*, 58–230. Paris: Picard, 1908.

Iamblichus. *The Exhortation to Philosophy*. Trans. Thomas M. Johnson. Grand Rapids, MI: Phanes Press, 1988. Greek: H. Pistelli, ed. *Iamblichi protrepticus ad fidem codicis*, 3–126. Leipzig: Teubner, 1888.

———. *Iamblichi Chalcidensis: In Platonis Dialogos Commentariorum Fragmenta*, 2nd ed. Ed. and trans. John M. Dillon. Wiltshire: The Prometheus Trust, 2009.

———. *Iamblichus De Anima*. Trans. John F. Finamore and John M. Dillon. Atlanta: Society of Biblical Literature Press, 2002.

———. *On the Mysteries*. Trans. Emma C. Clarke, John M. Dillon, and Jackson P. Hershbell. Atlanta: Society of Biblical Literature Press, 2003.

———. *On the Pythagorean Life*. Trans. Gillian Clark. Cambridge: Liverpool University Press, 1989. Greek: U. Klein and L. Deubner, eds. *De vita Pythagorica*. In *Iamblichi de vita Pythagorica liber*. Leipzig: Teubner, 1937.

Ignatius. *Epistle to the Ephesians*. In *Ignatius of Antioch: A Commentary on the Letters of Ignatius of Antioch*, ed. and trans. William R. Schoedel, 33–100.

———. *Epistle to the Romans*. In *Ignatius of Antioch: A Commentary on the Letters of Ignatius of Antioch*, ed. and trans. William R. Schoedel, 165–91.

Isocrates. *Against the Sophists (Orat. 13)*. In *Isocrates* II, trans. George Norlin and Laure Van Hook. Cambridge, MA: Harvard University Press, 1928.

Jerome. *Against Vigilantius*. In *NPNF* 6. Trans. W. H. Fremantle, G. Lewis, and W. G. Martley, 417–23.

John Chrysostom. *The Cult of the Saints*. Trans. Wendy Mayer. Crestwood, NY: St. Vladimir's Seminary Press, 2006.

———. "A Homily on the Holy Martyrs." Trans. Wendy Mayer. In *"Let Us Die That We May Live,"* ed. Johan Leemans et al., 115–26.

Julian. *Hymn to the King Helios (Orat. 4)*. In *Julian* I, trans. Wilmer C. Wright. Cambridge, MA: Harvard University Press, 2013.

———. *Hymn to the Mother of the Gods (Orat. 5)*. In *Julian* I, trans. Wilmer C. Wright. Cambridge, MA: Harvard University Press, 1913.

———. *Letters. Epigrams. Against the Galileans. Fragments*. In *Julian* III, trans. Wilmer C. Wright. Cambridge, MA: Harvard University Press, 1923.

Libanius. *Autobiography and Selected Letters*. Trans. A. F. Norman. Cambridge, MA: Harvard University Press, 1992.

———. *Reply to Aristides (Orat. 64)*, cited in Webb, *Demons and Dancers*. Greek: Richard Foerster, ed. *Libanii opera*, vols. 1–4, Leipzig: Teubner, 1903–1908.

Lucian. *The Dead Come to Life, or The Fisherman*. In *Lucian*, vol. 3, trans. A. M. Harmon, 2–81. Cambridge, MA: Harvard University Press, 1921.

Methodius. *The Symposium: A Treatise on Chastity*. Trans. Herbert Musurillo. New York: Newman Press, 1958.

Musurillo, Herbert, ed. and trans. *The Martyrdom of St. Polycarp*. In *The Acts of the Christian Martyrs*, vol. 2, 2–21. Oxford: Oxford University Press, 1972.

———, ed. and trans. *The Martyrs of Lyons*. In *The Acts of the Christian Martyrs*, vol. 2, 60–85. Oxford: Oxford University Press, 1972.

The New Oxford Annotated Bible with Apocrypha: New Revised Standard Version, 4th ed. Ed. Michael Coogan. Oxford: Oxford University Press, 2010. Greek: *Nestle-Aland Novum Testamentum Graece*. Stuttgart: Deutsche Bibelgesellschaft, 2012.

Origen. *Commentaire sur saint Jean*. Ed. C. Blanc. 5 vols. Paris: Éditions du Cerf, 1966–1992.

———. *Commentary on the Epistle to the Romans, Books 1–5, Books 6–10*. Trans. Thomas Scheck. Washington, DC: The Catholic University of America Press, 2001, 2002. Latin: *Der Römerbriefkommentar des Origenes: Kritische Ausgabe der Übersetzung Rufinus*. 3 vols. Ed. Caroline P. Hammond Bammel. Freiburg im Breisgau: Herder, 1990–1998.

———. *Commentary on the Gospel according to John, Books 1–10, Books 13–32*. Trans. Ronald E. Heine. Washington, DC: The Catholic University of America Press, 1989, 1993.

——. *Contra Celsum*. Trans. Henry Chadwick. Cambridge: Cambridge University Press, 1953. Greek: Marcel Borret, ed. *Contre Celse*. 4 vols. Paris: Éditions du Cerf, 1967–1969.

——. *Exhortation to Martyrdom*. In *Origen: An Exhortation to Martyrdom, Prayer and Selected Works*, trans. Rowan Greer, 41–79. Mahwah, NJ: Paulist Press, 1979. Greek: ΕΙΣ ΜΑΡΤΥΡΙΟΝ ΠΡΟΤΡΕΠΤΙΚΟΣ. In *Origenes Werke*, vol. 1, ed. P. Koetschau, 3–47.

——. *On First Principles*, vols. 1–2. Ed. and trans. John Behr. Oxford: Oxford University Press, 2017.

——. *On First Principles: Being Koetschau's Text of the De Principiis*. Trans. G. W. Butterworth. New York: Harper Torchbooks, 1966. Greek: Paul Koetschau, ed. *De Principiis*. Berlin: De Gruyter, 1913.

——. *Origenes Werke*. Ed. P. Koetschau. 12 vols. Leipzig: Hinrichs, 1899–.

——. *The Song of Songs: Commentary and Homilies*. Trans. R. P. Lawson. New York: Newman Press, 1956.

Philoponus. *Against Proclus On the Eternity of the World 1–5*. Trans. Michael Share. London: Bloomsbury, 2004.

Plato. *Critias*. Trans. R. B. Bury. In *Plato* XI. Cambridge, MA: Harvard University Press, 1929.

——. *Ion*. Trans. W. R. M. Lamb. In *Plato* VII. Cambridge, MA: Harvard University Press, 1925.

——. *Phaedrus*. Trans. Robin Waterfield. Oxford: Oxford University Press, 2002.

——. *Platonis Opera*. Ed. J. Burnet. 5 vols. Oxford: Clarendon Press, 1900–1906.

——. *The Republic of Plato*, 2nd ed. Trans. Allan Bloom. New York: Basic Books, 1991.

——. *Statesman*. Trans. Harold North Fowler and W. R. M. Lamb. In *Plato* VII. Cambridge, MA: Harvard University Press, 1925.

——. *Symposium*. Trans. W. R. M. Lamb. In *Plato* III. Cambridge, MA: Harvard University Press, 1925.

——. *Symposium*. Trans. Alexander Nehamas and Paul Woodruff. Indianapolis: Hackett, 1989.

——. *Timaeus*. Trans. R. G. Bury. In *Plato* XI. Cambridge, MA: Harvard University Press, 1929.

——. *Timaeus*. Trans. Peter Kalkavage. Newburyport, MA: Focus Publishing, 2001.

——. *Timaeus*. Trans. Donald J. Zeyl. Indianapolis: Hackett, 2000.

Plotinus. *Enneads*. Trans. A. H. Armstrong. 7 vols. Cambridge, MA: Harvard University Press, 1966–1988.

——. *The Enneads*. Ed. Lloyd P. Gerson. Trans. George Boys-Stones, John M. Dillon, Lloyd P. Gerson, R. A. H. King, Andrew Smith, and James Wilberding. Cambridge: Cambridge University Press, 2018. Greek: P. Henry and H.-R. Schwyzer, eds. *Plotini Opera*. 3 vols. Leiden: Brill, 1951–1973.

Porphyry. *The Life of Plotinus*. In Plotinus, *The Enneads*, ed. Lloyd P. Gerson, trans. George Boys-Stones et al., 17–37.

Proclus. *Commentary on Alcibiades*. In *Iamblichi Chalcidensis*, ed. and trans. John M. Dillon, 72–83.

——. *Commentary on Timaeus*. In *Iamblichi Chalcidensis*, ed. and trans. John M. Dillon, 106–205.

——. *The Elements of Theology*, 2nd ed. Ed. and trans. E. R. Dodds. Oxford: Oxford University Press, 1963.

——. *Proclus the Successor on Poetics and the Homeric Poems: Essays 5 and 6 of His Commentary on the Republic of Plato*. Trans. Robert Lamberton. Atlanta: Society of Biblical Literature Press, 2012.

Pseudo-Dionysius. *Corpus Dionysiacum I–II: Pseudo-Dionysius Areopagita*. Ed. Günter Heil and Adolf Martin Ritter. Berlin: De Gruyter, 1990–1991.

———. *The Works of Dionysius the Areopagite*. Trans. John Parker. 2 vols. Merrick, NY: Richwood Publishing Co., 1897–1899.

Quintilian. *The Orator's Education*. Trans. Donald A. Russell. Cambridge, MA: Harvard University Press, 2001.

Rufinus of Aquileia. *Inquiry about the Monks in Egypt*. Trans. Andrew Cain. Washington, DC: The Catholic University of America Press, 2019.

Seneca. *Ad Lucilium Epistulae Morales*. Trans. Richard M. Gummere. 3 vols. Cambridge, MA: Harvard University Press, 1979.

Socrates. *Church History*. Trans. A. C. Zeno. In *NPNF* 2, 1–178.

Sophocles. *Oedipus*. Ed. H. Lloyd-Jones and N. G. Wilson. In *Sophoclis fabulae*, 120–80. Oxford: Clarendon Press, 1990.

Sozomen. *Ecclesiastical History*. Trans. Chester D. Hartranft. In *NPNF* 2, 179–427.

Ward, Benedicta, ed. and trans. *The Desert Fathers: Sayings of the Early Christian Monks*. New York: Penguin, 2003.

———, ed. and trans. *The Sayings of the Desert Fathers: The Alphabetical Collection*. Trappist, KY: Cistercian Publications, 1975.

Xenophon. *Memorabilia*. Trans. E. C. Marchant and O. J. Todd. Cambridge, MA: Harvard University Press, 1923.

Secondary Sources

Addey, Crystal. *Divination and Theurgy in Neoplatonism: Oracles of the Gods*. Burlington, VT: Ashgate, 2014.

Afonasin, Eugene, John Dillon, and John F. Finamore, eds. *Iamblichus and the Foundations of Late Platonism*. Leiden: Brill, 2012.

Anatolios, Khaled. *Athanasius*. New York: Routledge, 2004.

———. *Athanasius: The Coherence of His Thought*. New York: Routledge, 1998.

———. *Retrieving Nicaea: The Development and Meaning of Trinitarian Doctrine*. Grand Rapids, MI: Baker Academic, 2011.

Asad, Talal. "Thinking About Religion, Belief, and Politics." In *The Cambridge Companion to Religious Studies*, ed. Robert A. Orsi, 36–57.

Athanassiadi, Polymnia. "Apamea and the Chaldaean Oracles: A Holy City and a Holy Book." In *The Philosopher and Society in Late Antiquity: Essays in Honour of Peter Brown*, ed. Andrew Smith, 117–43. Swansea: The Classical Press of Wales, 2005.

Attridge, Harold W., and Margot E. Fassler, eds. *Psalms in Community*. Atlanta: Society of Biblical Literature, 2003.

Auerbach, Erich. *Mimesis: The Representation of Reality in Western Literature*. Trans. Willard R. Trask. Princeton: Princeton University Press, 1953.

Ayres, Lewis. *Nicaea and Its Legacy: An Approach to Fourth-Century Trinitarian Theology*. Oxford: Oxford University Press, 2004.

Balás, David L. "Eternity and Time in Gregory of Nyssa's *Contra Eunomium*." In *Gregor Von Nyssa und die Philosophie*, ed. Heinrich Dörrie, Margarete Altenburger, and Uta Schramm, 128–55. Leiden: Brill, 1976.

———. *Μετουσία Θεοῦ: Man's Participation in God's Perfections according to Saint Gregory of Nyssa*. Rome: Pontificium Institutum S. Anselmi, 1966.

——. "Participation in the Specific Nature according to Gregory of Nyssa: Aristotelian Logic or Platonic Ontology?" In *Actes du Quatrième Congrès International de Philosophie Médiévale*, 1079–85. Montreal: Institut D'Études Médiévales, 1969.

Banchich, Thomas. Review of *Julian's Gods: Religion and Philosophy in the Thought and Action of Julian the Apostate*, by Rowland Smith. *Bryn Mawr Classical Review* 1997.03.22. https://bmcr.brynmawr.edu/1997/1997.03.22/.

Barnes, Michel René. *The Power of God: Δύναμις in Gregory of Nyssa's Trinitarian Theology*. Washington, DC: The Catholic University of America Press, 2001.

Barthes, Roland. *Camera Lucida*. Trans. Richard Howard. New York: Hill and Wang, 1981.

Behr, John. *The Nicene Faith*, Part 1 of *True God of True God*. Crestwood, NY: St. Vladimir's Seminary Press, 2004.

——. "The Rational Animal: A Rereading of Gregory of Nyssa's *De hominis opificio*." *Journal of Early Christian Studies* 7, no. 2 (1999): 219–47.

Beierwaltes, Werner. *Das wahre Selbst: Studien zu Plotins Begriff des Geistes und des Einen*. Frankfurt am Main: Vittorio Klostermann, 2001.

Bell, Catherine. *Ritual Theory, Ritual Practice*. Oxford: Oxford University Press, 1992.

Berzon, Todd. *Classifying Christians: Ethnography, Heresiology, and the Limits of Knowledge in Late Antiquity*. Berkeley: University of California Press, 2016.

Betancourt, Roland. *Sight, Touch, and Imagination in Byzantium*. Cambridge: Cambridge University Press, 2018.

Bitton-Ashkelony, Brouria. *Encountering the Sacred: The Debate on Christian Pilgrimage in Late Antiquity*. Berkeley: University of California Press, 2005.

Blanchot, Maurice. "Literature and the Right to Death." In *The Work of Fire*, trans. Lydia Davis, 300–44. Stanford: Stanford University Press, 1995.

Bloomer, W. Martin. "Schooling in Persona: Imagination and Subordination in Roman Education." *Classical Antiquity* 16, no. 1 (April 1997): 57–78.

Boersma, Hans. *Embodiment and Virtue in Gregory of Nyssa: An Anagogical Approach*. Oxford: Oxford University Press, 2013.

Bolman, Elizabeth S. "Mimesis, Metamorphosis, and Representation in Coptic Monastic Cells." *The Bulletin of the American Society of Papyrologists* 35, nos. 1/2 (1998): 65–77.

Børresen, Kari Elisabeth. "God's Image, Man's Image." In *The Image of God: Gender Models in Judaeo-Christian Tradition*, ed. Kari Elisabeth Børresen, 187–211. Oslo: Solum Forlag, 1991.

——. *Subordination and Equivalence: The Nature and Role of Women in Augustine and Thomas Aquinas*. Washington, DC: University Press of America, 1981.

Bourdieu, Pierre. *The Logic of Practice*. Trans. Richard Nice. Stanford: Stanford University Press, 1990.

Bowersock, Glen. *Hellenism in Late Antiquity*. Ann Arbor: University of Michigan Press, 1996.

——. *Julian the Apostate*. Cambridge: Cambridge University Press, 1978.

Brakke, David. *Athanasius and Asceticism*. Baltimore: Johns Hopkins University Press, 1998.

——. *Demons and the Making of the Monk: Spiritual Combat in Early Christianity*. Cambridge, MA: Harvard University Press, 2006.

——. "The Lady Appears: Materializations of 'Women' in Early Monastic Literature." *Journal of Medieval and Early Modern Studies* 33, no. 3 (2003): 387–402.

——, and Andrew Crislip. *Selected Discourses of Shenoute the Great: Community, Theology, and Social Conflict in Late Ancient Egypt*. Cambridge: Cambridge University Press, 2015.

———, Michael L. Satlow, and Steven Weitzman, eds. *Religion and the Self in Antiquity*. Bloomington: Indiana University Press, 2005.

Brightbill, Jeremy David. "Roman Declamation: Between Creativity and Constraints." PhD diss., University of Chicago, 2015.

Brooks, Peter. *Reading for the Plot*. New York: Knopf, 1984.

Brown, Peter. *The Body and Society: Men, Women, & Sexual Renunciation in Early Christianity*. Twentieth Anniversary Edition. New York: Columbia University Press, 2008.

———. *The Cult of the Saints: Its Rise and Function in Latin Christianity*. Chicago: University of Chicago Press, 1981.

———. "Enjoying the Saints in Late Antiquity." *Early Medieval Europe* 9, no. 1 (2000): 1–24.

———. "The Glow of Byzantium." *New York Review of Books* 63, no. 12 (July 14, 2016): 37–39.

———. "The Notion of Virginity in the Early Church." In *Christian Spirituality*, vol. 1, *Origins to the Twelfth Century*, ed. Bernard McGinn, John Meyendorff, and Jean LeClercq, 427–43. London: Routledge, 1985.

———. *Poverty and Leadership in the Later Roman Empire*. Hanover, NH: University Press of New England, 2002.

———. *Power and Persuasion in Late Antiquity: Towards a Christian Empire*. Madison: University of Wisconsin Press, 1992.

———. *The Ransom of the Soul: Afterlife and Wealth in Early Western Christianity*. Cambridge, MA: Harvard University Press, 2015.

———. "The Rise and Function of the Holy Man in Late Antiquity." *The Journal of Roman Studies* 61 (1971): 81–101.

———. "The Rise and Function of the Holy Man in Late Antiquity, 1971–1997." *Journal of Early Christian Studies* 6, no. 3 (Fall 1998): 353–76.

———. "The Saint as Exemplar in Late Antiquity." *Representations* 1, no. 2 (Spring 1983): 1–25.

———. *Through the Eye of a Needle: Wealth, the Fall of Rome, and the Making of Christianity in the West, 350–550 AD*. Princeton: Princeton University Press, 2012.

———. *The World of Late Antiquity*. New York: Norton, 1989.

———. "A World Winking with Messages." *New York Review of Books* 65, no. 20 (December 20, 2018). https://www.nybooks.com/articles/2018/12/20/early-christian-art-world-winking-with-messages/.

Burnyeat, M. F. "Aristotle on Learning to Be Good." In *Essays on Aristotle's Ethics*, ed. Amélie Oksenberg Rorty, 69–72. Berkeley: University of California Press, 1980.

———. "Culture and Society in Plato's Republic." *Tanner Lectures on Human Values* 20 (1999): 215–324.

Burrow, Colin. *Imitating Authors: Plato to Futurity*. Oxford: Oxford University Press, 2019.

Burrus, Virginia. *Ancient Christian Ecopoetics: Cosmologies, Saints, Things*. Philadelphia: University of Pennsylvania Press, 2019.

———. *"Begotten, Not Made": Conceiving Manhood in Late Antiquity*. Stanford: Stanford University Press, 2000.

———. *Chastity as Autonomy: Women in the Stories of Apocryphal Acts*. Lewiston, NY: Edwin Mellen Press, 1987.

———. "Gender, Eros, and Pedagogy: Macrina's Pious Household." In *Ascetic Culture: Essays in Honor of Philip Rousseau*, ed. Blake Leyerle and Robin Darling Young, 167–81. Notre Dame: University of Notre Dame Press, 2013.

———. "Is Macrina a Woman? Gregory of Nyssa's *Dialogue on the Soul and Resurrection*." In *The Blackwell Companion to Postmodern Theology*, ed. Graham Ward, 249–64. Malden, MA: Blackwell, 2001.

———. "Macrina's Tattoo." In *The Cultural Turn in Late Ancient Studies*, ed. Dale B. Martin and Patricia Cox Miller, 103–18.

———. "Mimicking Virgins: Colonial Ambivalence and the Ancient Romance." *Arethusa* 38, no. 1 (2005): 49–88.

———. "Queer Father: Gregory of Nyssa and the Subversion of Identity." In *Queer Theology: Rethinking the Western Body*, ed. Gerard Loughlin, 147–62. Malden, MA: Blackwell, 2007.

———. "Radical Orthodoxy and the Heresiological Habit: Engaging with Graham Ward's Christology." In *Interpreting the Postmodern*, ed. Marion Grau and Rosemary Radford Ruether, 36–53. New York: Continuum, 2006.

———. *The Sex Lives of Saints: An Erotics of Ancient Hagiography*. Philadelphia: University of Pennsylvania Press, 2004.

———, and Rebecca Lyman. "Shifting the Focus of History." In *Late Ancient Christianity*, vol. 2 of *A People's History of Christianity*, ed. Virginia Burrus, 1–23. Minneapolis: Fortress Press, 2005.

Burton-Christie, Douglas. "Early Monasticism." In *The Cambridge Companion to Christian Mysticism*, ed. Amy Hollywood and Patricia Z. Beckman, 37–58.

Butler, Judith. *Bodies That Matter: On the Discursive Limits of Sex*. New York: Routledge, 1993.

———. *Giving an Account of Oneself*. New York: Fordham, 2005.

Cadenhead, Raphael. *The Body and Desire; Gregory of Nyssa's Ascetical Theology*. Oakland: University of California Press, 2018.

Cahill, J. B. "The Date and Setting of Gregory's Commentary on the Song of Songs." *Journal of Theological Studies* 32, no. 2 (October 1981): 447–60.

Cain, Andrew. "Jerome's *Epitaphium Paulae*: Hagiography, Pilgrimage, and the Cult of Saint Paula." *Journal of Early Christian Studies* 18, no. 1 (Spring 2010): 105–39.

———, and Noel Lenski, eds. *The Power of Religion in Late Antiquity*. Burlington, VT: Ashgate, 2009.

Cameron, Averil. "Ascetic Closure and the End of Antiquity." In *Asceticism*, ed. Vincent Wimbush and Richard Valantasis, 147–61.

———. *Christianity and the Rhetoric of Empire: The Development of Christian Discourse*. Berkeley: University of California Press, 1991.

Canévet, Mariette. "Exégèse et théologie dans les traits spirituels de Grégoire de Nysse." In *Écriture et culture philosophique dans la pensée de Grégoire de Nyssa*, ed. Marguerite Harl, 169–96.

———. *Grégoire de Nysse et l'herméneutique biblique*. Paris: Études Augustiniennes, 1983.

Carlson, Thomas A. *The Indiscrete Image: Infinitude and Creation of the Human*. Chicago: University of Chicago Press, 2008.

Carruthers, Mary. *The Craft of Thought: Meditation, Rhetoric, and the Making of Images, 400–1200*. Cambridge: Cambridge University Press, 1998.

Carson, Anne. *Eros the Bittersweet*. Princeton: Princeton University Press, 1986.

———. *Grief Lessons: Four Plays*. New York: *New York Review of Books*, 2006.

Cassin, Matthieu. "*De deitate filii et spiritus sancti et in Abraham*." In *Gregory of Nyssa: The Minor Treatises on Trinitarian Theology and Apollinarism*, ed. Volker Henning Drecoll and Margitta Berghaus, 277–311. Leiden: Brill, 2011.

———. *L'écriture de la controverse chez Grégoire de Nysse. Polémique littéraire et exégèse dans le Contre Eunome.* Turnhout: Brepols, 2012.

———. "Text and Context: The Importance of Scholarly Reading. Gregory of Nyssa, *Contra Eunomium.*" In *Reading the Church Fathers,* ed. Scot Douglass and Morwenna Ludlow, 109–31.

———, and Hélèn Grelier, eds. *Grégoire de Nysse: La Bible dans la construction de son discours: Actes du colloque de Paris, 9–10 février 2007.* Paris: Institut d'Études Augustiniennes, 2008.

Casson, Lionel. *Travel in the Ancient World.* Baltimore: Johns Hopkins University Press, 1974.

Castelli, Elizabeth. *Imitating Paul: A Discourse of Power.* Louisville: Westminster Press, 1991.

———. *Martyrdom and Memory: Early Christian Culture Making.* New York: Columbia University Press, 2004.

Cazelles, Brigitte. *Le corps de sainteté d'après Jehan Bouche d'Or, Jehan Paulus et quelques vies des XIIe et XIIIe siècles.* Geneva: Droz, 1982.

Certeau, Michel de. "A Variant: Hagio-Graphical Edification." In *The Writing of History,* trans. Tom Conley, 269–83. New York: Columbia University Press, 1988.

Chin, C. M., and Moulie Vidas, eds. *Late Ancient Knowing: Explorations in Intellectual History.* Berkeley: University of California Press, 2015.

Clark, D. L. "Imitation: Theory and Practice in Roman Rhetoric." *Quarterly Journal of Speech* 37 (1951): 11–22.

Clark, Elizabeth A. "Holy Women, Holy Words: Early Christian Women, Social History and the 'Linguistic Turn.'" *Journal of Early Christian Studies* 6, no. 3 (Fall 1998): 413–30.

———. "Ideology, History, and the Construction of 'Woman' in Late Antique Christianity." *Journal of Early Christian Studies* 2, no. 2 (1994): 155–84.

———. "The Lady Vanishes: Dilemmas of a Feminist Historian After the 'Linguistic Turn.'" *Church History* 67, no. 1 (March 1998): 1–31.

———. *The Origenist Controversy: The Cultural Construction of an Early Christian Debate.* Princeton: Princeton University Press, 1992.

Clark, Stephen R. L. *Plotinus: Myth, Metaphor, and Philosophical Practice.* Chicago: University of Chicago Press, 2016.

Clarke, Emma C., ed. *De Mysteriis: A Manifesto of the Miraculous.* Burlington, VT: Ashgate, 2001.

Coakley, Sarah. "The Eschatological Body: Gender, Transformation, and God." *Modern Theology* 16, no. 1 (January 2000): 61–73.

———. *God, Sexuality, and the Self: An Essay "On the Trinity."* Cambridge: Cambridge University Press, 2013.

———. "Gregory of Nyssa." In *The Spiritual Senses: Perceiving God in Western Christianity,* ed. Paul L. Gavrilyuk and Sarah Coakley, 36–55. Cambridge: Cambridge University Press, 2014.

———. "Introduction—Gender, Trinitarian Analogies, and the Pedagogy of *The Song.*" In *Re-thinking Gregory of Nyssa,* 1–13. First published in *Modern Theology* 18, no. 4 (2002): 432–43.

———. *Powers and Submissions: Spirituality, Philosophy, Gender.* Oxford: Blackwell, 2002.

———, ed. *Re-thinking Gregory of Nyssa.* Oxford: Blackwell, 2003.

Collins, Adela Yarbro. "The Psalms and the Origins of Christology." In *Psalms in Community,* ed. Harold W. Attridge and Margot E. Fassler, 113–23.

Collins, James Henderson. *Exhortations to Philosophy: The Protreptics of Plato, Isocrates, and Aristotle*. Oxford: Oxford University Press, 2015.

Conway-Jones, Ann. *Gregory of Nyssa's Tabernacle Imagery in Its Jewish and Christian Contexts*. Oxford: Oxford University Press, 2014.

Cooper, Kate. *Band of Angels: The Forgotten World of Early Christian Women*. New York: Overlook Press, 2013.

———. *The Virgin and the Bride: Idealized Womanhood in Late Antiquity*. Cambridge, MA: Harvard University Press, 1996.

Corrigan, Kevin. *Evagrius and Gregory: Mind, Soul, and Body in the Fourth Century*. Burlington, VT: Ashgate, 2009.

———. "Ousia and Hypostasis in the Trinitarian Theology of the Cappadocian Fathers: Basil and Gregory of Nyssa." *Zeitschrift für Antikes Christentum* 12 (2008): 114–34.

———. *Reason, Faith and Otherness in Neoplatonic and Early Christian Thought*. Burlington, VT: Ashgate, 2013.

———, and Elena Glazov-Corrigan. *Plato's Dialectic at Play: Argument, Structure, and Myth in the* Symposium. University Park: Pennsylvania State University Press, 2004.

Coulter, James A. *The Literary Microcosm: Theories of Interpretation of the Later Neoplatonists*. Leiden: Brill, 1976.

Cribiore, Raffaella. *Gymnastics of the Mind: Greek Education in Hellenistic and Roman Egypt*. Princeton: Princeton University Press, 2001.

———. *The School of Libanius in Late Antique Antioch*. Princeton: Princeton University Press, 2007.

———. "The Value of a Good Education: Libanius and Public Authority." In *A Companion to Late Antiquity*, ed. Philip Rousseau, 233–45.

Crislip, Andrew. *Thorns in the Flesh: Illness and Sanctity in Late Ancient Christianity*. Philadelphia: University of Pennsylvania Press, 2012.

Crouzel, Henri. "L'imitation et la 'suite' de Dieu et du Christ dans les premiers siècles chrétiens ainsi que leurs sources gréco-romaines et hébraïques." *Jahrbuch für Antike und Christentum* 21 (1978): 7–41.

Daley, Brian. "Divine Transcendence and Human Transformation: Gregory of Nyssa's Anti-Apollinarian Christology." In *Re-thinking Gregory of Nyssa*, ed. Sarah Coakley, 67–76.

———. "Finding the Right Key: The Aims and Strategies of Early Christian Interpretation of the Psalms." In *Psalms in Community*, ed. Harold W. Attridge and Margot E. Fassler, 189–205.

Daniélou, Jean. "Akolouthia chez Grégoire de Nysse." *Revue des Sciences Religieuses* 27 (1953): 219–49.

———. *Bible et liturgie: la théologie biblique des sacrements et des fêtes d'après les Pères de l'Eglise*. Paris: Lex orandi, 1951.

———. "La chronologie des oeuvres de Grégoire de Nysse." *Studia Patristica* 7 (1966): 159–69.

———. *L'être et le temps chez Grégoire de Nysse*. Leiden: Brill, 1970.

———. Introduction to *From Glory to Glory: Texts from Gregory of Nyssa's Mystical Writings*, ed. and trans. Herbert Musurillo. Crestwood, NY: St. Vladimir's Seminary Press, 1997.

Davis, Stephen. *The Cult of Saint Thecla: A Tradition of Women's Piety in Late Antiquity*. Oxford: Oxford University Press, 2001.

DelCogliano, Mark. *Basil of Caesarea's Anti-Eunomian Theory of Names: Christian Theology and Late-Antique Philosophy in the Fourth Century Trinitarian Controversy*. Leiden: Brill, 2010.

Digeser, Elizabeth DePalma. "The Power of Religious Rituals: A Philosophical Quarrel on the Eve of the Great Persecution." In *The Power of Religion in Late Antiquity*, ed. Andrew Cain and Noel Lenski, 81–92.

Dillon, John. "Image, Symbol, and Analogy: Three Basic Concepts of Neoplatonic Allegorical Exegesis." In *The Significance of Neoplatonism*, ed. R. B. Harris, 247–63. Albany: State University of New York Press, 1979.

——. "The Letters of Iamblichus: Popular Philosophy in a Neoplatonic Mode." In *Iamblichus and the Foundations of Late Platonism*, ed. Eugene Afonasin, John Dillon, and John F. Finamore, 51–62.

——. "The Magical Power of Names in Origen and Later Platonism." In *Origeniana Tertia: Third International Colloquium for Origen Studies (University of Manchester, September 7th–11th, 1981)*, ed. Richard Hanson and Henri Crouzel, 203–16. Rome: Edizioni dell'Ateneo, 1985.

——. *The Middle Platonists, 80 B.C. to A.D. 220*. Ithaca: Cornell University Press, 1996.

——, and Wolfgang Polleichtner, eds. *Iamblichus of Chalcis: The Letters*. Atlanta: Society of Biblical Literature Press, 2009.

Dingeldein, Laura B. "Julian's Philosophy and His Religious Program." In *Religious Competition in the Greco-Roman World*, ed. Nathaniel P. DesRosiers and Lily C. Vuong, 119–29. Atlanta: Society of Biblical Literature Press, 2016.

Dörries, Hermann. "Griechentum und Christentum bei Gregor von Nyssa: Zu H. Langerbecks Edition des Hohelied-Kommentar in der Leidener Gregor-Ausgabe." *Theologische Literaturzeitung* 88 (1963): 582–92.

Douglass, Scot. "The Combinatory Detour: The Prefix Συν- in Gregory of Nyssa's Production of Theological Knowledge." In *Reading the Church Fathers*, ed. Scot Douglass and Morwenna Ludlow, 82–105.

——. *Theology of the Gap: Cappadocian Language Theory and the Trinitarian Controversy*. New York: Peter Lang, 2005.

——, and Morwenna Ludlow, eds. *Reading the Church Fathers*. London: T&T Clark, 2011.

Dünzl, Franz. "Formen der Kirchenväterrezeption am Beispiel der physischen Erlösungslehre des Gregor von Nyssa." *Theologie und Philosophie* 69 (1994): 161–81.

Edmonds III, Radcliffe G. *Drawing Down the Moon: Magic in the Ancient Greco-Roman World*. Princeton: Princeton University Press, 2019.

Edwards, Mark. *Religions of the Constantinian Empire*. Oxford: Oxford University Press, 2016.

Elm, Susanna. *Sons of Hellenism, Fathers of the Church: Emperor Julian, Gregory of Nazianzus, and the Vision of Rome*. Berkeley: University of California Press, 2012.

——. *"Virgins of God": The Making of Asceticism in Late Antiquity*. Oxford: Oxford University Press, 1994.

Elsner, Jaś. *Art and the Roman Viewer: The Transformation of Art from the Pagan World to Christianity*. Cambridge: Cambridge University Press, 1995.

——. "Beyond Compare: Pagan Saint and Christian God in Late Antiquity." *Critical Inquiry* 35 (Spring 2009): 655–83.

——. *Imperial Rome and Christian Triumph: The Art of the Roman Empire AD 100–450*. Oxford: Oxford University Press, 1998.

——. "Relic, Icon, and Architecture: The Material Articulation of the Holy in East Christian Art." In *Saints and Sacred Matter: The Cult of Relics in Byzantium and Beyond*, ed.

Cynthia Hahn and Holger A. Klein, 13–40. Washington, DC: Dumbarton Oaks Publications, 2015.

———. *Roman Eyes: Visuality and Subjectivity in Art and Text*. Princeton: Princeton University Press, 2007.

———, and Ian Rutherford, eds. *Pilgrimage in Graeco-Roman and Early Christian Antiquity: Seeing the Gods*. Oxford: Oxford University Press, 2005.

Emilsson, Eyjólfur. *Plotinus*. New York: Routledge, 2017.

———. *Plotinus on Sense-Perception: A Philosophical Study*. Cambridge: Cambridge University Press, 1984.

Falcasantos, Rebecca Stephens. *Constantinople: Ritual, Violence, and Memory in the Making of a Christian Imperial Capital*. Oakland: University of California Press, 2020.

———. "Wandering Wombs, Inspired Intellects: Christian Religious Travel in Late Antiquity." *Journal of Early Christian Studies* 25, no. 1 (Spring 2017): 89–117.

Fantham, Elaine. "Imitation and Evolution: The Discussion of Rhetorical Imitation in *De Orator* 2, 87–97." *Classical Philology* 73 (1978): 1–16.

———. *The Roman World of Cicero's* De Oratore. Oxford: Oxford University Press, 2004.

Ferrari, G. R. F. "Plato on Poetry." In *The Cambridge History of Literary Criticism*, vol. 1, ed. George Alexander Kennedy, 92–148. Cambridge: Cambridge University Press, 1989.

Finney, Paul Corby. *The Invisible God: The Earliest Christians on Art*. Oxford: Oxford University Press, 1994.

Fletcher, Emily. "*Aisthēsis*, Reason and Appetite in the *Timaeus*." *Phronesis* 61 (2016): 397–434.

Fontaine, Jacques, and Charles Kannengiesser, eds. *Épektasis: Mélanges patristiques offerts au Cardinal Jean Daniélou*. Paris: Beauchesne, 1972.

Foucault, Michel. "On the Genealogy of Ethics: An Overview of Work in Progress." In *The Foucault Reader*, ed. Paul Rabinow, 340–71. London: Penguin Books, 1991.

———. "Technologies of the Self." In *Technologies of the Self: A Seminar with Michel Foucault*, ed. Luther H. Martin, Huck Gutman, and Patrick H. Hutton, 16–49. Amherst: University of Massachusetts Press, 1988.

Fowden, Garth. *Before and After Muhammad: The First Millennium Refocused*. Princeton: Princeton University Press, 2014.

———. *The Egyptian Hermes: A Historical Approach to the Late Pagan Mind*. Princeton: Princeton University Press, 1986.

Fox, Robin Lane. *Augustine: Conversions to Confessions*. New York: Basic Books, 2015.

Francis, James A. "Late Antique Visuality: Blurring Boundaries Between Word and Image, Pagan and Christian." In *Shifting Cultural Frontiers in Late Antiquity*, ed. David Brakke, Deborah Deliyannis, and Edward Watts, 139–49. Burlington, VT: Ashgate, 2012.

———. "Living Icons: Tracing a Motif in Verbal and Visual Representation from the Second to Fourth Centuries C.E." *American Journal of Philology* 124, no. 4 (Winter 2003): 575–600.

———. "Visual and Verbal Representation: Image, Text, Person, and Power." In *A Companion to Late Antiquity*, ed. Philip Rousseau, 285–305.

Frank, Georgia. "Macrina's Scar: Homeric Allusion and Heroic Identity in Gregory of Nyssa's *Life of Macrina*." *Journal of Early Christian Studies* 8, no. 4 (2000): 511–30.

———. *The Memory of the Eyes: Pilgrims to Living Saints in Christian Late Antiquity*. Berkeley: University of California Press, 2000.

———. "The Memory Palace of Marcellinus: Athanasius and the Mirror of the Psalms." In *Ascetic Culture: Essays in Honor of Philip Rousseau*, ed. Blake Leyerle and Robin Darling Young, 167–81. Notre Dame: University of Notre Dame Press, 2013.

———. "Pilgrimage." In *The Oxford Handbook of Early Christian Studies*, ed. Susan Ashbrook Harvey and David G. Hunter, 826–41. Oxford: Oxford University Press, 2008.

———. "'Taste and See': The Eucharist and the Eyes of Faith in the Fourth Century." *Church History* 70, no. 4 (2001): 619–43.

Frankfurter, David, ed. *Guide to the Study of Ancient Magic*. Leiden: Brill, 2019.

Gargola, Daniel J. *The Shape of the Roman Order: The Republic and Its Spaces*. Chapel Hill: University of North Carolina Press, 2017.

Gebauer, Gunter, and Christoph Wulf. *Mimesis: Culture, Art, Society*. Trans. Don Reneau. Berkeley: University of California Press, 1995.

Geljon, Albert-Kees. "Divine Infinity in Gregory of Nyssa and Philo of Alexandria." *Vigiliae Christianae* 59, no. 2 (May 2005): 152–77.

Gerson, Lloyd P., ed. *Aristotle and Other Platonists*. Ithaca: Cornell University Press, 2005.

———, ed. *The Cambridge Companion to Plotinus*. Cambridge: Cambridge University Press, 1996.

———, ed. *The Cambridge History of Philosophy in Late Antiquity*, vol. 1. Cambridge: Cambridge University Press, 2010.

———. *From Plato to Platonism*. Ithaca: Cornell University Press, 2013.

———. *Plotinus*. New York: Routledge, 1994.

Giardina, Andrea. "The Transition to Late Antiquity." In *The Cambridge Economic History of the Greco-Roman World*, ed. Walter Scheidel, Ian Morris, and Richard Saller, 743–68. Cambridge: Cambridge University Press, 2007.

Gill, Christopher. *The Structured Self in Hellenistic and Roman Thought*. Oxford: Oxford University Press, 2006.

———, Tim Whitmarsh, and John Wilkins. *Galen and the World of Knowledge*. Cambridge: Cambridge University Press, 2009.

Giulea, Dragoş Andrei. "*Simpliciores, Eruditi*, and the Noetic Form of God: Pre-Nicene Christology Revisited." *Harvard Theological Review* 108, no. 2 (2015): 263–88.

Gordon, Jill. *Plato's Erotic World: From Cosmic Origins to Human Death*. Cambridge: Cambridge University Press, 2012.

Gray, Vivienne. "Mimesis in Greek Historical Theory." *American Journal of Philology* 108, no. 3 (1987): 467–86.

Greenblatt, Stephen. *Marvels and Possessions: The Marvels of the New World*. Chicago: University of Chicago Press, 2017.

Grig, Lucy. *Making Martyrs in Late Antiquity*. Liverpool: Duckworth, 2004.

Habinek, Thomas. *Ancient Rhetoric and Oratory*. Malden, MA: Blackwell, 2004.

———. *The World of Roman Song: From Ritualized Speech to Social Order*. Baltimore: Johns Hopkins University Press, 2005.

Hadot, Pierre. *Philosophy as a Way of Life: Spiritual Exercises from Socrates to Foucault*. Trans. Arnold Davidson. Oxford: Blackwell, 1995.

———. *Plotinus or the Simplicity of Vision*. Trans. Michael Chase. Chicago: University of Chicago Press, 1993.

———. "Théologie, exégèse, révélation, écriture dans la philosophie grecque." In *Les Règles de l'interprétation*, ed. Michel Tardieu, 13–34. Paris: Cerf, 1987.

Hägg, Tomas, and Philip Rousseau, eds. *Greek Biography and Panegyric in Late Antiquity.* Berkeley: University of California Press, 2000.

Hahn, Cynthia, and Holger A. Klein, eds. *Saints and Sacred Matter: The Cult of Relics in Byzantium and Beyond.* Washington, DC: Dumbarton Oaks Publications, 2015.

Halberstam, Jack. *The Queer Art of Failure.* Durham: Duke University Press, 2011.

Halliwell, Stephen. *The Aesthetics of Mimesis: Ancient Texts and Modern Problems.* Princeton: Princeton University Press, 2002.

———. *Aristotle's Poetics.* Chicago: University of Chicago Press, 1998.

———. *Between Ecstasy and Truth: Interpretations of Greek Poetics from Homer to Longinus.* Oxford: Oxford University Press, 2011.

Halperin, David M. "Platonic Erôs and What Men Call Love." *Ancient Philosophy* 5 (1985): 161–204.

———. "Why Is Diotima a Woman? Platonic Eros and the Figuration of Gender." In *One Hundred Years of Homosexuality and Other Essays on Greek Love,* ed. David Halperin, 113–51. New York: Routledge, 1990.

Hanson, R. P. C. *The Search for the Doctrine of God.* Edinburgh: T&T Clark, 1988.

———. "The Transformation of Images in the Trinitarian Theology of the Fourth Century." *Studia Patristica* 17, no. 1 (1982): 91–113.

Harl, Marguerite, ed. *Écriture et Culture Philosophique dans la Pensée de Grégoire de Nysse: Actes du colloque de Chevetogne (22–26 Septembre 1969).* Leiden: Brill, 1971.

———. "Moïse figure de l'évêque dans l'Eloge de Basile de Grégoire de Nysse (381): Un plaidoyer pour l'autorité épiscopale." In *The Biographical Works of Gregory of Nyssa,* ed. Andreas Spira, 71–119.

Harper, Kyle. *From Shame to Sin: The Christian Transformation of Sexual Morality in Late Antiquity.* Cambridge, MA: Harvard University Press, 2013.

Harpham, Geoffrey Galt. "Asceticism and the Compensations of Art." In *Asceticism,* ed. Vincent Wimbush and Richard Valantasis, 357–68.

Harris, William V. *Ancient Literacy.* Cambridge, MA: Harvard University Press, 1989.

Harrison, Carol. "Getting Carried Away: Why Did Augustine Sing?" *Augustinian Studies* 46, no. 1 (2015): 1–22.

Harrison, Verna E. F. "Gender, Generation, and Virginity in Cappadocian Theology." *Journal of Theological Studies* 47, no. 1 (April 1996): 38–68.

———. *Grace and Human Freedom according to St. Gregory of Nyssa.* Lewiston, NY: Edwin Mellen Press, 1992.

Hart, D. Bentley. "The Mirror of the Infinite: Gregory of Nyssa on the *Vestigia Trinitatis.*" In *Re-thinking Gregory of Nyssa,* ed. Sarah Coakley, 111–31.

———. "The 'Whole Humanity': Gregory of Nyssa's Critique of Slavery in Light of His Eschatology." *Scottish Journal of Theology* 54, no. 1 (2001): 51–69.

Harvey, David. "Space as a Key Word." In *Spaces of Global Capitalism: Towards a Theory of Uneven Geographical Development.* London: Verso, 2006.

Harvey, Susan Ashbrook. "Revisiting the Daughters of the Covenant: Women's Choirs and Sacred Song in Ancient Syriac Christianity." *Hugoye: Journal of Syriac Studies* 8, no. 2 (July 2005): 125–49.

———. *Scenting Salvation: Ancient Christianity and the Olfactory Imagination.* Berkeley: University of California Press, 2006.

———. *Song and Memory: Biblical Women in Syriac Tradition*. Milwaukee: Marquette University Press, 2010.

Haskins, Ekaterina V. "*Mimesis* Between Poetics and Rhetoric: Performance Culture and Civic Education in Plato, Isocrates and Aristotle." *Rhetoric Society Quarterly* 30, no. 3 (Summer 2000): 7–33.

Heine, Ronald. Introduction to *Gregory of Nyssa's Treatise on the Inscriptions of the Psalms*, trans. Ronald Heine, 1–80.

———. *Perfection in the Virtuous Life: A Study in the Relationship Between Edification and Polemical Theology in Gregory of Nyssa's* De vita Moysis. Cambridge, MA: Philadelphia Patristic Foundation, 1975.

Hollywood, Amy. Introduction to *The Cambridge Companion to Christian Mysticism*, ed. Amy Hollywood and Patricia Z. Beckman, 1–36.

———. "Performativity, Citationality, Ritualization." *History of Religions* 42, no. 2 (November 2002): 93–115.

———. "Song, Experience, and the Book in Benedictine Monasticism." In *The Cambridge Companion to Christian Mysticism*, ed. Amy Hollywood and Patricia Z. Beckman, 59–79.

———, and Patricia Z. Beckman, eds. *The Cambridge Companion to Christian Mysticism*. Cambridge: Cambridge University Press, 2012.

Holman, Susan R. *The Hungry Are Dying: Beggars and Bishops in Roman Cappadocia*. Oxford: Oxford University Press, 2001.

Horden, Peregrine. "The Earliest Hospitals in Byzantium, Western Europe, and Islam." *Journal of Interdisciplinary History* 35, no. 3 (Winter 2005): 361–89.

Hunter, Richard. "The Ugly Peasant and the Naked Virgins: Dionysius on Halicarnassus, *On Imitation*." In *Critical Moments in Classical Literature: Studies in the Ancient View of Literature and Its Uses*, 107–27. Cambridge: Cambridge University Press, 2009.

Inglebert, Hervé. "Introduction: Late Antique Conceptions of Late Antiquity." In *The Oxford Handbook of Late Antiquity*, ed. Scott Fitzgerald Johnson, 3–28.

Izmirlieva, Valentina. *All the Names of the Lord: Lists, Mysticism, and Magic*. Chicago: University of Chicago Press, 2008.

Jacob, Christian. *The Sovereign Map: Theoretical Approaches in Cartography Throughout History*. Trans. Tom Conley. Chicago: University of Chicago Press, 2006.

Jacobs, Andrew. *Epiphanius of Cyprus: A Cultural Biography of Late Antiquity*. Oakland: University of California Press, 2016.

———. *Remains of the Jews: The Holy Land and Christian Empire in Late Antiquity*. Stanford: Stanford University Press, 2004.

Jaeger, Werner. *Early Christianity and Greek Paideia*. Cambridge, MA: Harvard University Press, 1961.

———. *Two Rediscovered Works of Ancient Literature: Gregory of Nyssa and Macarius*. Leiden: Brill, 1954.

James, Liz. "'Pray Not to Fall into Temptation and Be on Your Guard': Pagan Statues in Christian Constantinople." *Gesta* 35, no. 1 (1996): 12–20.

———, and Ruth Webb. "'To Understand Ultimate Things and Enter Secret Places': Ekphrasis and Art in Byzantium." *Art History* 14, no. 1 (1991): 1–17.

James, William. *The Principles of Psychology*, vol. 1. New York: Dover, 1950.

Jefferson, Lee M., and Robin M. Jensen, eds. *The Art of Empire: Christian Art in Its Imperial Context*. Minneapolis: Fortress Press, 2015.

Jensen, Robin M. "Compiling Narratives: The Visual Strategies of Early Christian Visual Art." *Journal of Early Christian Studies* 23, no. 1 (Spring 2015): 1–26.

——. *Face to Face: Portraits of the Divine in Early Christianity*. Minneapolis: Fortress Press, 2005.

——. *Understanding Early Christian Art*. London: Routledge, 2000.

Johnson, Scott Fitzgerald. *Literary Territories: Cartographical Thinking in Late Antiquity*. Oxford: Oxford University Press, 2016.

——. "Travel, Cartography, and Cosmology." In *The Oxford Handbook of Late Antiquity*, ed. Scott Fitzgerald Johnson, 562–94.

——, ed. *The Oxford Handbook of Late Antiquity*. Oxford: Oxford University Press, 2014.

Johnston, Sarah Iles. "Animating Statues: A Case Study in Ritual." *Arethusa* 41 (2008): 445–77.

Jones Farmer, Tamsin. "Revealing the Invisible: Gregory of Nyssa on the Gift of Revelation." *Modern Theology* 21, no. 1 (January 2005): 67–85.

Jordan, Mark. "Ancient Philosophical Protreptic and the Problem of Persuasive Genres." *Rhetorica* 4, no. 4 (1986): 309–33.

——. *Teaching Bodies: Moral Formation in the Summa of Thomas Aquinas*. New York: Fordham University Press, 2017.

Jungkeit, Steven R. *Spaces of Modern Theology: Geography and Power in Schleiermacher's World*. New York: Palgrave MacMillan, 2012.

Keller, Catherine. *Cloud of the Impossible: Negative Theology and Planetary Entanglement*. New York: Columbia University Press, 2014.

Kelly, J. N. D. *Early Christian Creeds*, 3rd ed. London: Longmans, 1972.

Kennedy, George A. *Classical Rhetoric and Its Christian and Secular Tradition: From Ancient to Modern Times*, 2nd ed. Chapel Hill: University of North Carolina Press, 1999.

King, Karen. *The Secret Revelation of John*. Cambridge, MA: Harvard University Press, 2006.

Klein, Jacob. *A Commentary on Plato's* Meno. Chicago: University of Chicago Press, 1989.

Kominko, Maja. *The World of Kosmas: Illustrated Byzantine Codices of Christian Topography*. Cambridge: Cambridge University Press, 2013.

Krueger, Derek. *Liturgical Subjects: Christian Ritual, Biblical Narrative, and the Formation of the Self in Byzantium*. Philadelphia: University of Pennsylvania Press, 2014.

——. *Writing and Holiness: The Practice of Authorship in the Early Christian East*. Philadelphia: University of Pennsylvania Press, 2004.

——, and Robert S. Nelson, eds. *The New Testament in Byzantium*. Washington, DC: Dumbarton Oaks Research Library and Collection, 2016.

Kuhner, Matthew. "The 'Aspects of Christ' (*Epinoiai Christou*) in Origen's *Commentary on the Epistles to the Romans*." *Harvard Theological Review* 110 (January 2017): 7–9.

Laird, Martin. "The Fountain of His Lips: Desire and Divine Union in Gregory of Nyssa's *Homilies on the Song of Songs*." *Spiritus: A Journal of Christian Spirituality* 7, no. 1 (2007): 40–57.

——. *Gregory of Nyssa and the Grasp of Faith: Union, Knowledge, and Divine Presence*. Oxford: Oxford University Press, 2004.

——. "Under Solomon's Tutelage: The Education of Desire in the *Homilies on the Song of Songs*." In *Re-thinking Gregory of Nyssa*, ed. Sarah Coakley, 77–95.

Lakoff, George, and Mark Johnson. *Metaphors We Live By*. Chicago: University of Chicago Press, 1980.

Lamberton, Robert. *Homer the Theologian*. Berkeley: University of California Press, 1986.

Lampe, G. W. H. *A Patristic Greek Lexicon*. Oxford: Oxford University Press, 1969.

Langlands, Rebecca. "Roman *Exempla* and Situation Ethics: Valerius Maximus and Cicero *de Officiis*." *The Journal of Roman Studies* 101 (November 2011): 100–22.

Layne, Danielle A. "Cosmic Etiology and Demiurgic Mimesis in Proclus' Account of Prayer." In *Platonic Theories of Prayer*, ed. John M. Dillon and Andrei Timotin, 134–63. Leiden: Brill, 2015.

Lear, Jonathan. *Aristotle: The Desire to Understand*. Cambridge: Cambridge University Press, 1988.

Leemans, Johan, Wendy Mayer, Pauline Allen, and Boudewijn Dehandschutter, eds. *"Let Us Die That We May Live": Greek Homilies on Christian Martyrs from Asia Minor, Palestine and Syria (c. AD 350–450)*. New York: Routledge, 2003.

Lefebvre, Henri. *The Production of Space*. Trans. Donald Nicholson-Smith. Malden, MA: Blackwell, 1991.

Leyerle, Blake. "Mobility and the Traces of Empire." In *A Companion to Late Antiquity*, ed. Philip Rousseau, 110–24.

———. *Theatrical Shows and Ascetic Lives: John Chrysostom's Attack on Spiritual Marriage*. Berkeley: University of California Press, 2001.

Liddell, Henry George, and Robert Scott. *Liddell and Scott's Greek-English Lexicon*. Oxford: Clarendon Press, 1996.

Lieber, Laura S. "Setting the Stage: The Theatricality of Jewish Aramaic Poetry from Late Antiquity." *The Jewish Quarterly Review* 104, no. 4 (Fall 2014): 537–72.

Limberis, Vasiliki M. *Architects of Piety: The Cappadocian Fathers and the Cult of the Martyrs*. Oxford: Oxford University Press, 2011.

Lincoln, Bruce. *Theorizing Myth: Narrative, Ideology, and Scholarship*. Chicago: University of Chicago Press, 1999.

Lindbeck, George A. *The Nature of Doctrine: Religion and Theology in a Postliberal Age*. Louisville: Westminster John Knox Press, 1984.

Lindberg, David C. *Theories of Vision from Al-Kindi to Kepler*. Chicago: University of Chicago Press, 1996.

Lorenz, Hendrik. *The Brute Within: Appetitive Desire in Plato and Aristotle*. Oxford: Oxford University Press, 2006.

Louth, Andrew. "Apophatic and Cataphatic Theology." In *The Cambridge Companion to Christian Mysticism*, ed. Amy Hollywood and Patricia Z. Beckman, 137–46.

———. *The Origins of the Christian Mystical Tradition: From Plato to Denys*. Oxford: Clarendon Press, 1981.

Ludlow, Morwenna. "Anatomy: Investigating the Body of Texts in Origen and Gregory of Nyssa." In *Reading the Church Fathers*, ed. Scot Douglass and Morwenna Ludlow, 132–53.

———. "Divine Infinity and Eschatology: The Limits and Dynamics of Human Knowledge According to Gregory of Nyssa (CE II 67–170)." In *Contra Eunomium II: An English Version with Supporting Studies*, ed. Lenka Karfíková et al., 217–37.

———. *Gregory of Nyssa: Ancient and (Post)modern*. Oxford: Oxford University Press, 2007.

———. "Texts, Teachers and Pupils in the Writings of Gregory of Nyssa." In *Literature and Society in the Fourth Century AD: Performing Paideia, Constructing the Present, Presenting the Self*, ed. Lieve Van Hoof and Peter Van Nuffelen, 83–102.

———. "Theology and Allegory: Origen and Gregory of Nyssa on the Unity and Diversity of Scripture." *International Journal of Systematic Theology* 4, no. 1 (March 2002): 45–66.

———. *Universal Salvation: Eschatology in the Thought of Gregory of Nyssa and Karl Rahner.* Oxford: Oxford University Press, 2000.

MacDougall, Byron. "Gregory of Nazianzus and Christian Festival Rhetoric." PhD diss., Brown University, 2015.

Mango, Cyril. "Saints." In *The Byzantines*, ed. Guglielmo Cavallo, 255–80. Chicago: University of Chicago Press, 1996.

Martin, Dale B., and Patricia Cox Miller, eds. *The Cultural Turn in Late Ancient Studies: Gender, Asceticism and Historiography.* Durham: Duke University Press, 2005.

Marx-Wolf, Heidi. *Spiritual Taxonomies and Ritual Authority: Platonists, Priests, and Gnostics in the Third Century C.E.* Philadelphia: University of Pennsylvania Press, 2016.

Maspero, Giulio. *Trinity and Man: Gregory of Nyssa's Ad Ablabium.* Leiden: Brill, 2007.

Mateo-Seco, Lucas Francisco. "Imitación y seguimiento de Cristo en Gregorio de Nisa." *Scripta Theologica* 33, no. 3 (2001): 601–21.

———, and Giulio Maspero, eds. *The Brill Dictionary of Gregory of Nyssa.* Trans. Seth Cherney. Leiden: Brill, 2010.

Mathews, Thomas F. *The Clash of Gods: A Reinterpretation of Christian Art.* Cambridge: Cambridge University Press, 1993.

———. *The Dawn of Christian Art in Panel Paintings and Icons.* Los Angeles: The J. Paul Getty Museum, 2016.

Mattern, Susan. *The Prince of Medicine: Galen in the Roman Empire.* Oxford: Oxford University Press, 2013.

May, Gerhard. "Die Chronologie des Lebens und der Werke des Gregor von Nyssa." In *Écriture et culture philosophique dans la pensée de Grégoire de Nysse*, ed. Marguerite Harl, 51–67.

Mayer, Wendy. "Antioch and the Intersection Between Religious Factionalism, Place, and Power in Late Antiquity." In *The Power of Religion in Late Antiquity*, ed. Andrew Cain and Noel Lenski, 357–67.

———. Introduction to John Chrysostom, *The Cult of the Saints*, trans. Wendy Mayer, 11–19.

Mazur, Zeke. "Mystical Self-Reversion in Platonizing Sethian Gnosticism and Plotinus." http://kalyptos.org/Zeke/pdf/Mystical_Self-Reversion.pdf.

McCambley, Casimir (Brother Casimir). "Saint Gregory of Nyssa: ΠΕΡΙ ΤΕΛΕΙΟΤΗΤΟΣ—*On Perfection.*" *The Greek Orthodox Theological Review* 29, no. 4 (December 1984): 349–51.

McGinn, Bernard. *Foundations of Mysticism: Origins to the Fifth Century.* Vol. 1 of *The Presence of God: A History of Western Christian Mysticism.* New York: Crossroad, 1991.

McKeon, Richard. "Literary Criticism and the Concept of Imitation in Antiquity." *Modern Philology* 34 (1936): 1–35.

Meltzer, Françoise, and Jaś Elsner. *Saints: Faith Without Borders.* Chicago: University of Chicago Press, 2011.

Meredith, Anthony. *Gregory of Nyssa.* New York: Routledge, 1999.

———. "Gregory of Nyssa." In *The Cambridge History of Philosophy in Late Antiquity*, vol. 1, ed. Lloyd P. Gerson, 471–81.

———. "The Language of God and Human Language." In *Contra Eunomium II: An English Version with Supporting Studies*, ed. Lenka Karfíková et al., 247–56.

Michopoulos, Tasos Sarris. "Μιμισόμεθα Νόμον Θεοῦ: Gregory the Theologian's Ontology of Compassion." *The Greek Orthodox Theological Review* 39, no. 2 (1994): 109–21.

Milbank, John. *Being Reconciled: Ontology and Pardon*. London: Routledge, 2003.
———. "Can a Gift Be Given?" *Modern Theology* 11, no. 1 (January 1995): 119–61.
———. "The Force of Identity." In *The Word Made Strange: Theology, Language, Culture*, 194–218.
———. *The Word Made Strange: Theology, Language, Culture*. Oxford: Blackwell, 1997.
Miller, Patricia Cox. *Biography in Late Antiquity: A Quest for the Holy Man*. Berkeley: University of California Press, 1983.
———. *The Corporeal Imagination: Signifying the Holy in Late Ancient Christianity*. Philadelphia: University of Pennsylvania Press, 2009.
———. "Pleasure of the Text, Text of Pleasure: Eros and Language in Origen's Commentary on the Song of Songs." *Journal of the American Academy of Religion* 54, no. 2 (Summer 1986): 241–53.
———. "Strategies of Representation in Collective Biography: Constructing the Subject as Holy." In *Greek Biography and Panegyric in Late Antiquity*, ed. Tomas Hägg and Philip Rousseau, 209–54.
———. "Subtle Embodiments: Imagining the Holy in Late Antiquity." In *Apophatic Bodies*, ed. Chris Boesel and Catherine Keller, 45–58. New York: Fordham University Press, 2010.
Morrison, Karl F. *The Mimetic Tradition of Reform in the West*. Princeton: Princeton University Press, 1982.
Moss, Candida. *Ancient Christian Martyrdom: Diverse Practices, Theologies, and Traditions*. New Haven: Yale University Press, 2012.
———. "On the Dating of Polycarp: Rethinking the Place of the *Martyrdom of Polycarp* in the History of Christianity." *Early Christianity* 1 (2010): 539–74.
———. *The Other Christs: Imitating Jesus in Ancient Christian Ideologies of Martyrdom*. Oxford: Oxford University Press, 2010.
Moss, Jessica. "What Is Imitative Poetry and Why Is It Bad?" In *The Cambridge Companion to Plato's Republic*, ed. G. R. F. Ferrari, 415–44. Cambridge: Cambridge University Press, 2007.
Mosshammer, Alden A. "The Created and the Uncreated in Gregory of Nyssa's *Contra Eunomium* 1, 105–13." In *El "Contra Eunomium I" en la Producción Literaria de Gregorio de Nisa*, ed. Lucas F. Mateo-Seco and Juan L. Bastero, trans. Stuart G. Hall, 353–79.
———. "Disclosing but Not Disclosed: Gregory of Nyssa as Deconstructionist." In *Studien zu Gregor von Nyssa und der christlichen Spätantike*, ed. Hubertus Drobner and Christoph Klock, 99–123. Leiden: Brill, 1990.
———. "Gregory's Intellectual Development: A Comparison of the *Homilies on the Beatitudes* with the *Homilies on the Song of Songs*." In *Gregory of Nyssa: Homilies on the Beatitudes*, ed. Hubertus R. Drobner and Albert Viciano, 359–87.
Most, G. W. "What Ancient Quarrel Between Philosophy and Poetry?" In *Plato and the Poets*, ed. Pierre Destrée and Fritz-Gregor Herrmann, 1–20. Leiden: Brill, 2011.
Motia, Michael. "Gregory of Nyssa." In *The Oxford Handbook of Dionysius the Areopagite*, ed. Mark Edwards. Oxford: Oxford University Press, forthcoming.
———. "Language Is the Author of All These Emotions: Greek Novels and Christian Affect in Gregory of Nyssa's *Homilies on the Song of Songs*." *Studia Patristica*, forthcoming.
———. "Three Ways to Imitate Paul in Late Antiquity: Ekstasis, Ekphrasis, Epektasis." *Harvard Theological Review* 114, no. 1 (2021): 96–117.

Moutsoulas, Elias. "La 'sainteté' dans les oeuvres biographiques de Grégoire de Nysse." In *The Biographical Works of Gregory of Nyssa*, ed. Andreas Spira, 221–40.

Muckelbauer, John. "Imitation and Invention in Antiquity: An Historical-Theoretical Revision." *Rhetorica* 21, no. 2 (Spring 2003): 61–88.

Muehlberger, Ellen. "Salvage: Macrina and the Christian Project of Cultural Reclamation." *Church History* 81, no. 2 (June 2012): 271–97.

Mühlenberg, Ekkehard. "Die philosophische Bildung Gregors von Nyssa in den Büchern *Contra Eunomium*." In *Écriture et culture philosophique dans la pensée de Grégoire de Nysse*, ed. Marguerite Harl, 230–51.

———. "Synergism in Gregory of Nyssa." *Zeitschrift für die alttestamentliche Wissenschaft* 68, no. 1 (January 1977): 93–122.

———. *Die Unendlichkeit Gottes bei Gregor von Nyssa: Gregors Kritik am Gottesbegriff der klassischen Metaphysik*. Göttingen: Vandenhoeck und Ruprecht, 1966.

Münz-Manor, Ophir, and Thomas Arentzen. "Soundscapes of Salvation: Resounding Refrains in Jewish and Christian Liturgical Poems." *Studies in Late Antiquity* 3, no. 1 (2019): 36–55.

Nasrallah, Laura Salah. *Christian Responses to Roman Art and Architecture: The Second-Century Church Amid the Spaces of Empire*. Cambridge: Cambridge University Press, 2010.

Nehamas, Alexander. "Plato on Imitation and Poetry in *Republic* X." In *Virtues of Authenticity: Essays on Plato and Socrates*, 251–98. Princeton: Princeton University Press, 1999.

Neil, Bronwen, and Pauline Allen, eds. *Collecting Early Christian Letters: From the Apostle Paul to Late Antiquity*. Cambridge: Cambridge University Press, 2015.

Nelson, Robert S. "To Say and to See: Ekphrasis and Vision in Byzantium." In *Visuality Before and Beyond the Renaissance*, ed. Robert S. Nelson, 143–68. Cambridge: Cambridge University Press, 2000.

Nightingale, Andrea Wilson. "The Philosopher at the Festival: Plato's transformation of Traditional *Theōria*." In *Pilgrimage in Graeco-Roman and Early Christian Antiquity: Seeing the Gods*, ed. Jaś Elsner and Ian Rutherford, 151–80.

O'Meara, Dominic J. *Platonopolis*. Oxford: Oxford University Press, 2003.

———. "Plotinus." In *The Cambridge History of Philosophy in Late Antiquity*, vol. 1, ed. Lloyd P. Gerson, 301–24.

———. *Plotinus: An Introduction to the Enneads*. Oxford: Oxford University Press, 1993.

Orsi, Robert A., ed. *The Cambridge Companion to Religious Studies*. Cambridge: Cambridge University Press, 2012.

———, "The Problem of the Holy." In *The Cambridge Companion to Religious Studies*, ed. Robert A. Orsi, 84–105.

Orton, Robin. Introduction to *St. Gregory of Nyssa: Anti-Apollinarian Writings*, trans. Robin Orton, 3–88.

———, trans. *St. Gregory of Nyssa: Anti-Apollinarian Writings*. Washington, DC: The Catholic University of America Press, 2015.

Padilla Peralta, Dan-el. *Divine Institutions: Religion and Community in the Middle Roman Republic*. Princeton: Princeton University Press, 2020.

Penella, Robert J., ed. *Rhetorical Exercises from Late Antiquity: A Translation of Choricius of Gaza's Preliminary Talks and Declamations*. Cambridge: Cambridge University Press, 2009.

Peppard, Michael. "Was the Presence of Christ in Statues? The Challenge of Divine Media for a Jewish Roman God." In *The Art of Empire: Christian Art in Its Imperial Context*, ed. Lee M. Jefferson and Robin M. Jensen, 225–70.

Perkins, Judith. *The Suffering Self: Pain and Narrative Representation in the Early Christian Era*. New York: Routledge, 1995.

Perl, Eric D. *Theophany: The Neoplatonic Philosophy of Dionysius the Areopagite*. Albany: State University of New York Press, 2007.

Perry, Ellen. *The Aesthetics of Emulation in the Visual Arts of Ancient Rome*. Cambridge: Cambridge University Press, 2005.

Pfanner, Michael. "Über das Herstellen von Porträts: Ein Beitrag zu Rationalisierungsmaßnahmen und Produktionsmechanismen von Massenware im späten Hellenismus und in der römischen Kaiserzeit." *Jahrbuch des deutschen archäologischen Instituts* 104 (1989): 157–257.

Potolsky, Matthew. *Mimesis*. New York: Routledge, 2006.

Radde-Gallwitz, Andrew. *Basil of Caesarea, Gregory of Nyssa, and the Transformation of Divine Simplicity*. Oxford: Oxford University Press, 2009.

———. *Gregory of Nyssa's Doctrinal Works: A Literary Study*. Oxford: Oxford University Press, 2018.

Rancière, Jacques. *The Politics of Aesthetics: The Distribution of the Sensible*. Trans. Gabriel Rockhill. New York: Continuum, 2004.

Rapp, Claudia. *Holy Bishops in Late Antiquity: The Nature of Christian Leadership in an Age of Transition*. Berkeley: University of California Press, 2005.

———. "Storytelling as Spiritual Communication in Early Greek Hagiography: The Use of Diegesis." *Journal of Early Christian Studies* 6, no. 3 (1998): 431–48.

Rappe, Sara. *Reading Neoplatonism: Non-discursive Thinking in the Texts of Plotinus, Proclus, and Damascius*. Cambridge: Cambridge University Press, 2000.

Reale, Giovanni. *A History of Ancient Philosophy*, vol. 4. Trans. John R. Catan. Albany: State University of New York Press, 1990.

Remes, Pauliina. *Plotinus on Self: The Philosophy of the "We."* Cambridge: Cambridge University Press, 2007.

Rist, John. "The Indefinite Dyad and Intelligible Matter in Plotinus." *The Classical Quarterly* 12, no. 1 (May 1962): 99–107.

Rousseau, Philip. *Basil of Caesarea*. Berkeley: University of California Press, 1994.

———, ed. *A Companion to Late Antiquity*. Malden, MA: Wiley-Blackwell, 2012.

———. "The Pious Household and the Virgin Chorus: Reflections on Gregory of Nyssa's *Life of Macrina*." *Journal of Early Christian Studies* 13, no. 2 (Summer 2005): 165–66.

Rubenson, Samuel. "Philosophy and Simplicity: The Problem of Classical Education in Early Christian Biography." In *Greek Biography and Panegyric in Late Antiquity*, ed. Tomas Hägg and Philip Rousseau, 110–39.

Ruether, Rosemary Radford. "Imago Dei, Christian Tradition and Feminist Hermeneutics." In *The Image of God: Gender Models in Judaeo-Christian Tradition*, ed. Kari Elisabeth Børresen, 258–81. Oslo: Solum Forlag, 1991.

Russell, D. A. *Greek Declamation*. Cambridge: Cambridge University Press, 1983.

Schoedel, William R. *Ignatius of Antioch: A Commentary on the Letters of Ignatius of Antioch*. Philadelphia: Fortress Press, 1985.

Schoos, Daniel J. "Timaeus' Banquet." *Ancient Philosophy* 19 (1999): 97–107.

Schroeder, Frederic M. "Plotinus and Language." In *The Cambridge Companion to Plotinus*, ed. Lloyd P. Gerson, 336–55.

Schweiker, William. "Beyond Imitation: Mimetic Praxis in Gadamer, Ricoeur, and Derrida." *The Journal of Religion* 68, no. 1 (January 1988): 21–38.

Seligman, Adam B., Robert P. Weller, Michael J. Puett, and Bennett Simon. *Ritual and Its Consequences: An Essay on the Limits of Sincerity.* Oxford: Oxford University Press, 2008.

Shaw, Gregory. "Neoplatonic Theurgy and Dionysius the Areopagite." *Journal of Early Christian Studies* 7, no. 4 (1999): 573–99.

———. "The Role of *Aesthesis* in Theurgy." In *Iamblichus and the Foundations of Late Platonism*, ed. Eugene Afonasin, John Dillon, and John F. Finamore, 91–111.

———. "The Soul's Innate Gnosis of the Gods: Revelation in Iamblichean Theurgy." In *Revelation, Literature, and Community in Late Antiquity*, ed. P. Townsend and M. Vidas, 117–30. Tübingen: Mohr Siebeck, 2011.

———. "Taking the Shape of the Gods: A Theurgic Reading of Hermetic Rebirth." *Aries: Journal for the Study of Western Esotericism* 15 (2015): 136–69.

———. *Theurgy and the Soul: The Neoplatonism of Iamblichus*, 2nd ed. Kettering, OH: Angelico Press, 2014. Originally published as *Theurgy and the Soul: The Neoplatonism of Iamblichus.* University Park: Pennsylvania State University Press, 1995.

Shepardson, Christine. *Controlling Contested Places: Late Antique Antioch and the Spatial Politics of Religious Controversy.* Berkeley: University of California Press, 2014.

Shoemaker, Stephen, J. *Mary in Early Christian Faith and Devotion.* New Haven: Yale University Press, 2016.

Silvas, Anna M. *Macrina the Younger, Philosopher of God.* Turnhout: Brepols, 2008.

Smith, J. Warren. "The Body of Paradise and the Body of the Resurrection: Gender and the Angelic Life in Gregory of Nyssa's *De hominis opificio.*" *Harvard Theological Review* 99, no. 2 (April 2006): 207–28.

———. "A Just and Reasonable Grief: The Death and Function of a Holy Woman in Gregory of Nyssa's *Life of Macrina.*" *Journal of Early Christian Studies* 12, no. 1 (Spring 2004): 57–84.

———. "Macrina, Tamer of Horses and Healer of Souls: Grief and the Therapy of Hope in Gregory of Nyssa's *De anima et resurrectione.*" *Journal of Theological Studies* 52, no. 1 (April 2001): 37–60.

Smith, Jonathan Z. "The Influence of Symbols on Social Change: A Place on Which to Stand." In Jonathan Z. Smith, *Map Is Not Territory: Studies in the History of Religions*, 129–46. Chicago: University of Chicago Press, 1993.

———. *To Take Place: Toward Theory in Ritual.* Chicago: University of Chicago Press, 1987.

Sorabji, Richard. "The Mind-Body Relation in the Wake of Plato's *Timaeus.*" In *Plato's Timaeus as Cultural Icon*, ed. Gretchen J. Reydams-Schils, 152–62. Notre Dame: University of Notre Dame Press, 2002.

Srinivasan, Amia. "He, She, One, They, Ho, Hus, Hum, Ita." *London Review of Books* 42, no. 13 (July 2, 2020). https://www.lrb.co.uk/the-paper/v42/n13/amia-srinivasan/he-she-one -they-ho-hus-hum-ita.

Stang, Charles. *Apophasis and Pseudonymity in Dionysius the Areopagite: "No Longer I."* Oxford: Oxford University Press, 2012.

———. "'Being Neither Oneself Nor Someone Else': The Apophatic Anthropology of Dionysius the Areopagite." In *Apophatic Bodies*, ed. Chris Boesel and Catherine Keller, 59–78. New York: Fordham University Press, 2010.

——. *Our Divine Double*. Cambridge, MA: Harvard University Press, 2016.

——. "Writing." In *The Cambridge Companion to Christian Mysticism*, ed. Amy Hollywood and Patricia Z. Beckman, 252–63.

Stefaniw, Blossom. *Christian Reading: Language, Ethics, and the Order of Things*. Oakland: University of California Press, 2019.

——. "A Disciplined Mind in an Orderly World: Mimesis in Late Antique Ethical Regimes." In *Formen ethischer Begründungszusammenhänge im frühen Christentum*, ed. U. Volp, F. W. Horn, and R. Zimmermann, 235–56. Tübingen: Mohr Siebeck, 2016.

——. "The Oblique Ethics of the Letters of Antony." In *L'identité à travers l'éthique: Nouvelles perspectives sur la formation des identités collectives dans le monde Greco-romain*, ed. Katell Berthelot et al., 169–85. Turnhout: Brepols, 2015.

Sterk, Andrea. *Renouncing the World Yet Leading the Church: The Monk-Bishop in Late Antiquity*. Cambridge, MA: Harvard University Press, 2004.

Stewart, Columba. "Imageless Prayer and the Theological Vision of Evagrius Ponticus." *Journal of Early Christian Studies* 9, no. 2 (Summer 2001): 173–204.

Stewart-Sykes, Alistair. *The Life of Polycarp: An Anonymous Vita from Third-Century Smyrna*. Sydney: St. Pauls, 2002.

Storin, Bradley K. *Self-Portrait in Three Colors: Gregory of Nazianzus's Epistolary Autobiography*. Oakland: University of California Press, 2019.

Struck, Peter T. "Allegory and Ascent in Neoplatonism." In *The Cambridge Companion to Allegory*, ed. Rita Copeland and Peter T. Struck, 57–70. Cambridge: Cambridge University Press, 2010.

——. *Birth of the Symbol: Ancient Readers at the Limits of Their Texts*. Princeton: Princeton University Press, 2004.

Taft, Robert. "Christian Liturgical Psalmody: Origins, Development, Decomposition, Collapse." In *Psalms in Community*, ed. Harold W. Attridge and Margot E. Fassler, 7–32.

Tanaseanu-Döbler, Ilinca. *Theurgy in Late Antiquity*. Göttingen: Vandenhoeck and Ruprecht, 2013.

Tannous, Jack. *The Making of the Medieval Middle East: Religion, Society, and Simple Believers*. Princeton: Princeton University Press, 2018.

Tarrant, Harold. "Platonism Before Plotinus." In *The Cambridge History of Philosophy in Late Antiquity*, vol. 1, ed. Lloyd P. Gerson, 63–99.

Teitler, H. C. *The Last Pagan Emperor: Julian the Apostate and the War Against Christianity*. Oxford: Oxford University Press, 2017.

Terrieux, Jean. *Grégoire de Nysse, Sur l'âme et la résurrection*. Paris: Éditions du Cerf, 1995.

Timotin, Andrei. "La Théorie de la Prière chez Jamblique: sa fonction et sa place dans l'histoire du Platonisme." *Laval théologique et philosophique* 70, no. 3 (October 2014): 563–77.

Tollefsen, Torstein Theodor. *Activity and Participation in Late Antique and Early Christian Thought*. Oxford: Oxford University Press, 2012.

Torrance, Alexis. "Individuality and Identity-formation in Late Antique Monasticism." In *Individuality in Late Antiquity*, ed. Alexis Torrance and Johannes Zachhuber, 111–28.

——, and Johannes Zachhuber, eds. *Individuality in Late Antiquity*. Burlington, VT: Ashgate, 2014.

Trimble, Jennifer, and Jaś Elsner. "If You Need an Actual Statue . . ." *Art History* 29, no. 2 (2006): 201–12.

Turcescu, Lucian. *Gregory of Nyssa and the Concept of Divine Persons*. Oxford: Oxford University Press, 2005.

Turner, Peter. *Truthfulness, Realism, Historicity: A Study in Late Antique Spiritual Literature.* Burlington, VT: Ashgate, 2012.

Urbano, Arthur. *The Philosophical Life: Biography and the Crafting of Intellectual Identity in Late Antiquity.* Washington, DC: The Catholic University of America Press, 2013.

Vaggione, Richard Paul. *Eunomius of Cyzicus and the Nicene Revolution.* Oxford: Oxford University Press, 2000.

Van Dam, Raymond. *Becoming Christian: The Conversion of Roman Cappadocia.* Philadelphia: University of Pennsylvania Press, 2003.

———. *Families and Friends in Late Roman Cappadocia.* Philadelphia: University of Pennsylvania Press, 2003.

van der Poel, Marc. "The Use of *exempla* in Roman Declamation." *Rhetorica* 27, no. 3 (2009): 332–53.

Van Hoof, Lieve, and Peter Van Nuffelen, eds. *Literature and Society in the Fourth Century AD: Performing Paideia, Constructing the Present, Presenting the Self.* Leiden: Brill, 2014.

Vasiliu, Anca. *Eikôn. L'image dans le discours des trois Cappadociens.* Paris: Presses universitaires de France, 2010.

———. "L'icône et le regard de Narcisse." *Chôra. Revue d'études anciennes et médiévales* 1 (2003): 9–38.

Vivian, Tim. "St. Antony the Great and the Monastery of St. Antony at the Red Sea, ca. AD 251 to 1232/1233." In *Monastic Visions: Wall Paintings in the Monastery of St. Antony at the Red Sea,* ed. Elizabeth S. Bolman, 3–20. New Haven: Yale University Press, 2002.

Völker, Walther. *Gregor von Nyssa als mystiker.* Wiesbaden: Steiner, 1955.

von Balthasar, Hans Urs. *Presence and Thought: An Essay on the Religious Philosophy of Gregory of Nyssa.* Trans. Mark Sebanc. San Francisco: Ignatius Press, 1995.

Watts, Edward J. *City and School in Late Antique Athens and Alexandria.* Berkeley: University of California Press, 2008.

———. *The Final Pagan Generation.* Berkeley: University of California Press, 2015.

Webb, Ruth. "Accomplishing the Picture: Ekphrasis, Mimesis, and Martyrdom in Asterios of Amaseia." In *Art and Text in Byzantine Culture,* ed. Liz James, 13–32. Cambridge: Cambridge University Press, 2007.

———. "The Aesthetics of Sacred Space: Narrative, Metaphor, and Motion in Ekphraseis of Church Buildings." *Dumbarton Oaks Papers* 53 (1999): 59–74.

———. *Demons and Dancers: Performance in Late Antiquity.* Cambridge, MA: Harvard University Press, 2008.

———. "*Ekphrasis* Ancient and Modern: The Invention of a Genre." *Word and Image* 15, no. 1 (1999): 7–18.

———. *Ekphrasis, Imagination and Persuasion in Ancient Rhetorical Theory and Practice.* Burlington, VT: Ashgate, 2009.

———. "Rhetorical and Theatrical Fictions in Chorikios of Gaza." In *Greek Literature in Late Antiquity,* illustrated edition, ed. Scott Fitzgerald Johnson, 107–24. Burlington, VT: Ashgate, 2006.

Weedman, Mark. "The Polemical Context of Gregory of Nyssa's Doctrine of Divine Infinity." *Journal of Early Christian Studies* 18, no. 1 (Spring 2010): 81–104.

Wendt, Heidi. *At the Temple Gates: The Religion of Freelance Experts in the Roman Empire.* Oxford: Oxford University Press, 2016.

Whitmarsh, Tim. *Greek Literature and the Roman Empire: The Politics of Imitation*. Oxford: Oxford University Press, 2001.

Wickham, L. R. "Homily 4." In *Homilies on Ecclesiastes: An English Version with Supporting Studies*, ed. and trans. Stuart G. Hall, 177–84.

———. "The *Syntagmation* of Aetius the Anomean." *Journal of Theological Studies* 19 (1968): 532–69.

Wiemer, Hans-Ulrich. *Libanios und Julian*. Munich: Beck, 1995.

Wilkin, Robert L. *The Land Called Holy: Palestine in Christian History and Thought*. New Haven: Yale University Press, 1992.

Williams, Michael Stuart. *Authorised Lives in Early Christian Biography: Between Eusebius and Augustine*. Cambridge: Cambridge University Press, 2008.

Williams, Rowan. *Arius: Heresy and Tradition*. Grand Rapids, MI: Eerdmans, 2002.

———. *The Edge of Words: God and the Habits of Language*. London: Bloomsbury, 2014.

———. "Macrina's Deathbed Revisited: Gregory of Nyssa on Mind and Passion." In *Christian Faith and Greek Philosophy in Late Antiquity*, ed. L. Wickham and C. Bammel, 227–46. Leiden: Brill, 1993.

———. *On Christian Theology*. Malden, MA: Blackwell, 2000.

———. "Saving Time: Thoughts on Practice, Patience, and Vision." *New Blackfriars* 73, no. 861 (1992): 319–26.

———. *The Wound of Knowledge: Christian Spirituality from the New Testament to Saint John of the Cross*, 2nd ed. London: Darton, Longman & Todd, 1990.

Wimbush, Vincent, and Richard Valantasis, eds. *Asceticism*. Oxford: Oxford University Press, 1998.

Wyschogrod, Edith. *Saints and Postmodernism: Revisioning Moral Philosophy*. Chicago: University of Chicago Press, 1990.

Young, Frances M. *Biblical Exegesis and the Formation of Christian Culture*. Peabody, MA: Hendrickson, 2002.

———. *From Nicaea to Chalcedon: A Guide to the Literature and Its Background*, 2nd ed. Grand Rapids, MI: Baker Academic, 2010.

———. *God's Presence: A Contemporary Recapitulation of Early Christianity*. Cambridge: Cambridge University Press, 2013.

Zachhuber, Johannes. "Christological Titles—Conceptually Applied? (*CE* II 294–358)." In *Contra Eunomium II: An English Version with Supporting Studies*, ed. Lenka Karfíková et al., 257–78.

———. *Human Nature in Gregory of Nyssa: Philosophical Background and Theological Significance*. Leiden: Brill, 2000.

———. "Individuality and the Theological Debate About 'Hypostasis.'" In *Individuality in Late Antiquity*, ed. Alexis Torrance and Johannes Zachhuber, 91–109.

Zanker, Paul. *The Power of Images in the Age of Augustus*. Trans. Alan Shapiro. Ann Arbor: University of Michigan Press, 1988.

———. *Roman Art*. Trans. Henry Heitmann-Gordon. Los Angeles: J. Paul Getty Museum, 2010.

Zlomislic, Marko, and Neal DeRoo, eds. *Cross and Khôra: Deconstruction and Christianity in the Work of John D. Caputo*. Eugene, OR: Pickwick, 2010.

Zuckert, Catherine H. *Plato's Philosophers: The Coherence of the Dialogues*. Chicago: University of Chicago Press, 2009.

INDEX

In this Index "GN" refers to Gregory of Nyssa.

ACKNOWLEDGMENTS

For Gregory of Nyssa, the key to living well was to choose the right examples and to sit with them for long enough that you might catch their halo. He imitated those examples, but he also lived in their world. It is overwhelming to know that I have lived in a world made by people who were kinder, smarter, and more generous than I had any right to expect.

My first thanks go to Charles Stang and Amy Hollywood. They taught me to think and read, and how to care about academia without losing my soul. Charlie introduced me to oysters, stirred cocktails, and the world of late antiquity. He poured over drafts and consistently made time to talk through problems or cool overheating anxieties. He has endured my ill-conceived ideas and rough drafts with patience, wisdom, and clarity. His friendship, advising, and even childcare have made my writing and my life better than I know how to thank him. Reading Jacques Derrida with Amy may be as close to a conversion moment as one can have in an academic life. Since then, her mentorship has grounded me and taken me through philosophy, psychoanalysis, contemporary literature, and medieval worlds. Our alchemical conversations and her detailed, incisive comments made this project far better. She remains the best book recommender I've ever known.

Mark Jordan read early drafts of the entire manuscript, and his feel for translation, attention to Plato's literary techniques, and subtle habits of reading with an eye toward ethical formation have underpinned and improved much of this project. Susan Harvey welcomed me to Providence with characteristic warmth, ensured I found academic community here in Rhode Island, and offered consistently generous critiques on much of this project. Georgia Frank's comments and guidance have buoyed both this book and my spirits. Stephanie Paulsell, Arthur Urbano, Andrew Jacobs, Jae Han, Rebecca Falcasantos, Margaret Mitchell, Erin Walsh, Craig

Tichelkamp, Filipe Maia, Michael Mango, Cassie Houtz, John Portlock, and Josh Cohen gave me helpful feedback on various parts of this work. Todd Berzon and Greg Given each read multiple chapters (sometimes multiple times) and have been indispensable interlocutors. AnnMarie Bridges was often my first and last reader. Annewies van den Hoek spent many Monday mornings with me translating Gregory. Michelle Sanchez and Burns Stanfield have been rocks of support. Large chunks of this project were formed in cherished car rides between Scranton, New Haven, and Cambridge with Steve Jungkeit. Teaching at UMass Boston has allowed me to work with dedicated students and kind colleagues, especially Ken Rothwell and Jason von Ehrenkrook.

I am grateful to have presented portions of this work to the North American Patristics Society, the Byzantine Studies Association of North America, and the Boston and Providence Patristics Groups. Portions of the Introduction first appeared as a Dissertation Spotlight in *Ancient Jew Review* (January 9, 2018): https://www.ancientjewreview.com/articles/2017/12/30/dissertation-spotlight-michael-motia. Sections of Chapter 5 first appeared in an earlier form as "Gregory of Nyssa's Shifting Scenes of Instruction," *Journal of Orthodox Christian Studies* 3, no. 1 (June 2020): 51–69. Copyright © 2020 Johns Hopkins University Press.

My editor at Divinations, Jerry Singerman, patiently initiated me into the book publishing world. The series editors, Daniel Boyarin, Virginia Burrus, and Derek Krueger, had been scholarly models for years before they, Derek primarily, encouraged me to publish, and sharpened many blunt arguments. Scott Johnson and Alexis Torrance both reviewed the manuscript in full, and their comments were generous and detailed, often saving me from embarrassing oversights.

But in the end, as Gregory writes, "Grace begins at home." Nothing has changed my life more or for the better than my daughter, Mae. Much of this book was written with an ear toward the baby monitor or with her crawling around my office, especially during the COVID pandemic. The book might have been finished earlier without her, but I would have been much less happy. From baseball games to close readings of Iamblichus, my dad, Farhad, has never let not understanding what I do get in the way of supporting me more than I deserve. No one who knows him is surprised that he is a wonderful grandfather, but seeing him interact with Mae has been one of the great joys of my life. My brother Matthew's love of the Dodgers, quick wit, and kitchen skills made for good meals and great days, often when I needed them most. To say that my mom, Marty, has been supportive of this project is an understatement worthy of her limitless grace, care, and humility. And, finally, my wife, Morgan, has taught me more about endlessly expanding love than Gregory ever could.

CPSIA information can be obtained
at www.ICGtesting.com
Printed in the USA
JSHW031046231021
19806JS00004B/5

9 780812 253139